SB
Shojo Beat

ST. DRAGON GIRL

VOLUME TWO

Story & Art by **Natsumi Matsumoto**

CHARACTERS

Ron-Ron
A stuffed animal Momoka treasures. ♥

Ryuga Kou
Momoka's childhood friend and magic master.

Momoka Sendou
She's possessed by a dragon spirit Ryuga called forth. When the seal on the dragon is broken, she becomes an invincible dragon girl.

Kouryu Kou
Ryuga's relative. A genius of sorcery in the Kou clan.

Shunran
Ryuga's cousin and Momoka's best friend. Has psychic abilites.

STORY THUS FAR

Momoka is a student and a member of the kenpo club at Yokohama's Tourin Academy. She's the daughter of a martial artist and is an expert at kenpo herself. Her nickname is "Dragon Girl." Her childhood friend Ryuga is adept at predicting the future and casting spells. Momoka likes him.

Only Ryuga can seal and release the dragon spirit inside of Momoka. In an attempt to defeat the serpent king, Ryuga called forth the dragon for himself. However, the dragon ended up possessing Momoka instead.

Then Kouryu arrived from China. He tried to pressure Momoka to become his. That didn't seem to bother Ryuga at all, so an angry Momoka agreed to go on a date with Kouryu. Apparently Kouryu wanted her because she was possessed by a dragon. Just when it seemed he would take Momoka to China against her will, Ryuga saved her in the nick of time.

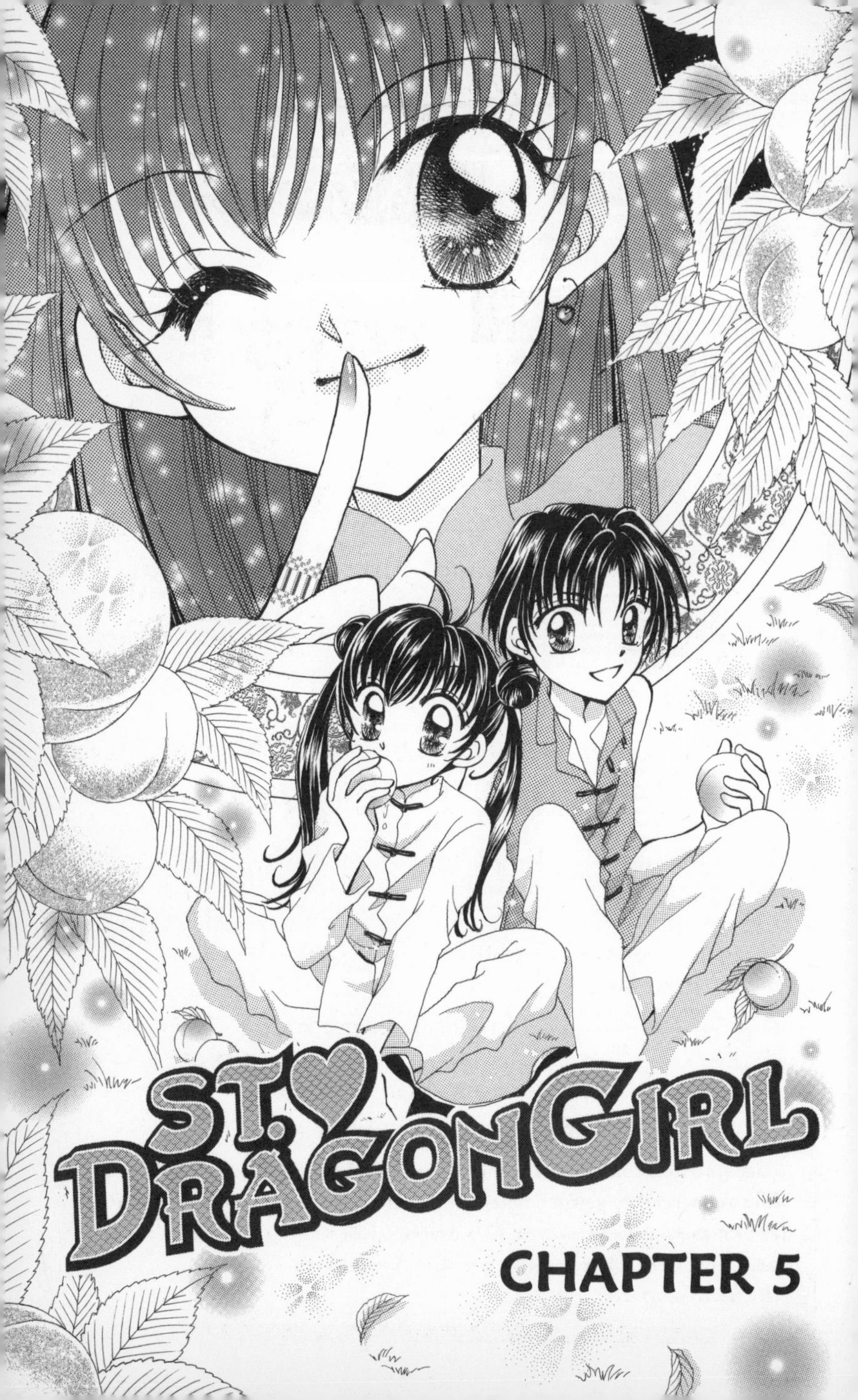
ST.♥DRAGONGIRL
CHAPTER 5

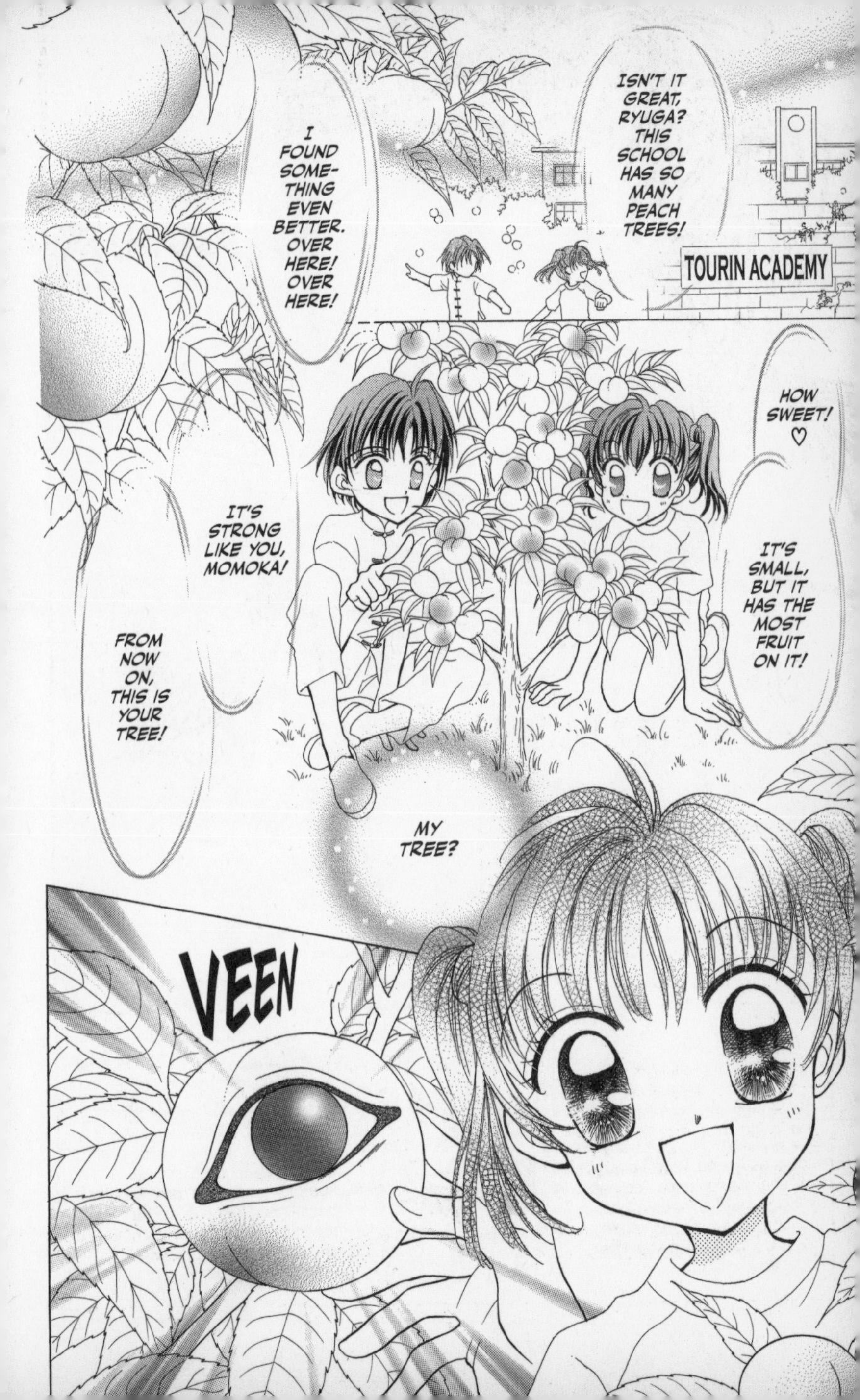
TOURIN ACADEMY
ISN'T IT GREAT, RYUGA? THIS SCHOOL HAS SO MANY PEACH TREES!
I FOUND SOME-THING EVEN BETTER. OVER HERE! OVER HERE!
HOW SWEET! ♡
IT'S SMALL, BUT IT HAS THE MOST FRUIT ON IT!
IT'S STRONG LIKE YOU, MOMOKA!
FROM NOW ON, THIS IS YOUR TREE!
MY TREE?
VEEN

AAAH!
WHAT'S WRONG, MOMOKA?
I HAD A BAD DREAM.
You shouldn't be sleep-ing here.
WE'RE HERE FOR THE KENPO CLUB'S TRAINING CAMP.
SHABBY
TONIGHT WE'LL BE SLEEPING IN THE OLD SCHOOL BUILDING...

Shunran Kou

She has a very gentle personality and is somewhat timid. She is easily possessed by spirits and demons, so Momoka and Ryuga have always protected her. She is just as popular among readers as Ageha. People always ask if she has romantic feelings for Ryuga, but I think he might be a little scary for her. I think someone a little older would be better for her.

naturally curly

Born March 17.
Pisces, Blood Type: A.
Member of the kenpo club.
Half Chinese, half Japanese.
She's Ryuga's cousin and Momoka's best friend. Because of her psychic abilities, she's staying with the Kou family in Yokohama.
Her hobby is knitting.

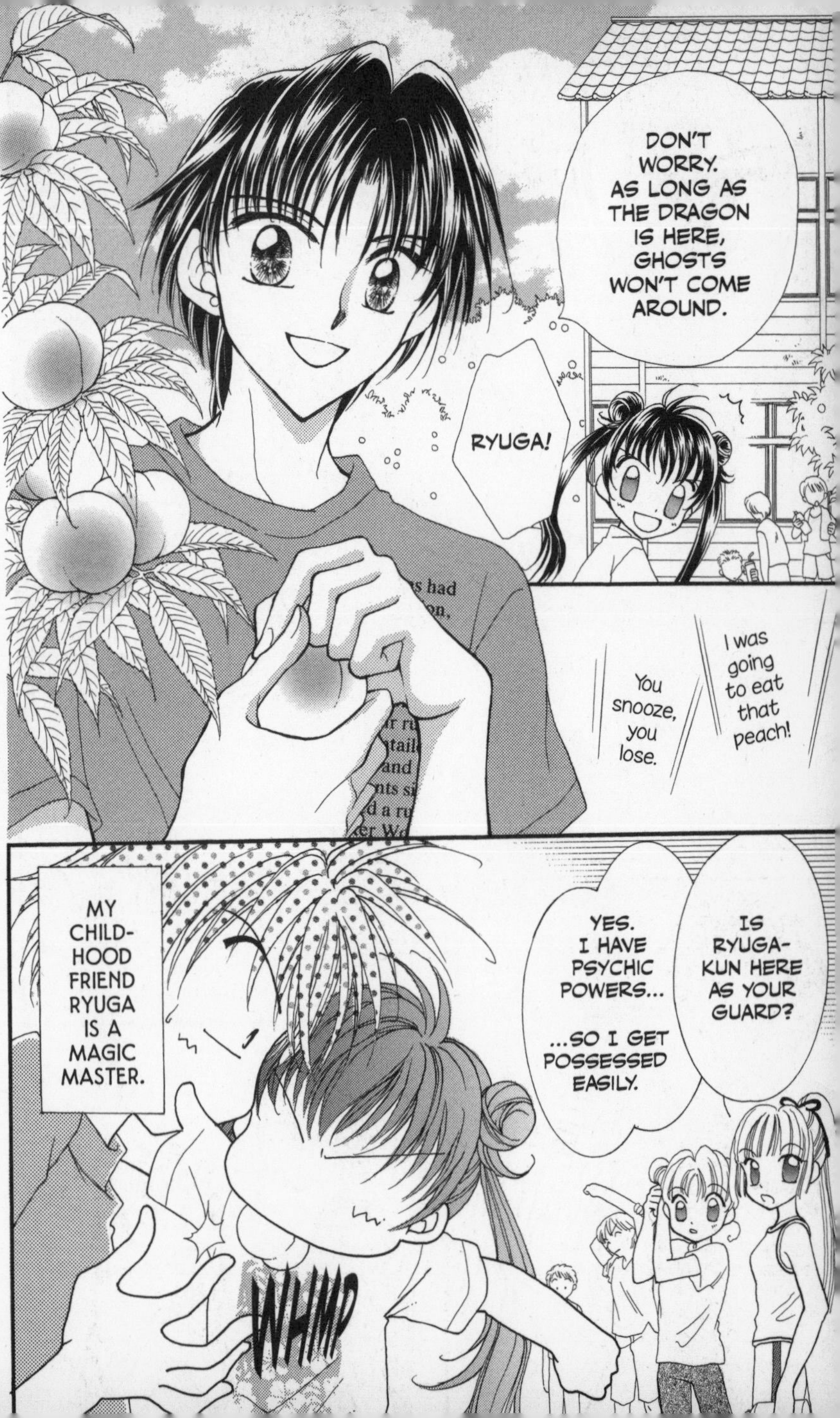
DON'T WORRY. AS LONG AS THE DRAGON IS HERE, GHOSTS WON'T COME AROUND.
RYUGA!
I was going to eat that peach!
You snooze, you lose.
IS RYUGA-KUN HERE AS YOUR GUARD?
YES. I HAVE PSYCHIC POWERS...
...SO I GET POSSESSED EASILY.
MY CHILD-HOOD FRIEND RYUGA IS A MAGIC MASTER.
WHIMP

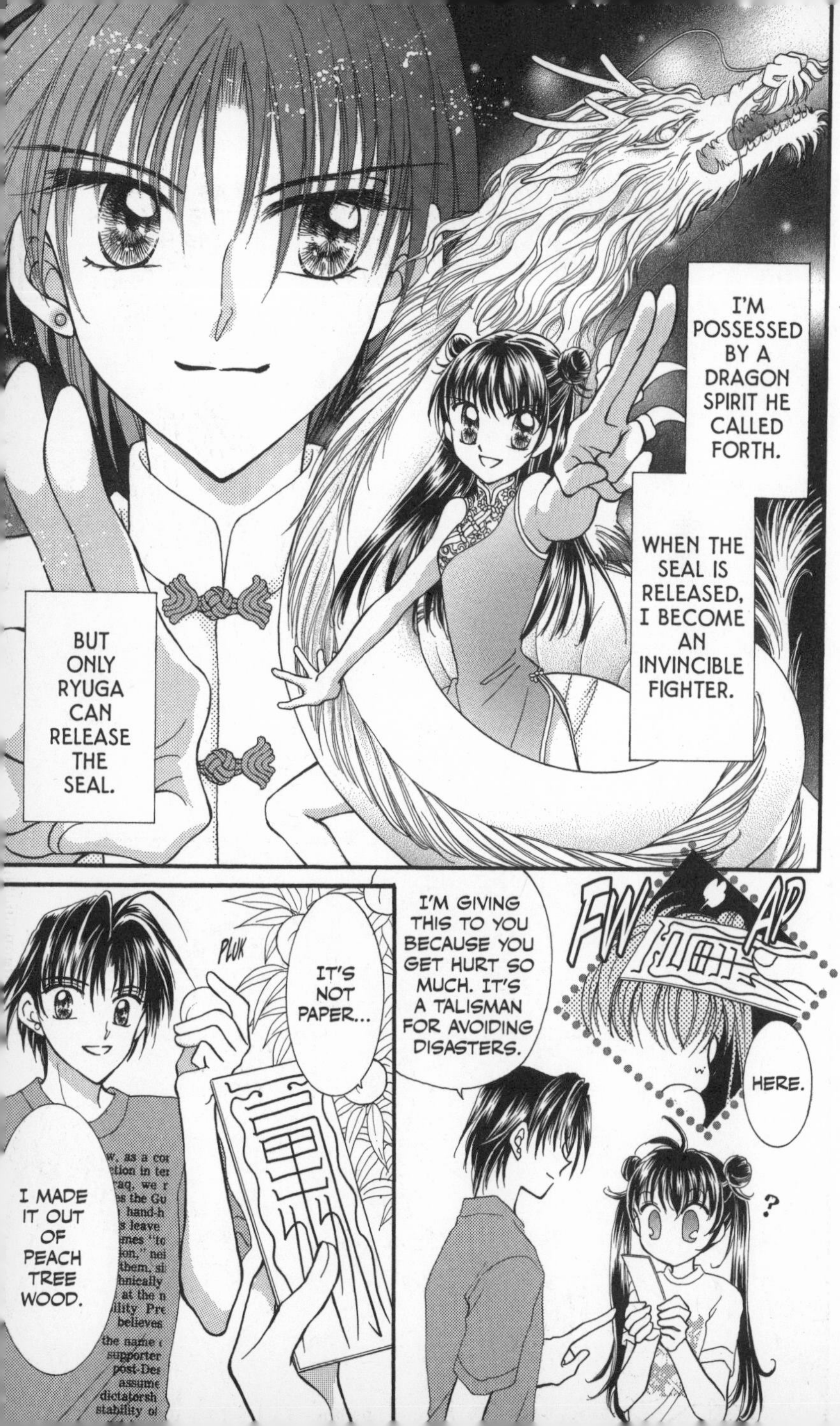
I'M POSSESSED BY A DRAGON SPIRIT HE CALLED FORTH.
WHEN THE SEAL IS RELEASED, I BECOME AN INVINCIBLE FIGHTER.
BUT ONLY RYUGA CAN RELEASE THE SEAL.
FWAP
HERE.
?
I'M GIVING THIS TO YOU BECAUSE YOU GET HURT SO MUCH. IT'S A TALISMAN FOR AVOIDING DISASTERS.
IT'S NOT PAPER...
PLUK
I MADE IT OUT OF PEACH TREE WOOD.

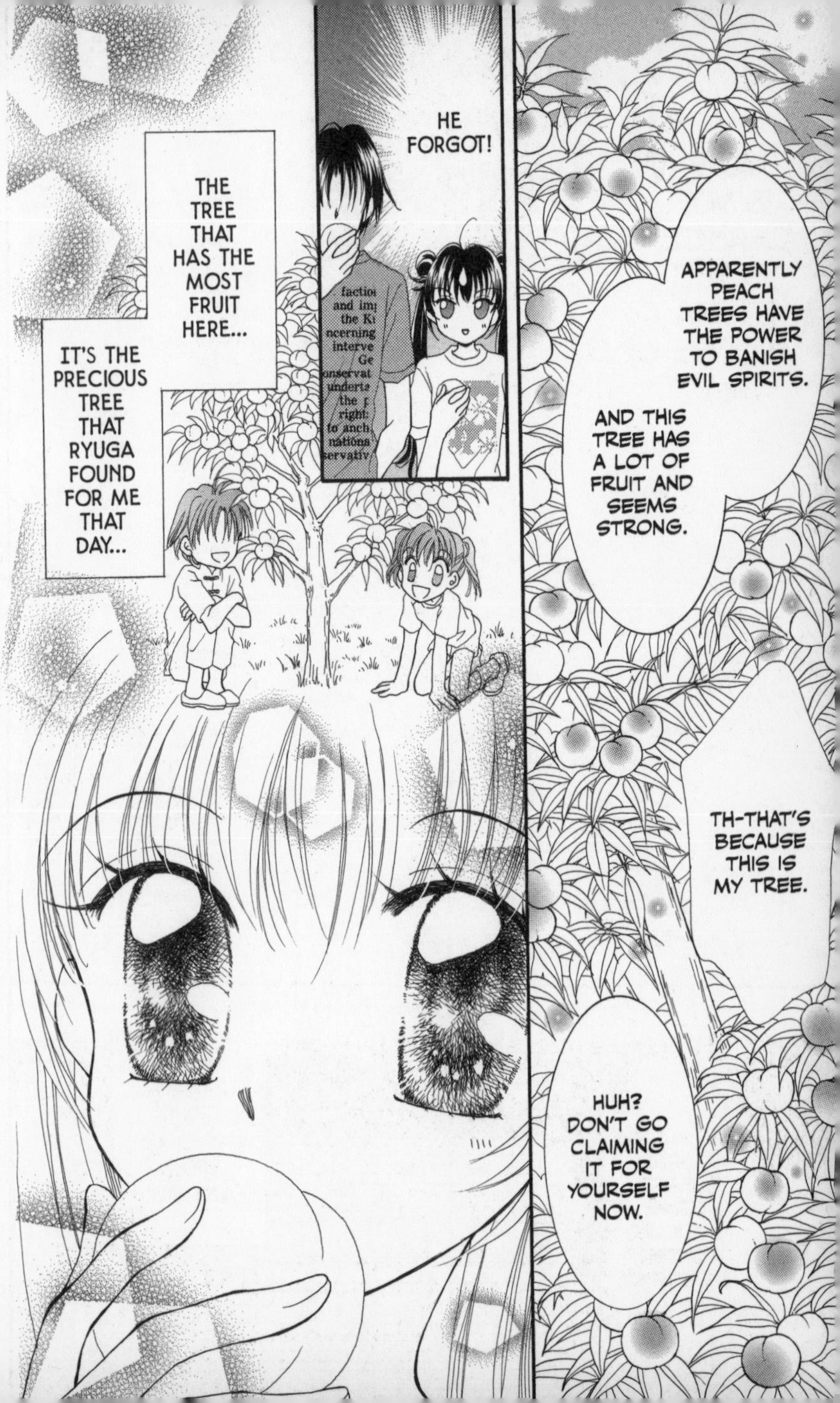
APPARENTLY PEACH TREES HAVE THE POWER TO BANISH EVIL SPIRITS.
AND THIS TREE HAS A LOT OF FRUIT AND SEEMS STRONG.
TH-THAT'S BECAUSE THIS IS MY TREE.
HUH? DON'T GO CLAIMING IT FOR YOURSELF NOW.
HE FORGOT!
THE TREE THAT HAS THE MOST FRUIT HERE...
IT'S THE PRECIOUS TREE THAT RYUGA FOUND FOR ME THAT DAY...

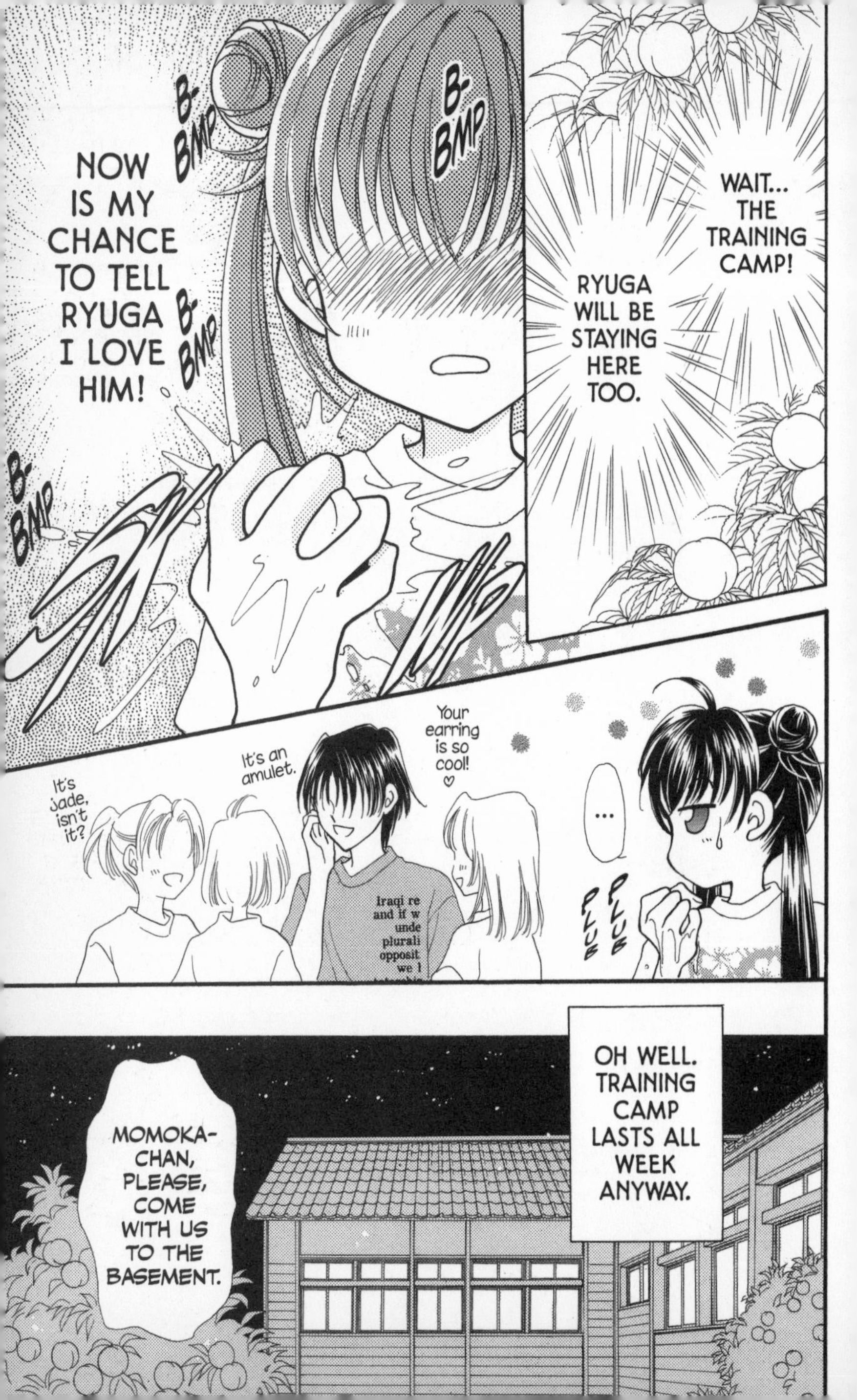
WAIT... THE TRAINING CAMP!
RYUGA WILL BE STAYING HERE TOO.
B-BMP
B-BMP
NOW IS MY CHANCE TO TELL RYUGA I LOVE HIM!
B-BMP
B-BMP
...
PLUB PLUB
Your earring is so cool!
It's an amulet.
It's jade, isn't it?
OH WELL. TRAINING CAMP LASTS ALL WEEK ANYWAY.
MOMOKA-CHAN, PLEASE, COME WITH US TO THE BASEMENT.

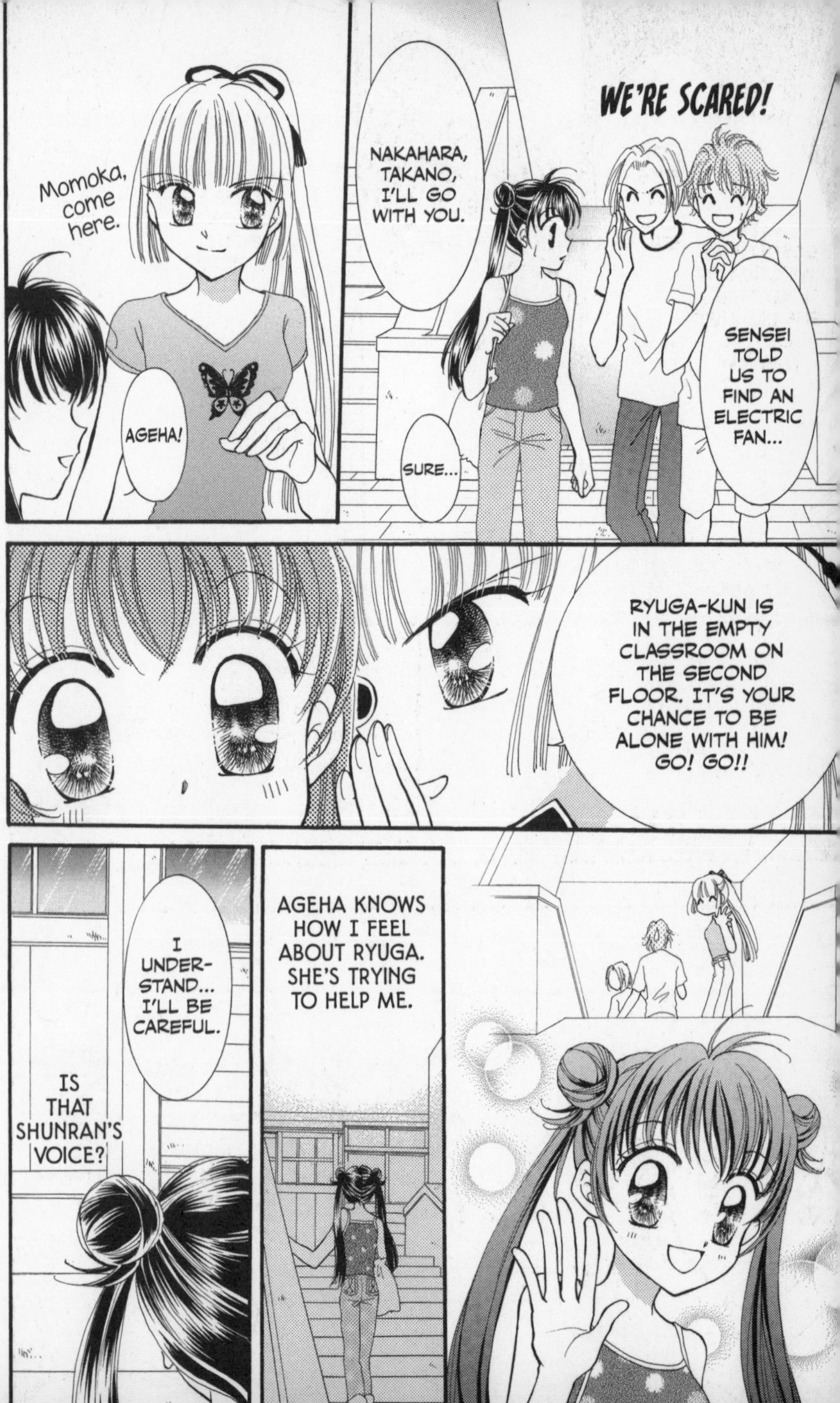
WE'RE SCARED!
NAKAHARA, TAKANO, I'LL GO WITH YOU.
SENSEI TOLD US TO FIND AN ELECTRIC FAN...
SURE...
Momoka, come here.
AGEHA!
RYUGA-KUN IS IN THE EMPTY CLASSROOM ON THE SECOND FLOOR. IT'S YOUR CHANCE TO BE ALONE WITH HIM! GO! GO!!
AGEHA KNOWS HOW I FEEL ABOUT RYUGA. SHE'S TRYING TO HELP ME.
I UNDER-STAND... I'LL BE CAREFUL.
IS THAT SHUNRAN'S VOICE?

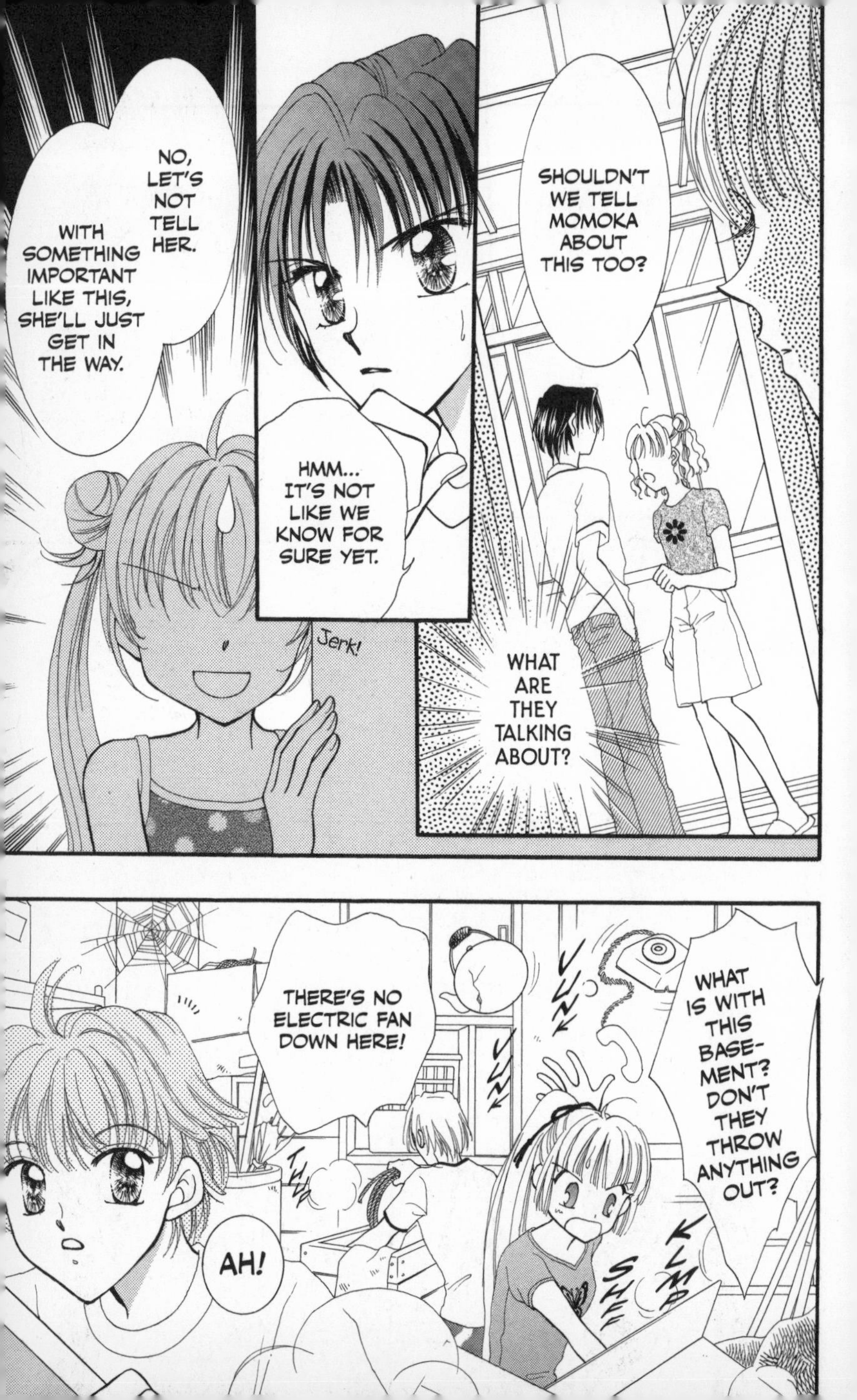
SHOULDN'T WE TELL MOMOKA ABOUT THIS TOO?
HMM... IT'S NOT LIKE WE KNOW FOR SURE YET.
NO, LET'S NOT TELL HER.
WITH SOMETHING IMPORTANT LIKE THIS, SHE'LL JUST GET IN THE WAY.
WHAT ARE THEY TALKING ABOUT?
Jerk!
WHAT IS WITH THIS BASEMENT? DON'T THEY THROW ANYTHING OUT?
KLMP
SHFF
JUN
JUN
THERE'S NO ELECTRIC FAN DOWN HERE!
THMP
AH!

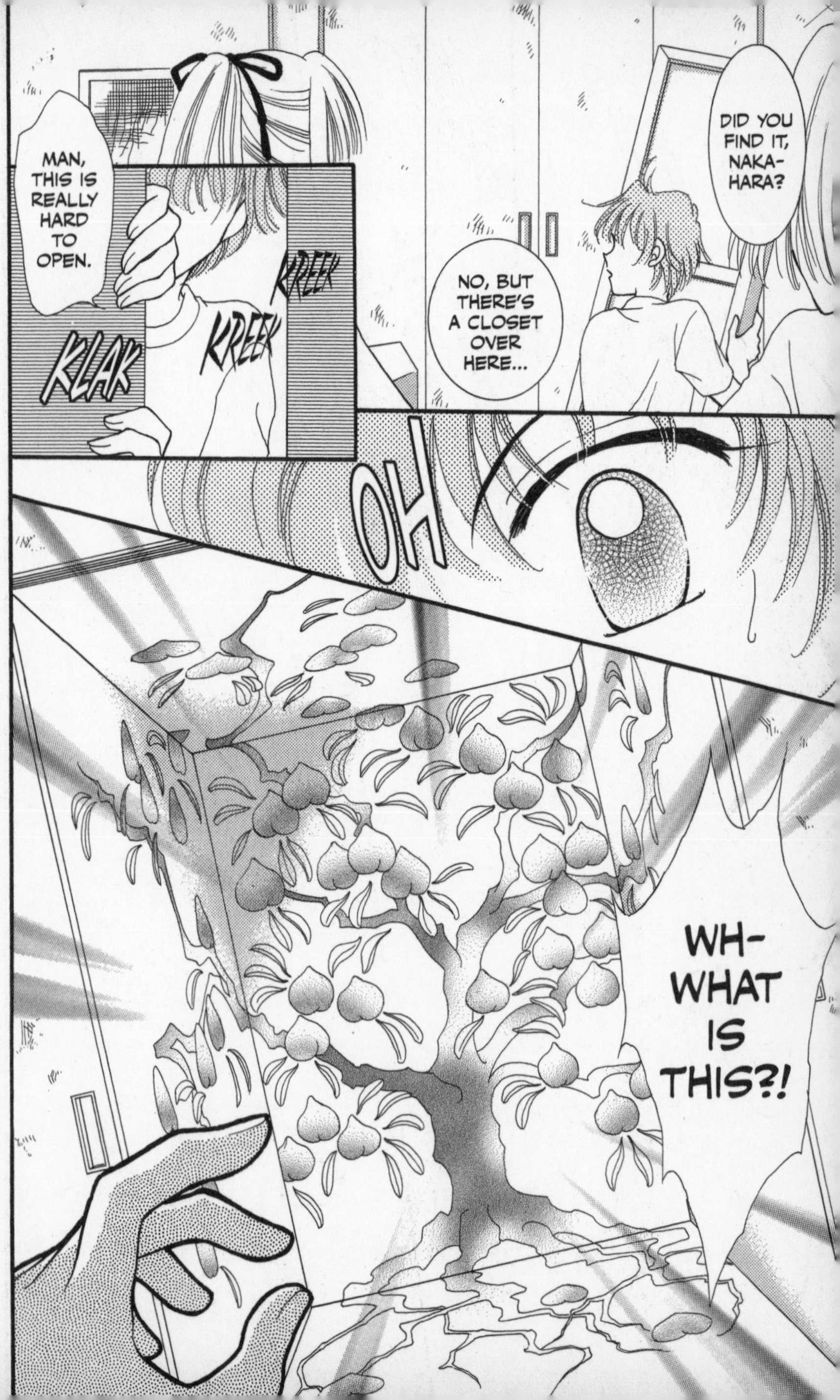
DID YOU FIND IT, NAKA-HARA?
NO, BUT THERE'S A CLOSET OVER HERE...
MAN, THIS IS REALLY HARD TO OPEN.
KREEK
KREEK
KLAK
OH
WH-WHAT IS THIS?!

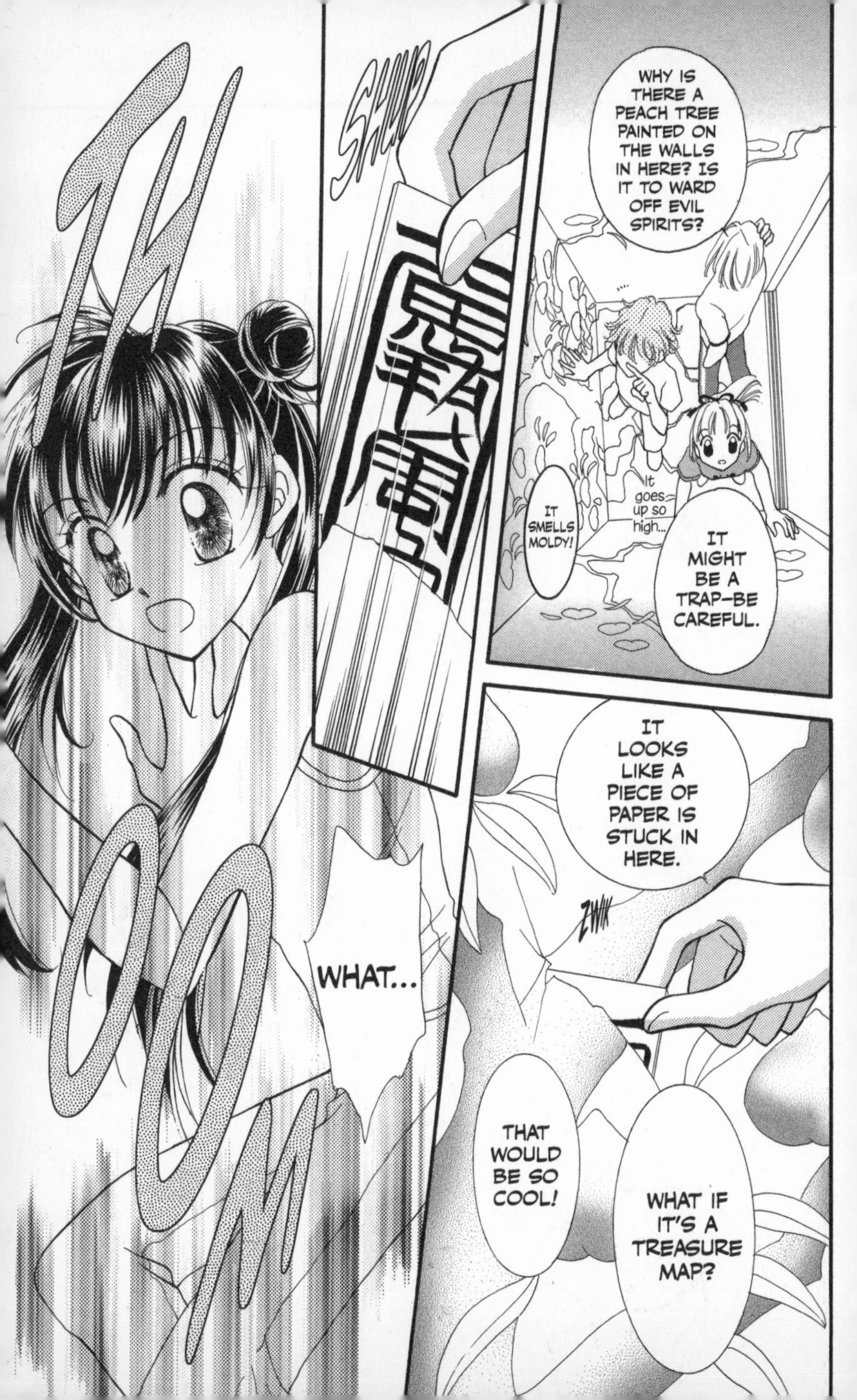

WHY IS THERE A PEACH TREE PAINTED ON THE WALLS IN HERE? IS IT TO WARD OFF EVIL SPIRITS?
IT MIGHT BE A TRAP—BE CAREFUL.
It goes up so high...
IT SMELLS MOLDY!
IT LOOKS LIKE A PIECE OF PAPER IS STUCK IN HERE.
ZWIK
WHAT IF IT'S A TREASURE MAP?
THAT WOULD BE SO COOL!
SHUP
WHAT...

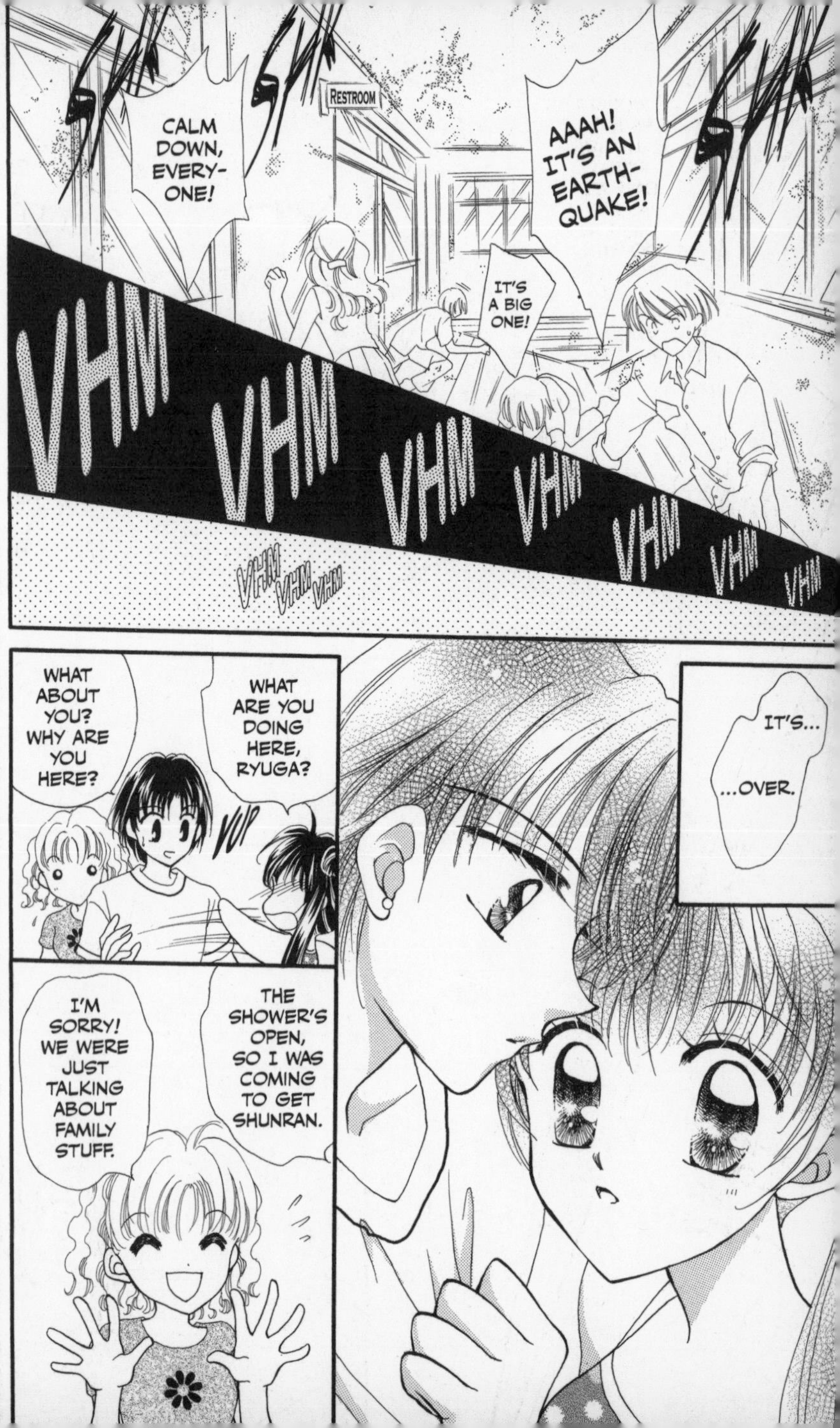
AAAH! IT'S AN EARTH-QUAKE!
RESTROOM
CALM DOWN, EVERY-ONE!
IT'S A BIG ONE!
VHM VHM VHM VHM VHM VHM VHM
VHM VHM VHM
IT'S...
...OVER.
WHAT ARE YOU DOING HERE, RYUGA?
VUP
WHAT ABOUT YOU? WHY ARE YOU HERE?
THE SHOWER'S OPEN, SO I WAS COMING TO GET SHUNRAN.
I'M SORRY! WE WERE JUST TALKING ABOUT FAMILY STUFF.

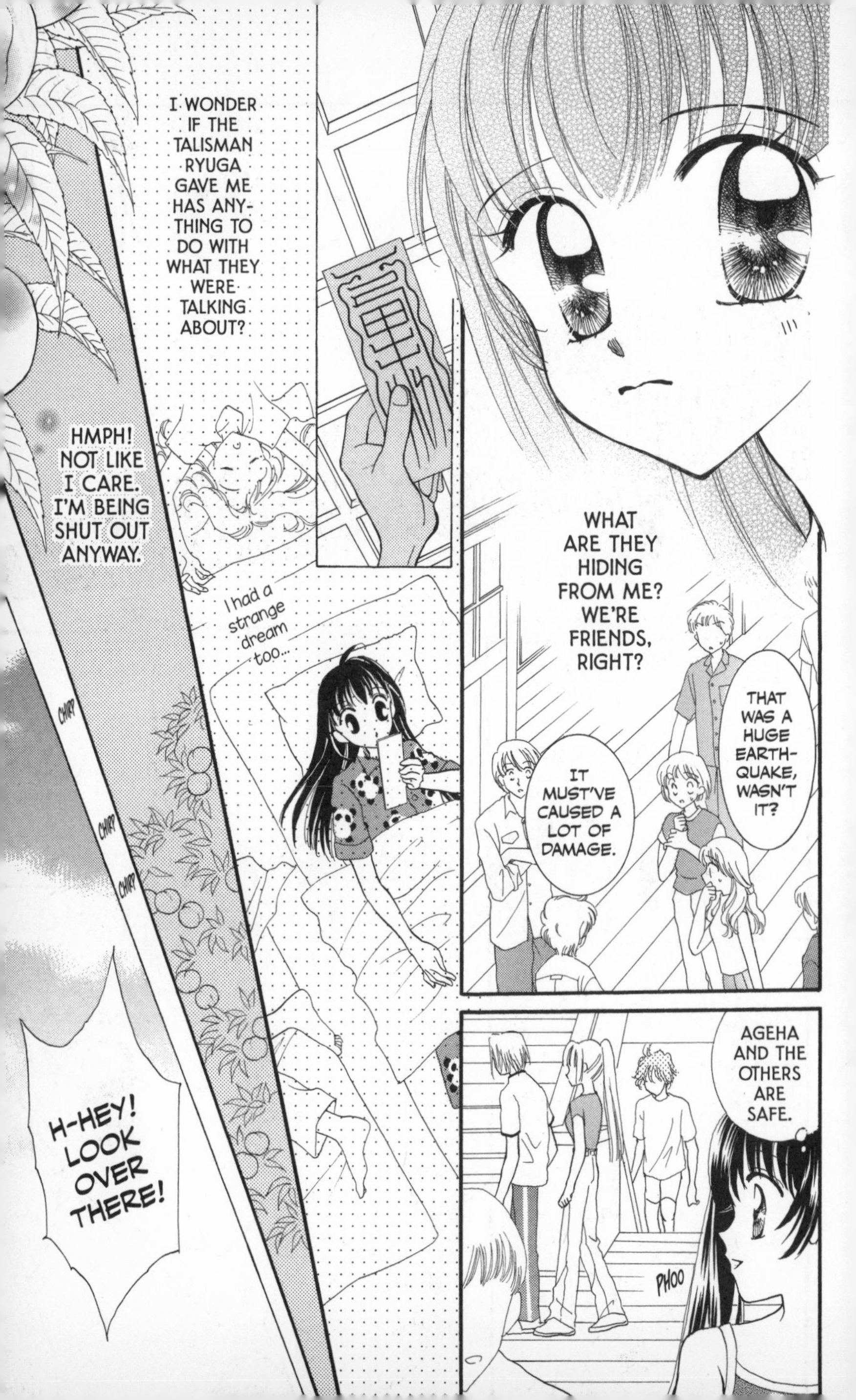
WHAT ARE THEY HIDING FROM ME? WE'RE FRIENDS, RIGHT?
THAT WAS A HUGE EARTHQUAKE, WASN'T IT?
IT MUST'VE CAUSED A LOT OF DAMAGE.
AGEHA AND THE OTHERS ARE SAFE.
PHOO
I WONDER IF THE TALISMAN RYUGA GAVE ME HAS ANYTHING TO DO WITH WHAT THEY WERE TALKING ABOUT?
I had a strange dream too...
HMPH! NOT LIKE I CARE. I'M BEING SHUT OUT ANYWAY.
CHIRP
CHIRP
CHIRP
H-HEY! LOOK OVER THERE!

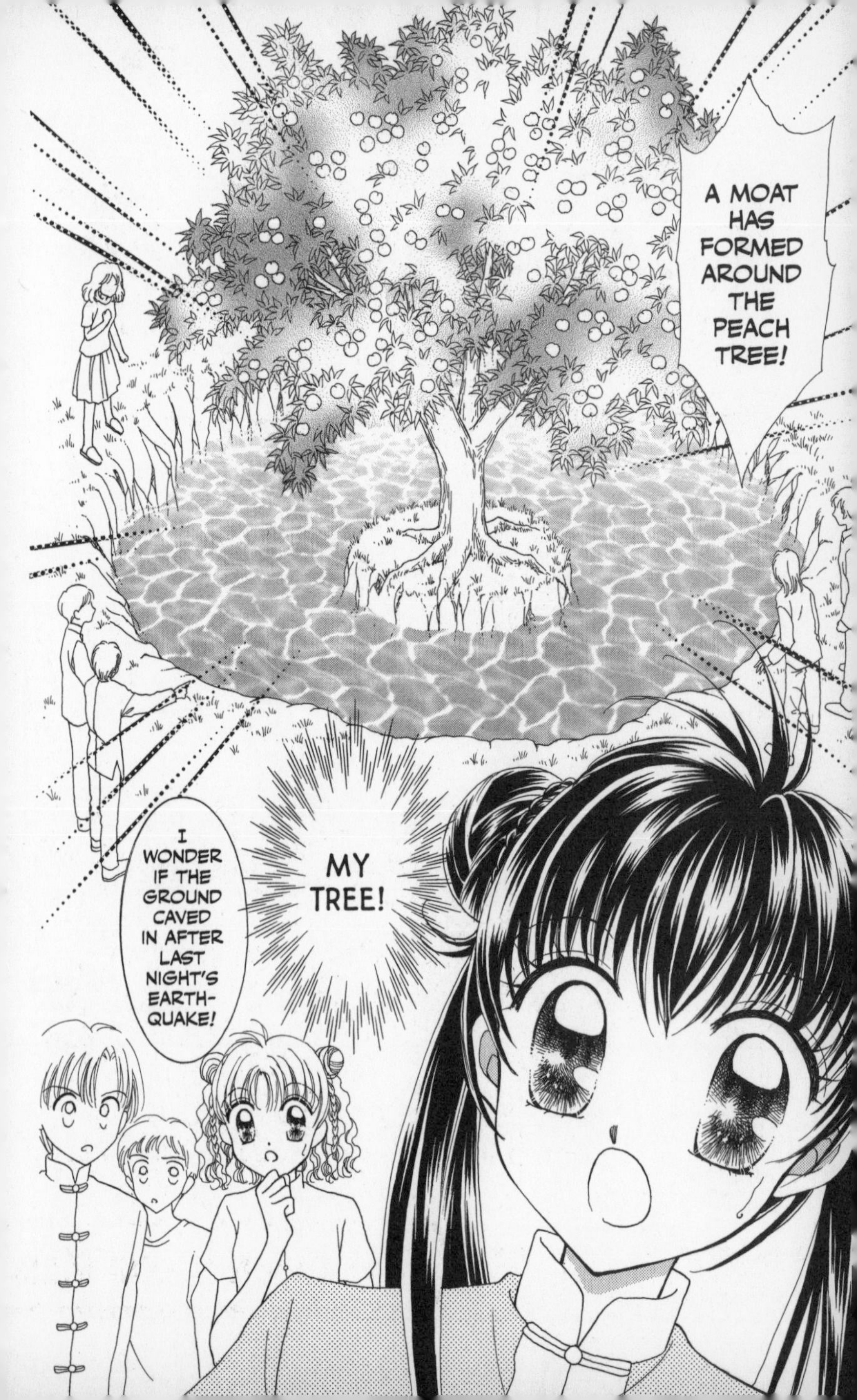
A MOAT HAS FORMED AROUND THE PEACH TREE!
MY TREE!
I WONDER IF THE GROUND CAVED IN AFTER LAST NIGHT'S EARTH-QUAKE!

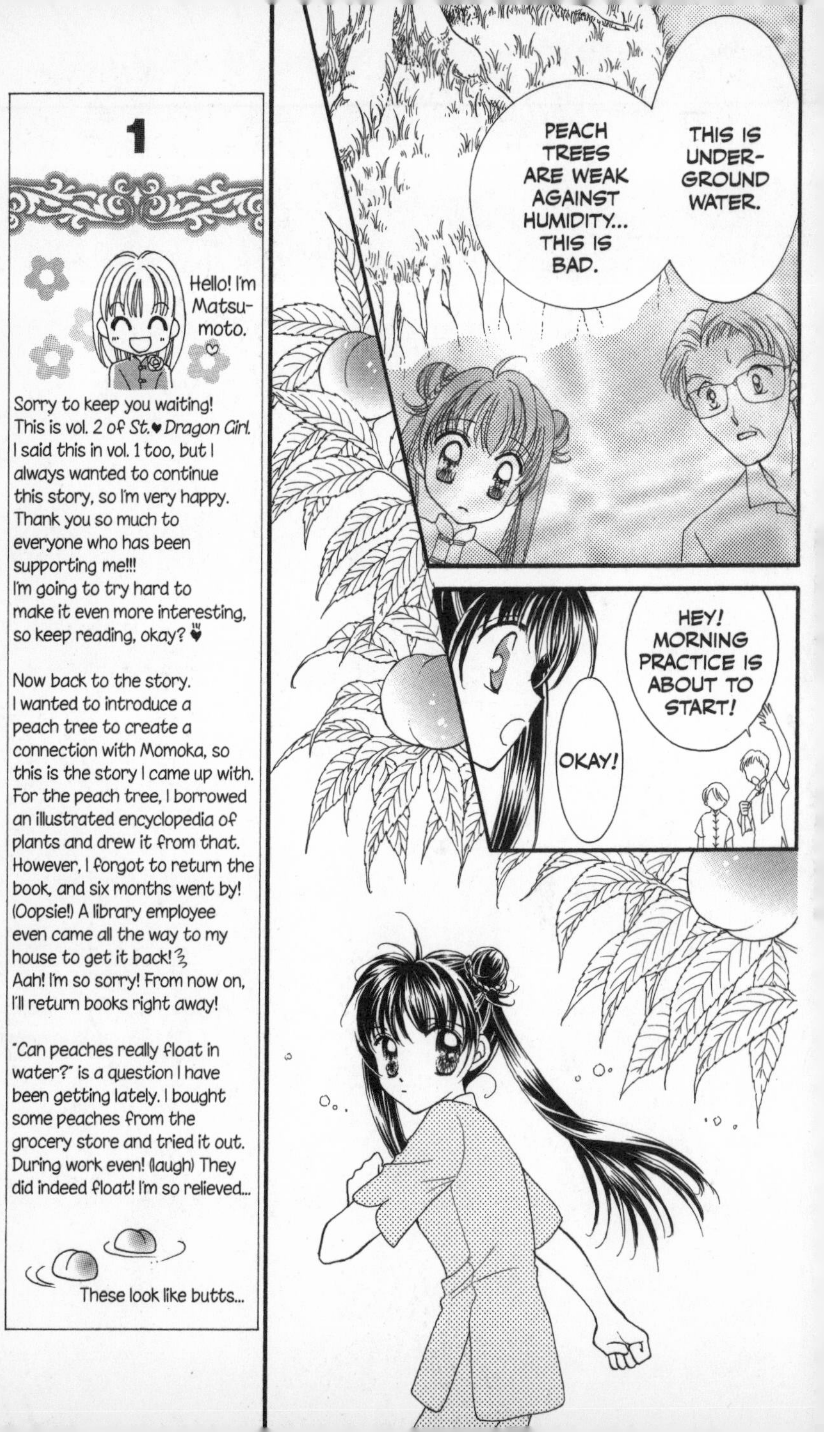
THIS IS UNDER-GROUND WATER.
PEACH TREES ARE WEAK AGAINST HUMIDITY... THIS IS BAD.
HEY! MORNING PRACTICE IS ABOUT TO START!
OKAY!

1

Hello! I'm Matsu-moto. ♡

Sorry to keep you waiting! This is vol. 2 of *St.♥Dragon Girl*. I said this in vol. 1 too, but I always wanted to continue this story, so I'm very happy. Thank you so much to everyone who has been supporting me!!! I'm going to try hard to make it even more interesting, so keep reading, okay? ♥

Now back to the story. I wanted to introduce a peach tree to create a connection with Momoka, so this is the story I came up with. For the peach tree, I borrowed an illustrated encyclopedia of plants and drew it from that. However, I forgot to return the book, and six months went by! (Oopsie!) A library employee even came all the way to my house to get it back! Aah! I'm so sorry! From now on, I'll return books right away!

"Can peaches really float in water?" is a question I have been getting lately. I bought some peaches from the grocery store and tried it out. During work even! (laugh) They did indeed float! I'm so relieved...

These look like butts...

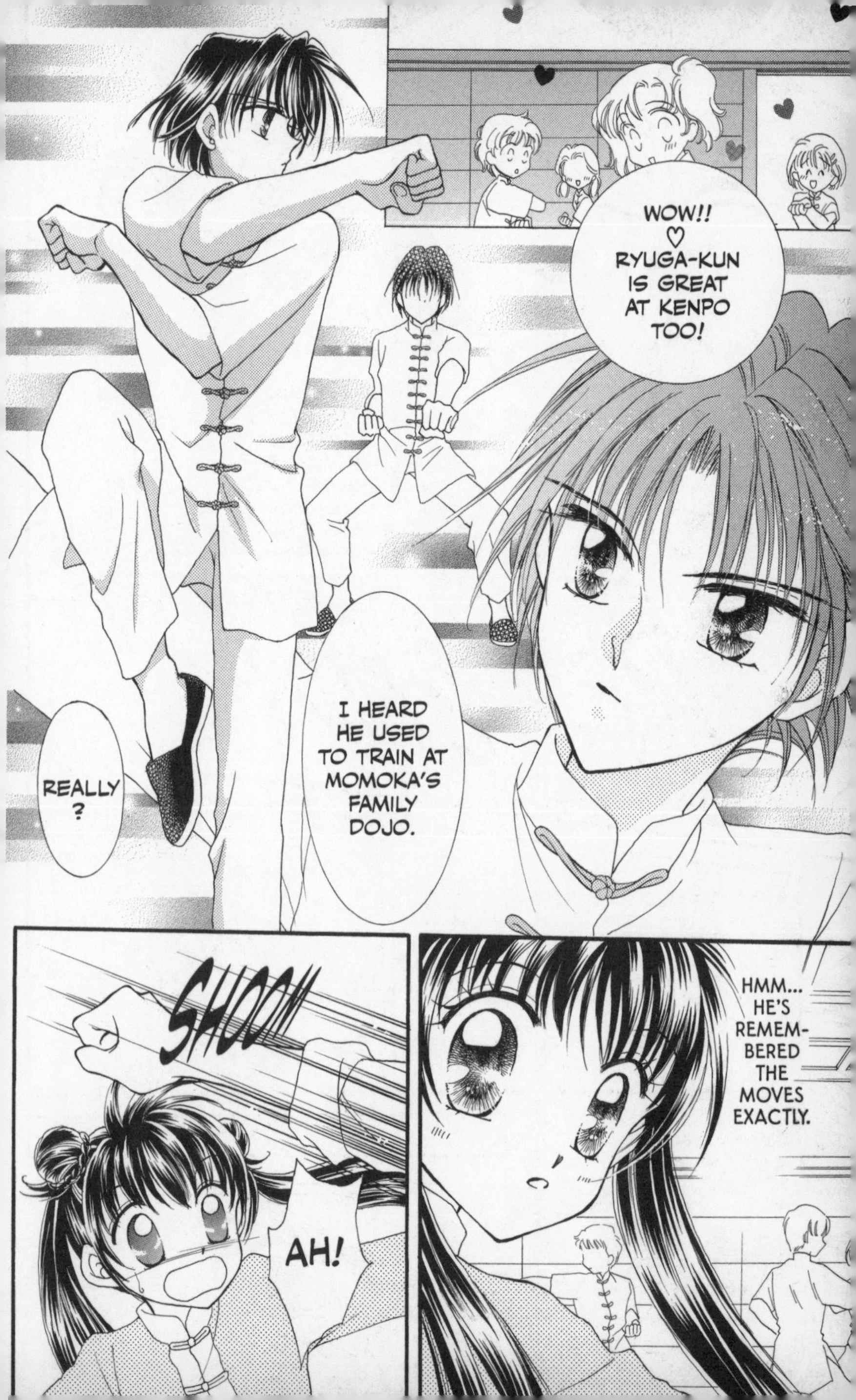
WOW!! ♡ RYUGA-KUN IS GREAT AT KENPO TOO!
I HEARD HE USED TO TRAIN AT MOMOKA'S FAMILY DOJO.
REALLY?
HMM... HE'S REMEMBERED THE MOVES EXACTLY.
SHOO
AH!

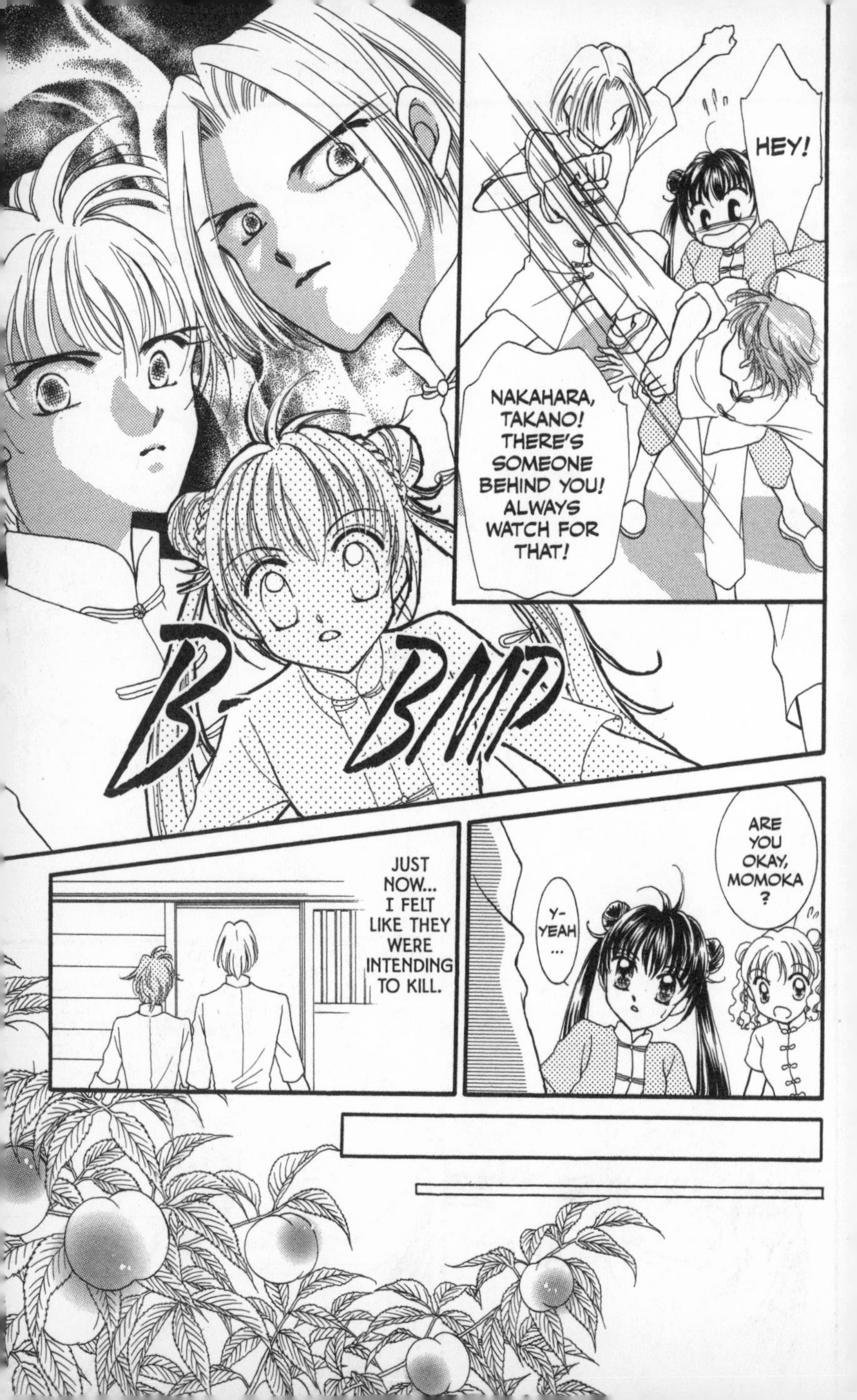
HEY!
NAKAHARA, TAKANO! THERE'S SOMEONE BEHIND YOU! ALWAYS WATCH FOR THAT!
B-BMP
ARE YOU OKAY, MOMOKA?
Y-YEAH...
JUST NOW... I FELT LIKE THEY WERE INTENDING TO KILL.

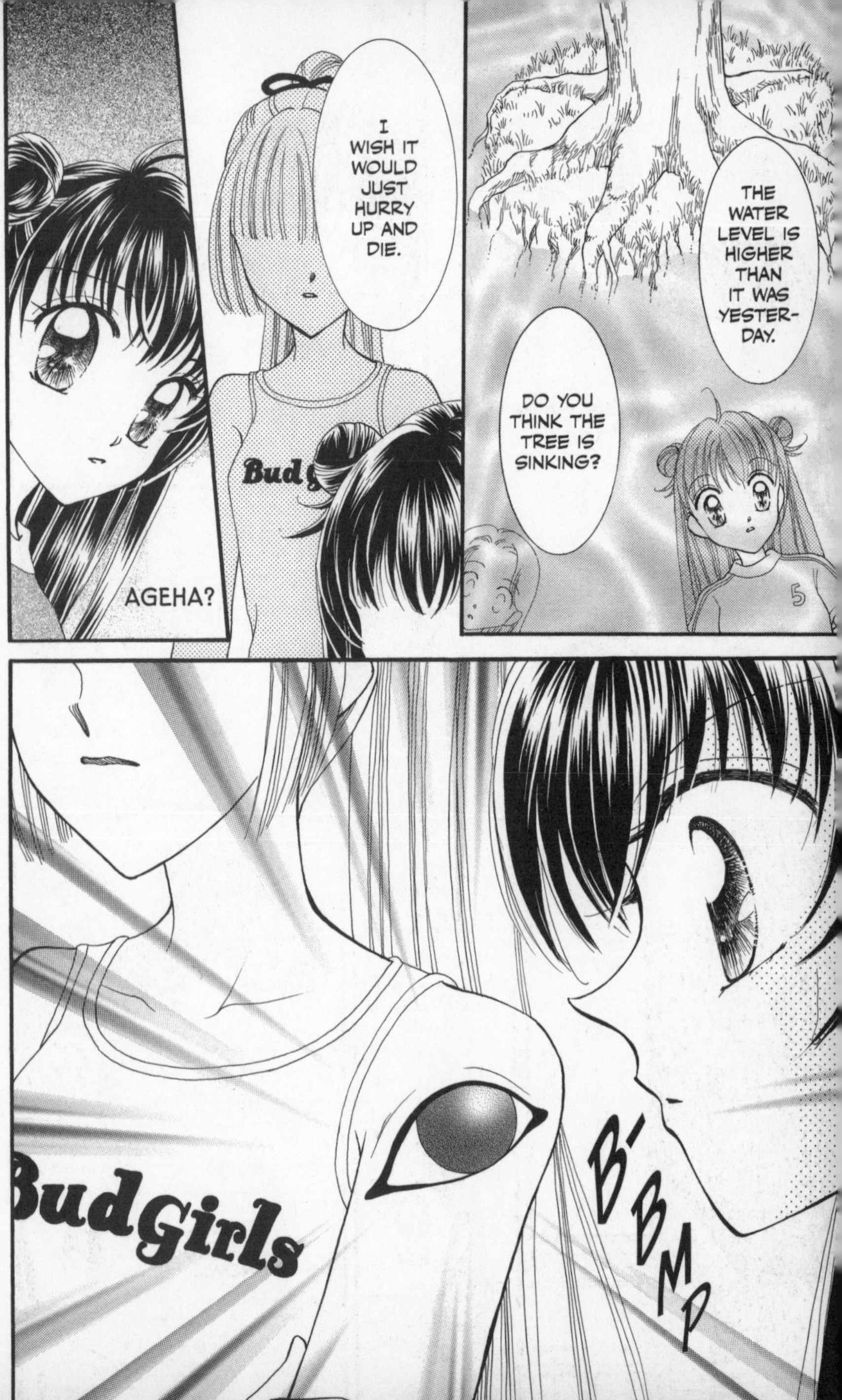
THE WATER LEVEL IS HIGHER THAN IT WAS YESTERDAY.
DO YOU THINK THE TREE IS SINKING?
I WISH IT WOULD JUST HURRY UP AND DIE.
AGEHA?
B-BMP
BudGirls

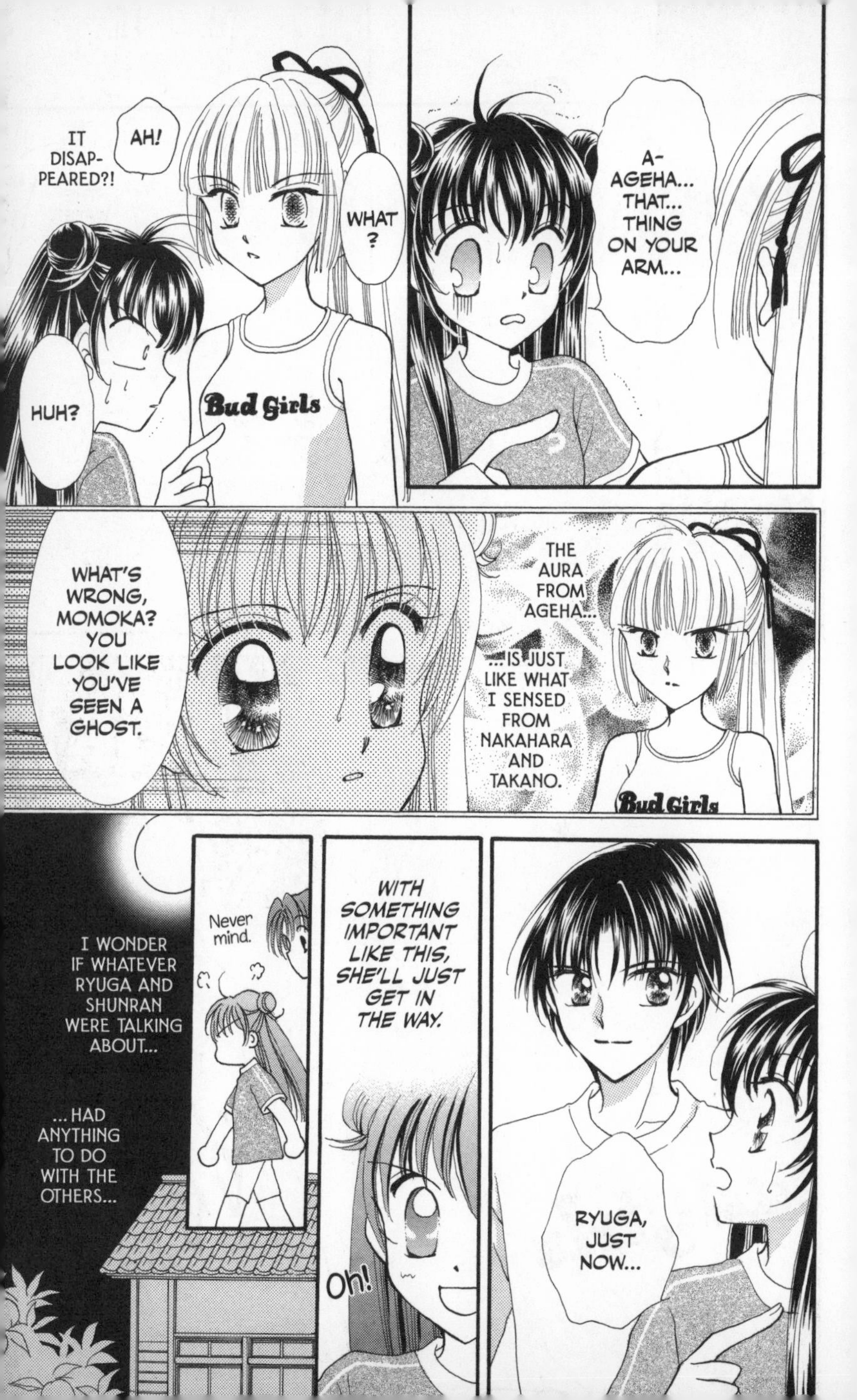
A- AGEHA... THAT... THING ON YOUR ARM...
WHAT?
AH!
IT DISAPPEARED?!
HUH?
THE AURA FROM AGEHA...
...IS JUST LIKE WHAT I SENSED FROM NAKAHARA AND TAKANO.
WHAT'S WRONG, MOMOKA? YOU LOOK LIKE YOU'VE SEEN A GHOST.
RYUGA, JUST NOW...
WITH SOMETHING IMPORTANT LIKE THIS, SHE'LL JUST GET IN THE WAY.
Oh!
Never mind.
I WONDER IF WHATEVER RYUGA AND SHUNRAN WERE TALKING ABOUT...
...HAD ANYTHING TO DO WITH THE OTHERS...

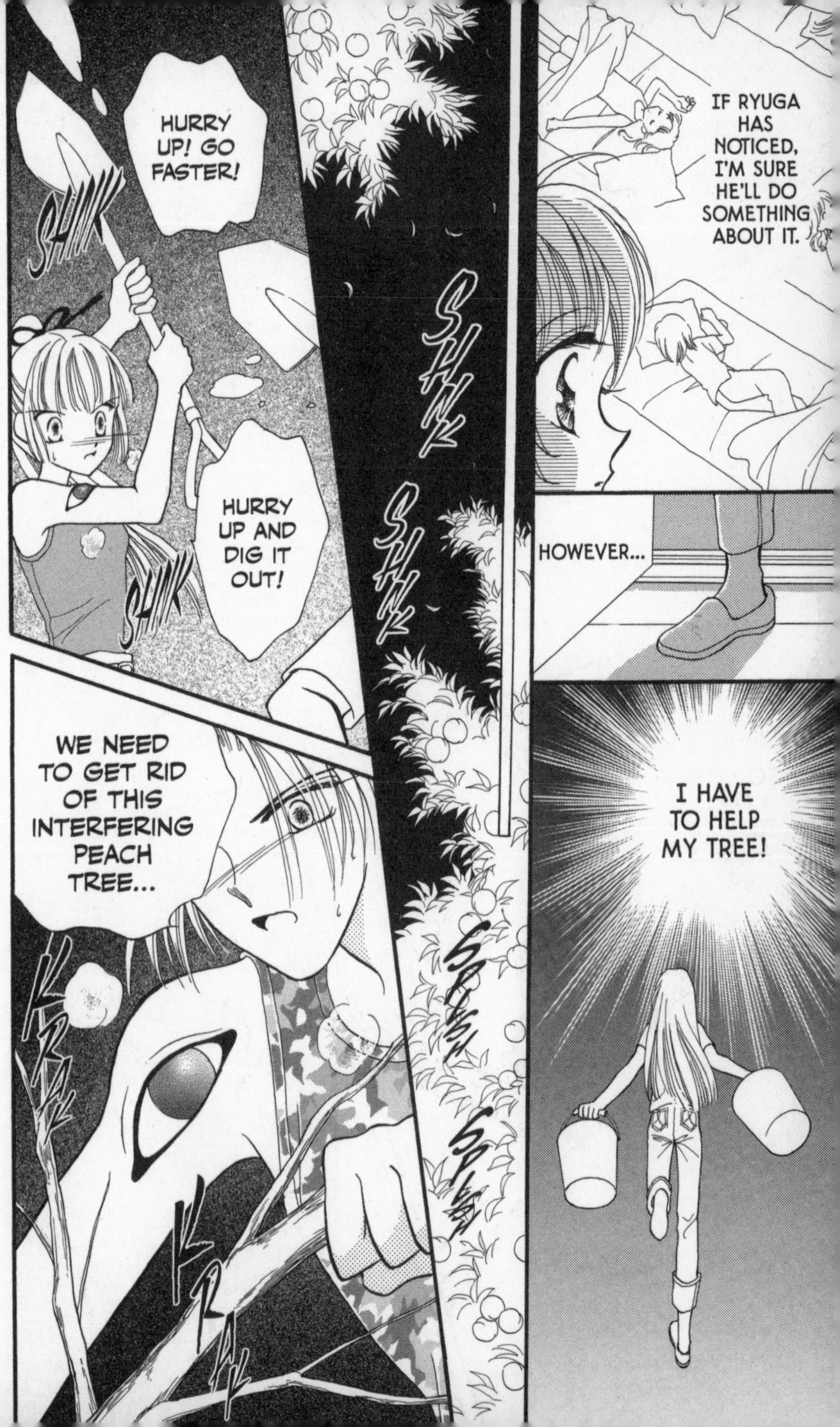
IF RYUGA HAS NOTICED, I'M SURE HE'LL DO SOMETHING ABOUT IT.
HOWEVER...
I HAVE TO HELP MY TREE!
SHHNK
SHHNK
HURRY UP! GO FASTER!
HURRY UP AND DIG IT OUT!
WE NEED TO GET RID OF THIS INTERFERING PEACH TREE...

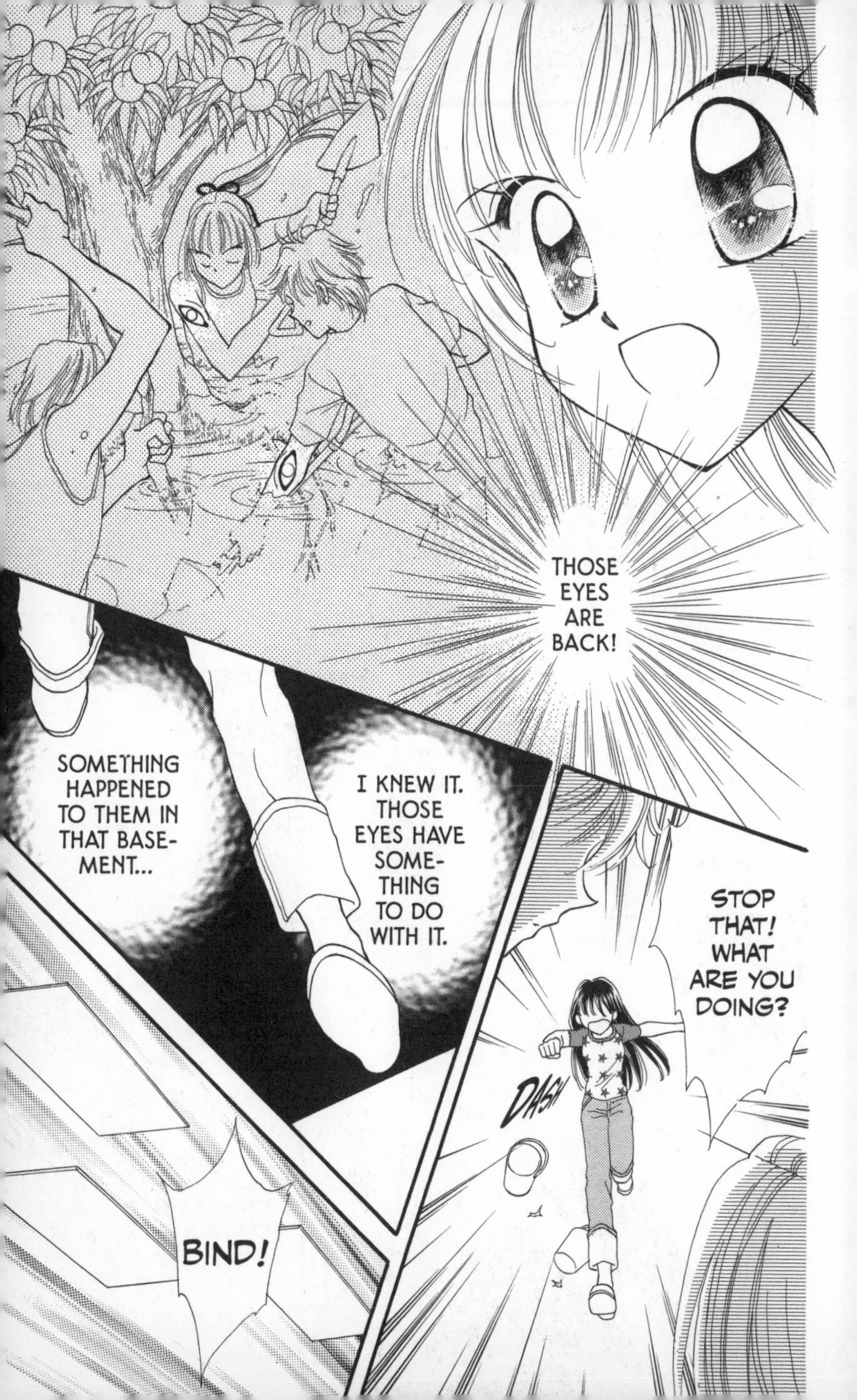
THOSE EYES ARE BACK!
STOP THAT! WHAT ARE YOU DOING?
DASH
I KNEW IT. THOSE EYES HAVE SOME-THING TO DO WITH IT.
SOMETHING HAPPENED TO THEM IN THAT BASE-MENT...
BIND!

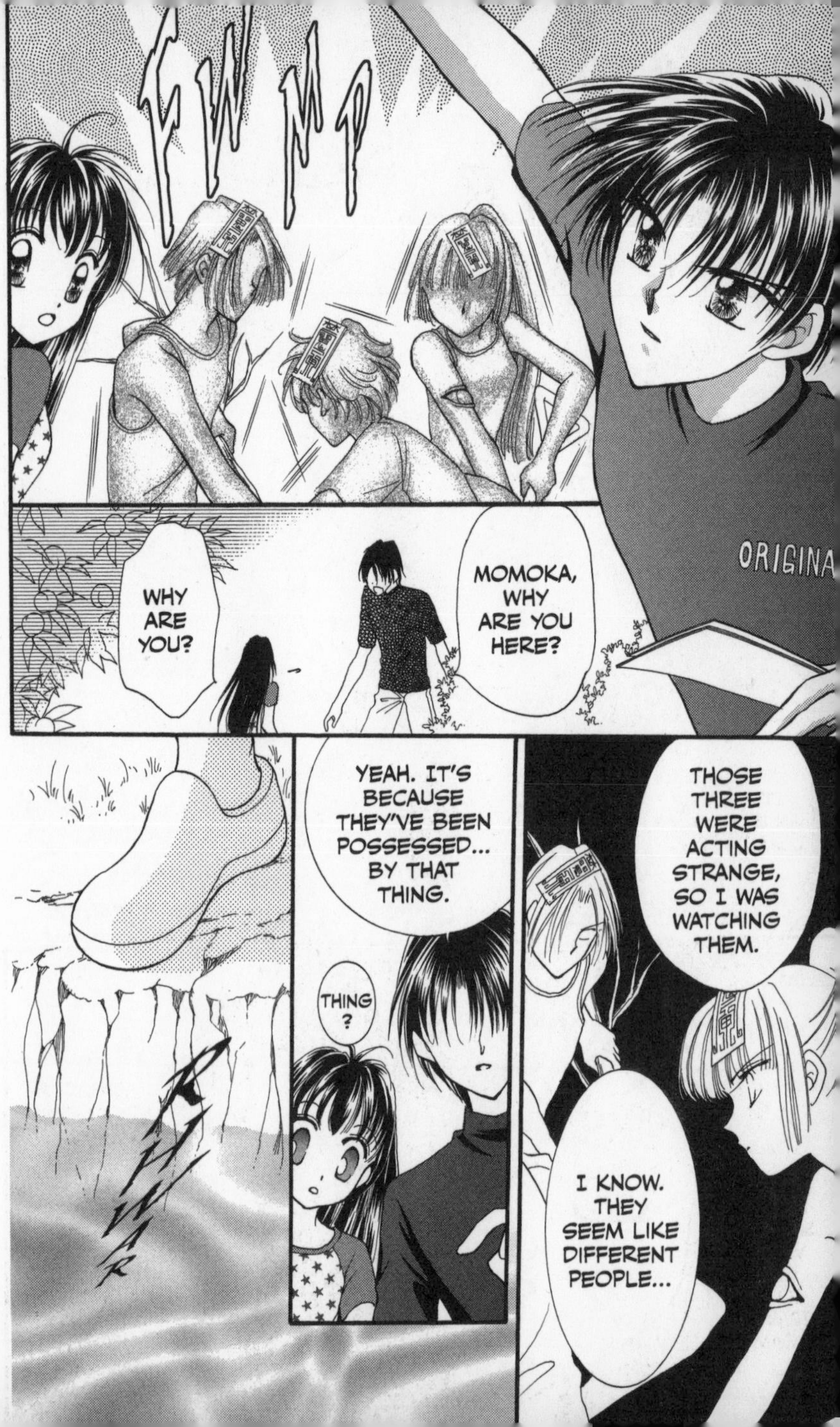
FWMP
ORIGINA
MOMOKA, WHY ARE YOU HERE?
WHY ARE YOU?
THOSE THREE WERE ACTING STRANGE, SO I WAS WATCHING THEM.
I KNOW. THEY SEEM LIKE DIFFERENT PEOPLE...
YEAH. IT'S BECAUSE THEY'VE BEEN POSSESSED... BY THAT THING.
THING?

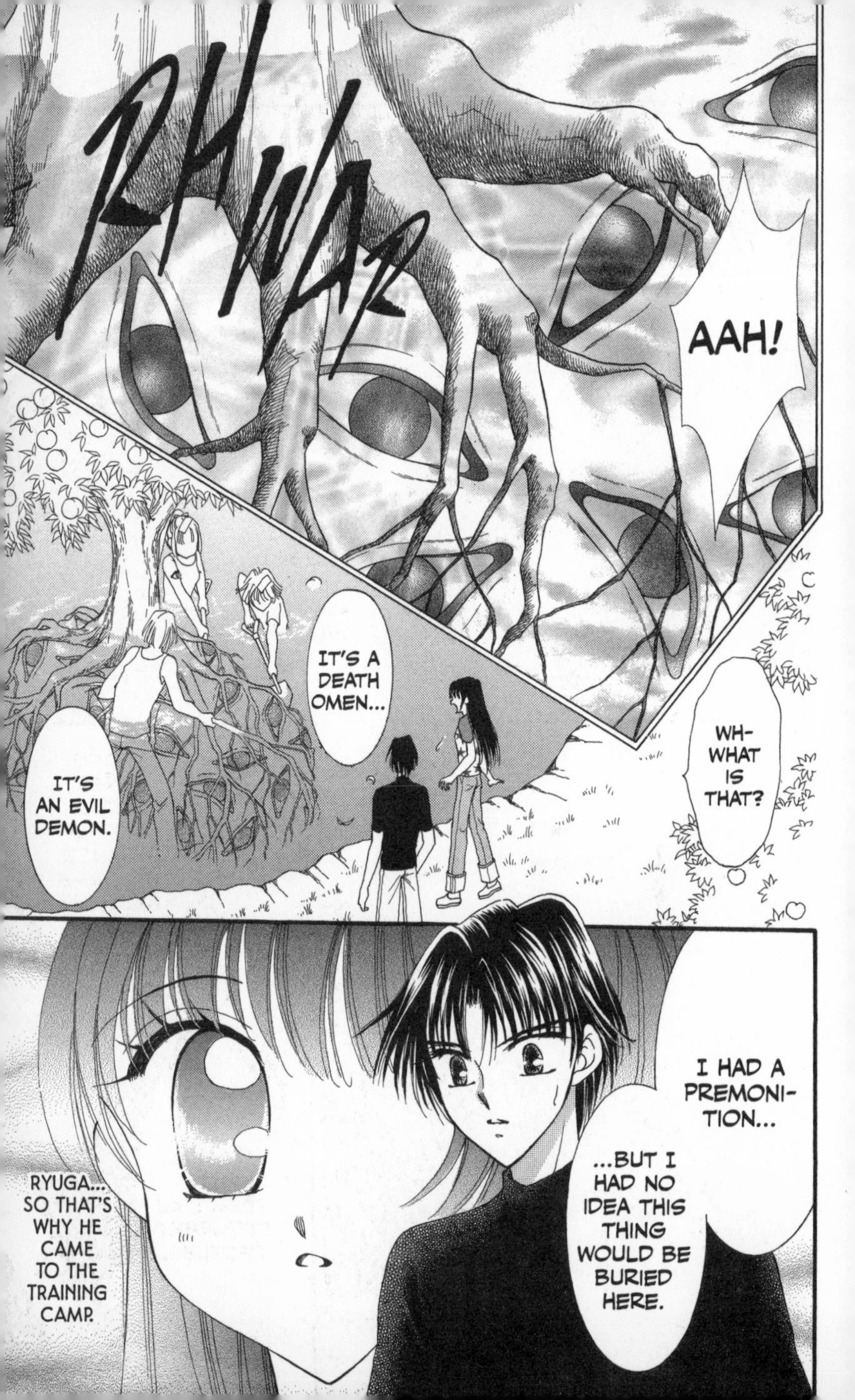
RHWAR
AAH!
WH-WHAT IS THAT?
IT'S A DEATH OMEN...
IT'S AN EVIL DEMON.
I HAD A PREMONITION...
...BUT I HAD NO IDEA THIS THING WOULD BE BURIED HERE.
RYUGA... SO THAT'S WHY HE CAME TO THE TRAINING CAMP.

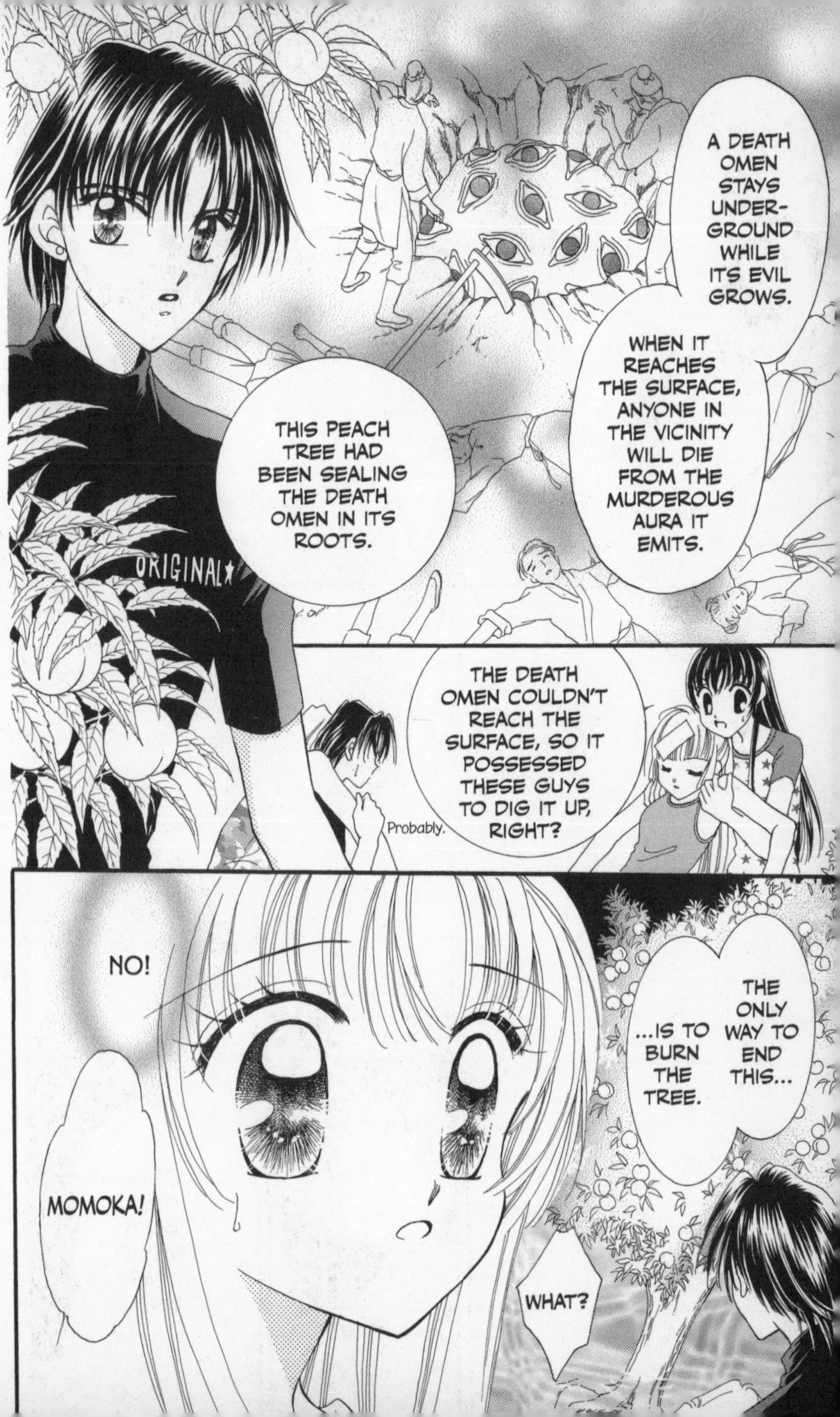
A DEATH OMEN STAYS UNDERGROUND WHILE ITS EVIL GROWS.
WHEN IT REACHES THE SURFACE, ANYONE IN THE VICINITY WILL DIE FROM THE MURDEROUS AURA IT EMITS.
THIS PEACH TREE HAD BEEN SEALING THE DEATH OMEN IN ITS ROOTS.
ORIGINAL
THE DEATH OMEN COULDN'T REACH THE SURFACE, SO IT POSSESSED THESE GUYS TO DIG IT UP, RIGHT?
Probably.
THE ONLY WAY TO END THIS...
...IS TO BURN THE TREE.
WHAT?
NO!
MOMOKA!

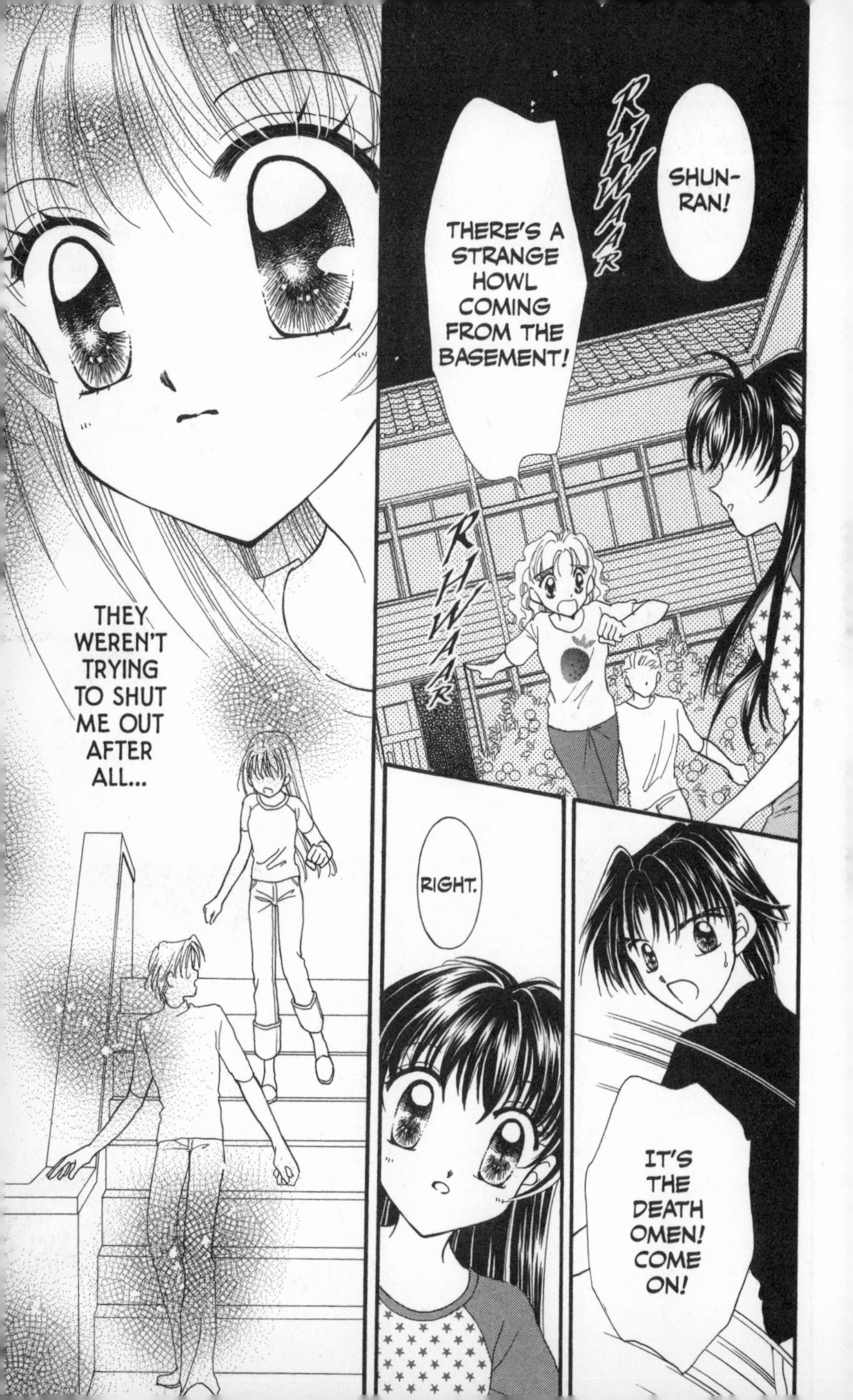
SHUN-RAN!
RHWAAR
THERE'S A STRANGE HOWL COMING FROM THE BASEMENT!
RHWAAR
IT'S THE DEATH OMEN! COME ON!
RIGHT.
THEY WEREN'T TRYING TO SHUT ME OUT AFTER ALL...

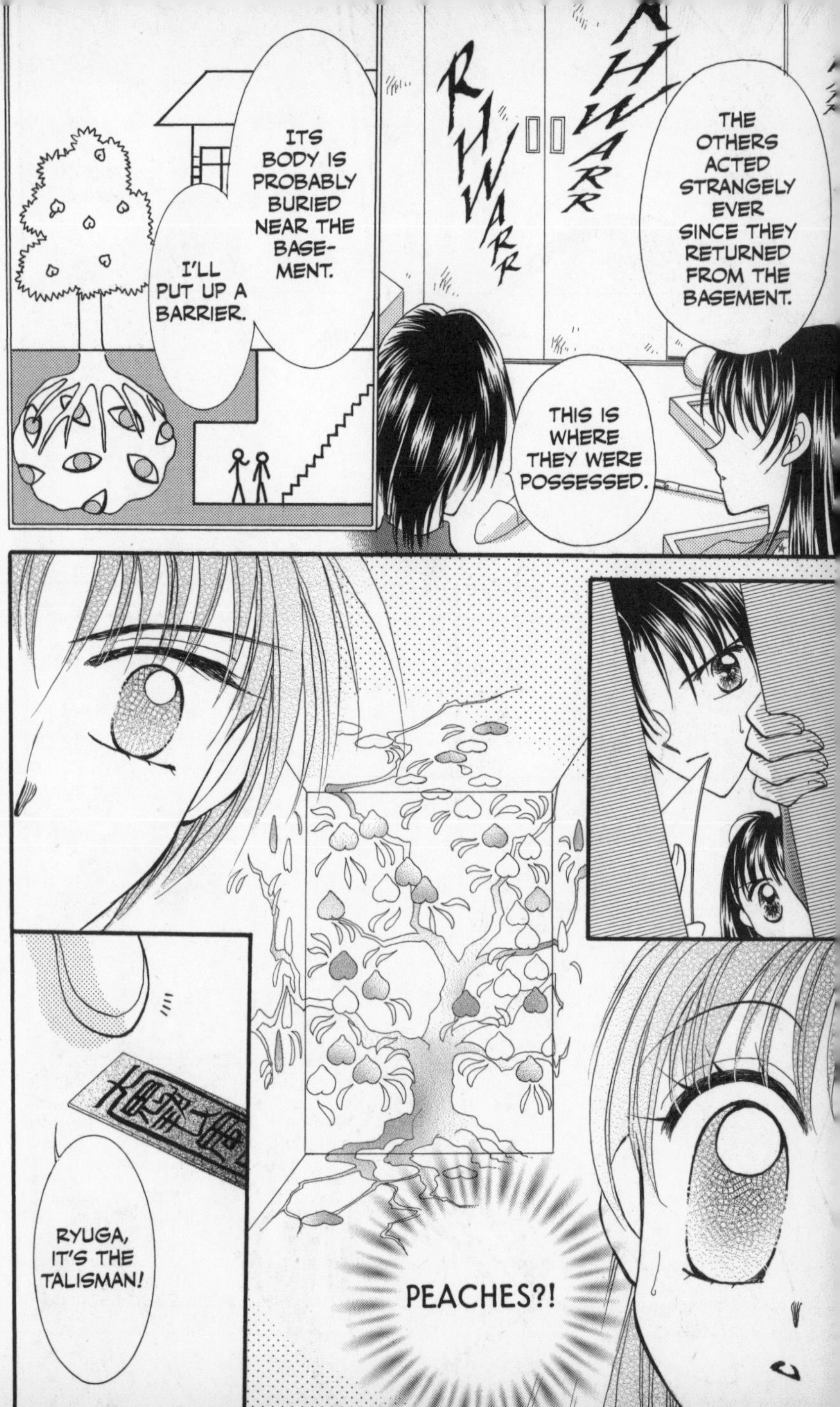
THE OTHERS ACTED STRANGELY EVER SINCE THEY RETURNED FROM THE BASEMENT.
AHWARR
RHWARR
THIS IS WHERE THEY WERE POSSESSED.
ITS BODY IS PROBABLY BURIED NEAR THE BASE-MENT.
I'LL PUT UP A BARRIER.
PEACHES?!
RYUGA, IT'S THE TALISMAN!

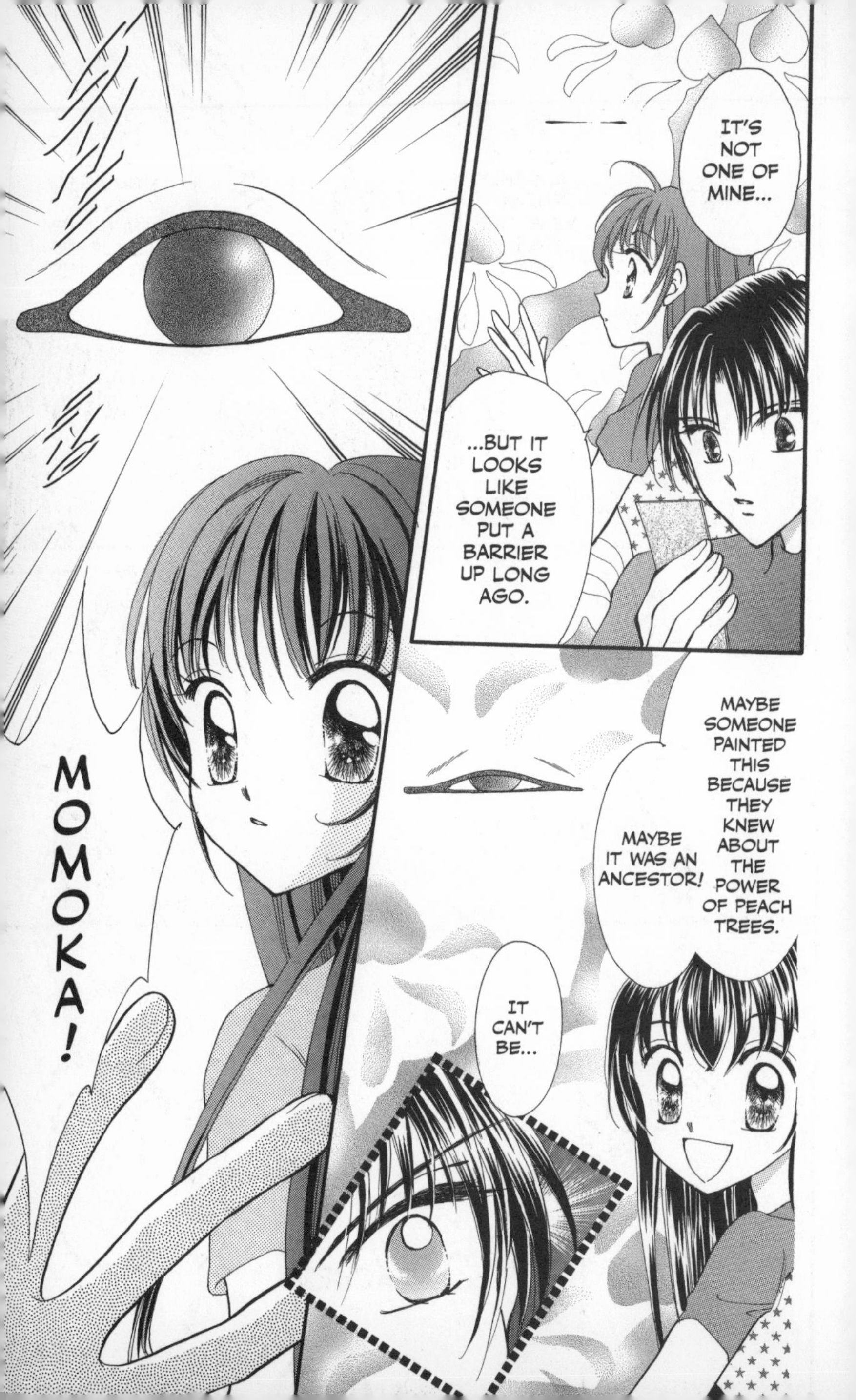
IT'S NOT ONE OF MINE...
...BUT IT LOOKS LIKE SOMEONE PUT A BARRIER UP LONG AGO.
MAYBE SOMEONE PAINTED THIS BECAUSE THEY KNEW ABOUT THE POWER OF PEACH TREES.
MAYBE IT WAS AN ANCESTOR!
IT CAN'T BE...
MOMOKA!

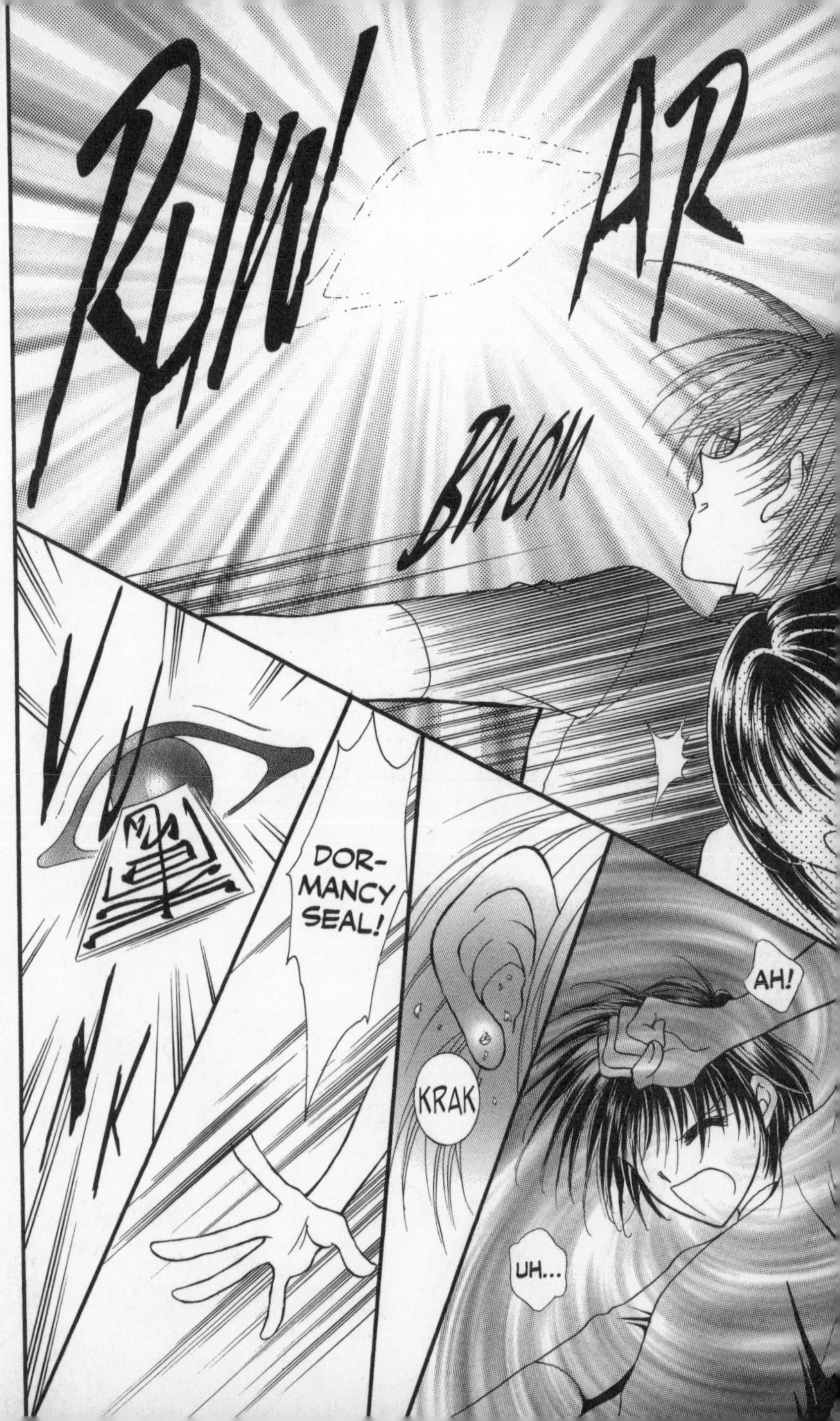
RUMBLE... ROAR
BWOM
DORMANCY SEAL!
VWNK
AH!
KRAK
UH...

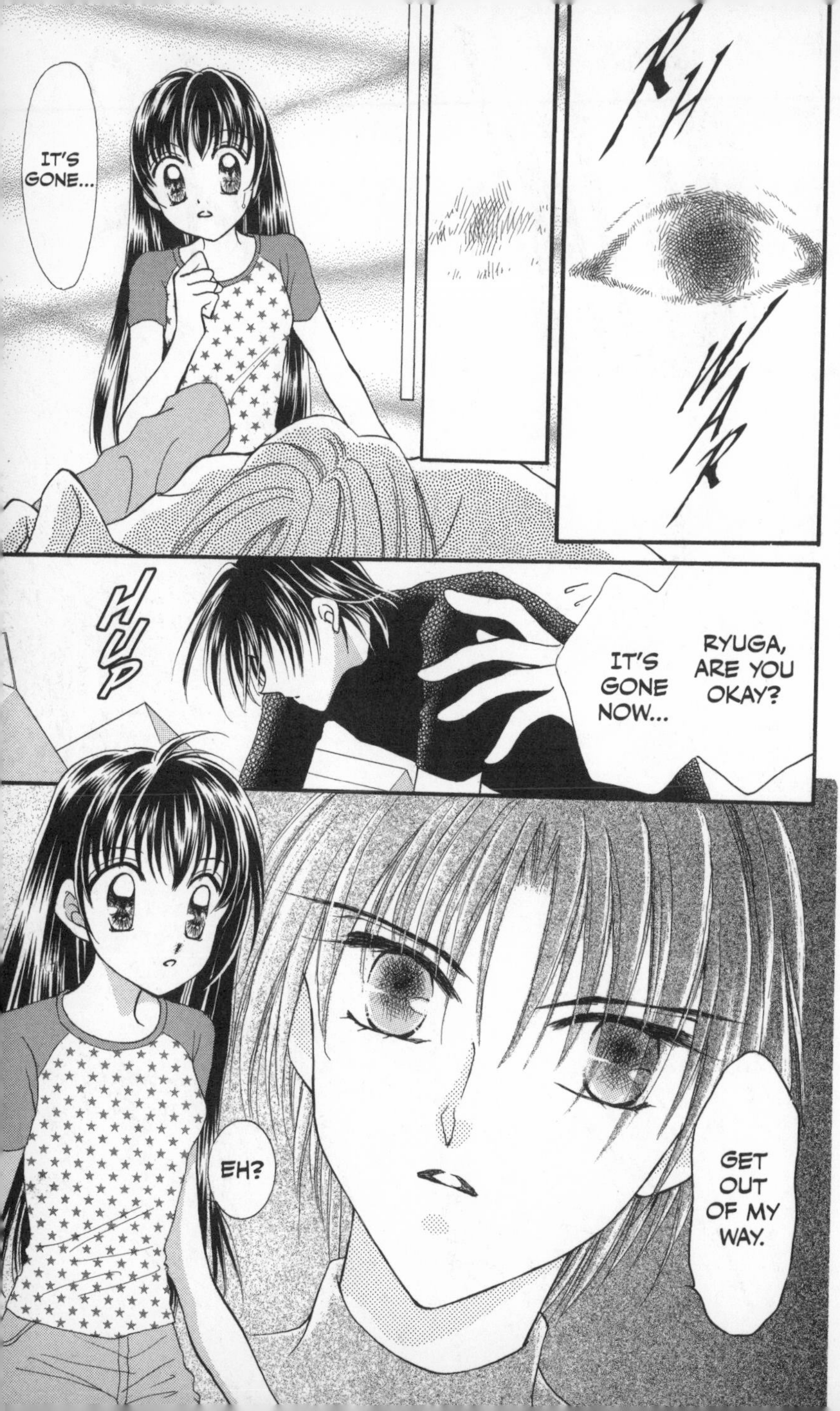
RHWAR
IT'S GONE...
RYUGA, ARE YOU OKAY?
IT'S GONE NOW...
HUP
GET OUT OF MY WAY.
EH?

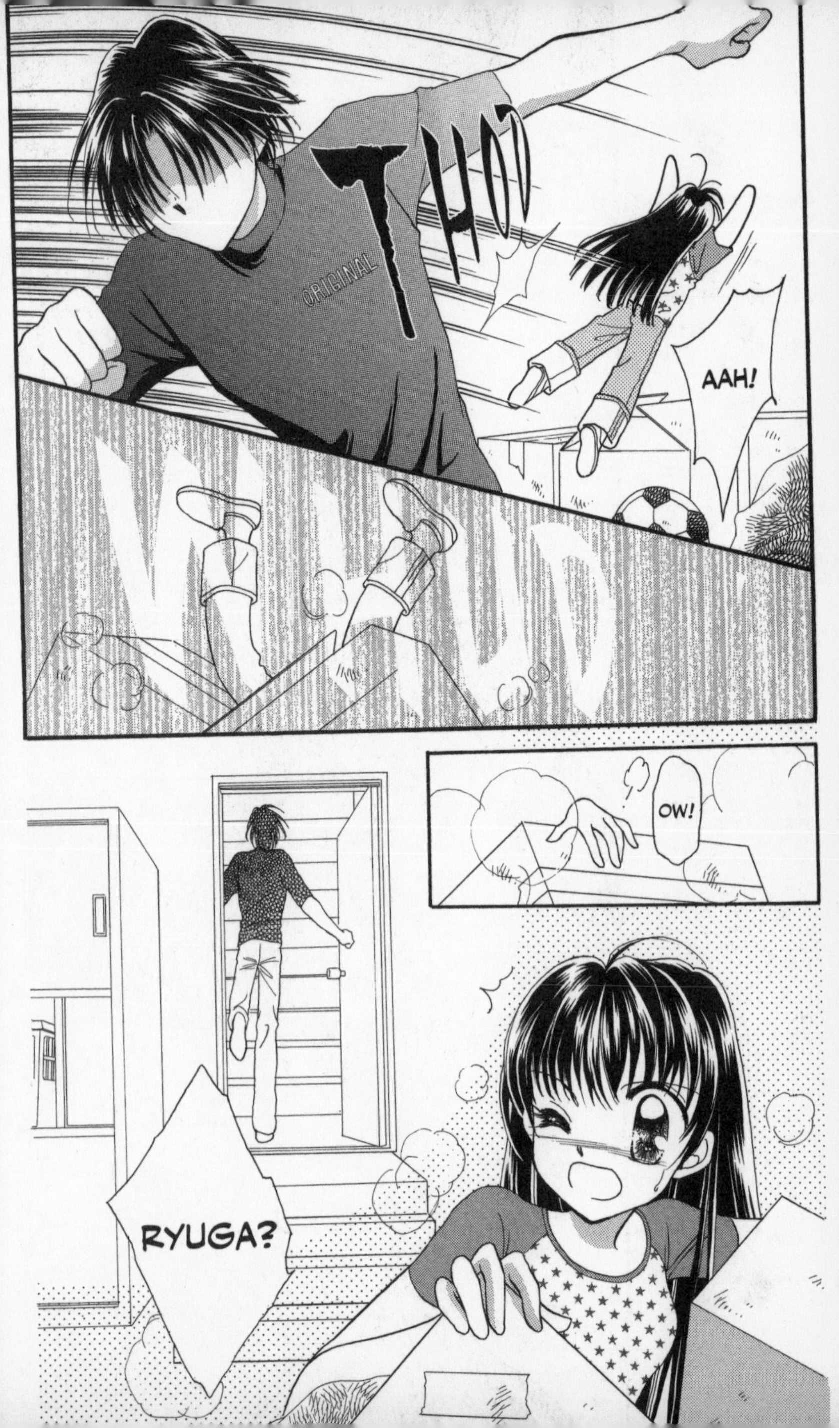
ORIGINAL
AAH!
OW!
RYUGA?

2

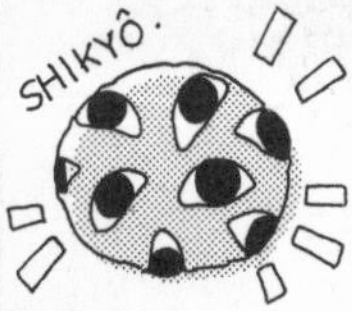
SHIKYÔ

Death Omen

The Death Omen was very popular here at my office! (laugh) My assistants said, "When all the eyes leer and smile all at once, it's really gross, isn't it?♥" They wanted to make the eyeliner thicker. They really seemed to enjoy it.

This demon is one of my personal favorites. If there were a miniature version of it that wouldn't hurt me, I'd try to keep a Death Omen as a pet! I'd ask its advice for all my worries, just like in that commercial. All the eyes would scowl at the same time...

The title page is a memorable scene for me—I was happy to draw the young Momoka and Ryuga.

In the special issue I had fun writing about a childhood story of theirs, so if I have a chance I'd like to write about the time they first met.

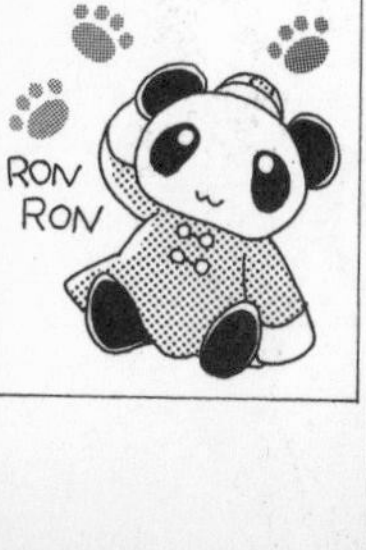
RON RON

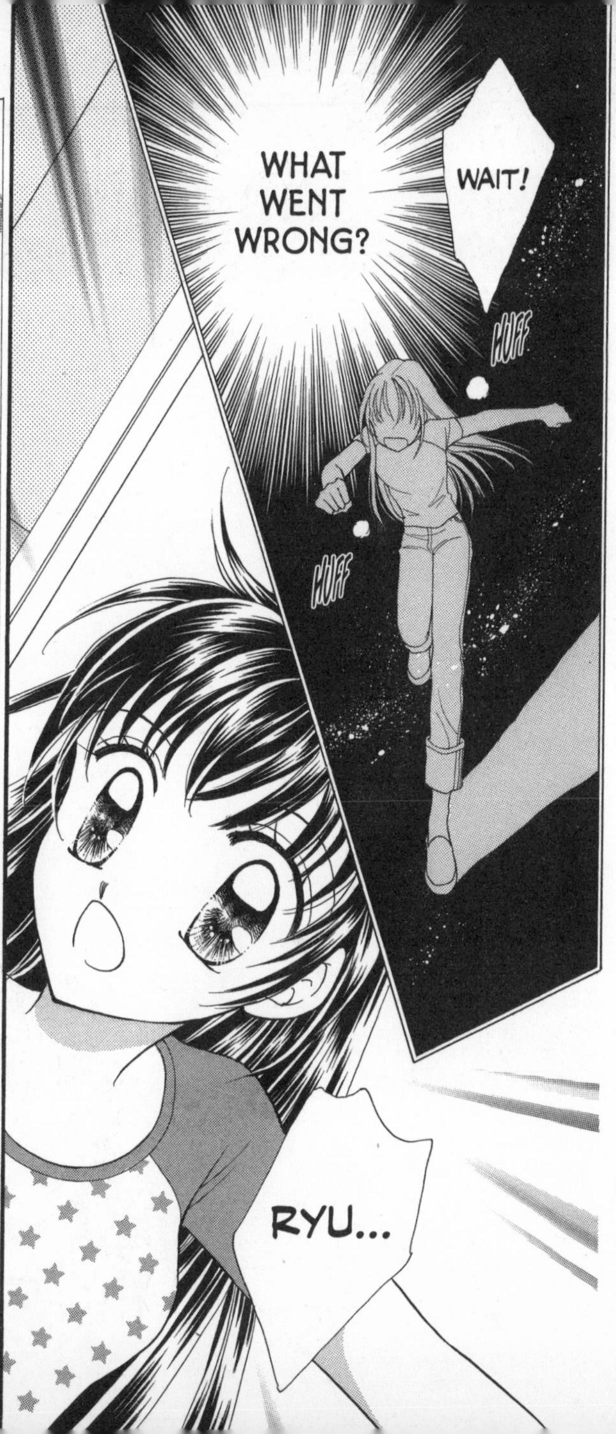
WAIT!
HUFF
HUFF
WHAT WENT WRONG?
RYU...

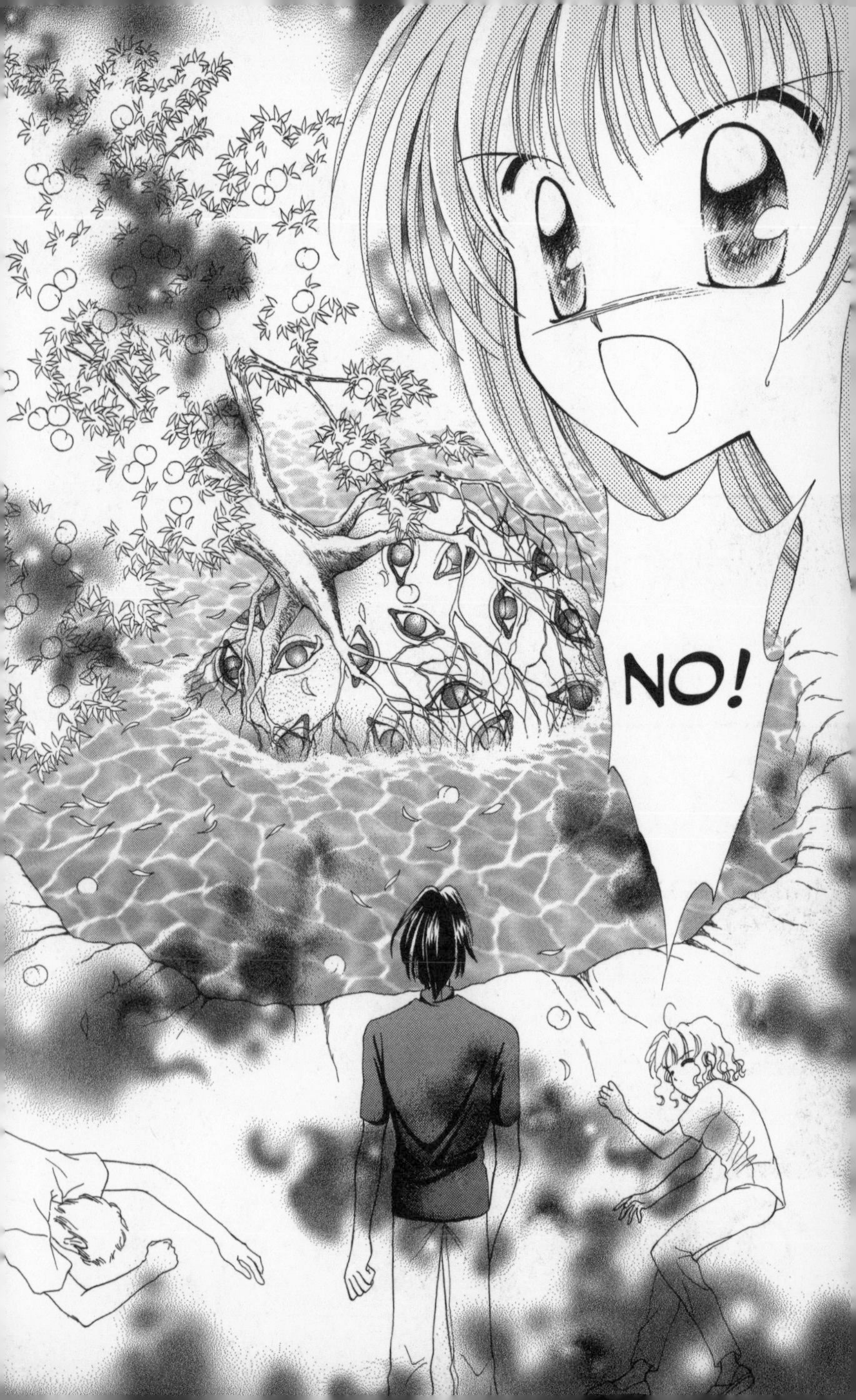
NO!

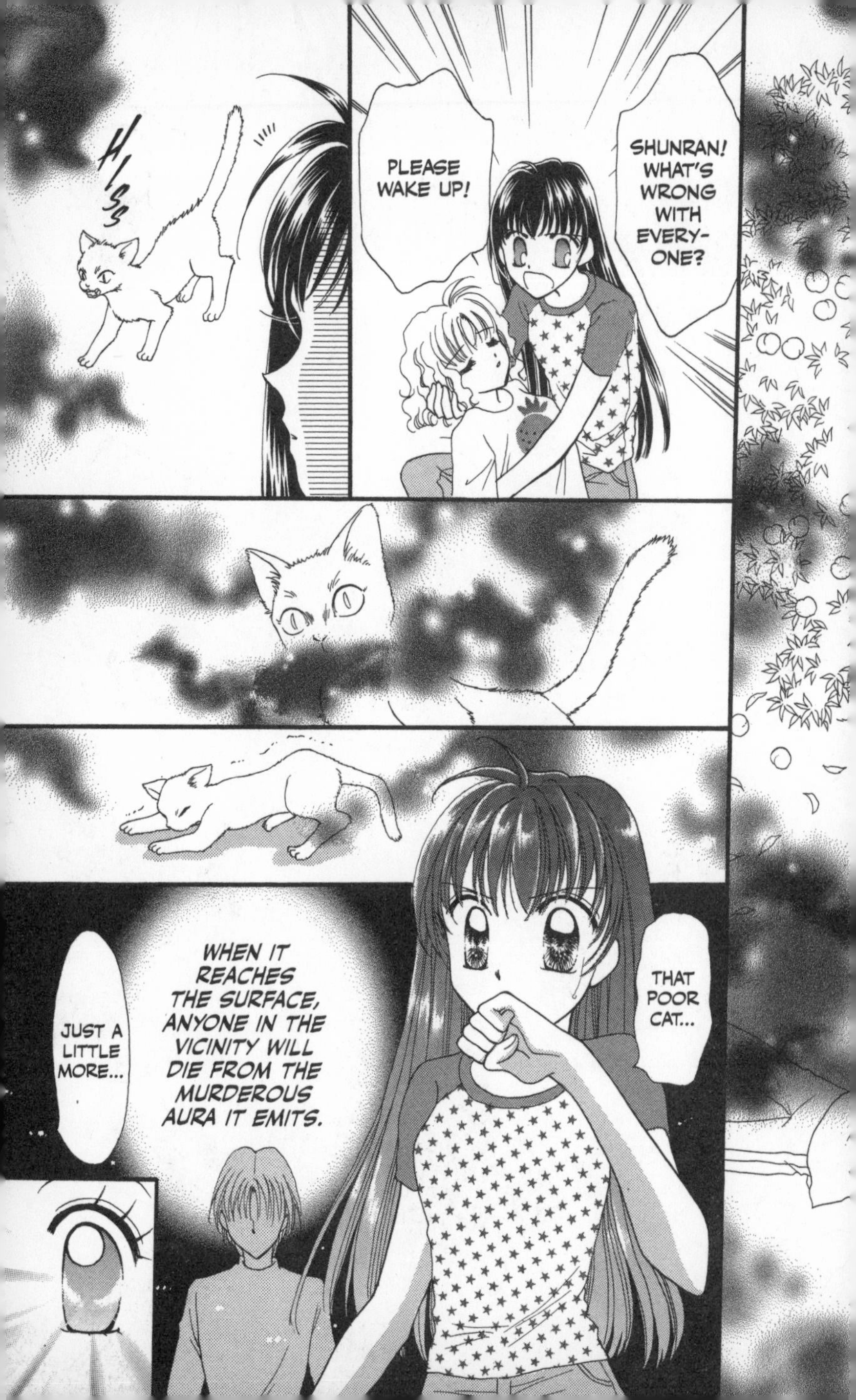
SHUNRAN! WHAT'S WRONG WITH EVERY-ONE?
PLEASE WAKE UP!
HISS
THAT POOR CAT...
WHEN IT REACHES THE SURFACE, ANYONE IN THE VICINITY WILL DIE FROM THE MURDEROUS AURA IT EMITS.
JUST A LITTLE MORE...

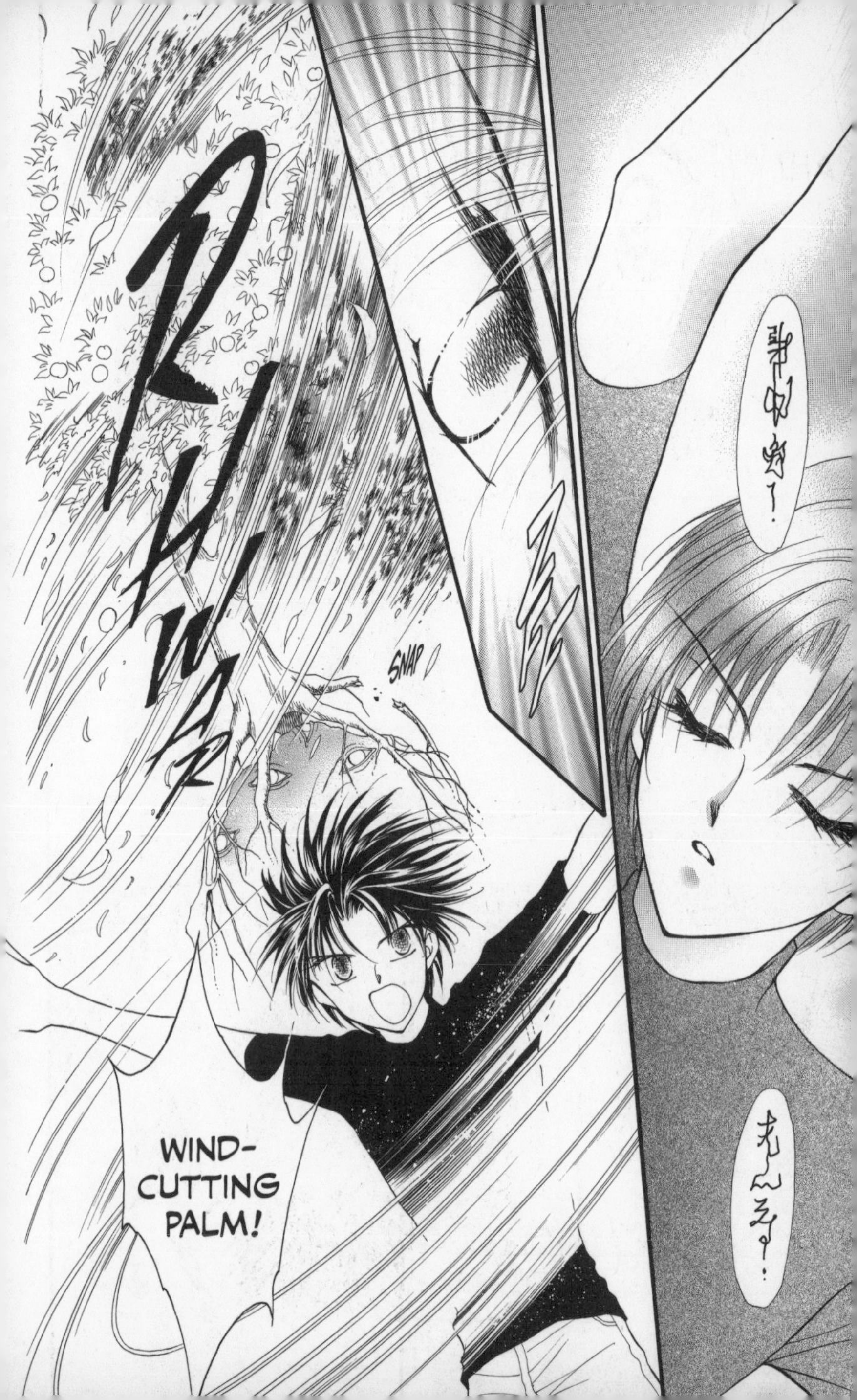
SNAP
WIND-CUTTING PALM!

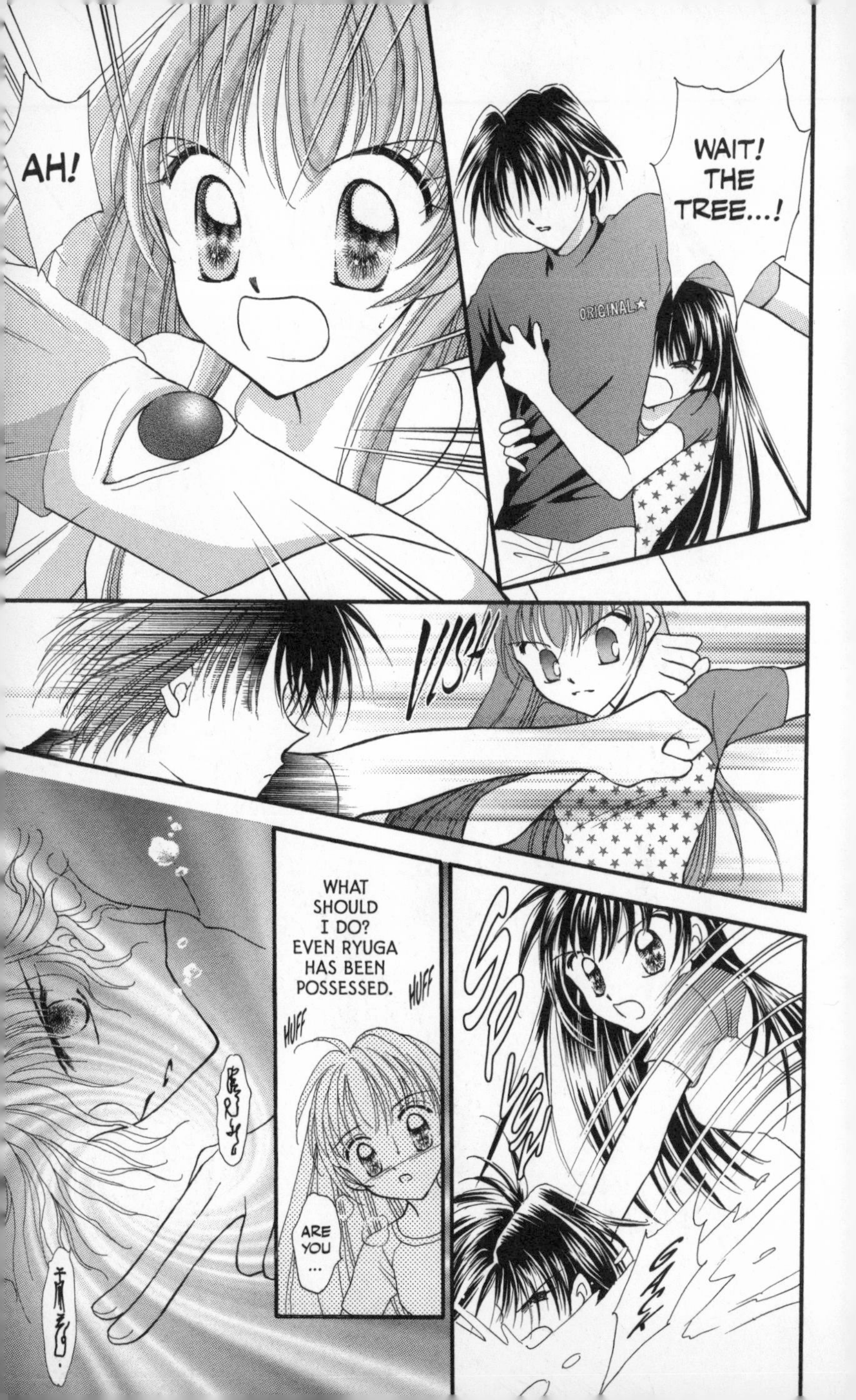
WAIT! THE TREE...!
AH!
VISH
WHAT SHOULD I DO? EVEN RYUGA HAS BEEN POSSESSED.
HUFF
HUFF
ARE YOU ...

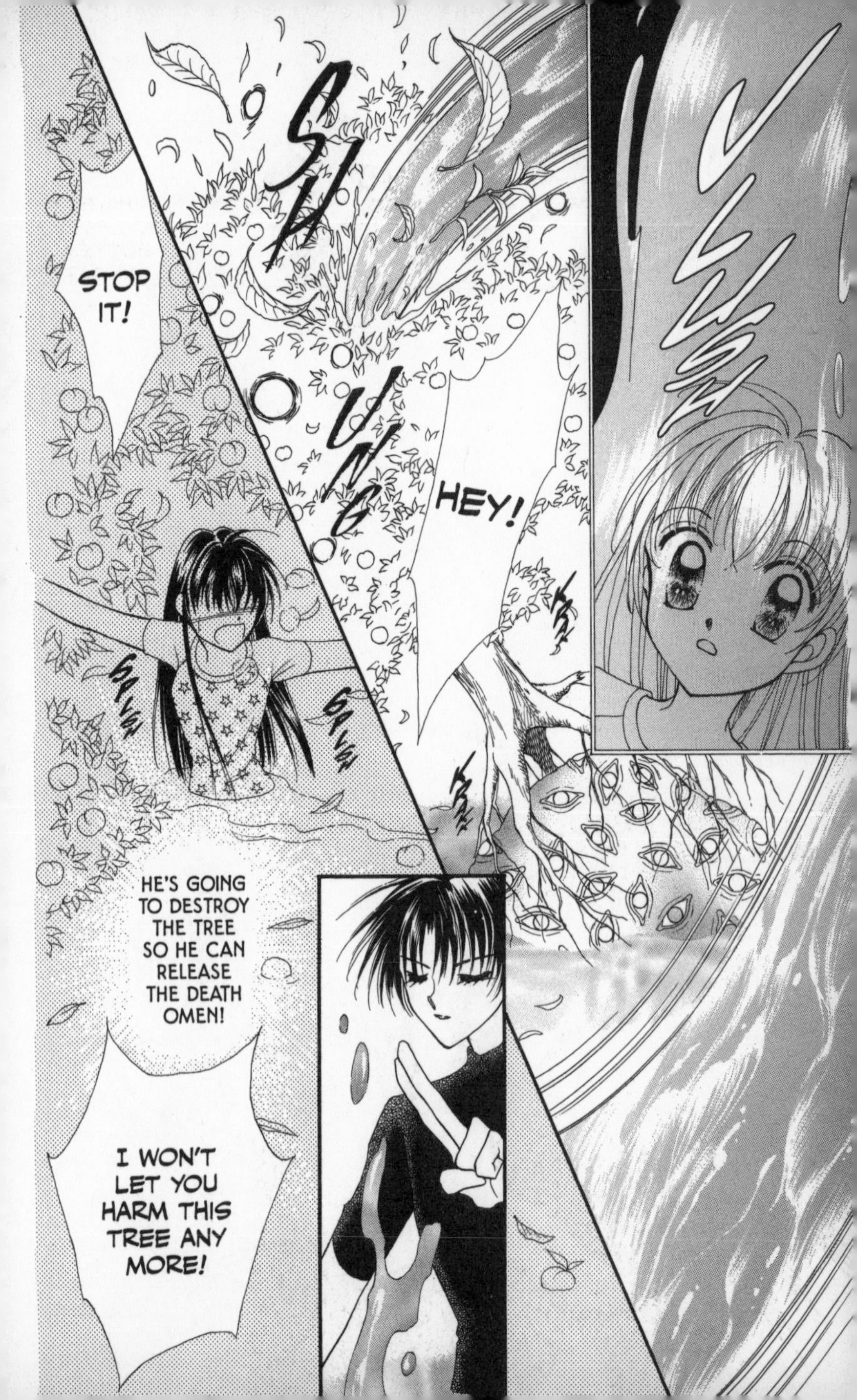
HEY!
STOP IT!
HE'S GOING TO DESTROY THE TREE SO HE CAN RELEASE THE DEATH OMEN!
I WON'T LET YOU HARM THIS TREE ANY MORE!

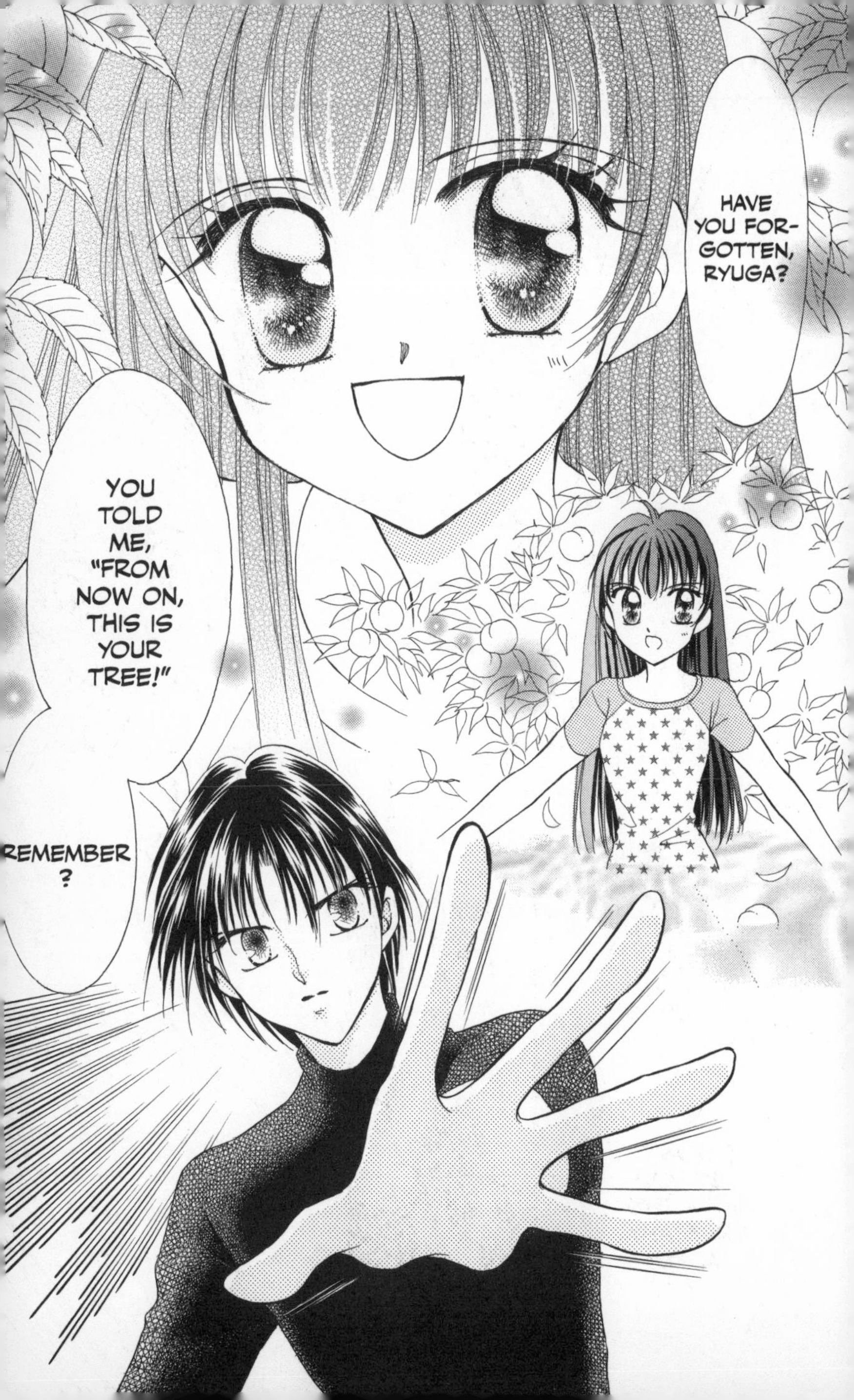
HAVE YOU FOR-GOTTEN, RYUGA?
YOU TOLD ME, "FROM NOW ON, THIS IS YOUR TREE!"
REMEMBER?

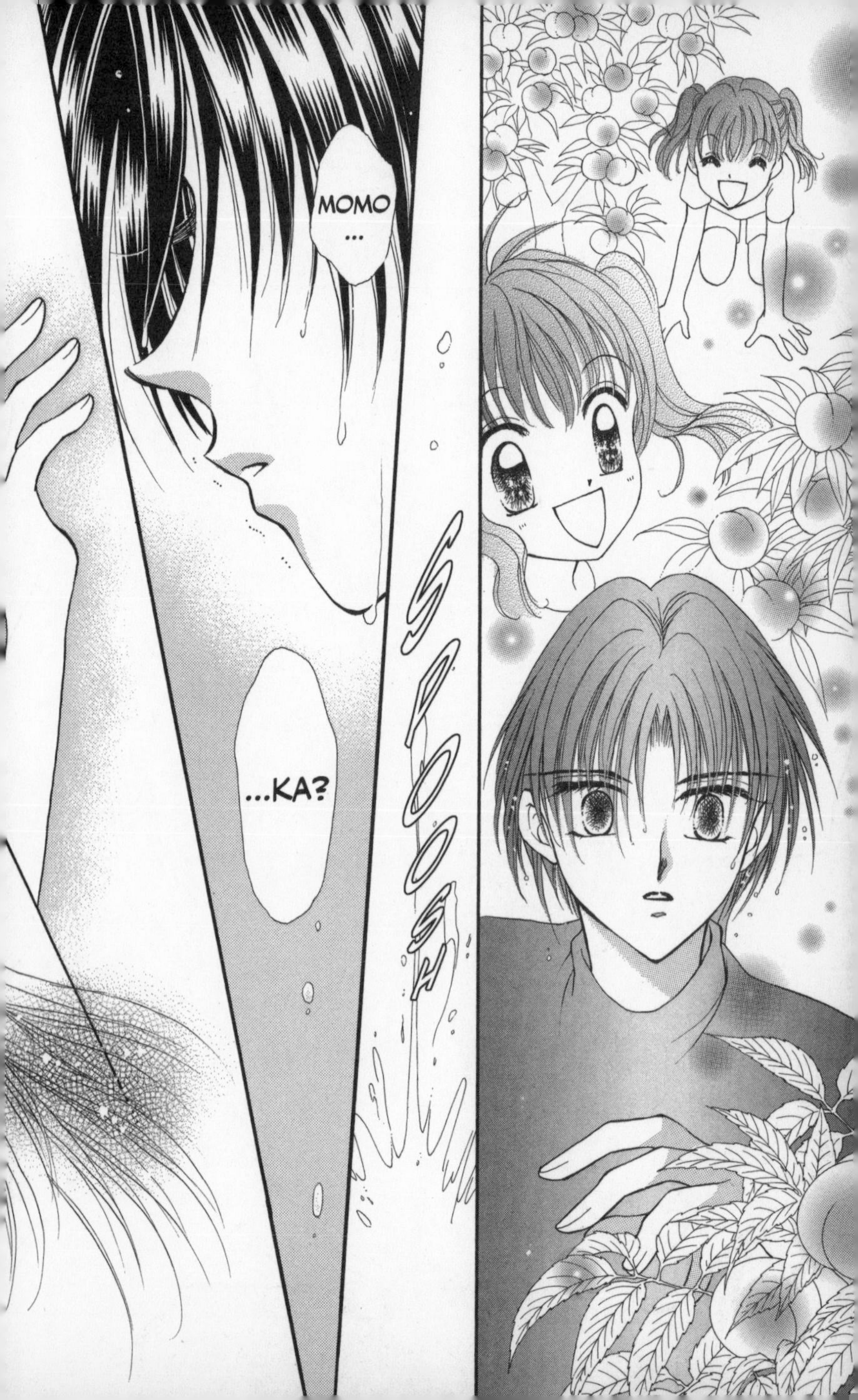
MOMO ...
...KA?
SPLOOSH

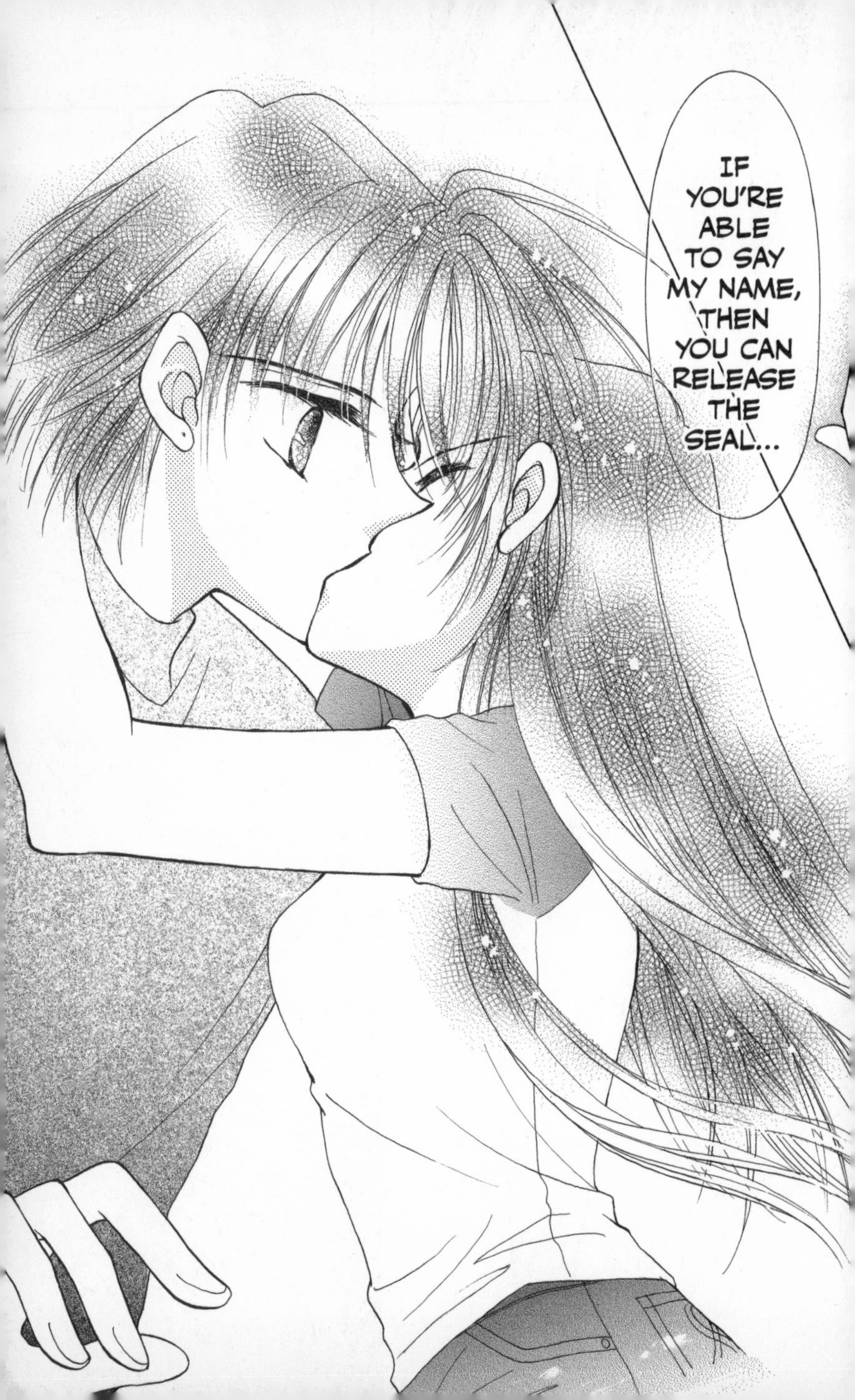
IF YOU'RE ABLE TO SAY MY NAME, THEN YOU CAN RELEASE THE SEAL...

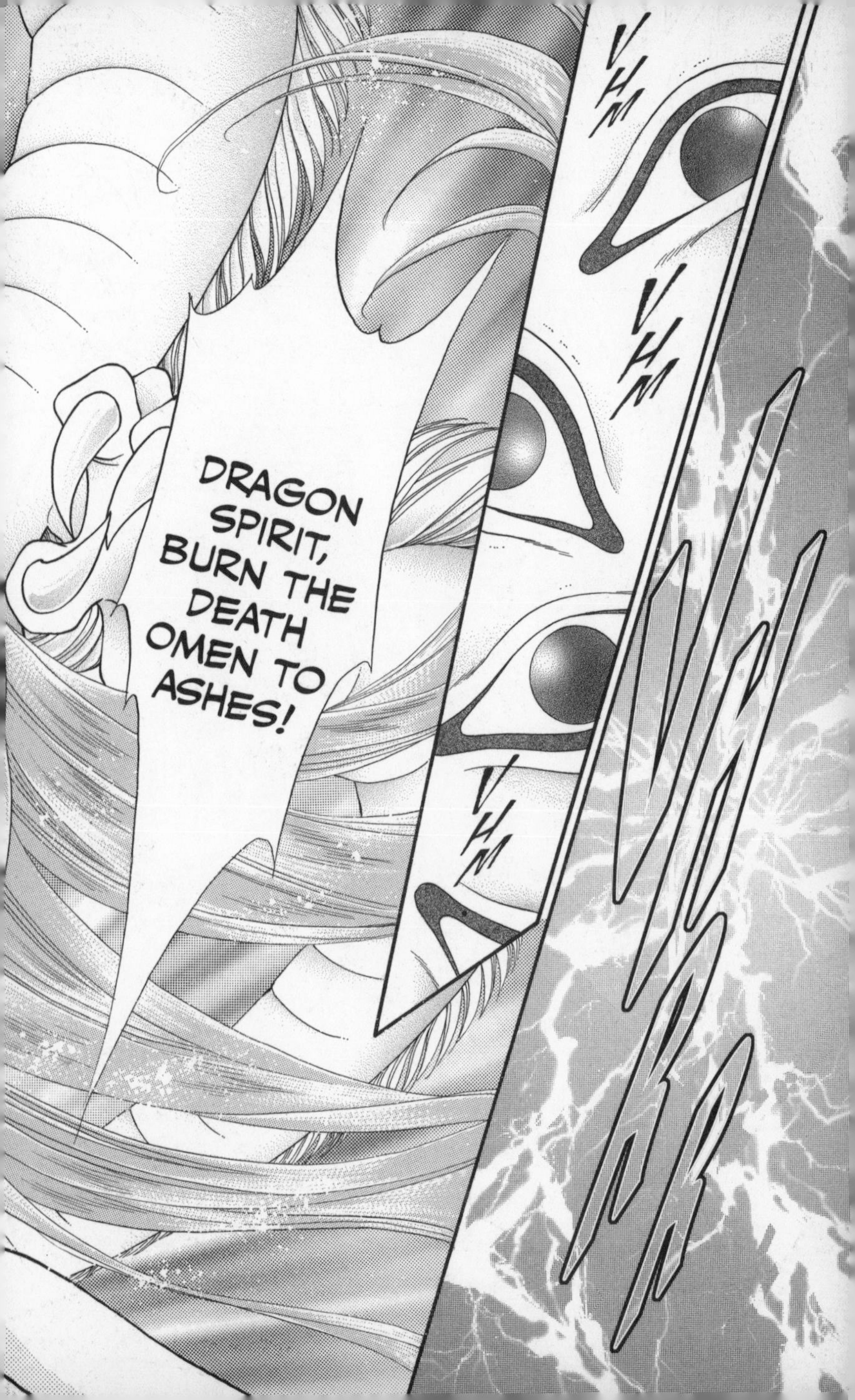
VHM
VHM
DRAGON SPIRIT, BURN THE DEATH OMEN TO ASHES!
VHM

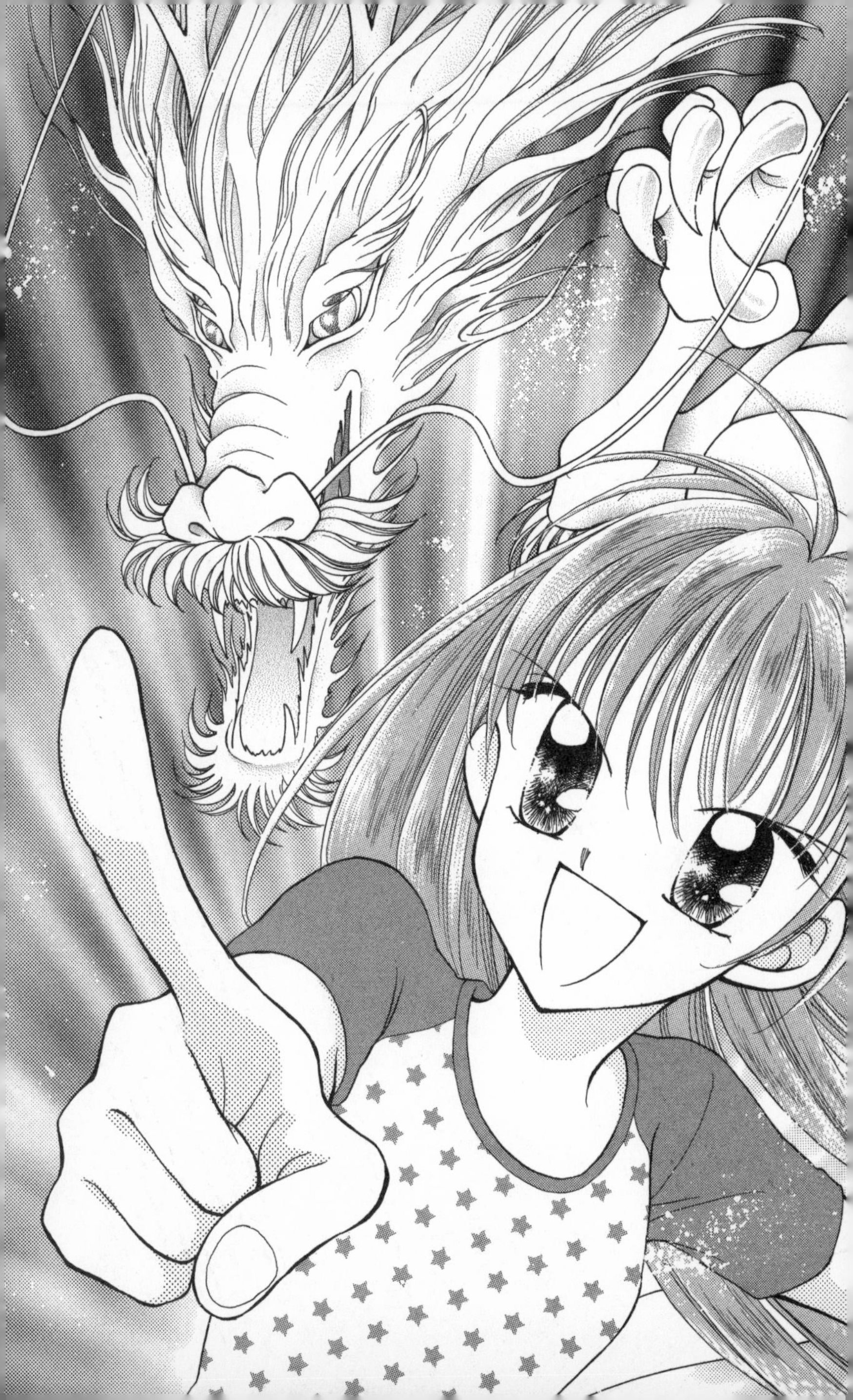

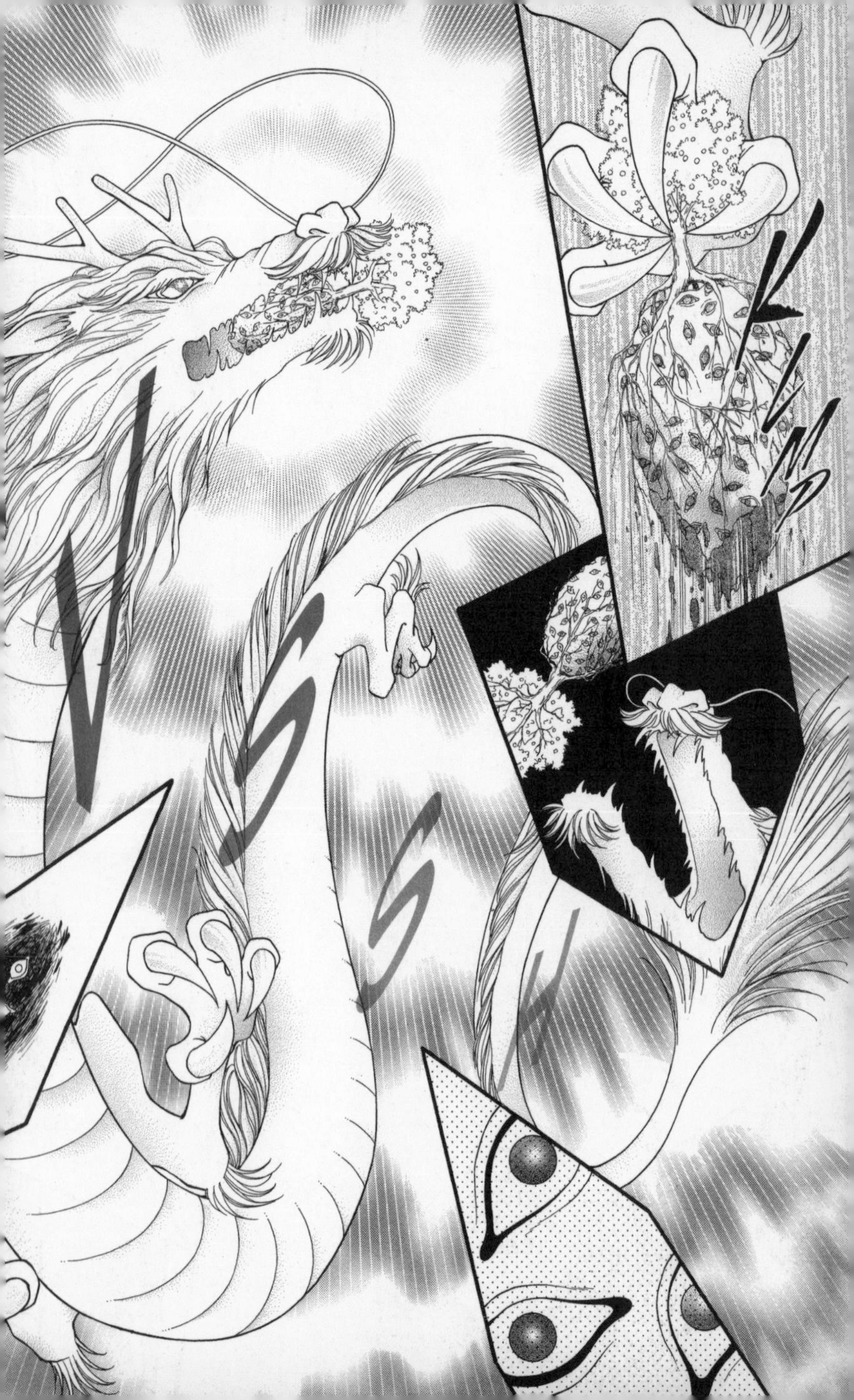
VSSH

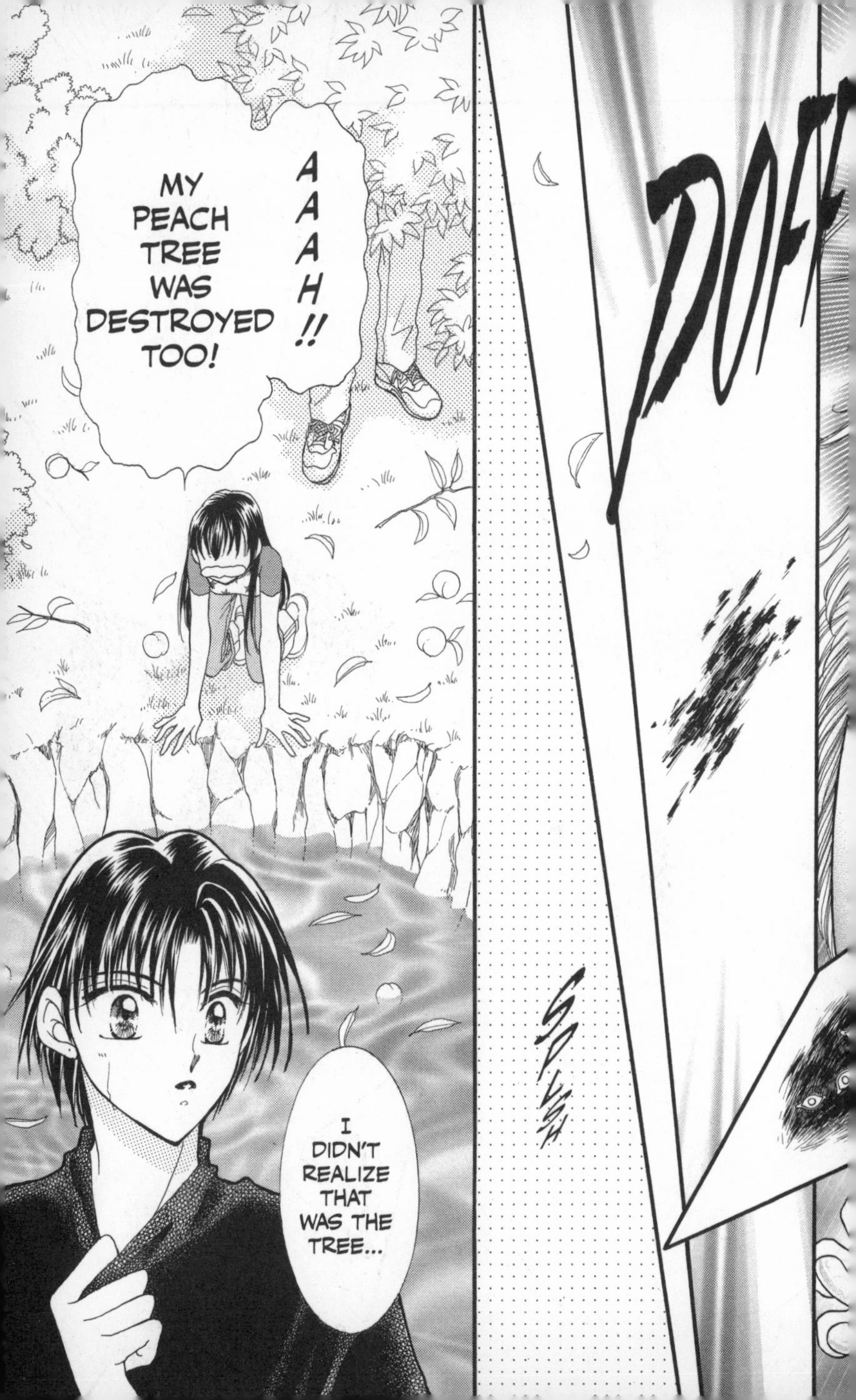
AAAAH!!
MY PEACH TREE WAS DESTROYED TOO!
I DIDN'T REALIZE THAT WAS THE TREE...

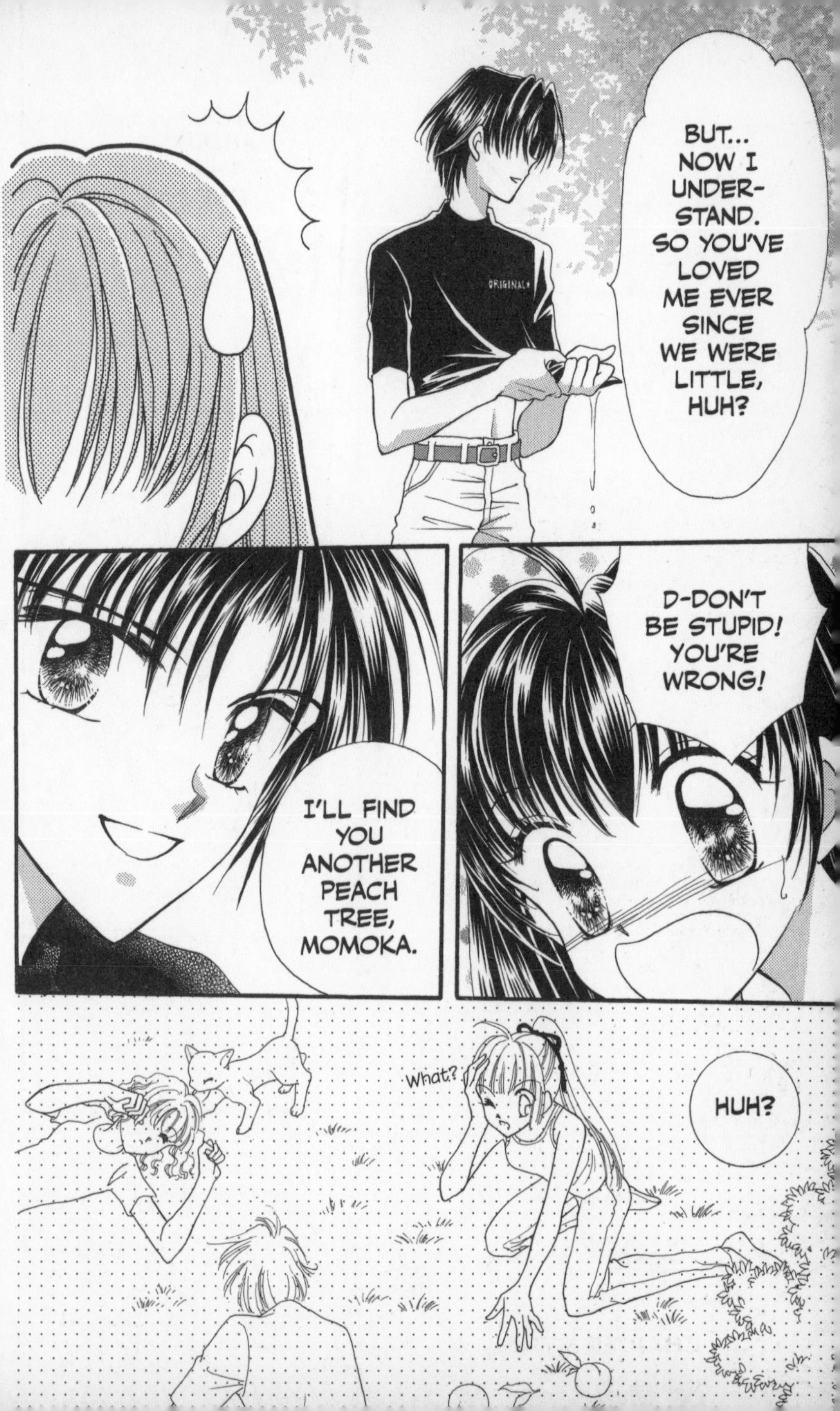
BUT... NOW I UNDER-STAND. SO YOU'VE LOVED ME EVER SINCE WE WERE LITTLE, HUH?
ORIGINAL
D-DON'T BE STUPID! YOU'RE WRONG!
I'LL FIND YOU ANOTHER PEACH TREE, MOMOKA.
HUH?
What?

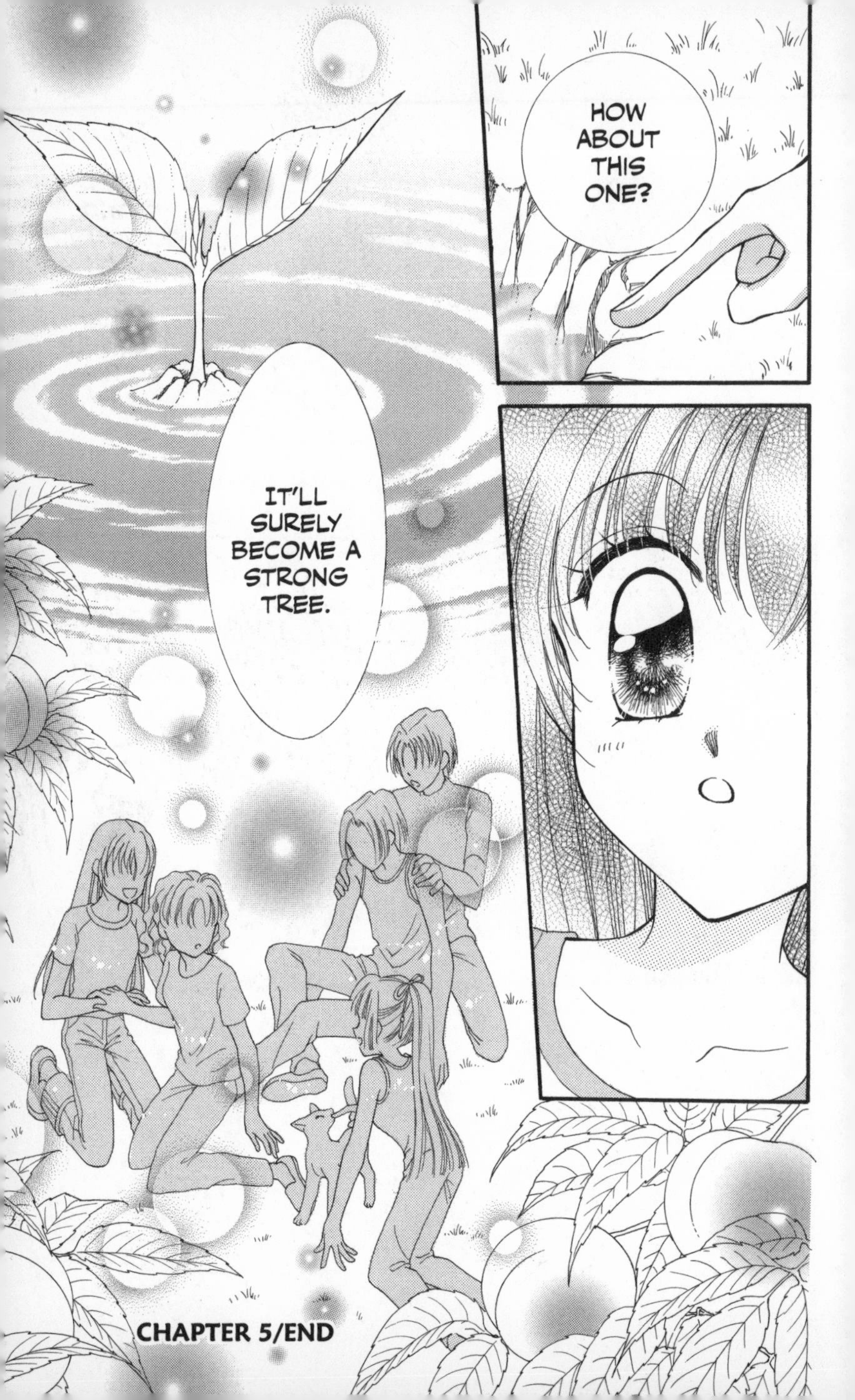
HOW ABOUT THIS ONE?
IT'LL SURELY BECOME A STRONG TREE.
CHAPTER 5/END

GON GIRL

CHAPTER 6

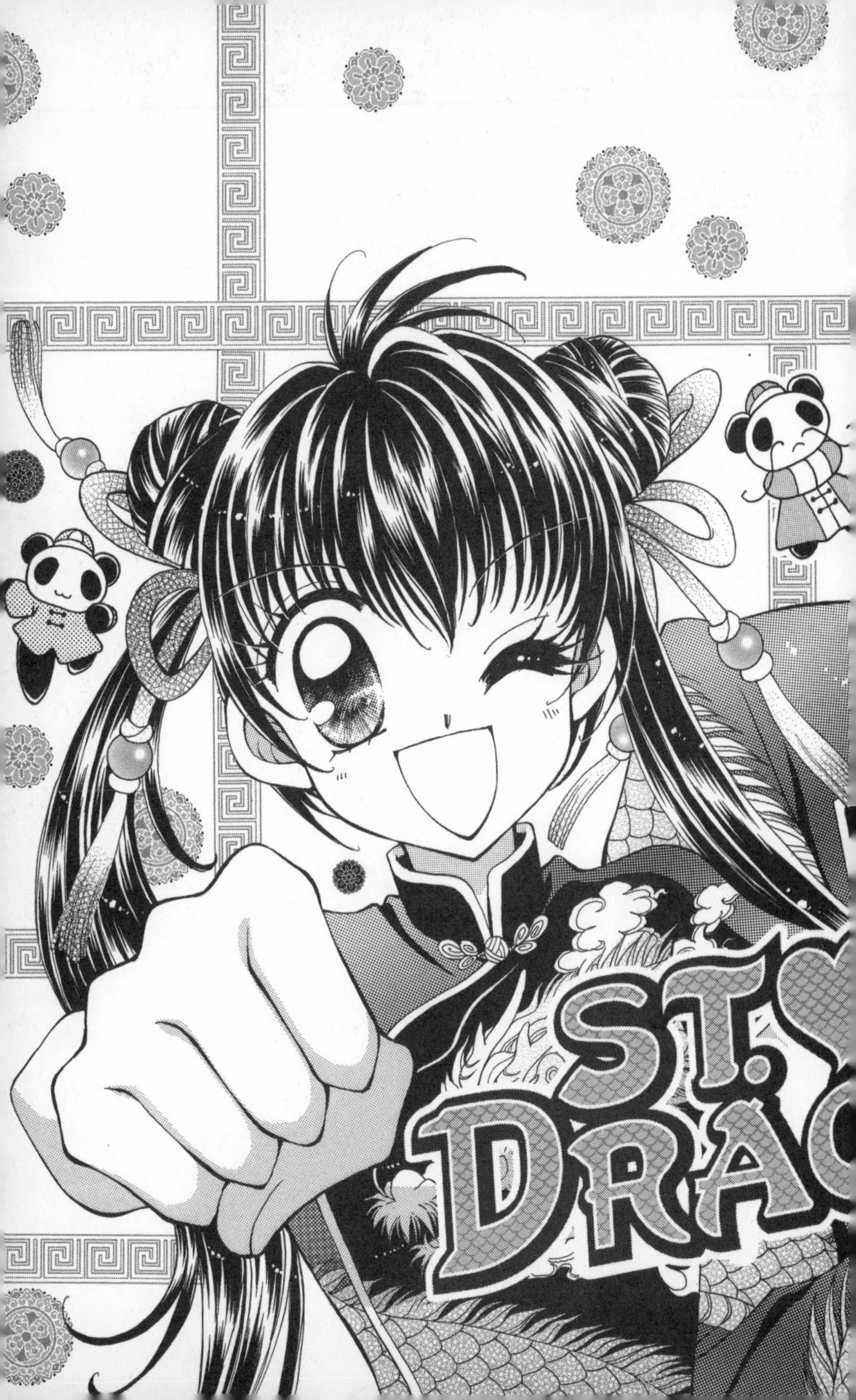
ST.
DRA

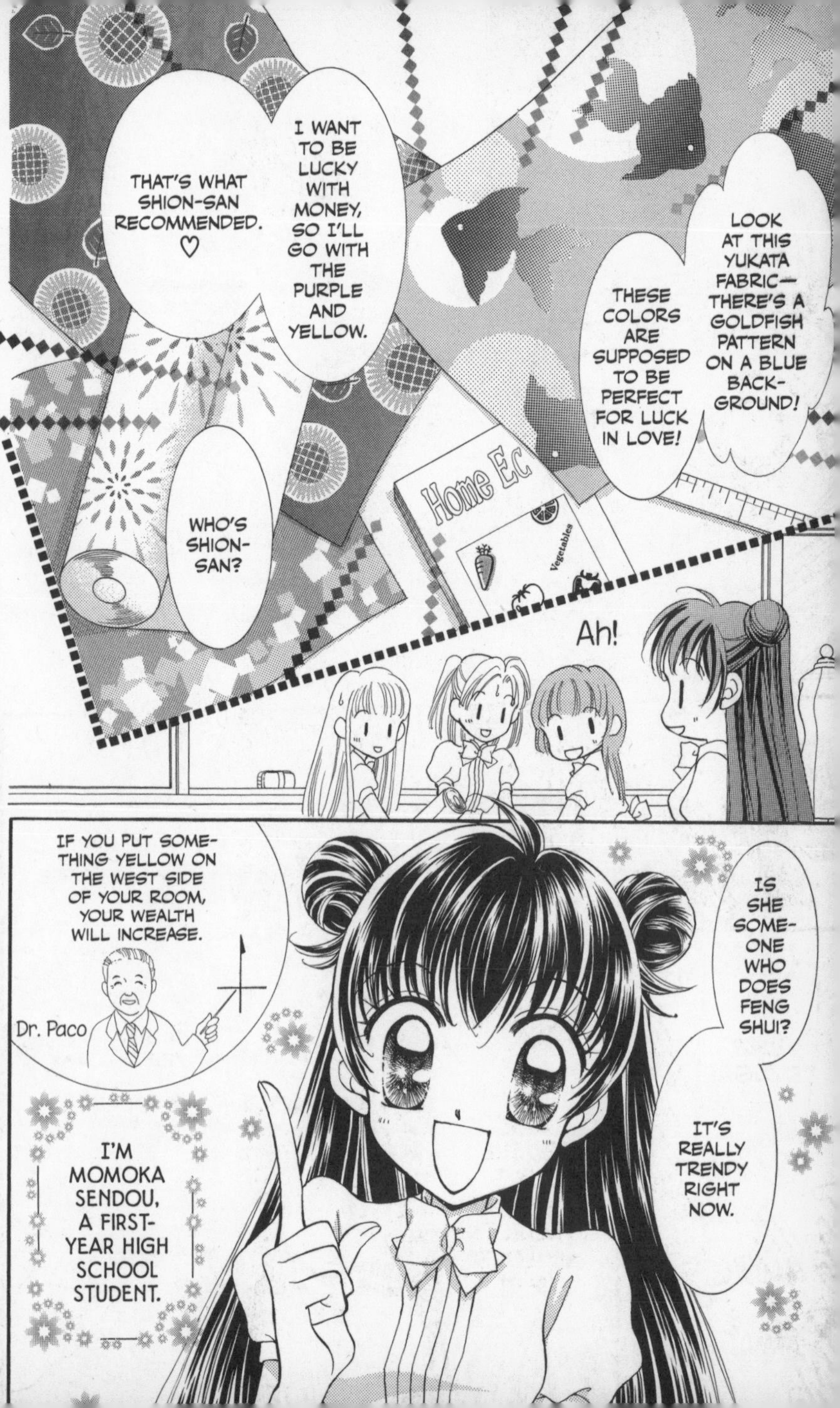
LOOK AT THIS YUKATA FABRIC—THERE'S A GOLDFISH PATTERN ON A BLUE BACKGROUND!
THESE COLORS ARE SUPPOSED TO BE PERFECT FOR LUCK IN LOVE!
Home Ec
Vegetables
I WANT TO BE LUCKY WITH MONEY, SO I'LL GO WITH THE PURPLE AND YELLOW.
THAT'S WHAT SHION-SAN RECOMMENDED. ♡
WHO'S SHION-SAN?
Ah!
IS SHE SOMEONE WHO DOES FENG SHUI?
IT'S REALLY TRENDY RIGHT NOW.
IF YOU PUT SOMETHING YELLOW ON THE WEST SIDE OF YOUR ROOM, YOUR WEALTH WILL INCREASE.
Dr. Paco
I'M MOMOKA SENDOU, A FIRST-YEAR HIGH SCHOOL STUDENT.

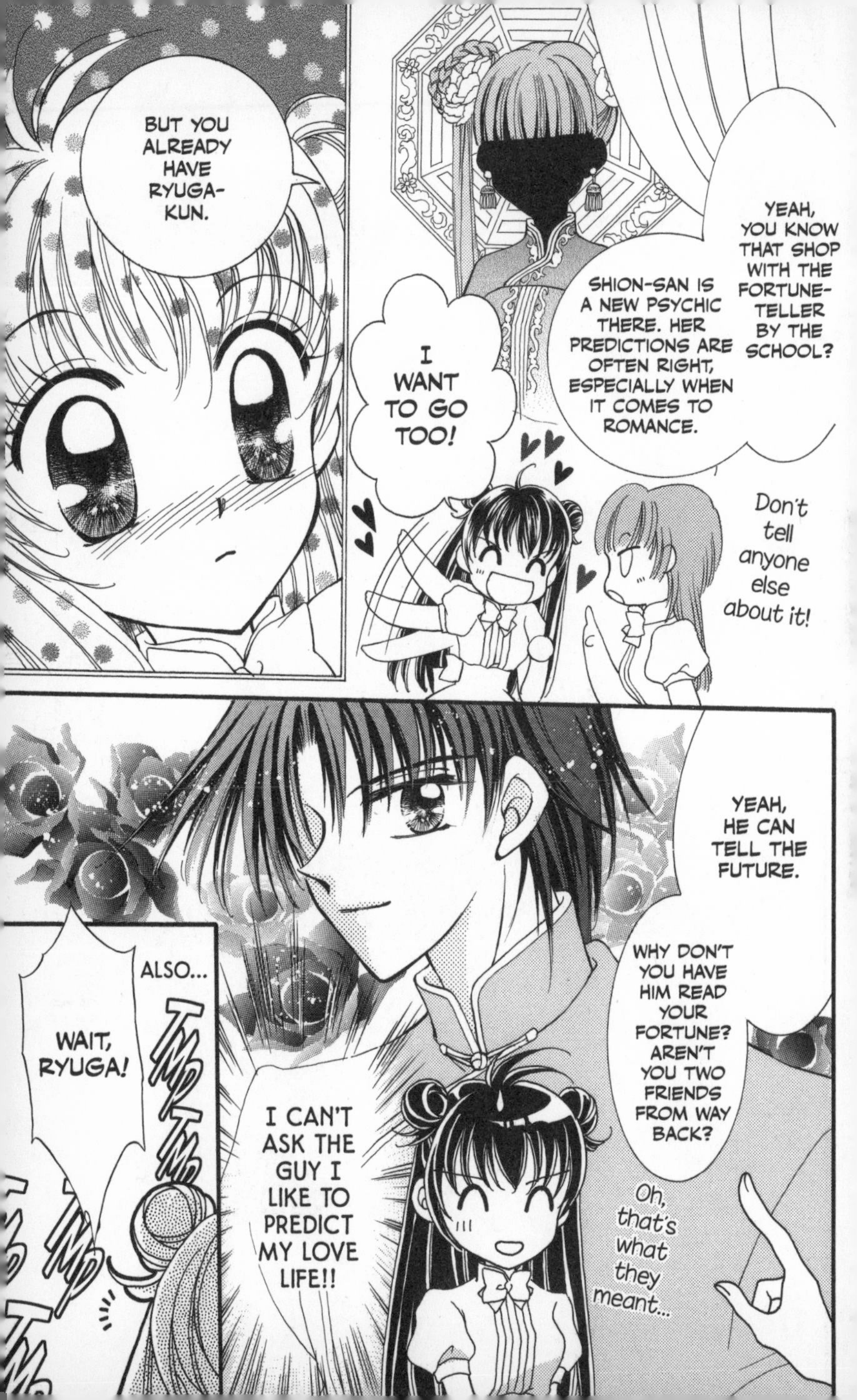
YEAH, YOU KNOW THAT SHOP WITH THE FORTUNE-TELLER BY THE SCHOOL?
SHION-SAN IS A NEW PSYCHIC THERE. HER PREDICTIONS ARE OFTEN RIGHT, ESPECIALLY WHEN IT COMES TO ROMANCE.
I WANT TO GO TOO!
Don't tell anyone else about it!
BUT YOU ALREADY HAVE RYUGA-KUN.
YEAH, HE CAN TELL THE FUTURE.
WHY DON'T YOU HAVE HIM READ YOUR FORTUNE? AREN'T YOU TWO FRIENDS FROM WAY BACK?
Oh, that's what they meant...
I CAN'T ASK THE GUY I LIKE TO PREDICT MY LOVE LIFE!!
ALSO...
WAIT, RYUGA!

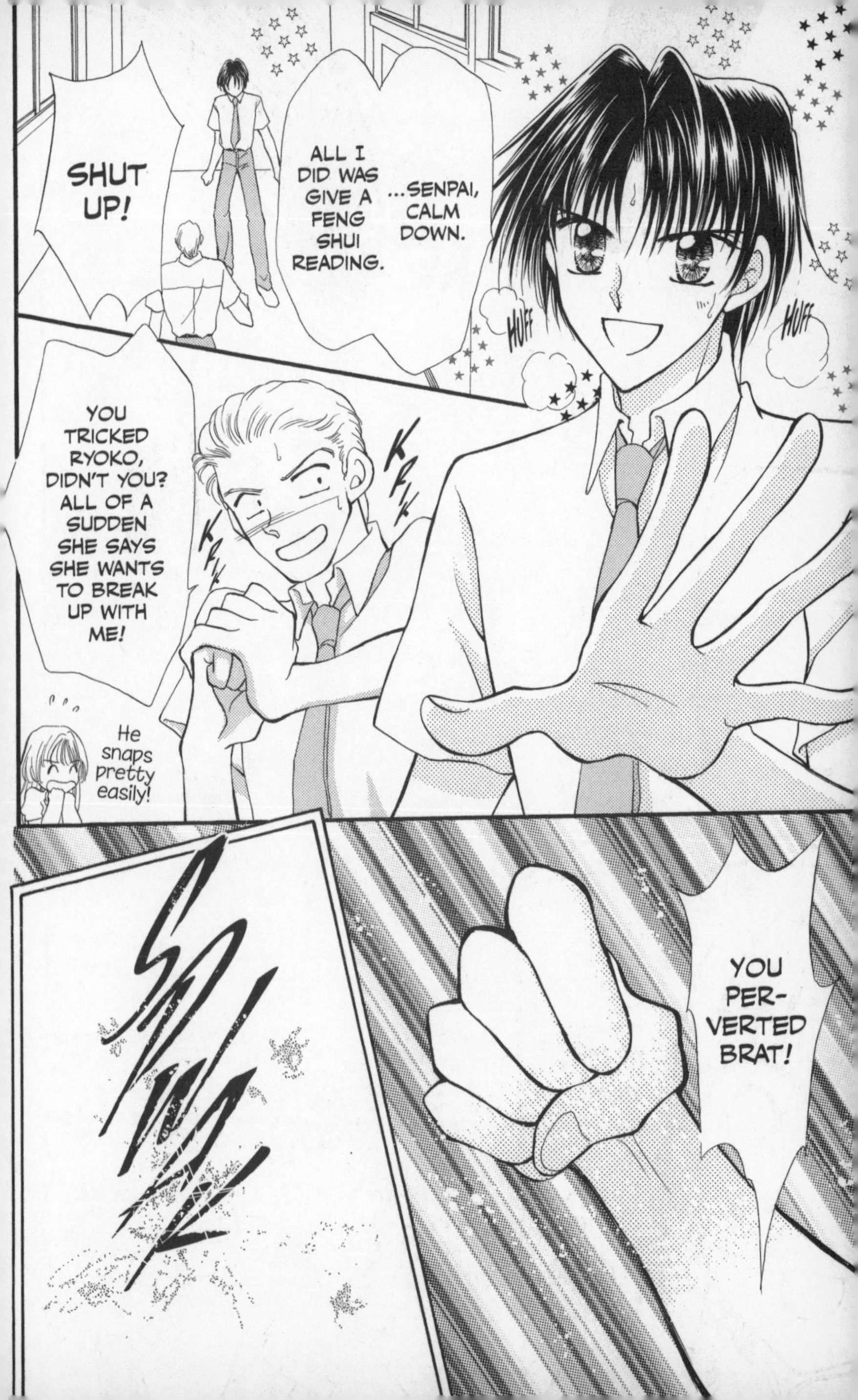
HUFF
HUFF
...SENPAI, CALM DOWN.
ALL I DID WAS GIVE A FENG SHUI READING.
SHUT UP!
YOU TRICKED RYOKO, DIDN'T YOU? ALL OF A SUDDEN SHE SAYS SHE WANTS TO BREAK UP WITH ME!
He snaps pretty easily!
YOU PER-VERTED BRAT!

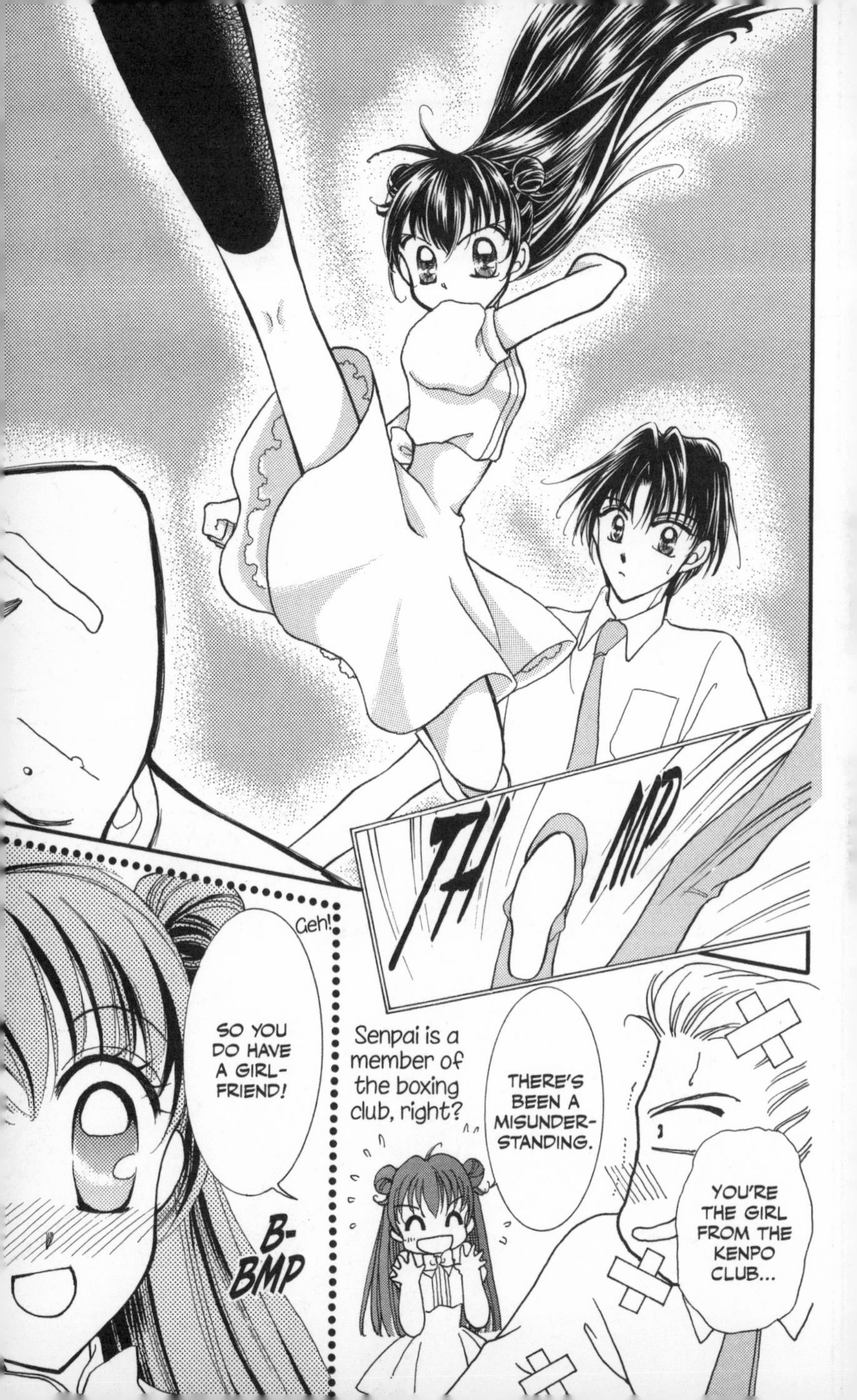
THOMP
YOU'RE THE GIRL FROM THE KENPO CLUB...
THERE'S BEEN A MISUNDERSTANDING.
Senpai is a member of the boxing club, right?
Geh!
SO YOU DO HAVE A GIRLFRIEND!
B-BMP

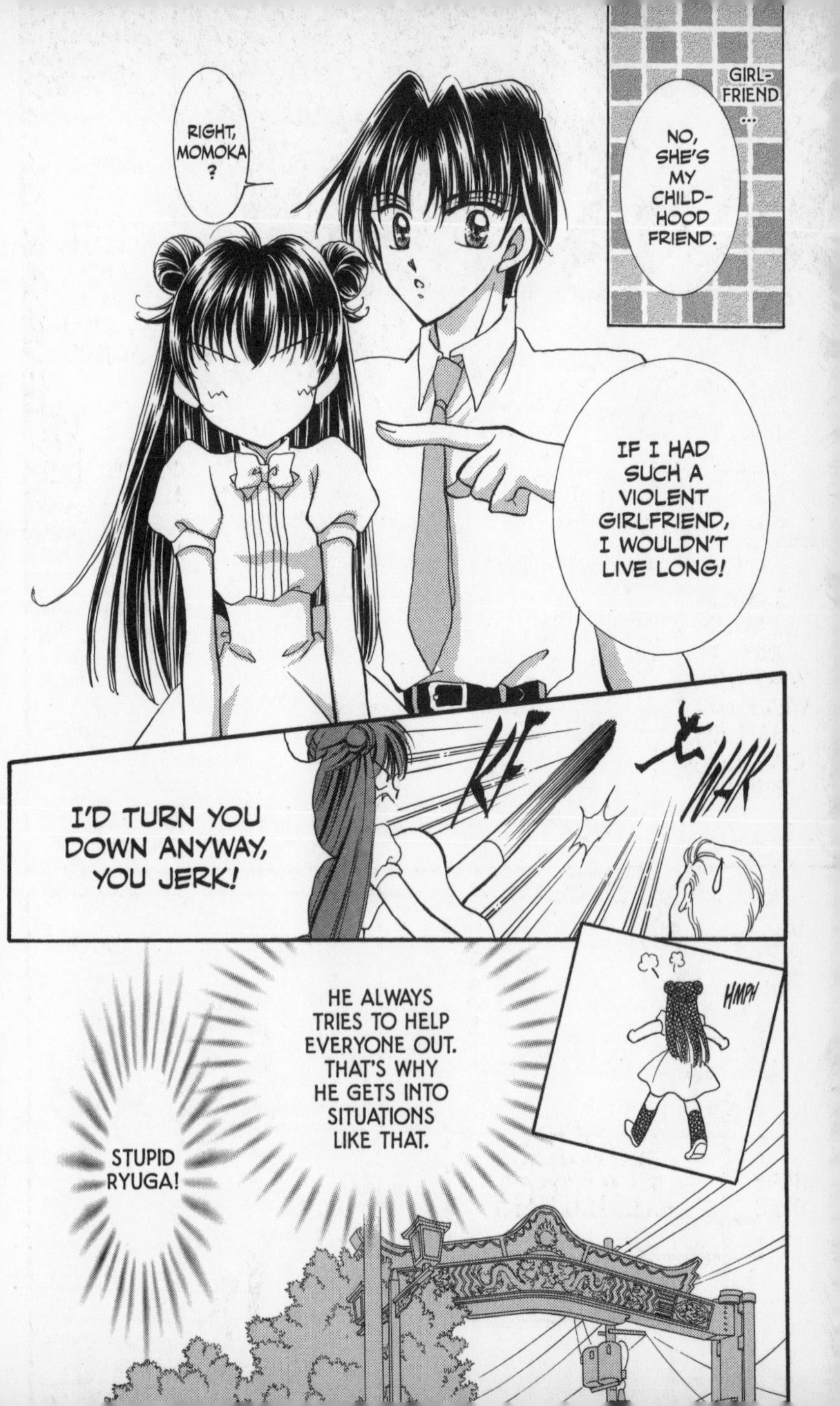
GIRL-FRIEND ...
NO, SHE'S MY CHILD-HOOD FRIEND.
IF I HAD SUCH A VIOLENT GIRLFRIEND, I WOULDN'T LIVE LONG!
RIGHT, MOMOKA ?
I'D TURN YOU DOWN ANYWAY, YOU JERK!
HMPH
HE ALWAYS TRIES TO HELP EVERYONE OUT. THAT'S WHY HE GETS INTO SITUATIONS LIKE THAT.
STUPID RYUGA!

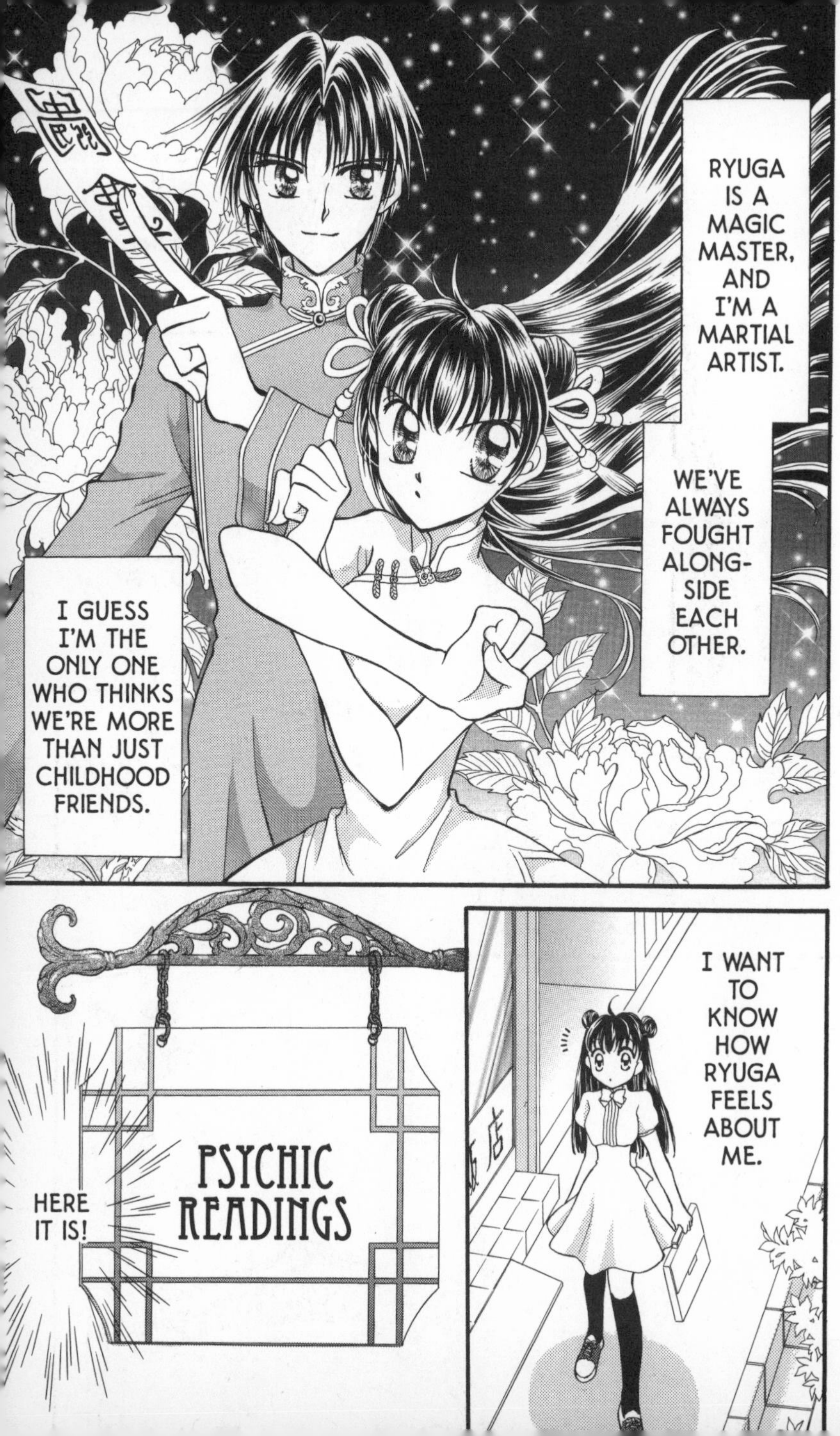
RYUGA IS A MAGIC MASTER, AND I'M A MARTIAL ARTIST.
WE'VE ALWAYS FOUGHT ALONG-SIDE EACH OTHER.
I GUESS I'M THE ONLY ONE WHO THINKS WE'RE MORE THAN JUST CHILDHOOD FRIENDS.
I WANT TO KNOW HOW RYUGA FEELS ABOUT ME.
PSYCHIC READINGS
HERE IT IS!

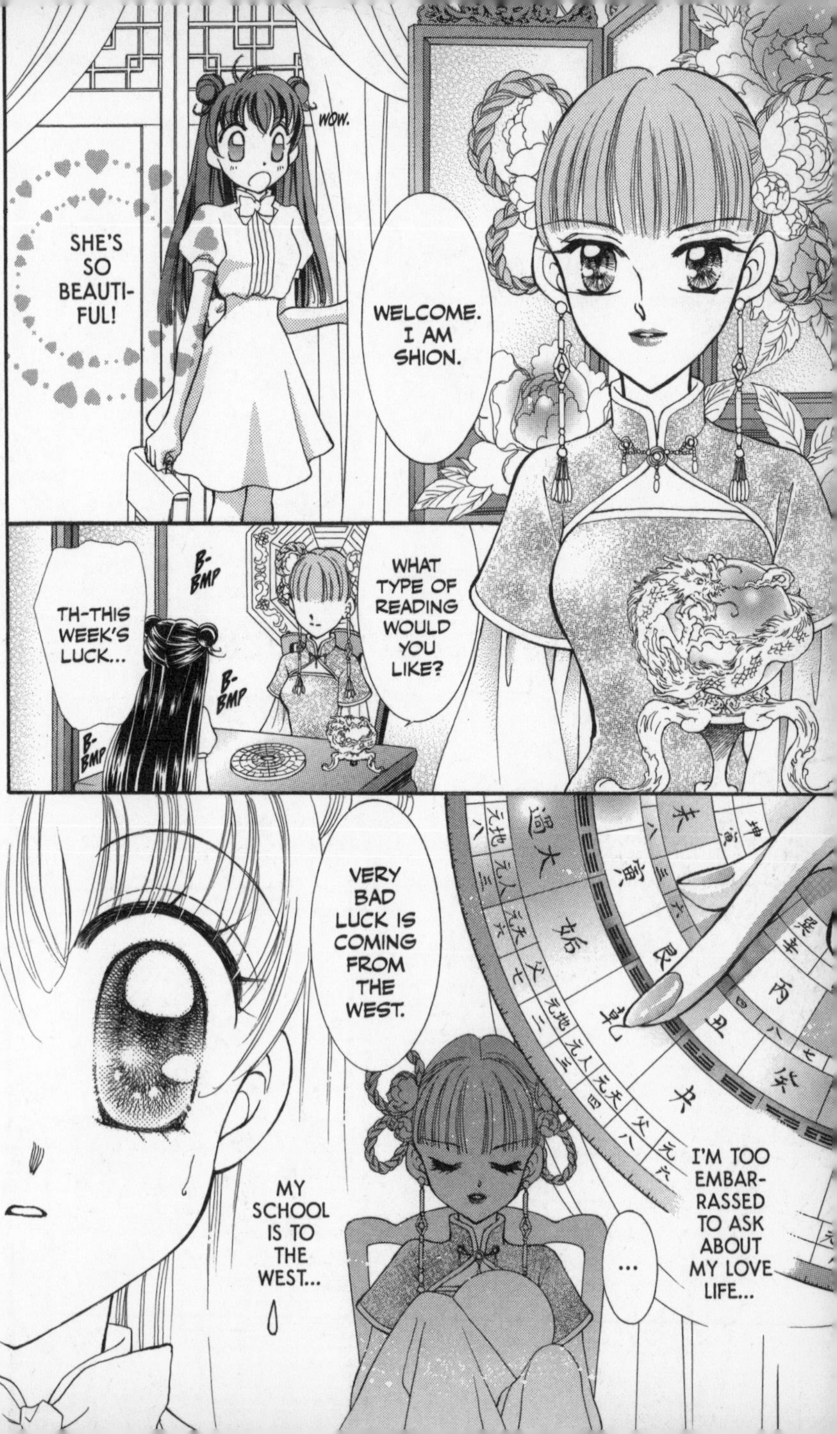
WELCOME. I AM SHION.
WOW.
SHE'S SO BEAUTIFUL!
WHAT TYPE OF READING WOULD YOU LIKE?
B-BMP
B-BMP
B-BMP
TH-THIS WEEK'S LUCK...
VERY BAD LUCK IS COMING FROM THE WEST.
I'M TOO EMBARRASSED TO ASK ABOUT MY LOVE LIFE...
...
MY SCHOOL IS TO THE WEST...

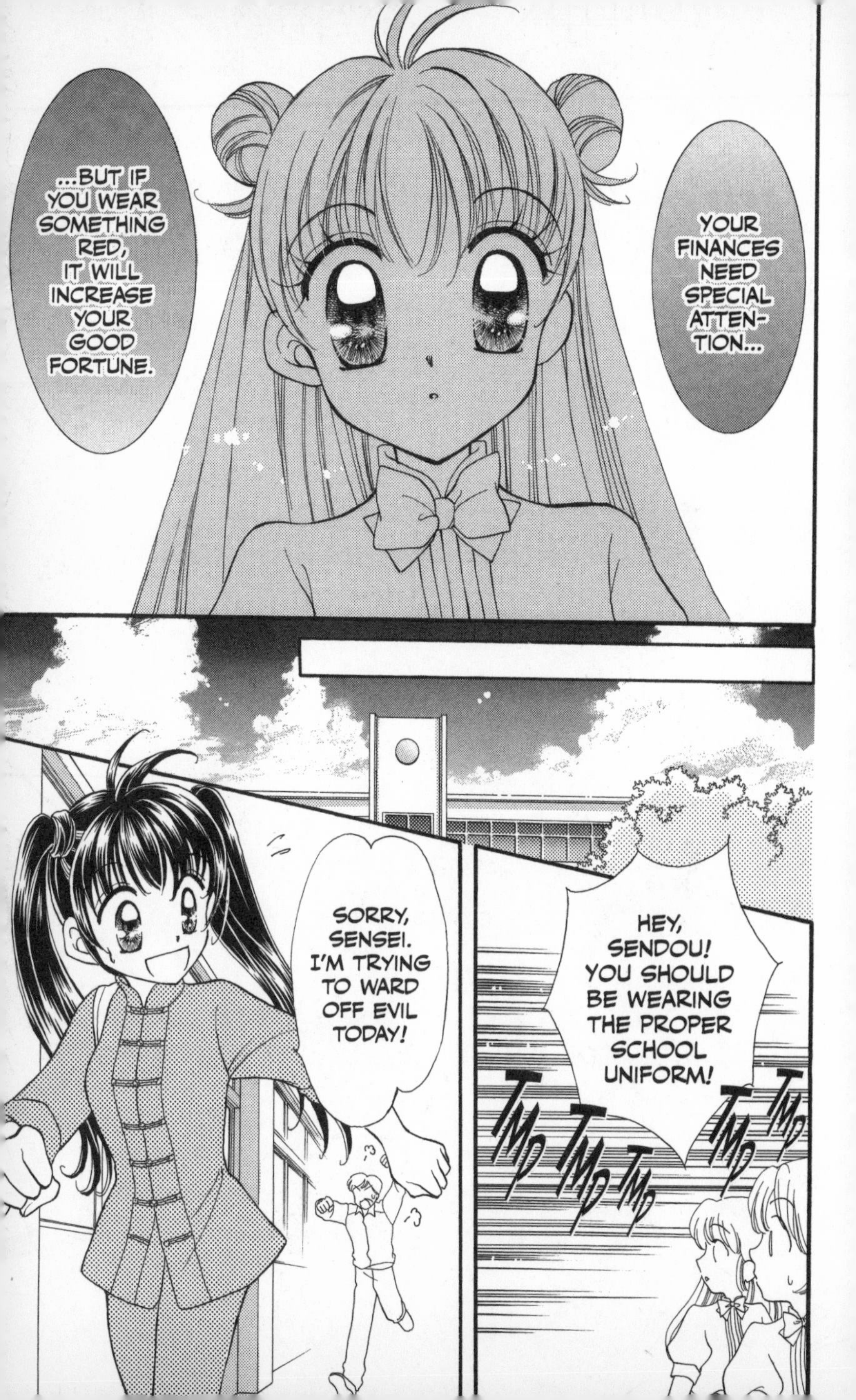
YOUR FINANCES NEED SPECIAL ATTEN-TION...
...BUT IF YOU WEAR SOMETHING RED, IT WILL INCREASE YOUR GOOD FORTUNE.
HEY, SENDOU! YOU SHOULD BE WEARING THE PROPER SCHOOL UNIFORM!
TMP TMP
TMP TMP TMP
SORRY, SENSEI. I'M TRYING TO WARD OFF EVIL TODAY!

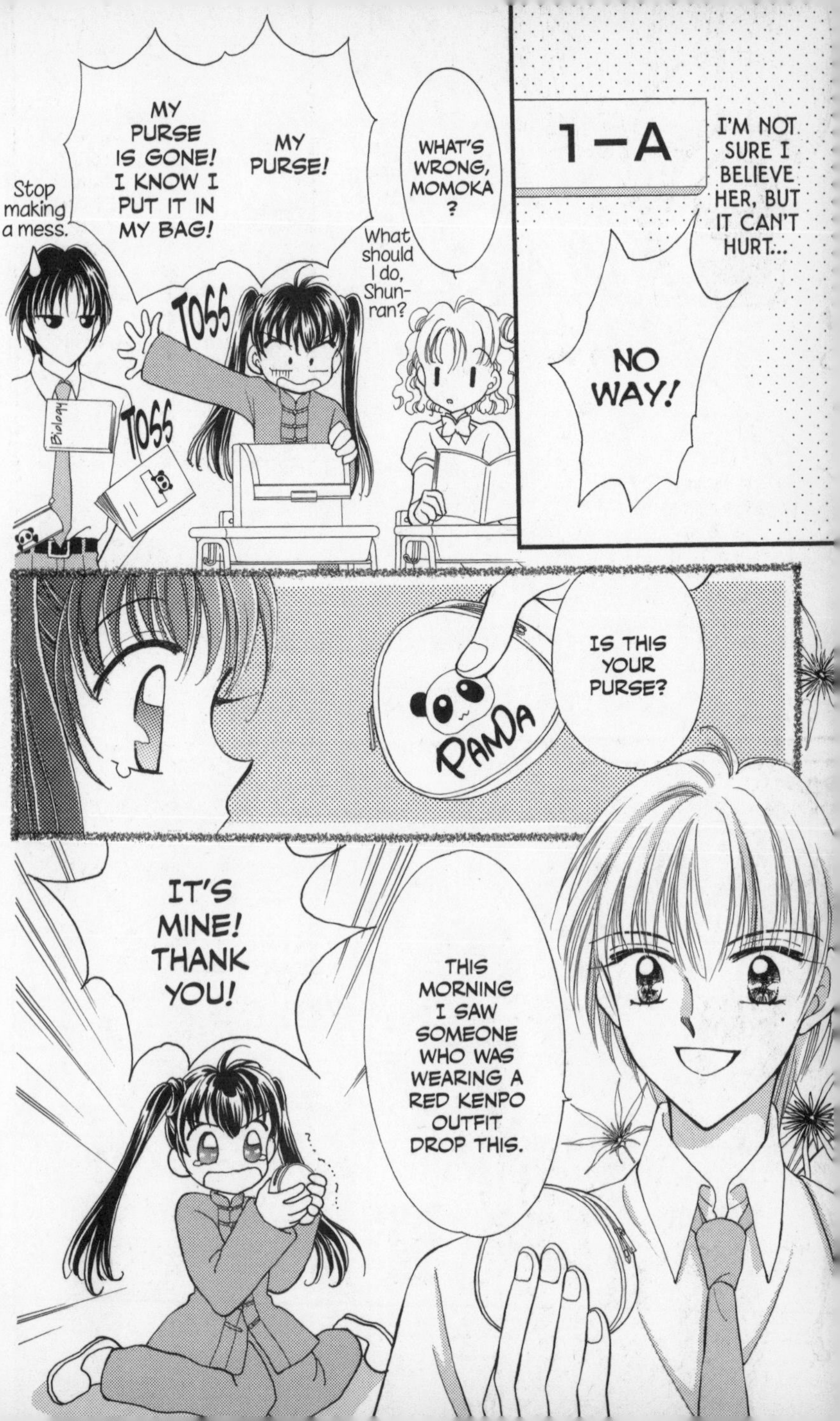
1-A
I'M NOT SURE I BELIEVE HER, BUT IT CAN'T HURT...
NO WAY!
WHAT'S WRONG, MOMOKA?
MY PURSE!
MY PURSE IS GONE! I KNOW I PUT IT IN MY BAG!
What should I do, Shun-ran?
Stop making a mess.
TOSS
Biology
TOSS
IS THIS YOUR PURSE?
PANDA
THIS MORNING I SAW SOMEONE WHO WAS WEARING A RED KENPO OUTFIT DROP THIS.
IT'S MINE! THANK YOU!

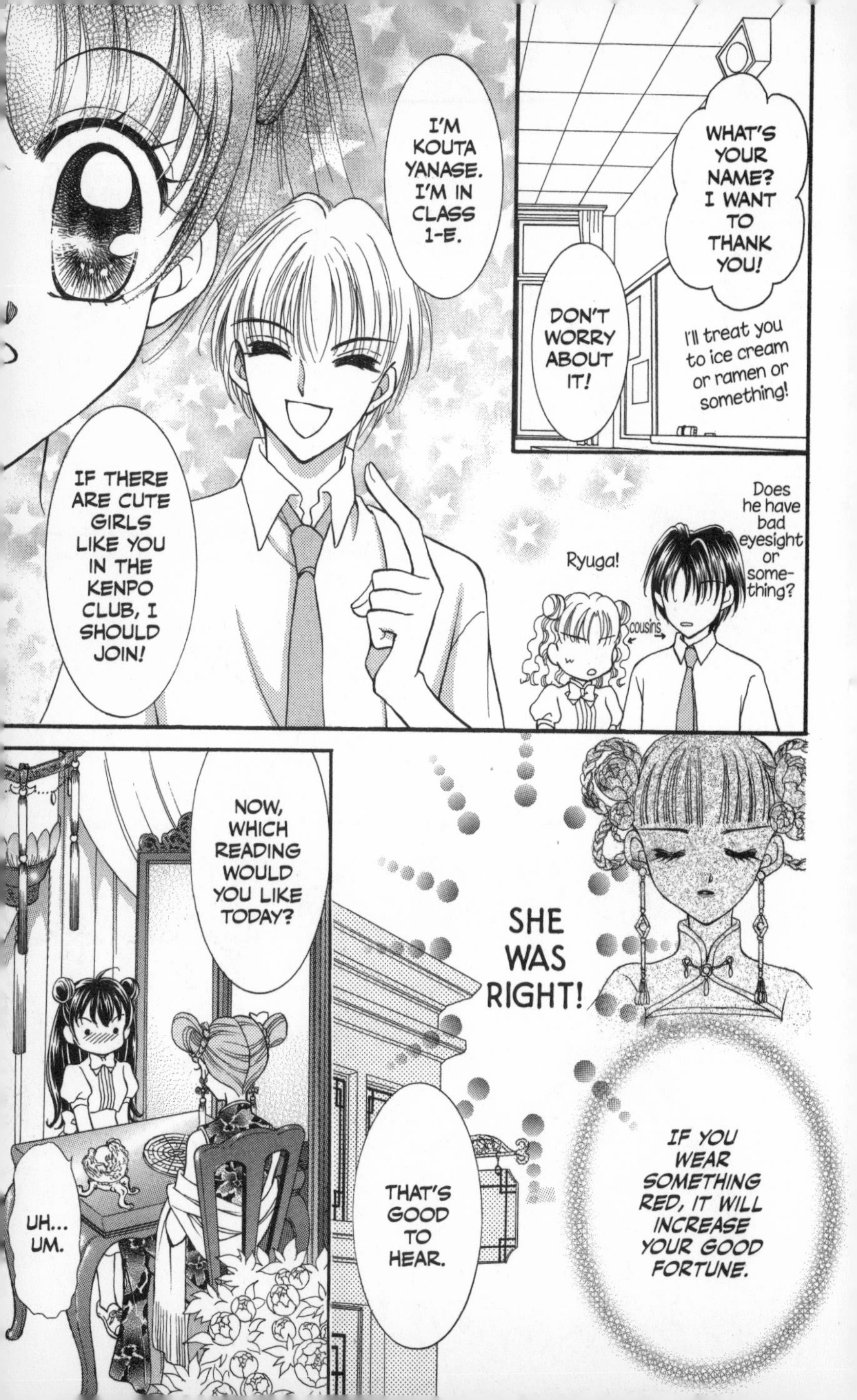
WHAT'S YOUR NAME? I WANT TO THANK YOU!
I'll treat you to ice cream or ramen or something!
DON'T WORRY ABOUT IT!
I'M KOUTA YANASE. I'M IN CLASS 1-E.
IF THERE ARE CUTE GIRLS LIKE YOU IN THE KENPO CLUB, I SHOULD JOIN!
Does he have bad eyesight or some-thing?
Ryuga!
cousins
SHE WAS RIGHT!
IF YOU WEAR SOMETHING RED, IT WILL INCREASE YOUR GOOD FORTUNE.
NOW, WHICH READING WOULD YOU LIKE TODAY?
THAT'S GOOD TO HEAR.
UH... UM.

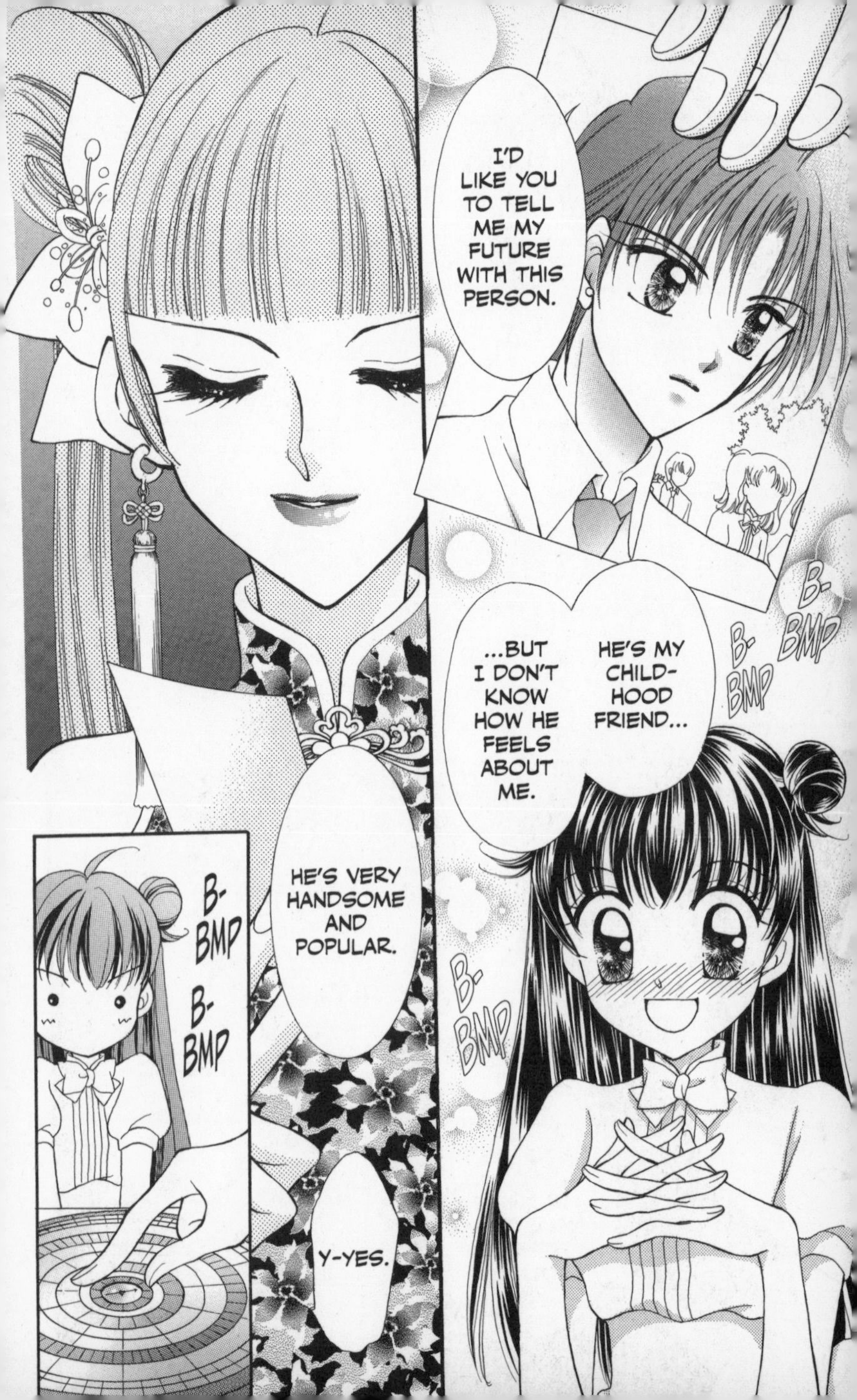
I'D LIKE YOU TO TELL ME MY FUTURE WITH THIS PERSON.
B-BMP
B-BMP
HE'S MY CHILD-HOOD FRIEND...
...BUT I DON'T KNOW HOW HE FEELS ABOUT ME.
B-BMP
HE'S VERY HANDSOME AND POPULAR.
Y-YES.
B-BMP
B-BMP

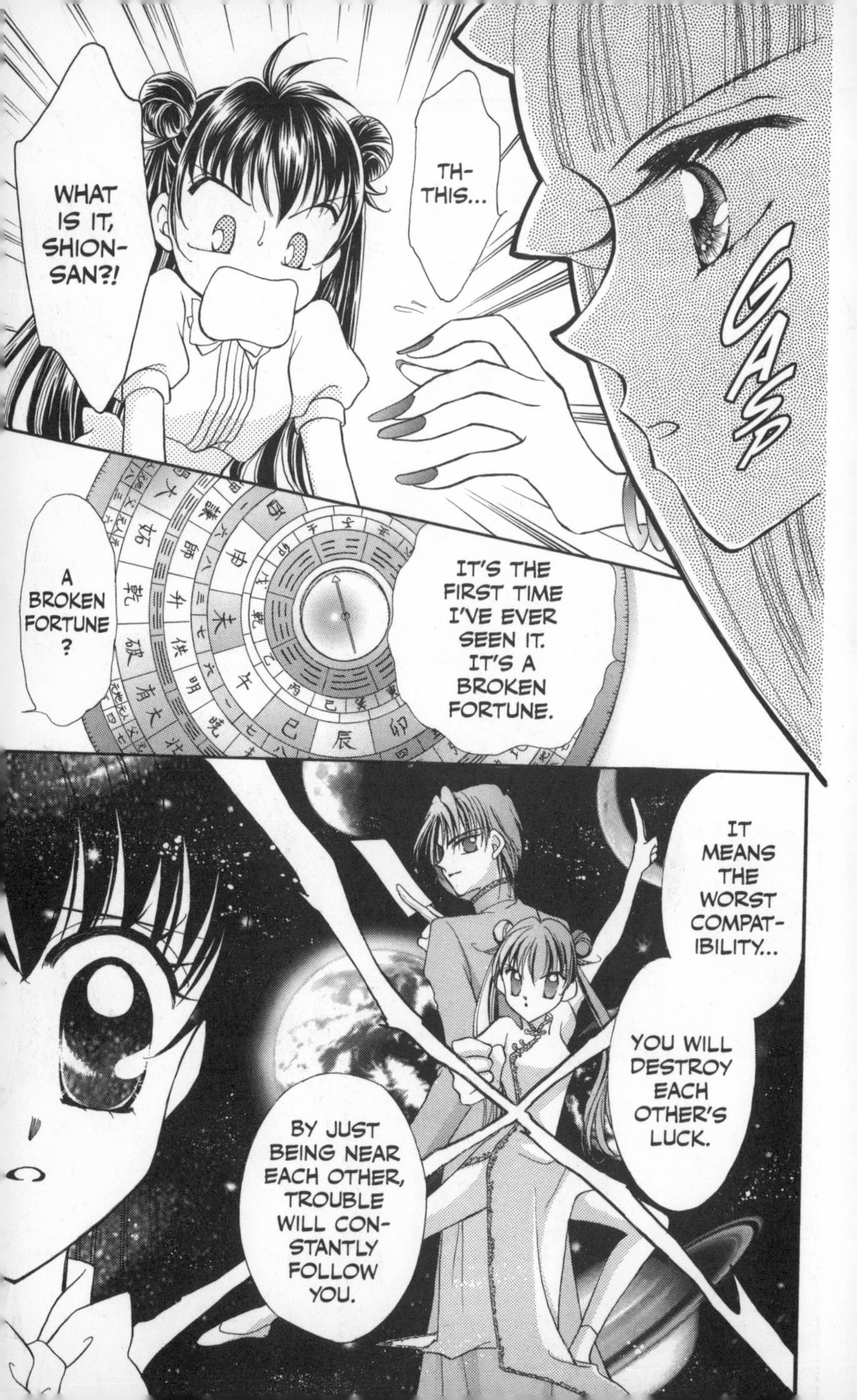
GASP
TH-THIS...
WHAT IS IT, SHION-SAN?!
IT'S THE FIRST TIME I'VE EVER SEEN IT. IT'S A BROKEN FORTUNE.
A BROKEN FORTUNE?
IT MEANS THE WORST COMPAT-IBILITY...
YOU WILL DESTROY EACH OTHER'S LUCK.
BY JUST BEING NEAR EACH OTHER, TROUBLE WILL CON-STANTLY FOLLOW YOU.

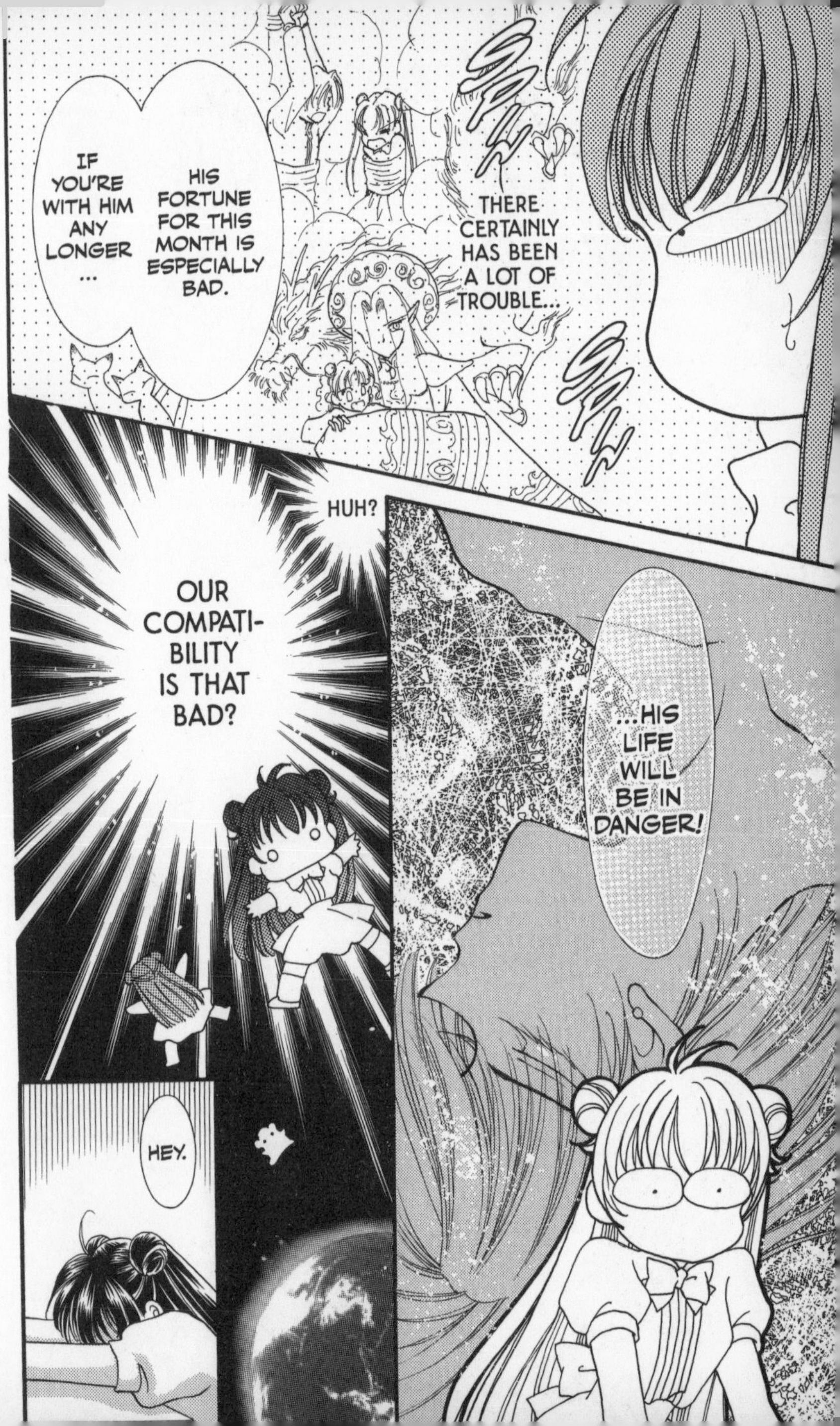
THERE CERTAINLY HAS BEEN A LOT OF TROUBLE...
HIS FORTUNE FOR THIS MONTH IS ESPECIALLY BAD.
IF YOU'RE WITH HIM ANY LONGER ...
...HIS LIFE WILL BE IN DANGER!
HUH?
OUR COMPATI-BILITY IS THAT BAD?
HEY.

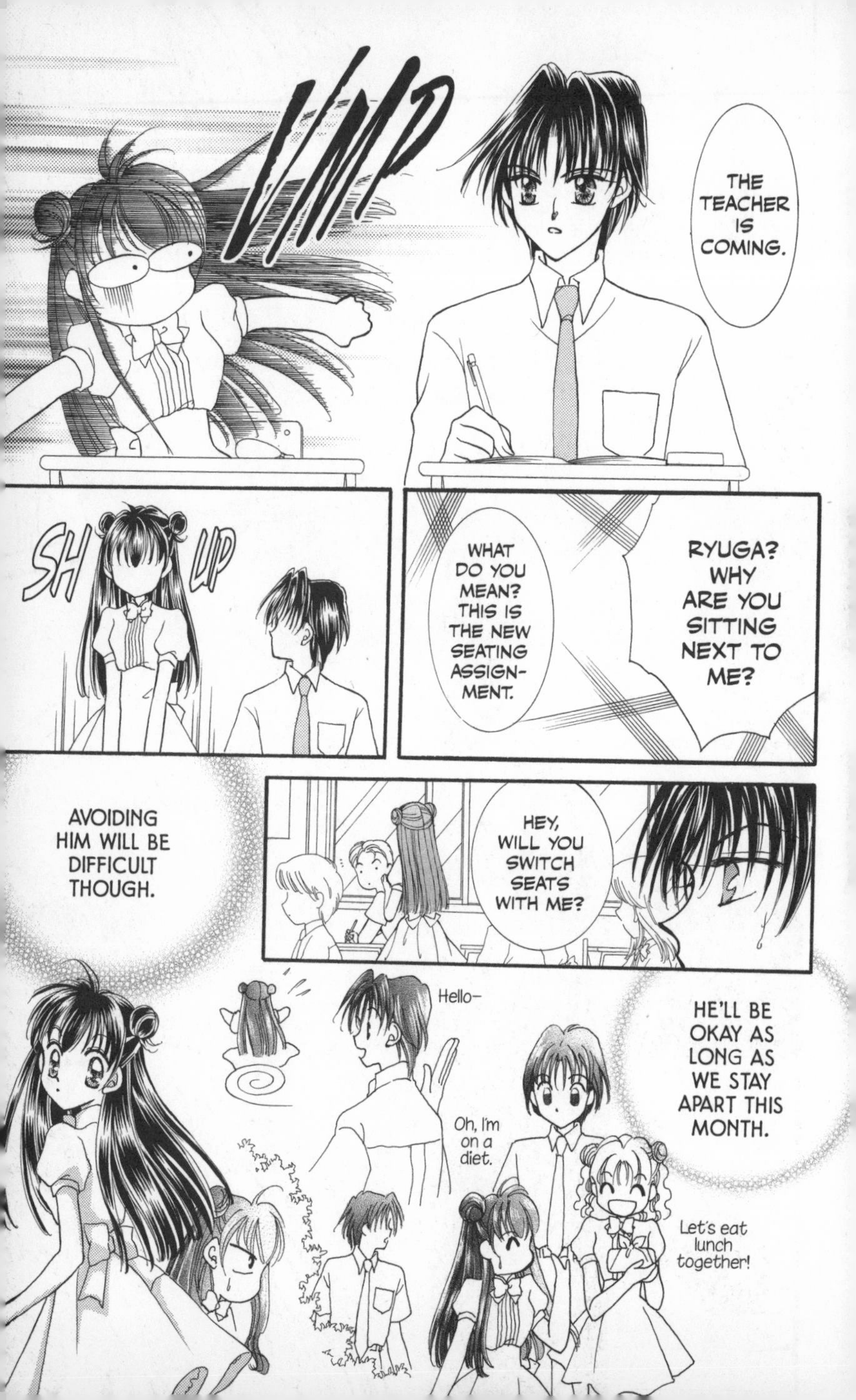
THE TEACHER IS COMING.
VMP
RYUGA? WHY ARE YOU SITTING NEXT TO ME?
WHAT DO YOU MEAN? THIS IS THE NEW SEATING ASSIGN-MENT.
SH UP
HEY, WILL YOU SWITCH SEATS WITH ME?
AVOIDING HIM WILL BE DIFFICULT THOUGH.
HE'LL BE OKAY AS LONG AS WE STAY APART THIS MONTH.
Let's eat lunch together!
Oh, I'm on a diet.
Hello–

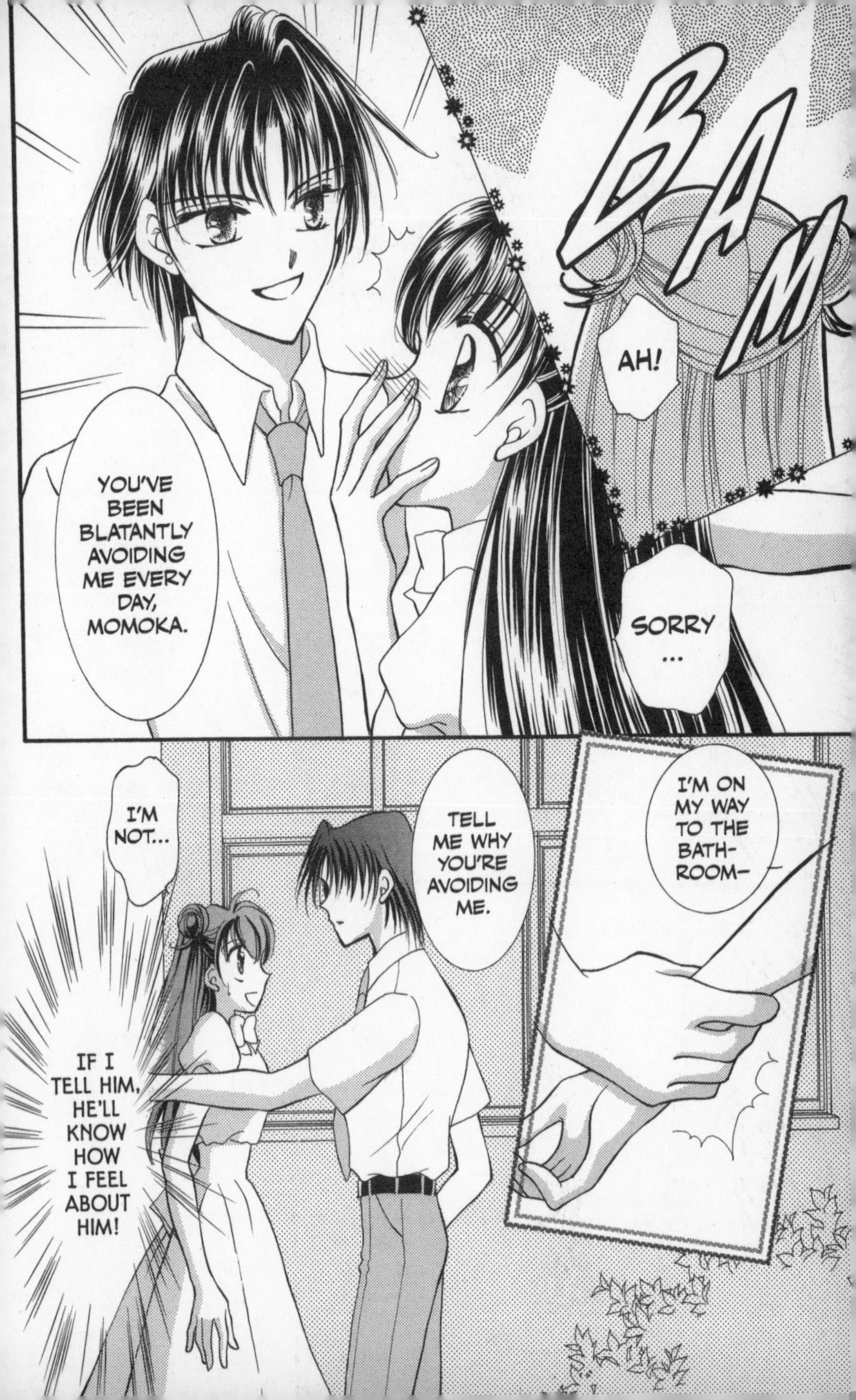
BAM
AH!
SORRY ...
YOU'VE BEEN BLATANTLY AVOIDING ME EVERY DAY, MOMOKA.
I'M ON MY WAY TO THE BATH-ROOM-
TELL ME WHY YOU'RE AVOIDING ME.
I'M NOT...
IF I TELL HIM, HE'LL KNOW HOW I FEEL ABOUT HIM!

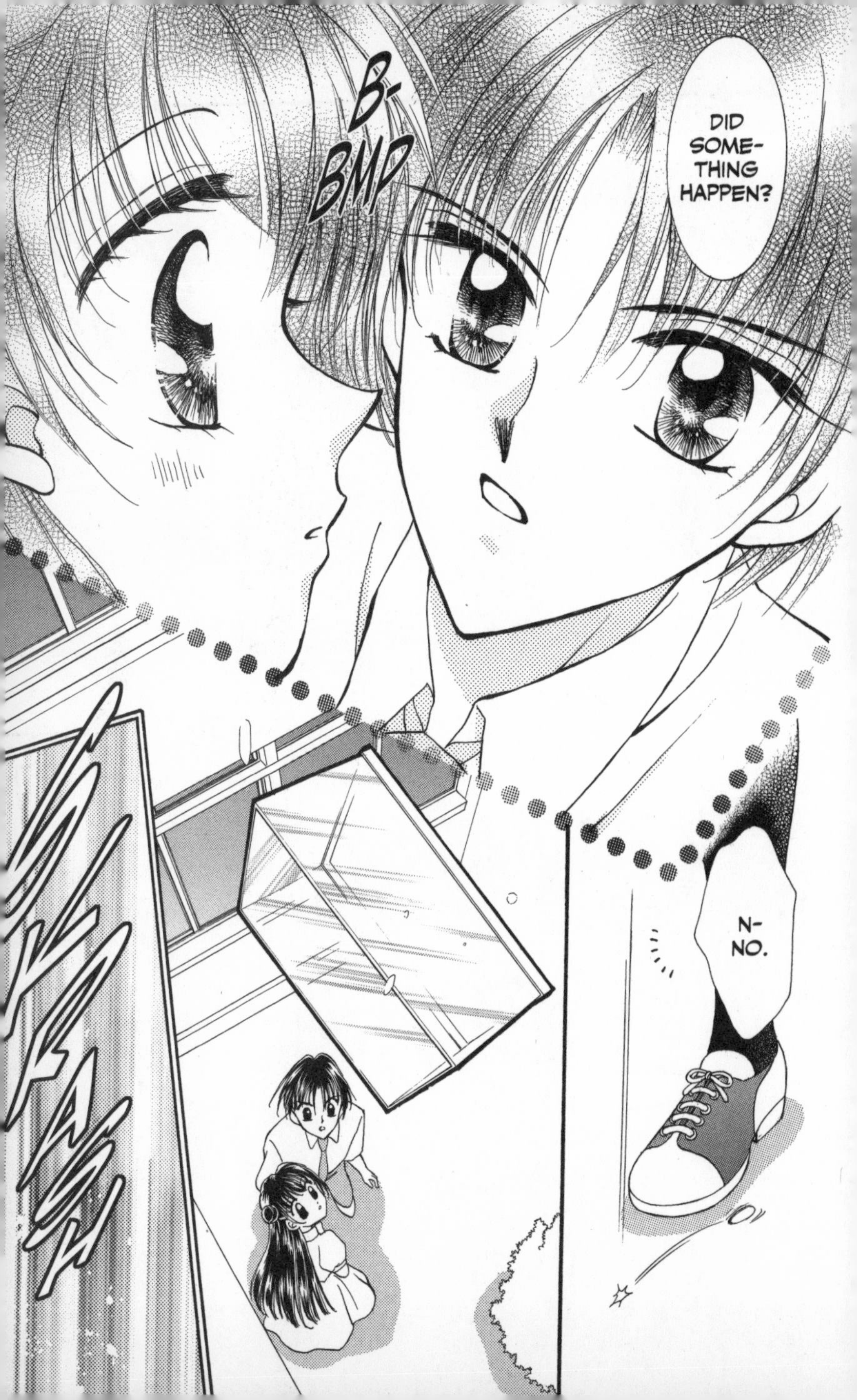
DID SOME-THING HAPPEN?
B-BMP
N-NO.

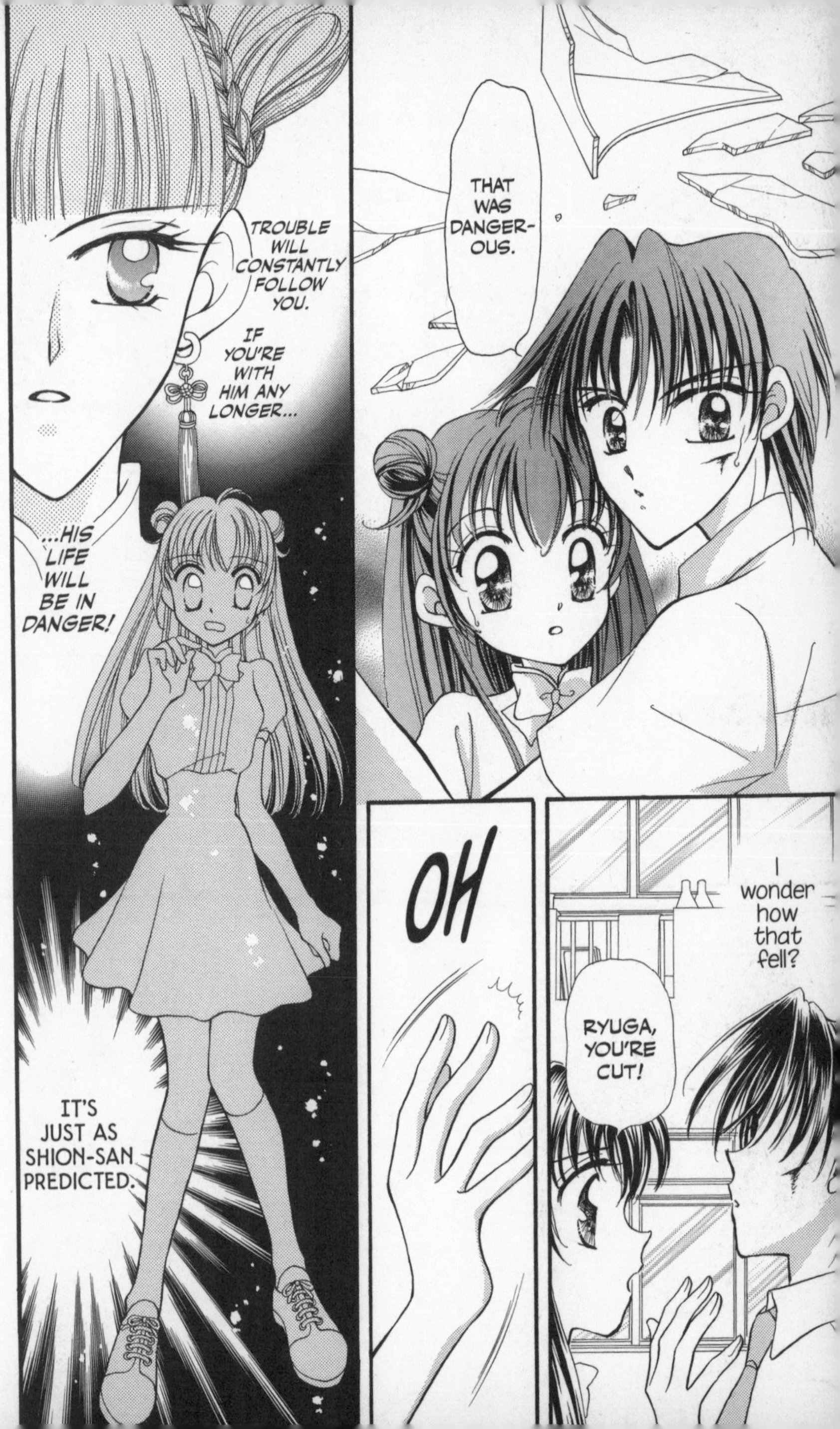
THAT WAS DANGER-OUS.
I wonder how that fell?
RYUGA, YOU'RE CUT!
OH
TROUBLE WILL CONSTANTLY FOLLOW YOU.
IF YOU'RE WITH HIM ANY LONGER...
...HIS LIFE WILL BE IN DANGER!
IT'S JUST AS SHION-SAN PREDICTED.

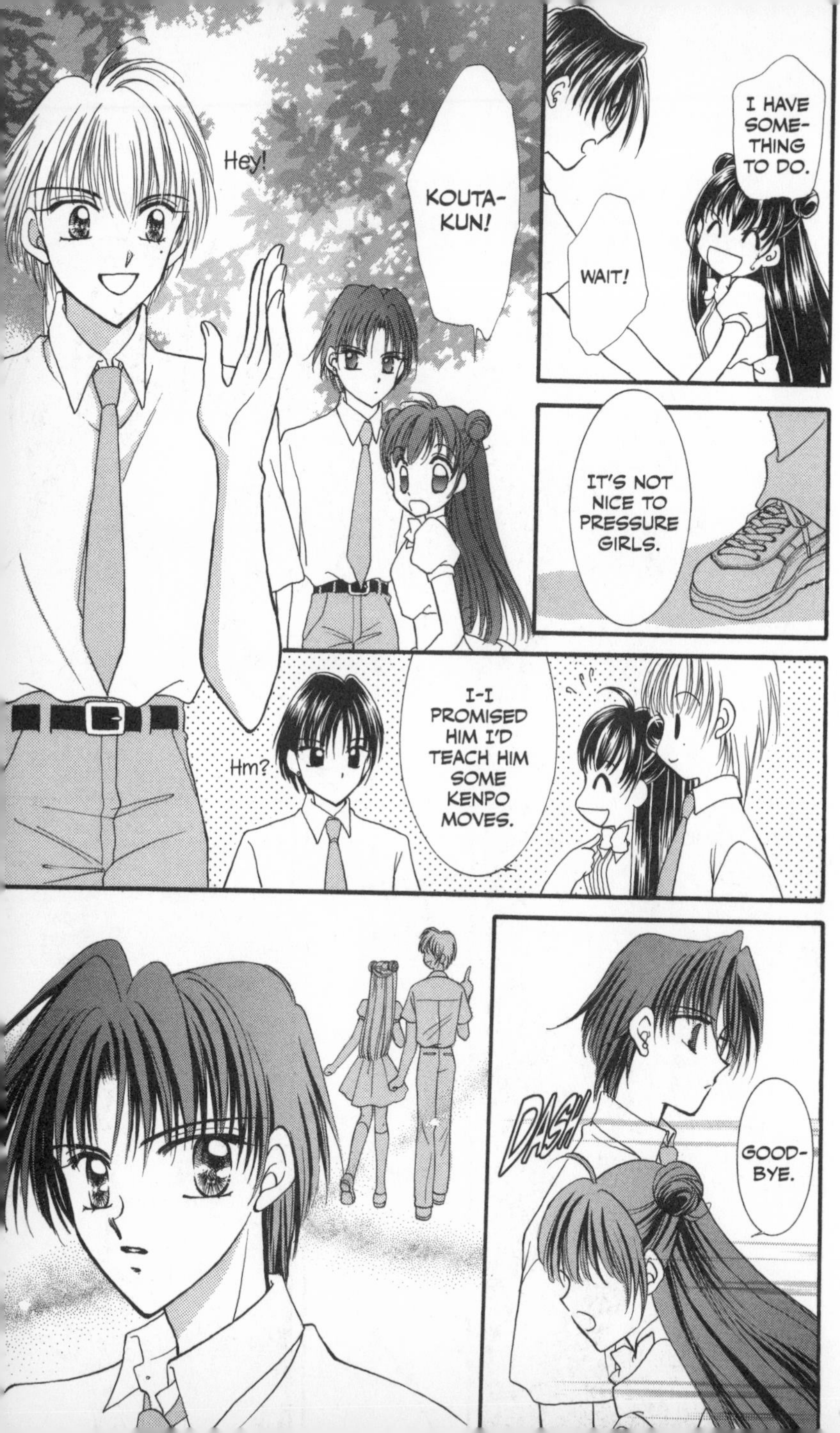
I HAVE SOME-THING TO DO.
WAIT!
IT'S NOT NICE TO PRESSURE GIRLS.
I-I PROMISED HIM I'D TEACH HIM SOME KENPO MOVES.
Hm?
KOUTA-KUN!
Hey!
GOOD-BYE.
DASH

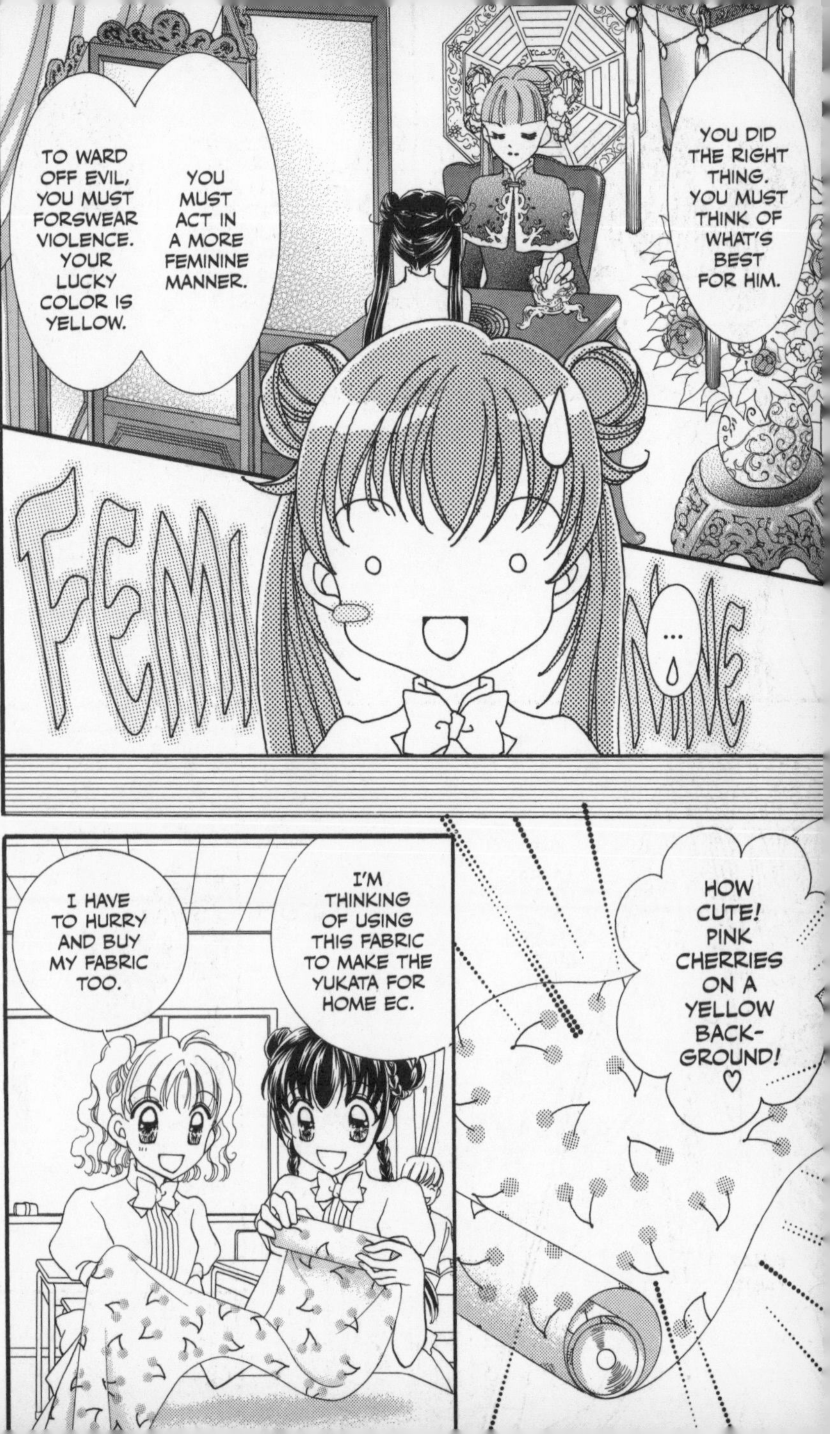
YOU DID THE RIGHT THING. YOU MUST THINK OF WHAT'S BEST FOR HIM.
YOU MUST ACT IN A MORE FEMININE MANNER.
TO WARD OFF EVIL, YOU MUST FORSWEAR VIOLENCE. YOUR LUCKY COLOR IS YELLOW.
FEMI
NINE
...
HOW CUTE! PINK CHERRIES ON A YELLOW BACK-GROUND! ♡
I'M THINKING OF USING THIS FABRIC TO MAKE THE YUKATA FOR HOME EC.
I HAVE TO HURRY AND BUY MY FABRIC TOO.

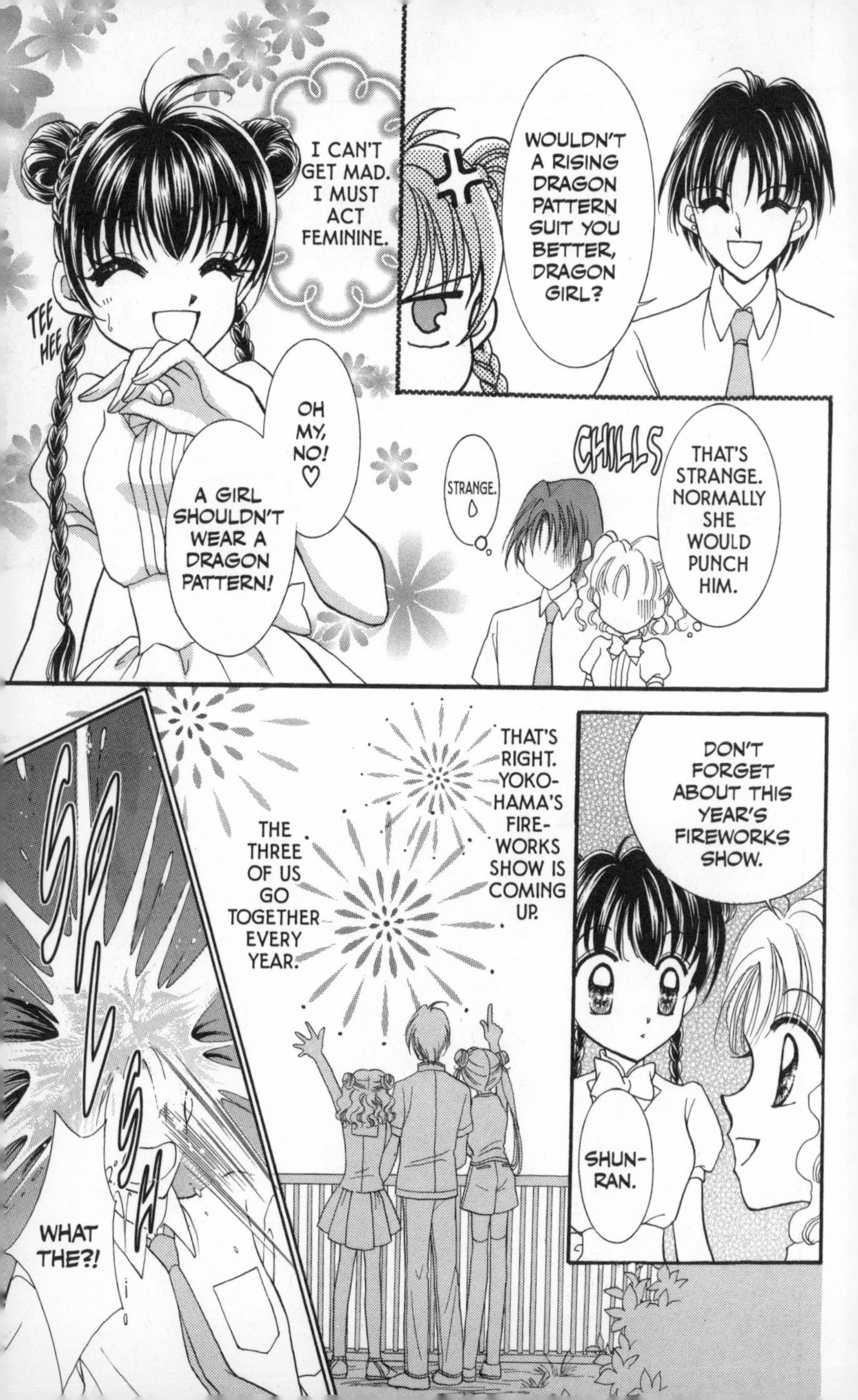
WOULDN'T A RISING DRAGON PATTERN SUIT YOU BETTER, DRAGON GIRL?
CHILLS
THAT'S STRANGE. NORMALLY SHE WOULD PUNCH HIM.
STRANGE.
I CAN'T GET MAD. I MUST ACT FEMININE.
TEE HEE
OH MY, NO! ♡
A GIRL SHOULDN'T WEAR A DRAGON PATTERN!
DON'T FORGET ABOUT THIS YEAR'S FIREWORKS SHOW.
SHUN-RAN.
THAT'S RIGHT. YOKO-HAMA'S FIRE-WORKS SHOW IS COMING UP.
THE THREE OF US GO TOGETHER EVERY YEAR.
WHAT THE?!

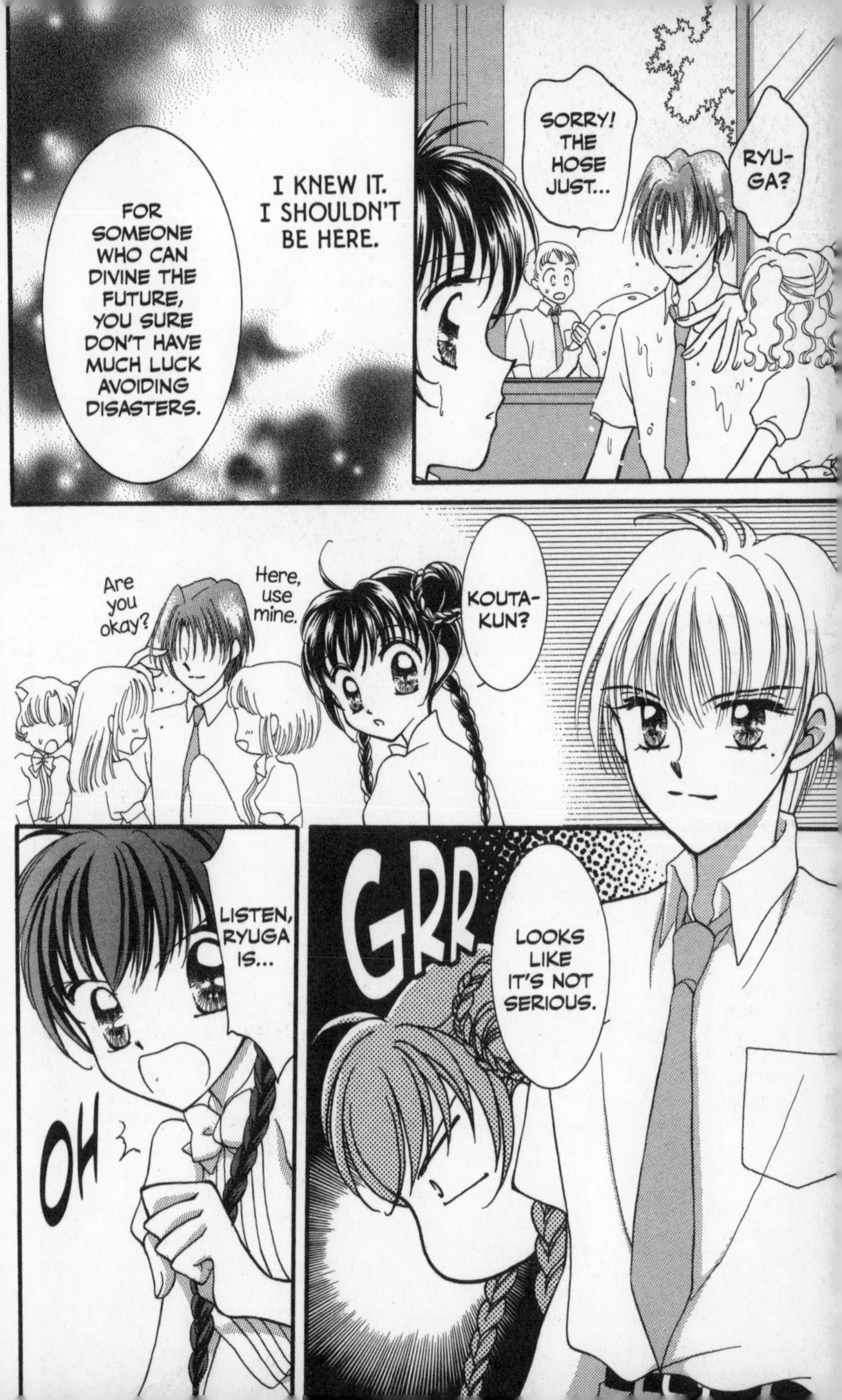
RYU-GA?
SORRY! THE HOSE JUST...
I KNEW IT. I SHOULDN'T BE HERE.
FOR SOMEONE WHO CAN DIVINE THE FUTURE, YOU SURE DON'T HAVE MUCH LUCK AVOIDING DISASTERS.
KOUTA-KUN?
Here, use mine.
Are you okay?
LOOKS LIKE IT'S NOT SERIOUS.
GRR
LISTEN, RYUGA IS...
OH

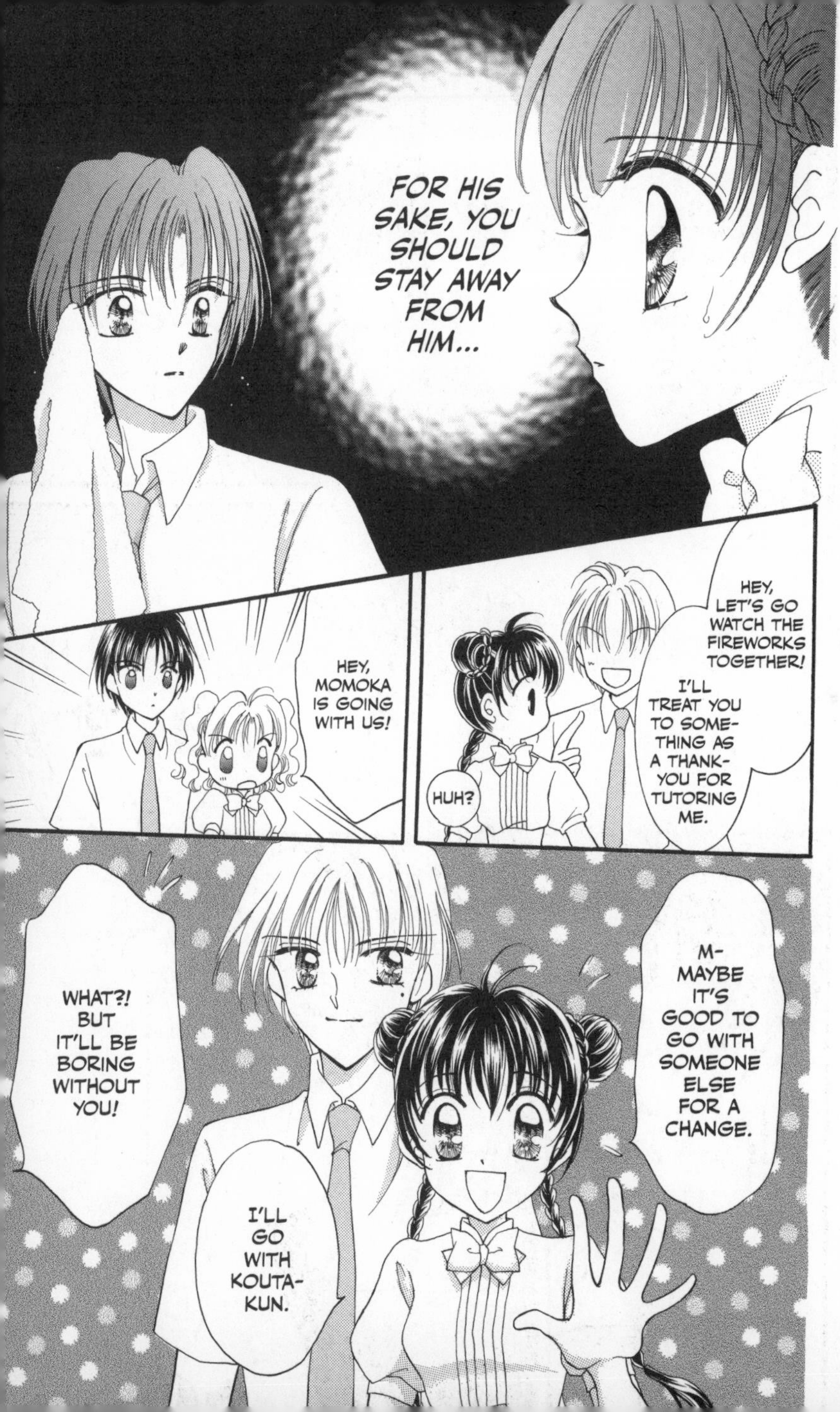
FOR HIS SAKE, YOU SHOULD STAY AWAY FROM HIM...
HEY, LET'S GO WATCH THE FIREWORKS TOGETHER!
I'LL TREAT YOU TO SOMETHING AS A THANK-YOU FOR TUTORING ME.
HUH?
HEY, MOMOKA IS GOING WITH US!
M-MAYBE IT'S GOOD TO GO WITH SOMEONE ELSE FOR A CHANGE.
WHAT?! BUT IT'LL BE BORING WITHOUT YOU!
I'LL GO WITH KOUTA-KUN.

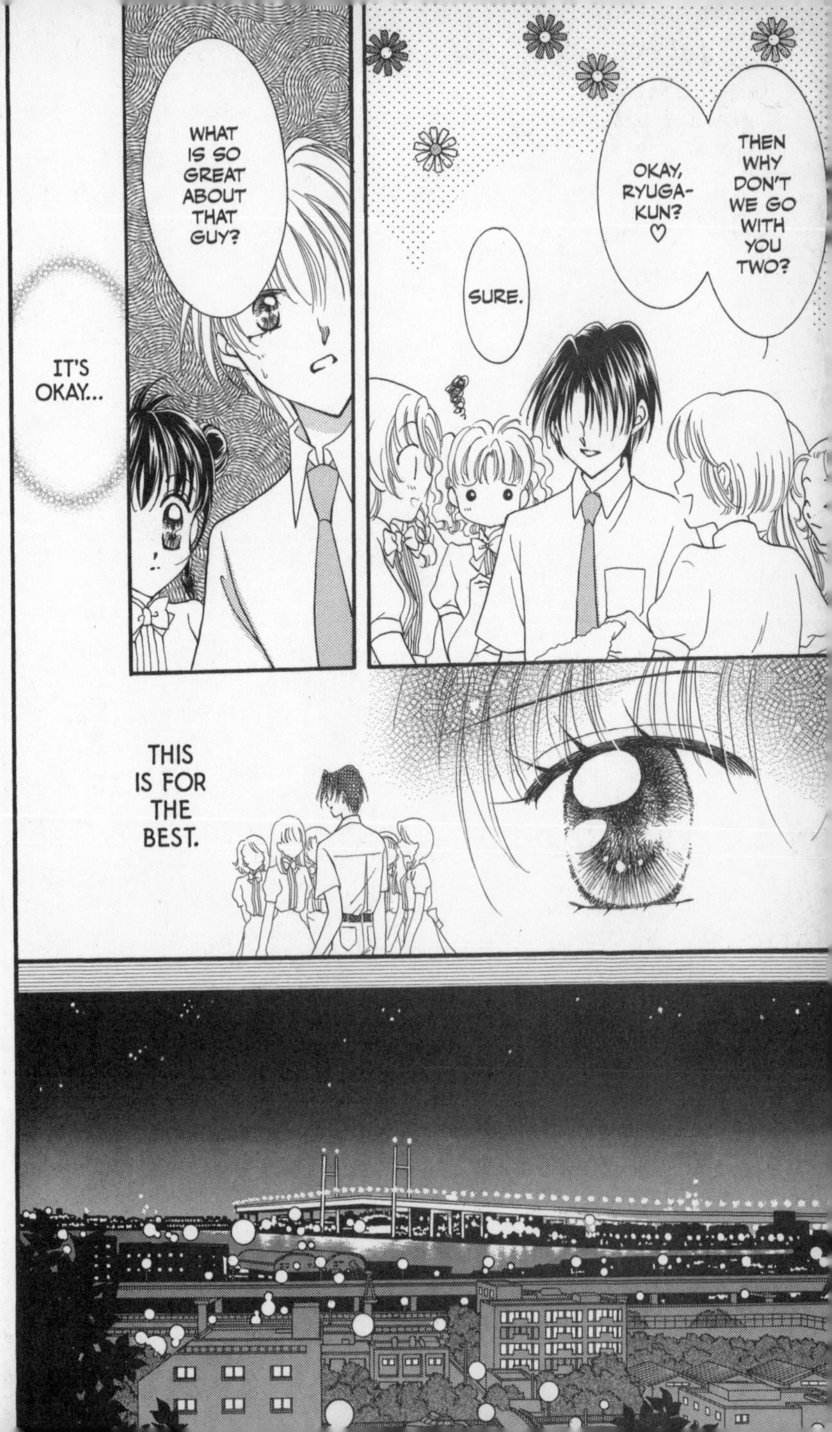
THEN WHY DON'T WE GO WITH YOU TWO?
OKAY, RYUGA-KUN? ♡
SURE.
WHAT IS SO GREAT ABOUT THAT GUY?
IT'S OKAY...
THIS IS FOR THE BEST.

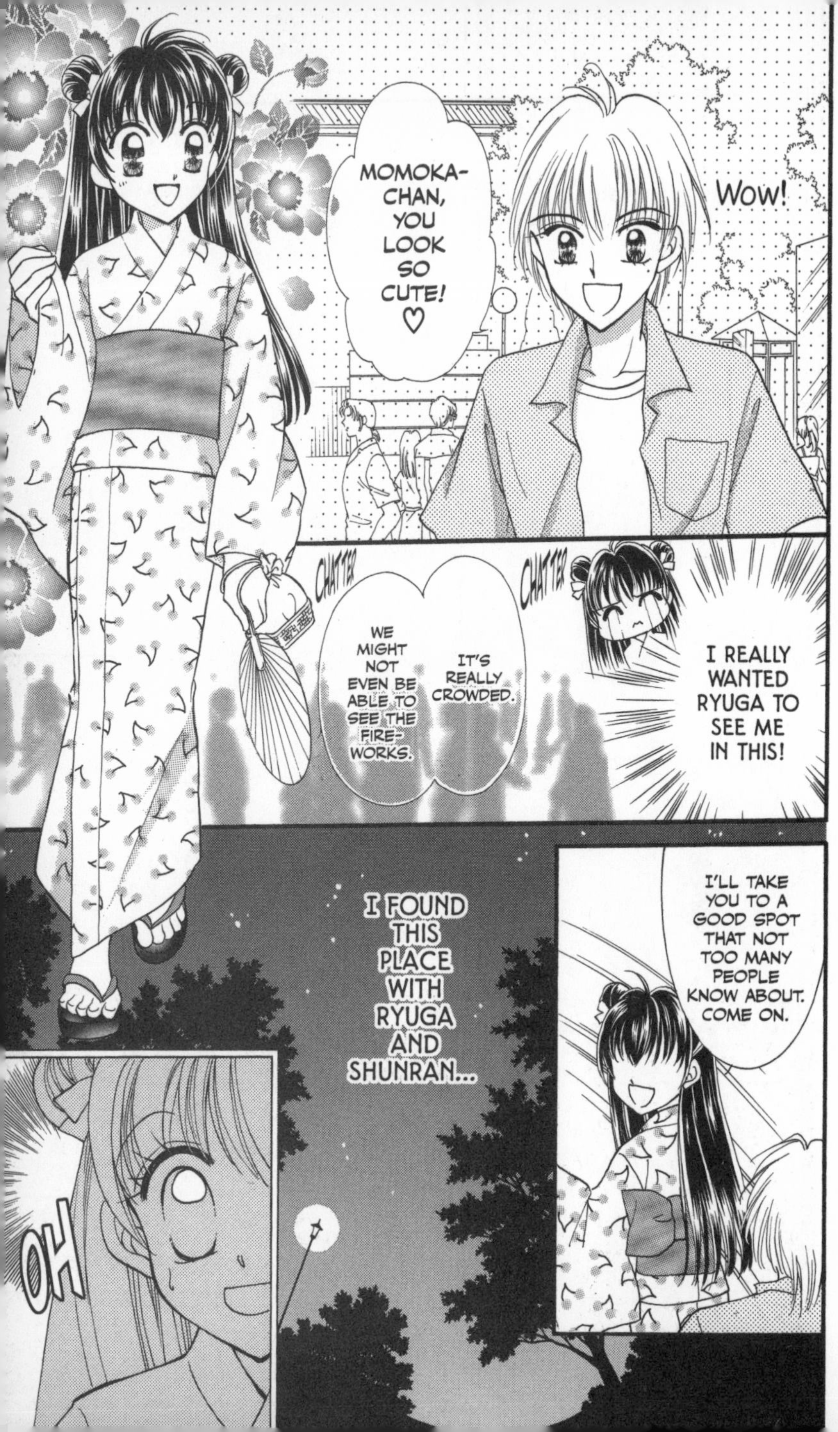
WOW!
MOMOKA-CHAN, YOU LOOK SO CUTE! ♡
I REALLY WANTED RYUGA TO SEE ME IN THIS!
CHATTER
IT'S REALLY CROWDED.
WE MIGHT NOT EVEN BE ABLE TO SEE THE FIRE-WORKS.
CHATTER
I'LL TAKE YOU TO A GOOD SPOT THAT NOT TOO MANY PEOPLE KNOW ABOUT. COME ON.
I FOUND THIS PLACE WITH RYUGA AND SHUNRAN...
OH

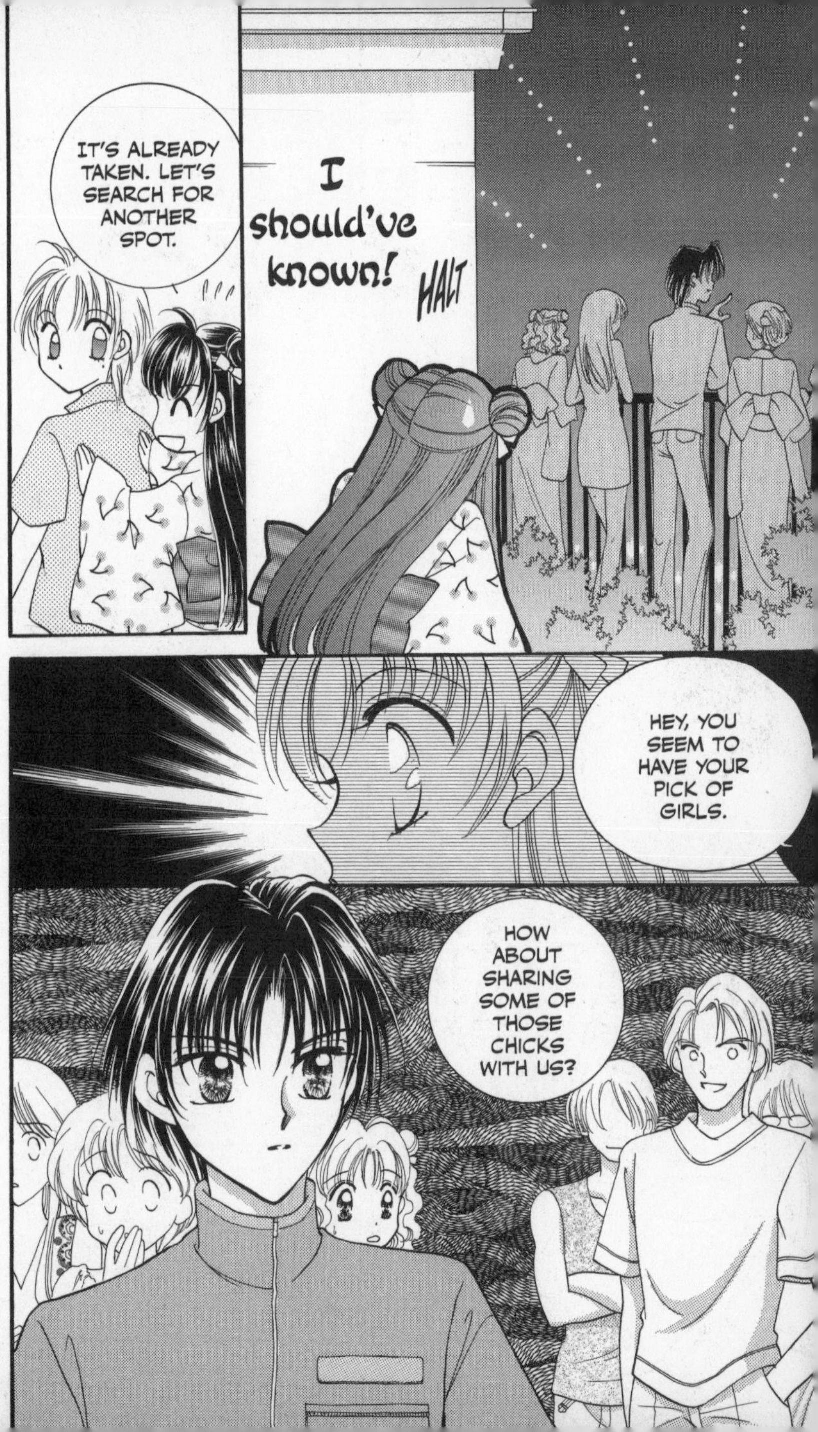
HALT
I should've known!
IT'S ALREADY TAKEN. LET'S SEARCH FOR ANOTHER SPOT.
HEY, YOU SEEM TO HAVE YOUR PICK OF GIRLS.
HOW ABOUT SHARING SOME OF THOSE CHICKS WITH US?

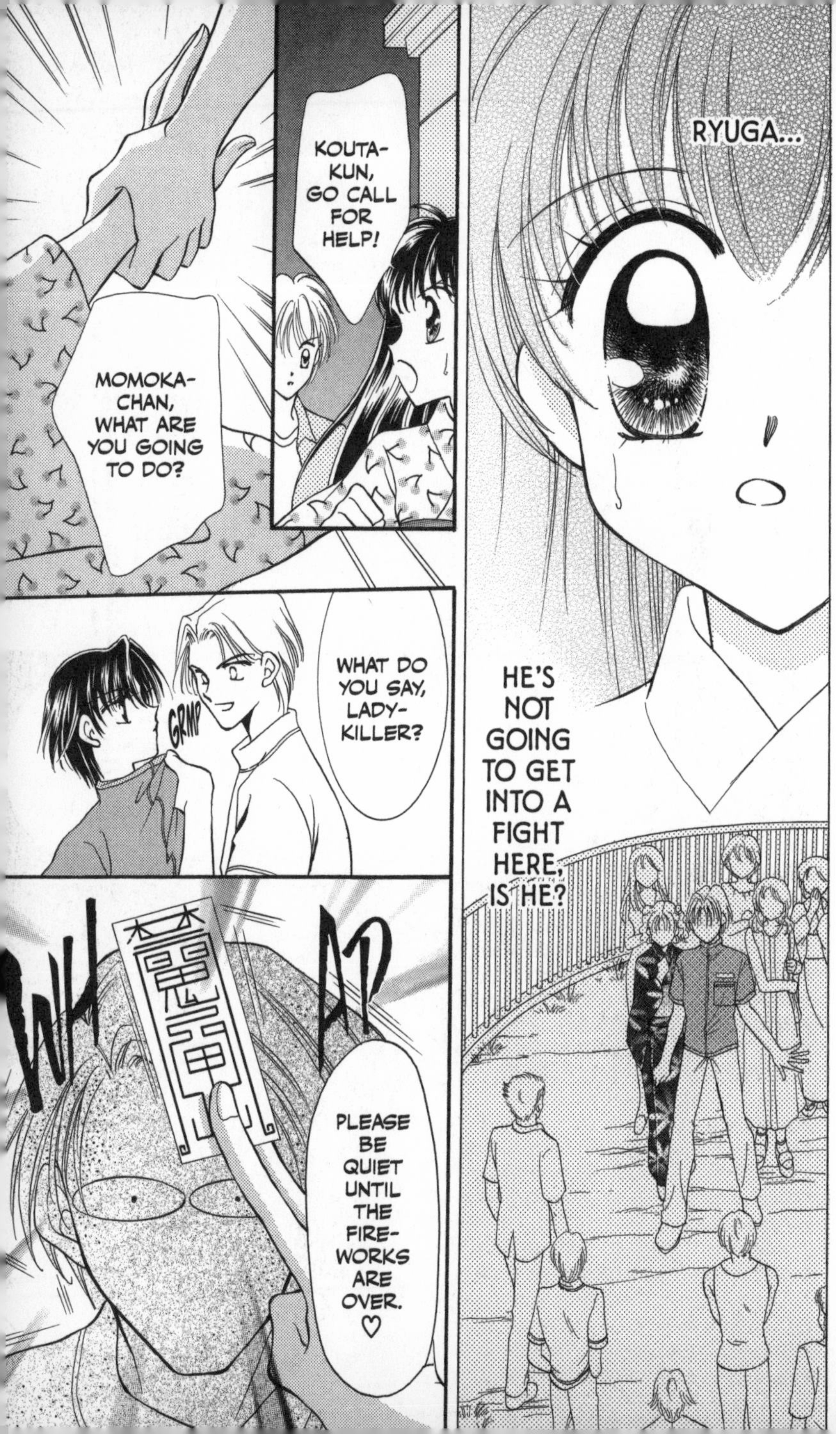
RYUGA...
HE'S NOT GOING TO GET INTO A FIGHT HERE, IS HE?
KOUTA-KUN, GO CALL FOR HELP!
MOMOKA-CHAN, WHAT ARE YOU GOING TO DO?
WHAT DO YOU SAY, LADY-KILLER?
GRMP
WHAP
PLEASE BE QUIET UNTIL THE FIRE-WORKS ARE OVER. ♡

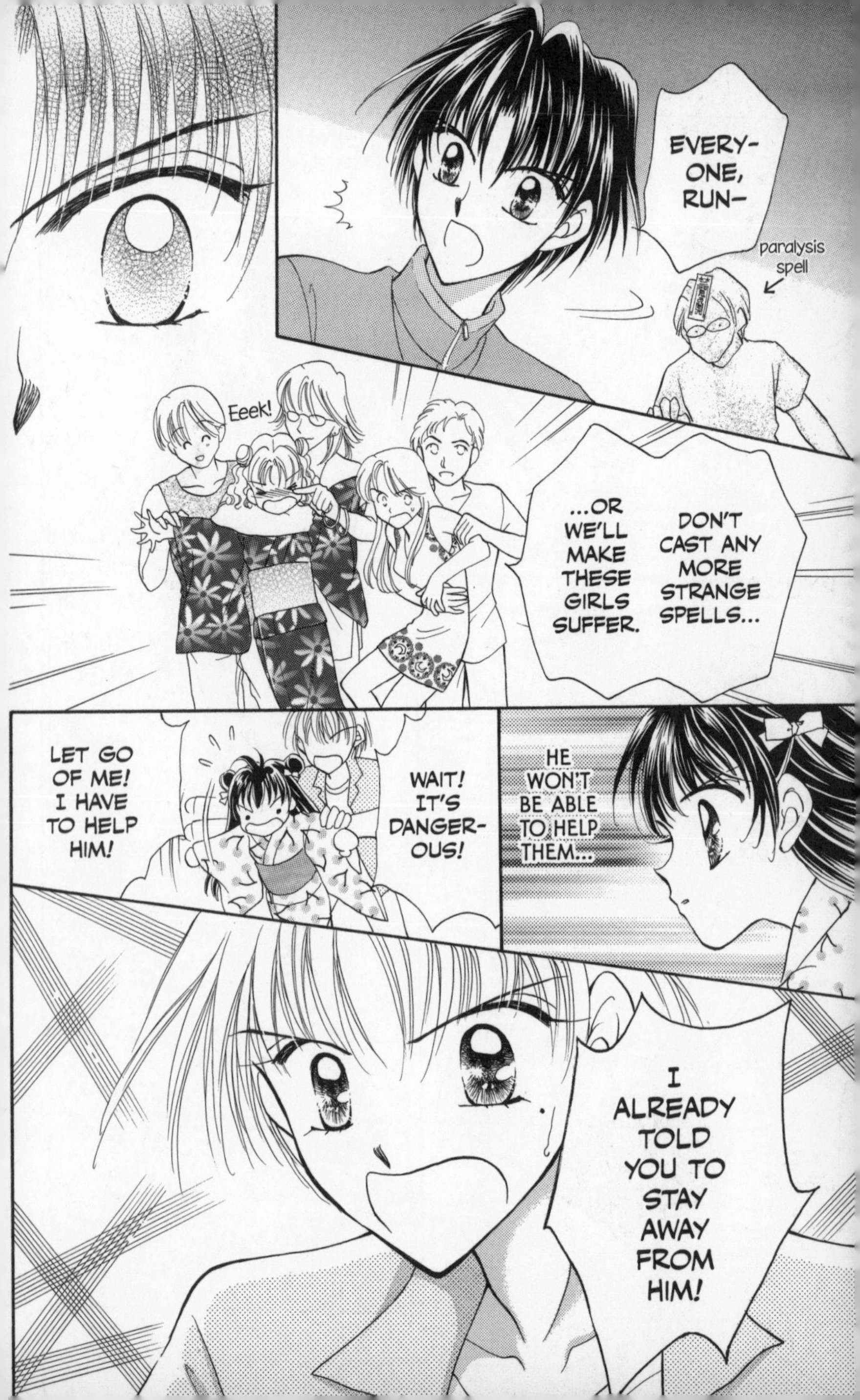
EVERYONE, RUN—
paralysis spell
Eeek!
DON'T CAST ANY MORE STRANGE SPELLS...
...OR WE'LL MAKE THESE GIRLS SUFFER.
HE WON'T BE ABLE TO HELP THEM...
WAIT! IT'S DANGEROUS!
LET GO OF ME! I HAVE TO HELP HIM!
I ALREADY TOLD YOU TO STAY AWAY FROM HIM!

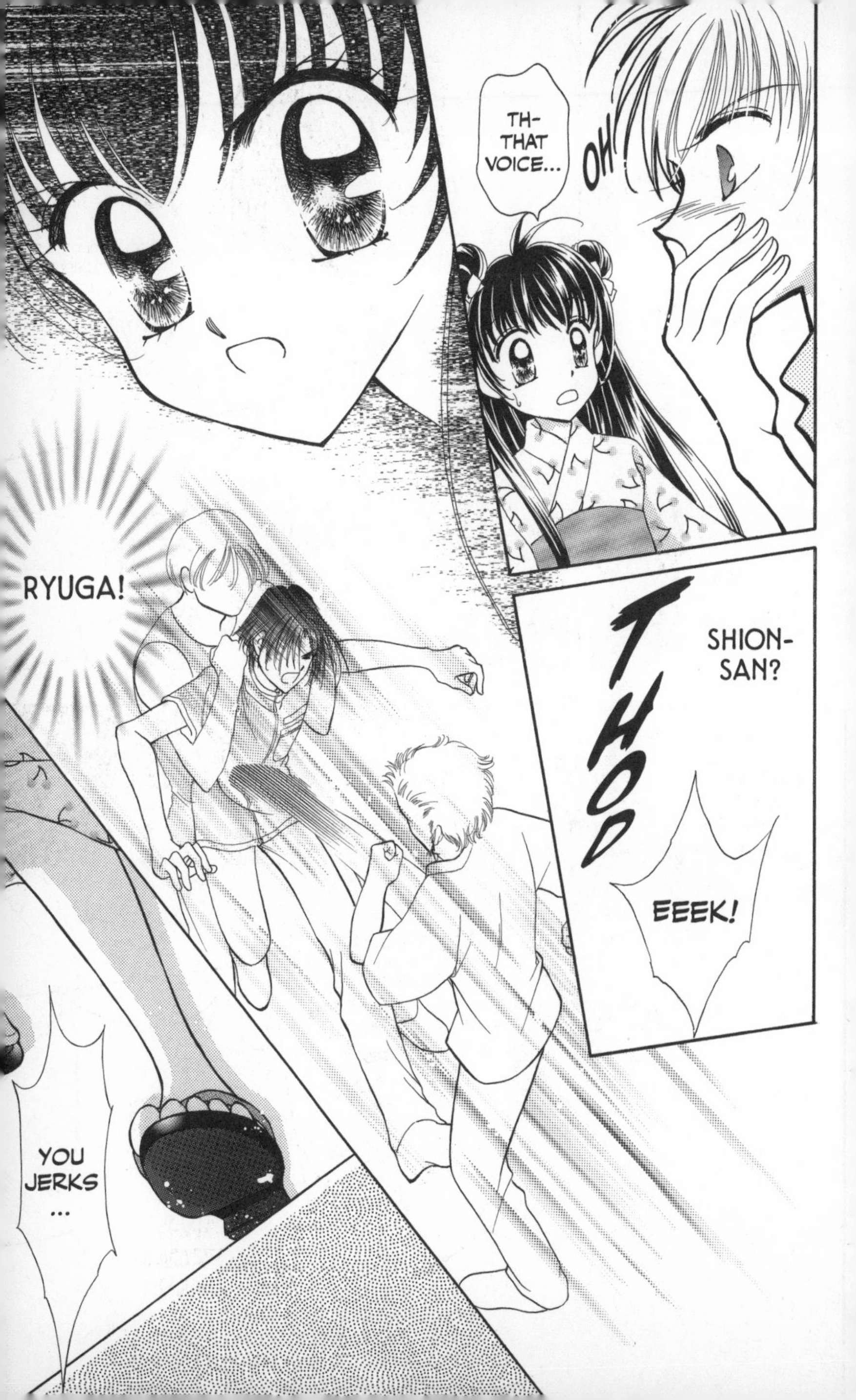
OH
TH-THAT VOICE...
SHION-SAN?
THOD
EEEK!
RYUGA!
YOU JERKS...

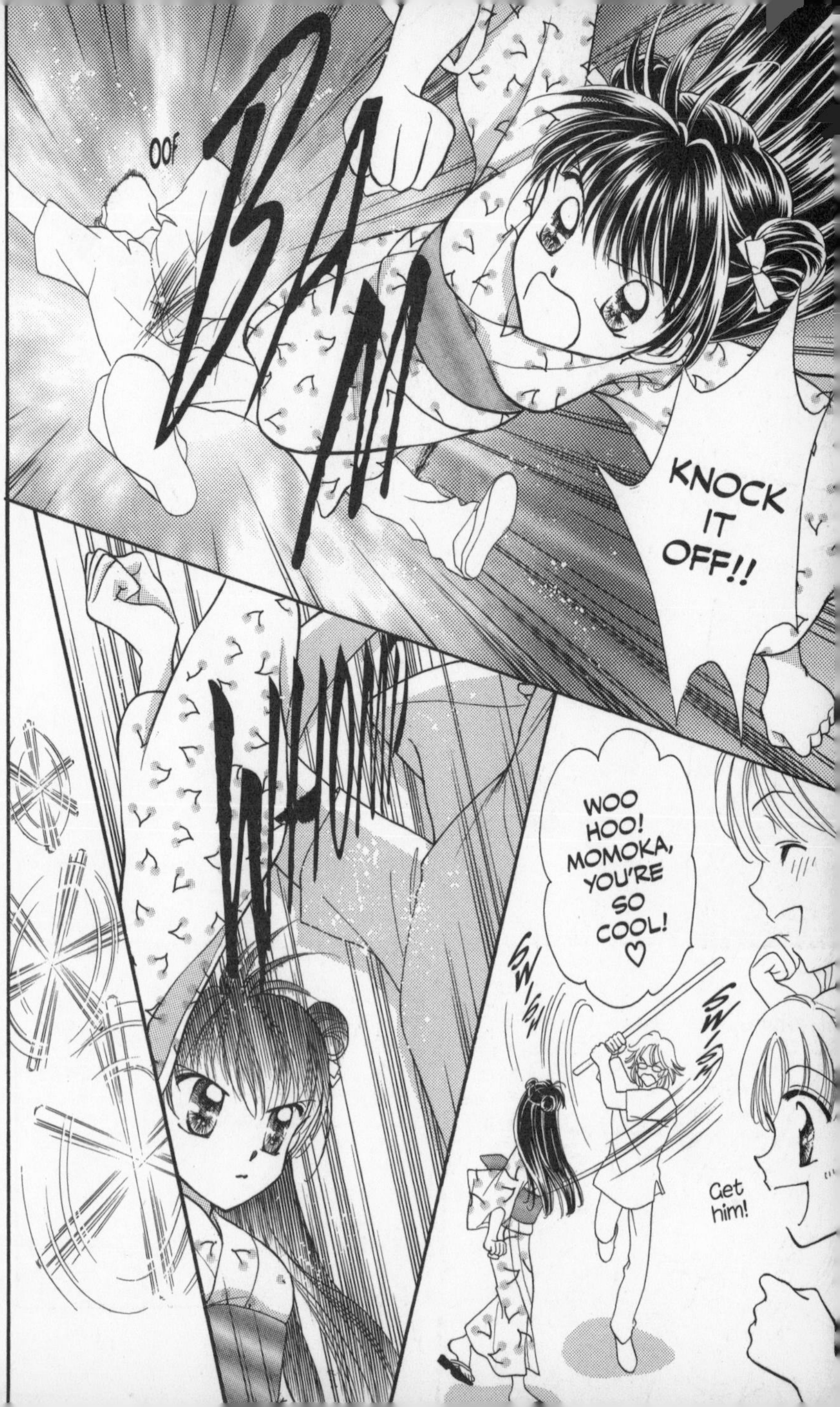
KNOCK IT OFF!!
BAM
OOF
WOO HOO! MOMOKA, YOU'RE SO COOL! ♡
SWISH
SWISH
Get him!
WHOMP

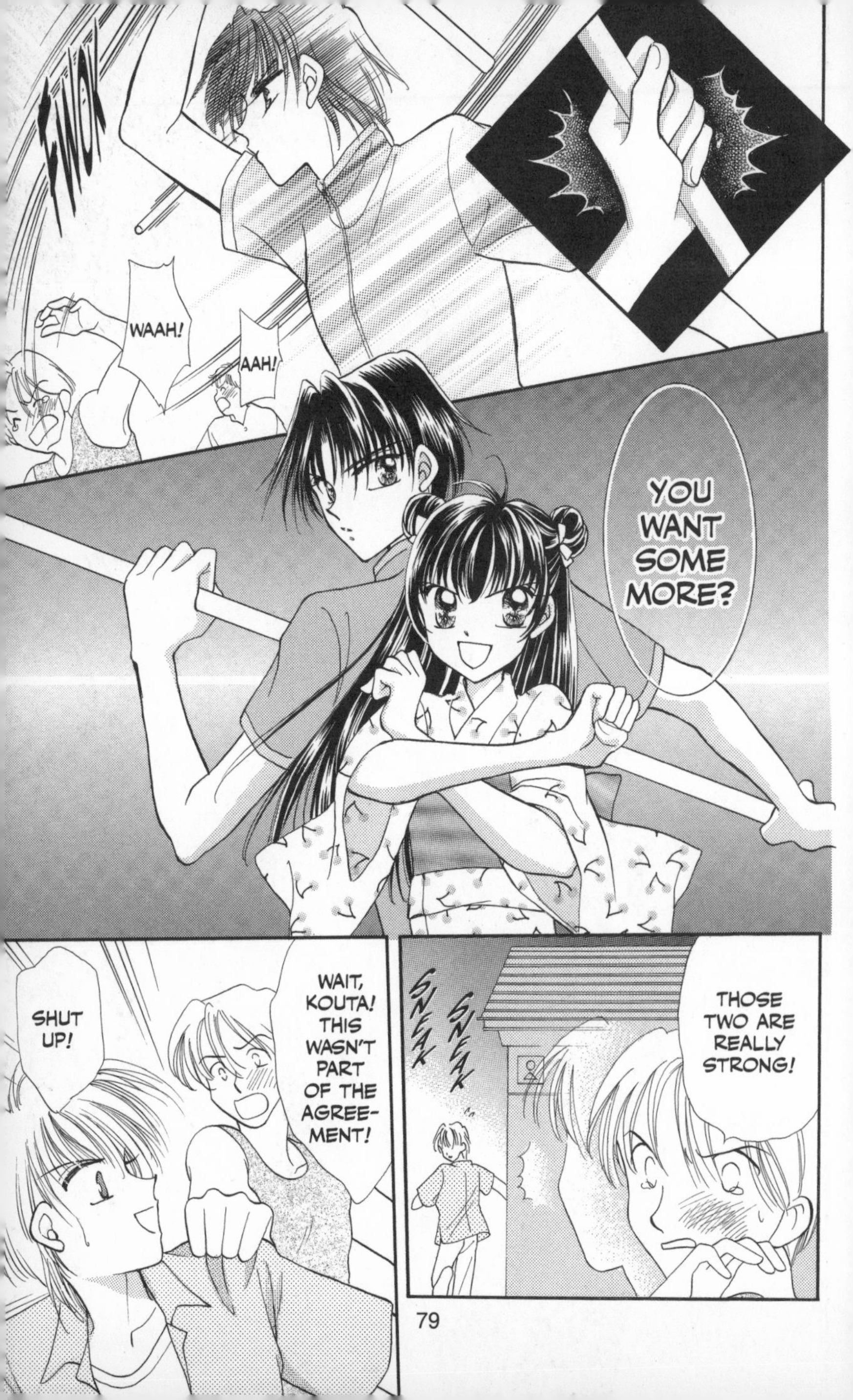
FWOK
AAH!
WAAH!
YOU WANT SOME MORE?
THOSE TWO ARE REALLY STRONG!
SNEAK
SNEAK
WAIT, KOUTA! THIS WASN'T PART OF THE AGREE-MENT!
SHUT UP!

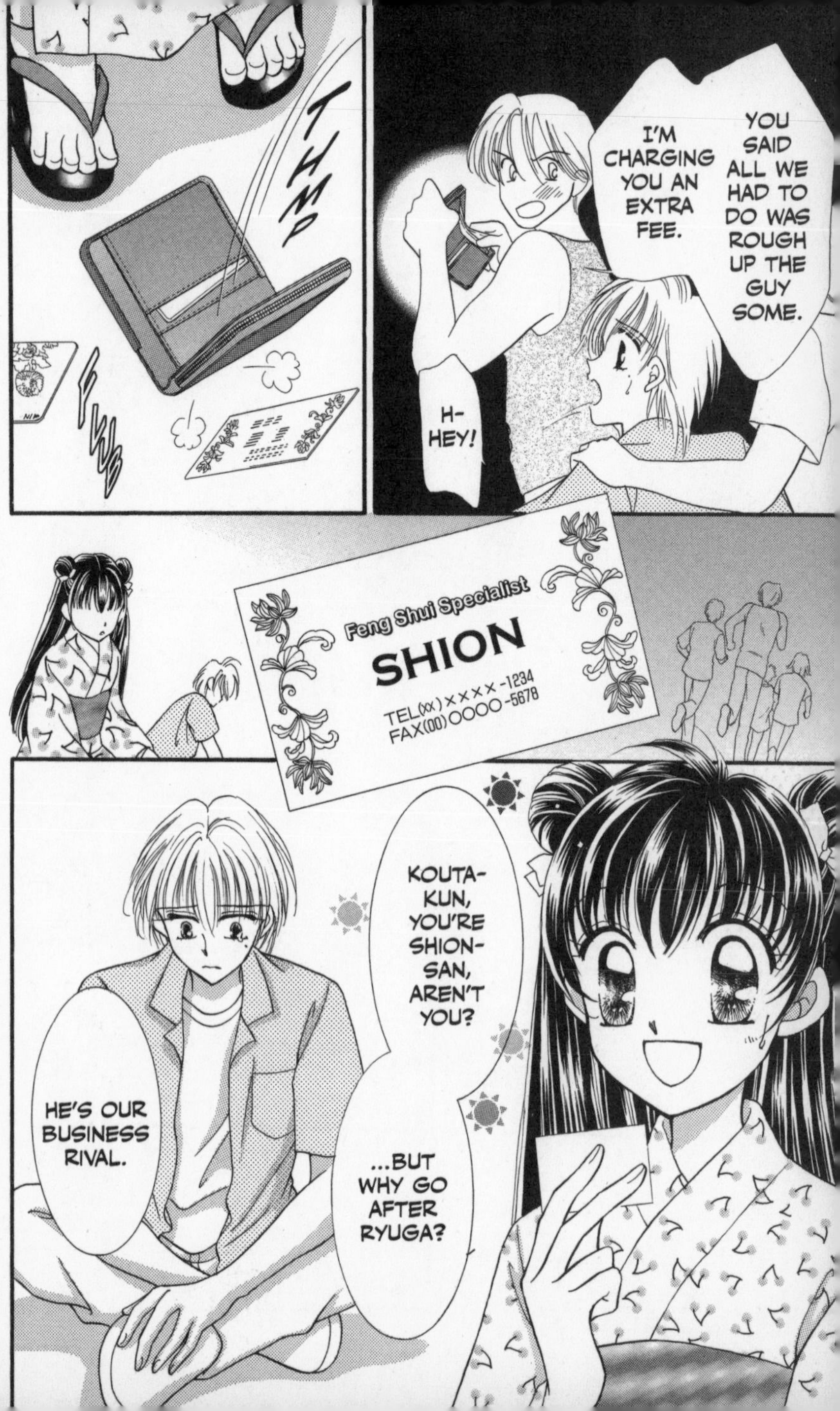
YOU SAID ALL WE HAD TO DO WAS ROUGH UP THE GUY SOME.
I'M CHARGING YOU AN EXTRA FEE.
H-HEY!
THUMP
FWUB
Feng Shui Specialist
SHION
TEL(xx)××××-1234
FAX(00)0000-5678
KOUTA-KUN, YOU'RE SHION-SAN, AREN'T YOU?
...BUT WHY GO AFTER RYUGA?
HE'S OUR BUSINESS RIVAL.

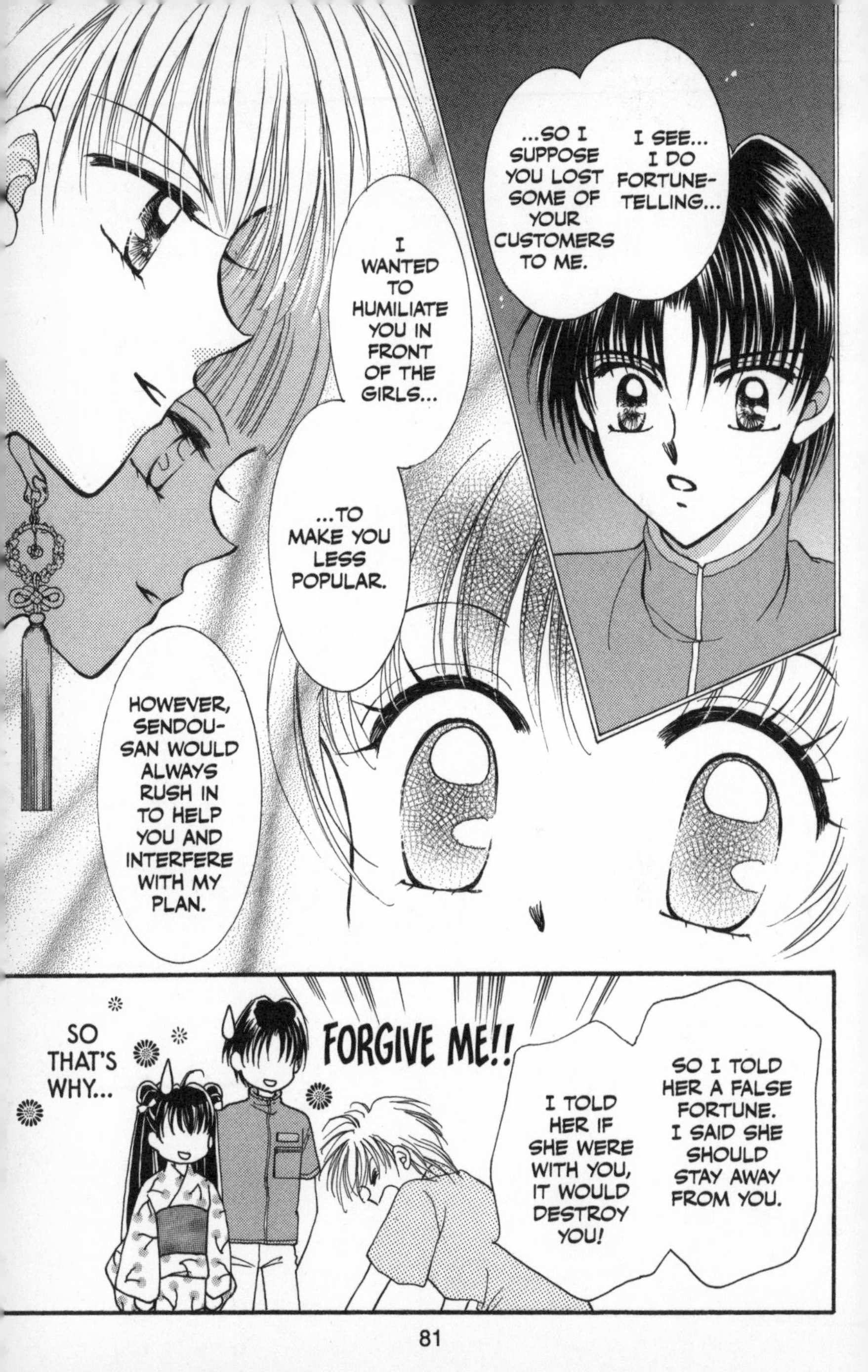
I SEE... I DO FORTUNE-TELLING...
...SO I SUPPOSE YOU LOST SOME OF YOUR CUSTOMERS TO ME.
I WANTED TO HUMILIATE YOU IN FRONT OF THE GIRLS...
...TO MAKE YOU LESS POPULAR.
HOWEVER, SENDOU-SAN WOULD ALWAYS RUSH IN TO HELP YOU AND INTERFERE WITH MY PLAN.
SO I TOLD HER A FALSE FORTUNE. I SAID SHE SHOULD STAY AWAY FROM YOU.
I TOLD HER IF SHE WERE WITH YOU, IT WOULD DESTROY YOU!
FORGIVE ME!!
SO THAT'S WHY...

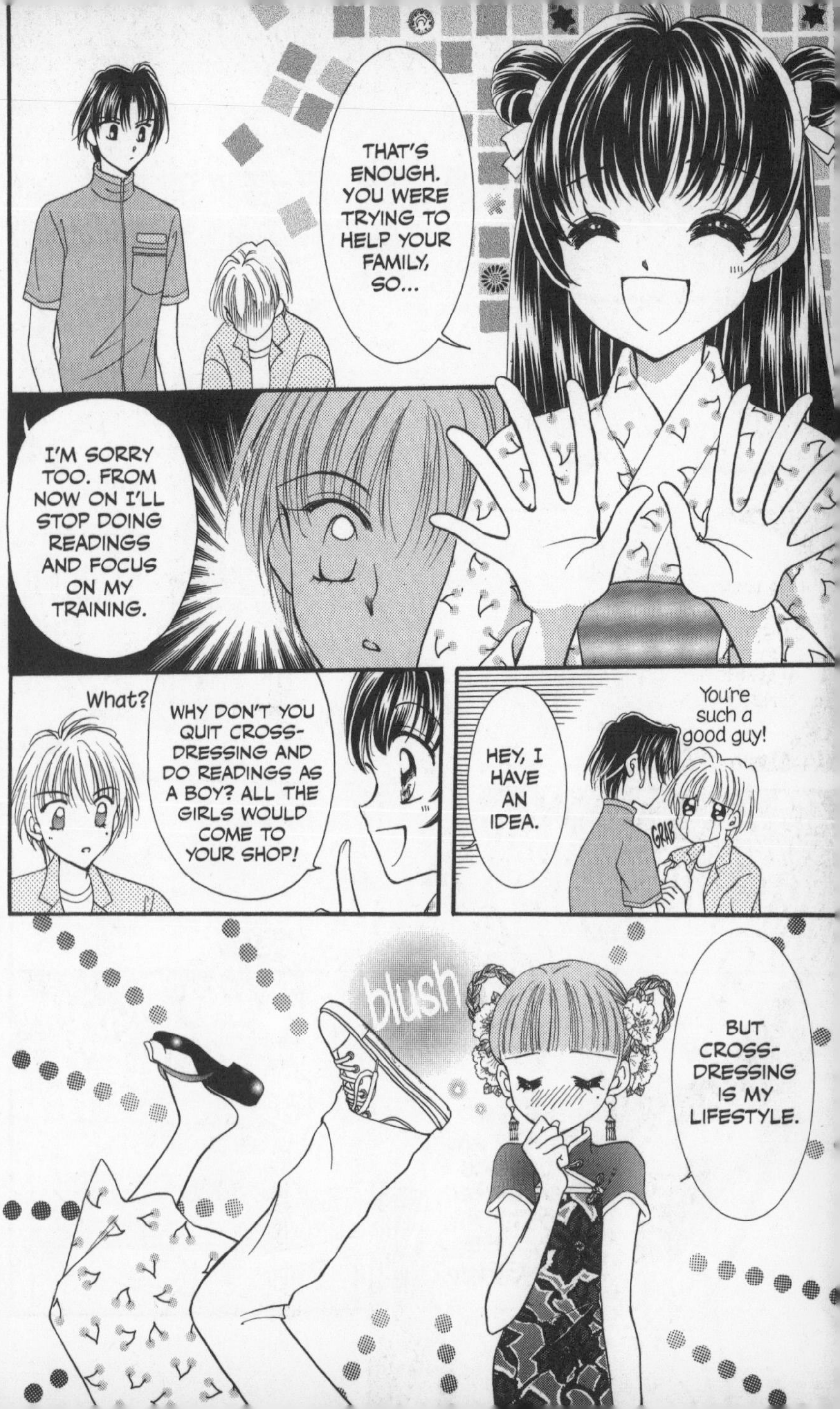
THAT'S ENOUGH. YOU WERE TRYING TO HELP YOUR FAMILY, SO...
I'M SORRY TOO. FROM NOW ON I'LL STOP DOING READINGS AND FOCUS ON MY TRAINING.
You're such a good guy!
GRAB
HEY, I HAVE AN IDEA.
WHY DON'T YOU QUIT CROSS-DRESSING AND DO READINGS AS A BOY? ALL THE GIRLS WOULD COME TO YOUR SHOP!
What?
BUT CROSS-DRESSING IS MY LIFESTYLE.
blush

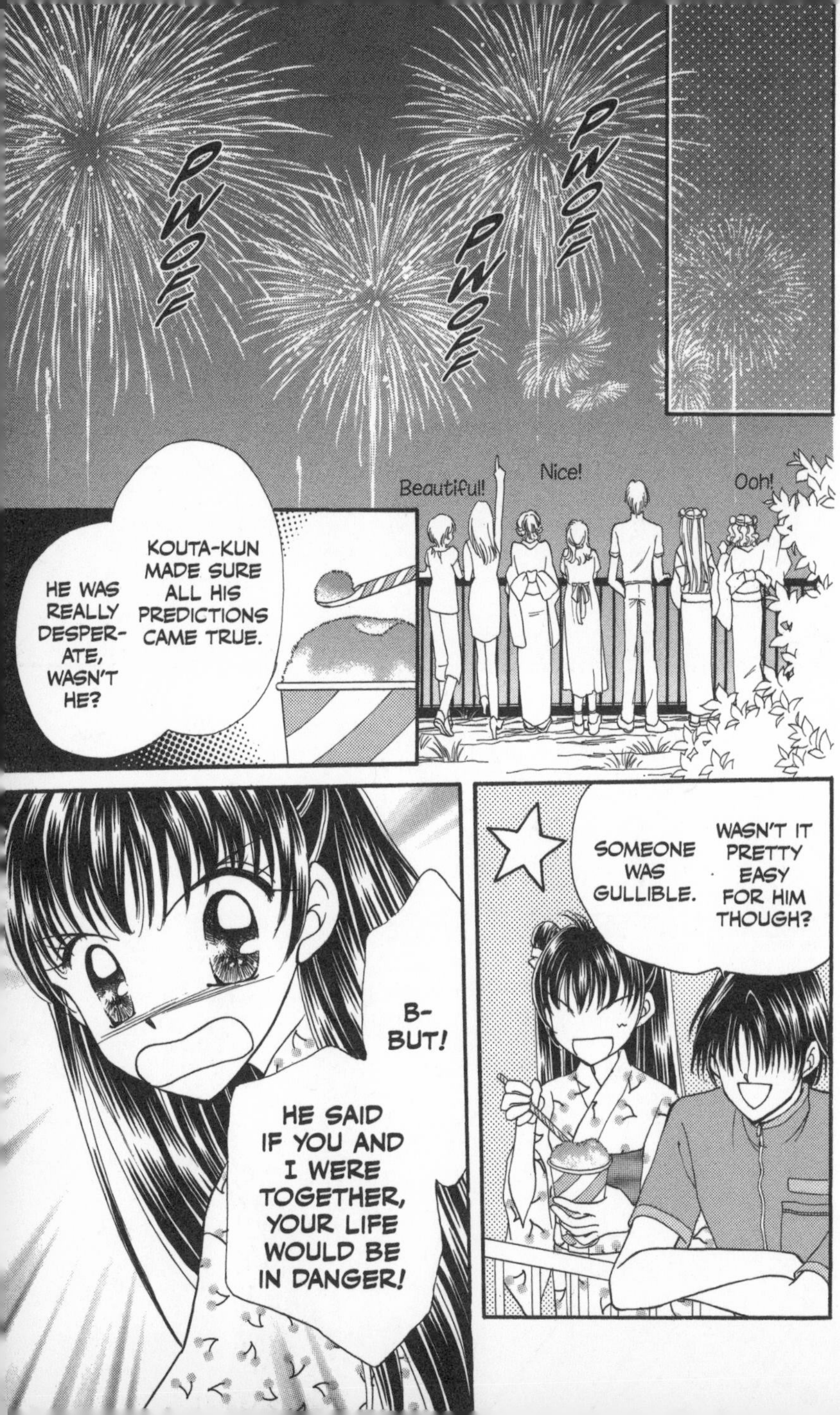
PWOFF
PWOFF
PWOFF
Ooh!
Nice!
Beautiful!
KOUTA-KUN MADE SURE ALL HIS PREDICTIONS CAME TRUE.
HE WAS REALLY DESPER-ATE, WASN'T HE?
WASN'T IT PRETTY EASY FOR HIM THOUGH?
SOMEONE WAS GULLIBLE.
B-BUT!
HE SAID IF YOU AND I WERE TOGETHER, YOUR LIFE WOULD BE IN DANGER!

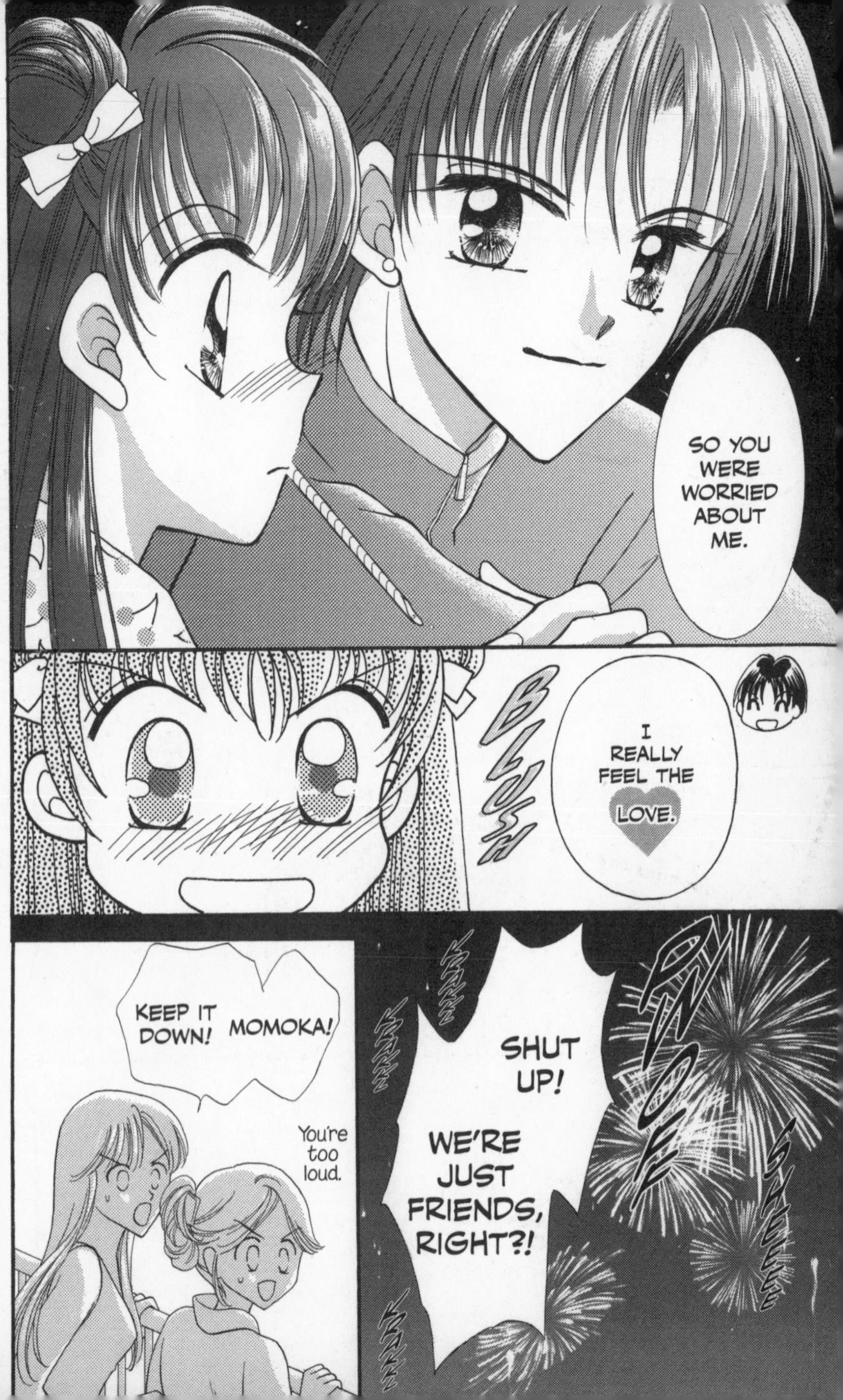
SO YOU WERE WORRIED ABOUT ME.
BLUSH
I REALLY FEEL THE LOVE.
SHUT UP!
WE'RE JUST FRIENDS, RIGHT?!
KEEP IT DOWN! MOMOKA!
You're too loud.

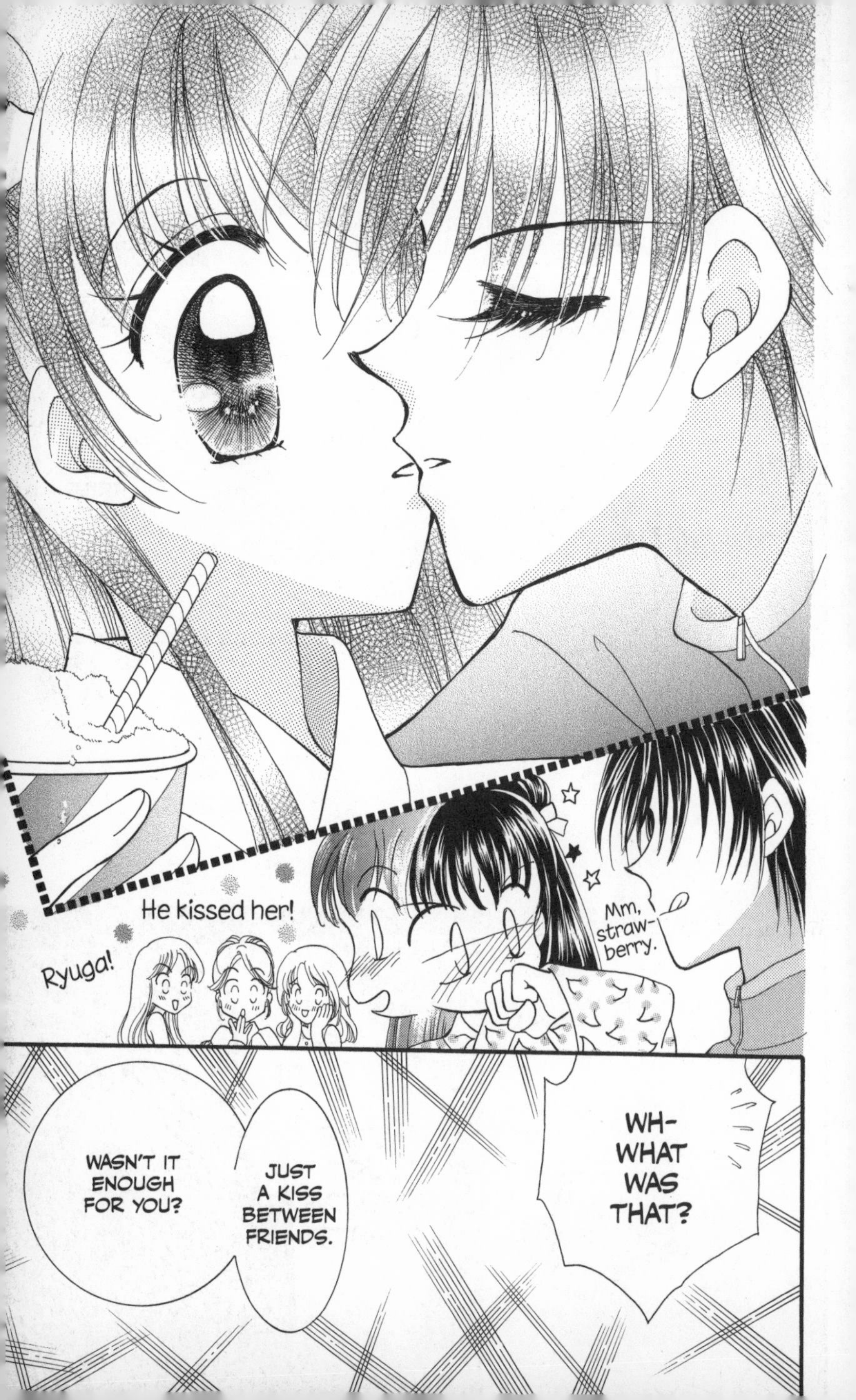
Mm, straw-berry.
He kissed her!
Ryuga!
WH-WHAT WAS THAT?
JUST A KISS BETWEEN FRIENDS.
WASN'T IT ENOUGH FOR YOU?

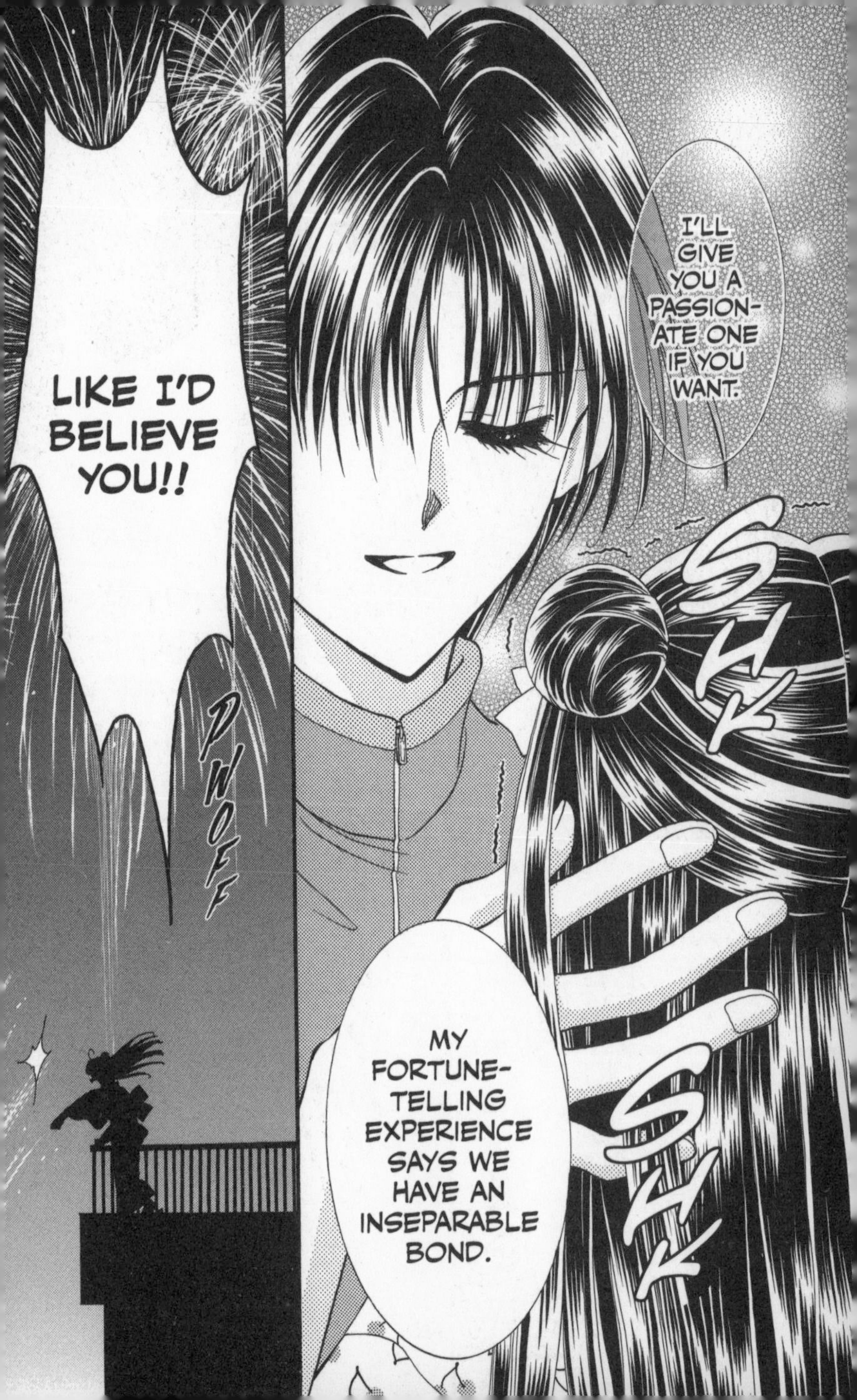
I'LL GIVE YOU A PASSION-ATE ONE IF YOU WANT.
SHK
MY FORTUNE-TELLING EXPERIENCE SAYS WE HAVE AN INSEPARABLE BOND.
SHK
LIKE I'D BELIEVE YOU!!
DWOFF

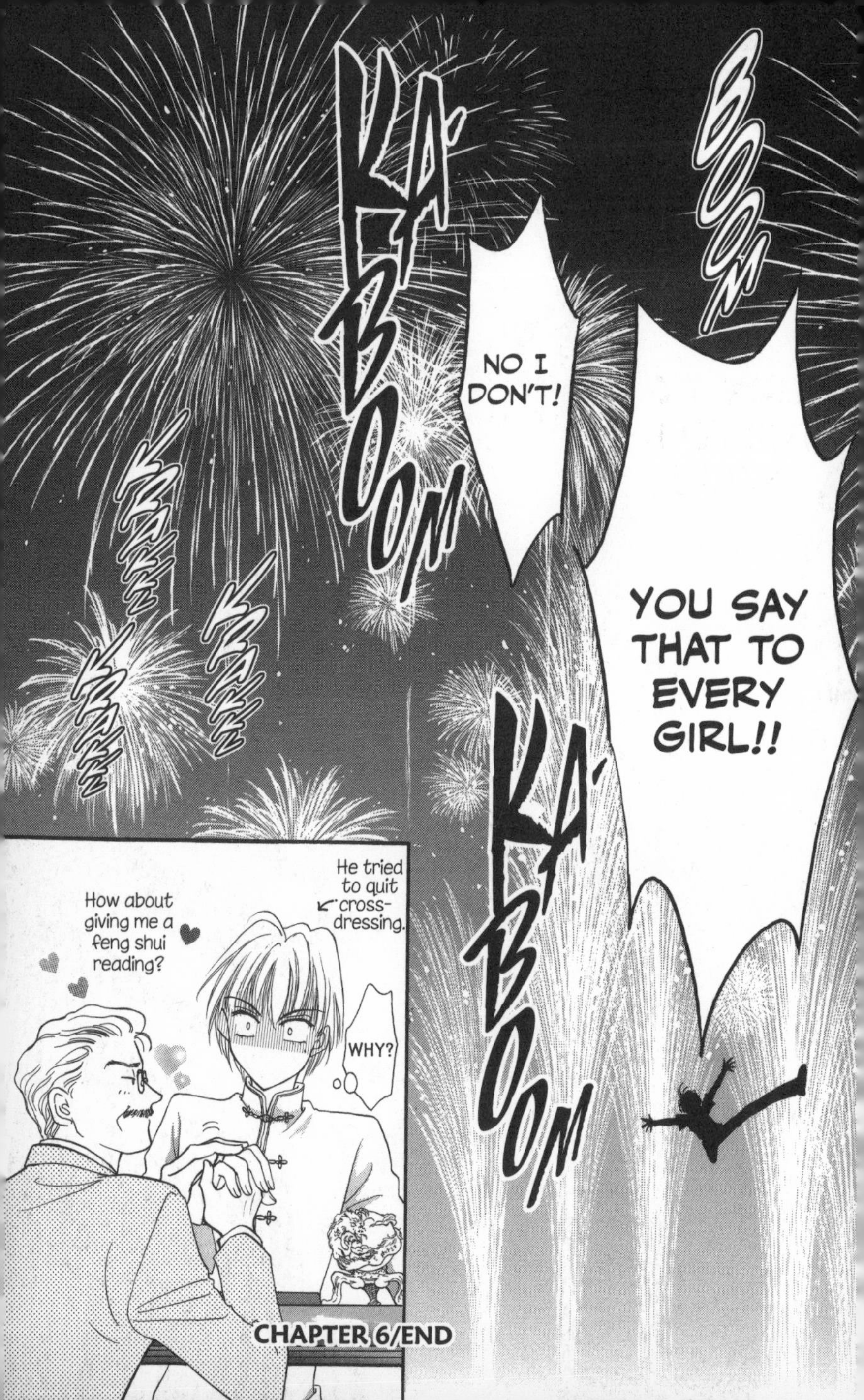
YOU SAY THAT TO EVERY GIRL!!
KA-BOOM
NO I DON'T!
KA-BOOM
He tried to quit cross-dressing.
How about giving me a feng shui reading?
WHY?

CHAPTER 6/END

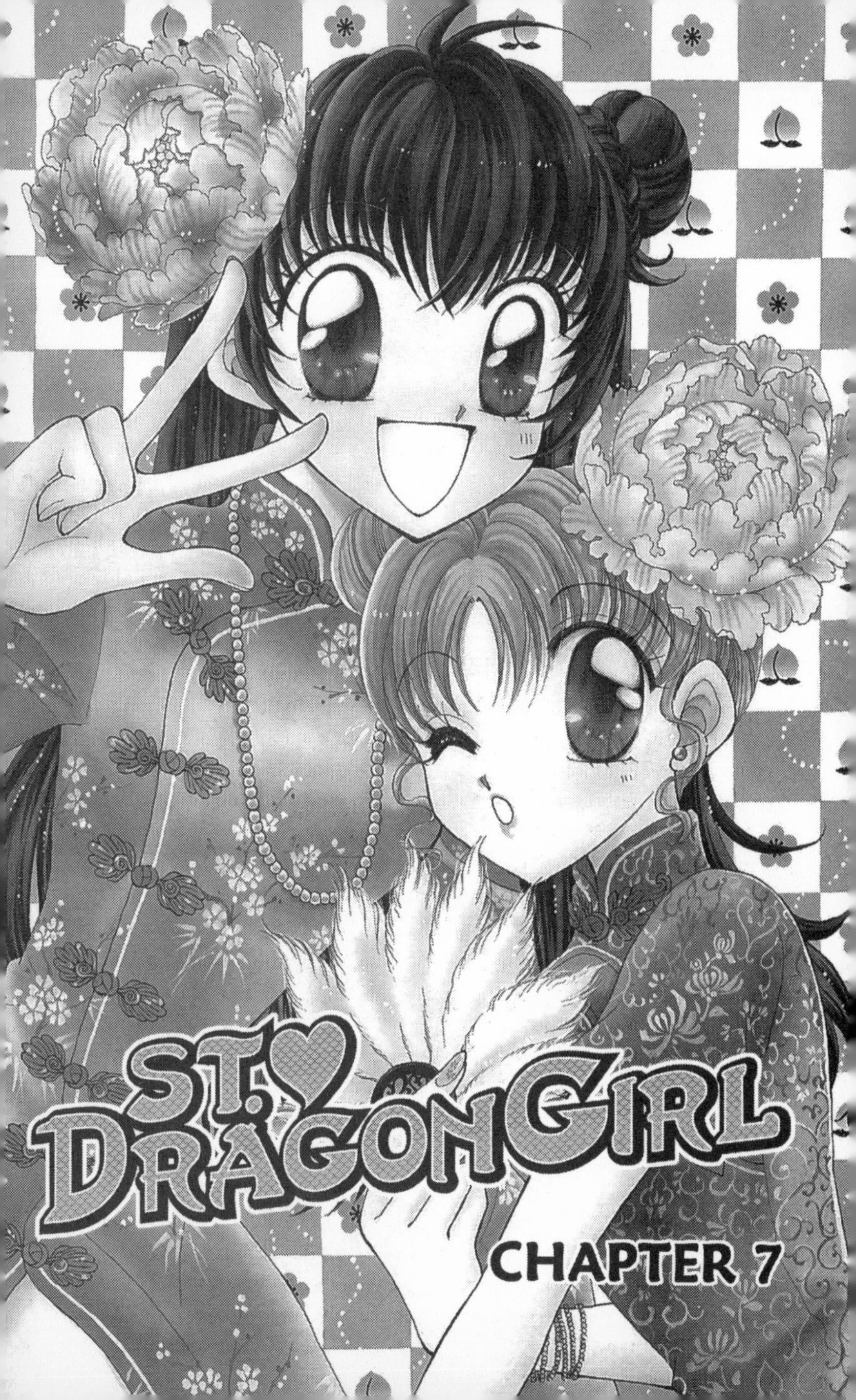
ST. DRAGON GIRL
CHAPTER 7

MWA HA HA! YOU'RE AT A DEAD END, DRAGON!
SUR-RENDER... ...AND HAND OVER THE PRINCESS AND THE TREASURED SWORD!
I REFUSE!
IT'S MY RESPONSIBILITY TO ESCORT HER SAFELY TO HER ROOM. I'VE GIVEN MY WORD!

Even though she is a girl, she uses the pronoun *boku*. She's not possessed by a dragon, but she can call forth the Thunder Dragon. However, there are concerns that she can't control the dragon. Her special skills include piano, kenpo, calligraphy, and making sushi—she's very versatile.

Raika Kou

Birthday: April 10.
Aries. Blood Type: AB.
Raised in Hong Kong.
When she gets too excited, she loses control of her power and emits electrical energy. Because of that, she has never gone to school. She is very intelligent, however.

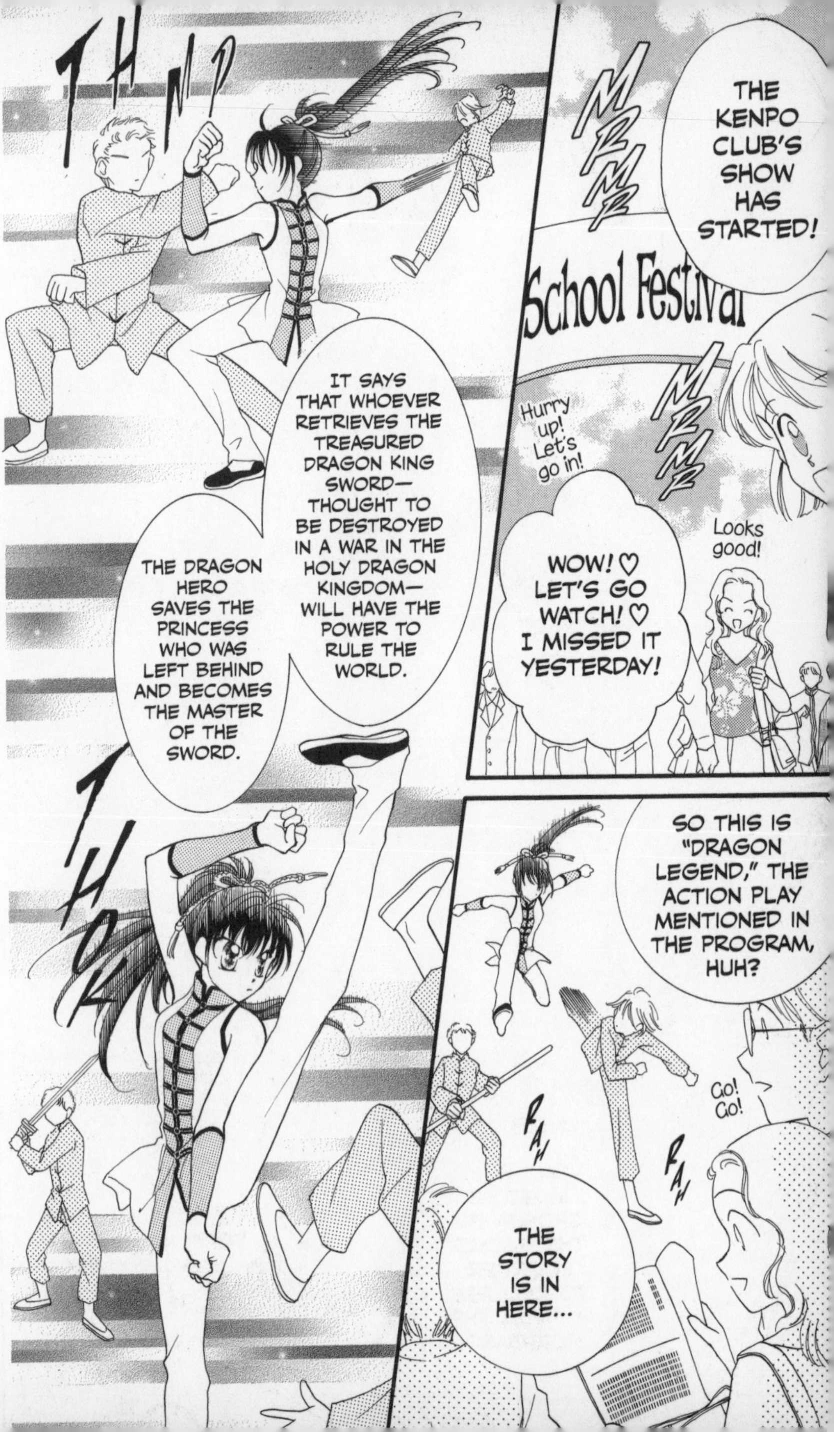
THE KENPO CLUB'S SHOW HAS STARTED!
MRMR
School Festival
MRMR
Hurry up! Let's go in!
Looks good!
WOW! ♡ LET'S GO WATCH! ♡ I MISSED IT YESTERDAY!
SO THIS IS "DRAGON LEGEND," THE ACTION PLAY MENTIONED IN THE PROGRAM, HUH?
Go! Go!
RAH
RAH
THE STORY IS IN HERE...
THMP
IT SAYS THAT WHOEVER RETRIEVES THE TREASURED DRAGON KING SWORD—THOUGHT TO BE DESTROYED IN A WAR IN THE HOLY DRAGON KINGDOM—WILL HAVE THE POWER TO RULE THE WORLD.
THE DRAGON HERO SAVES THE PRINCESS WHO WAS LEFT BEHIND AND BECOMES THE MASTER OF THE SWORD.
THOK

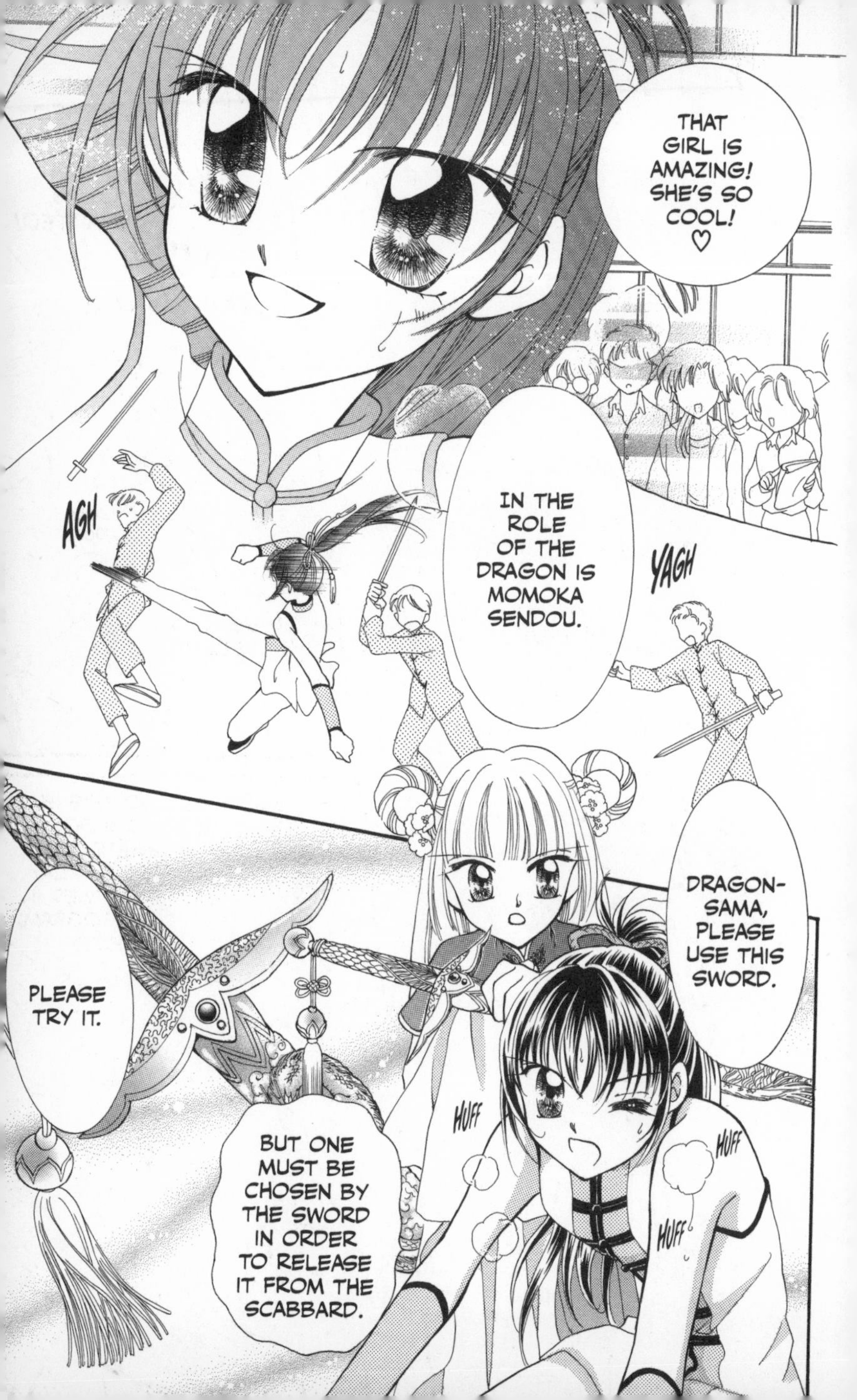
THAT GIRL IS AMAZING! SHE'S SO COOL! ♡
IN THE ROLE OF THE DRAGON IS MOMOKA SENDOU.
YAGH
AGH
DRAGON-SAMA, PLEASE USE THIS SWORD.
PLEASE TRY IT.
HUFF
HUFF
HUFF
BUT ONE MUST BE CHOSEN BY THE SWORD IN ORDER TO RELEASE IT FROM THE SCABBARD.

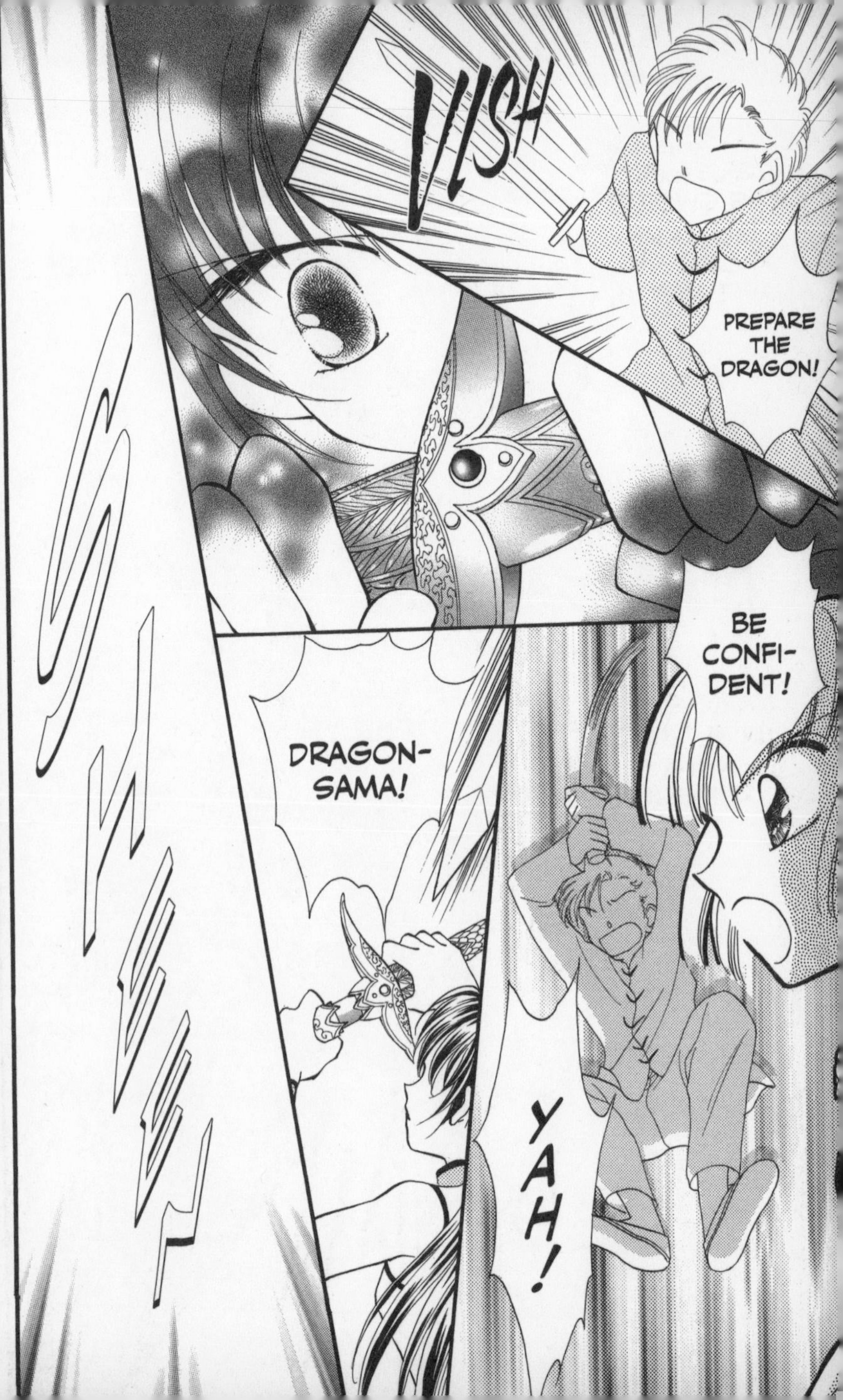
VISH
PREPARE THE DRAGON!
BE CONFI-DENT!
YAH!
DRAGON-SAMA!

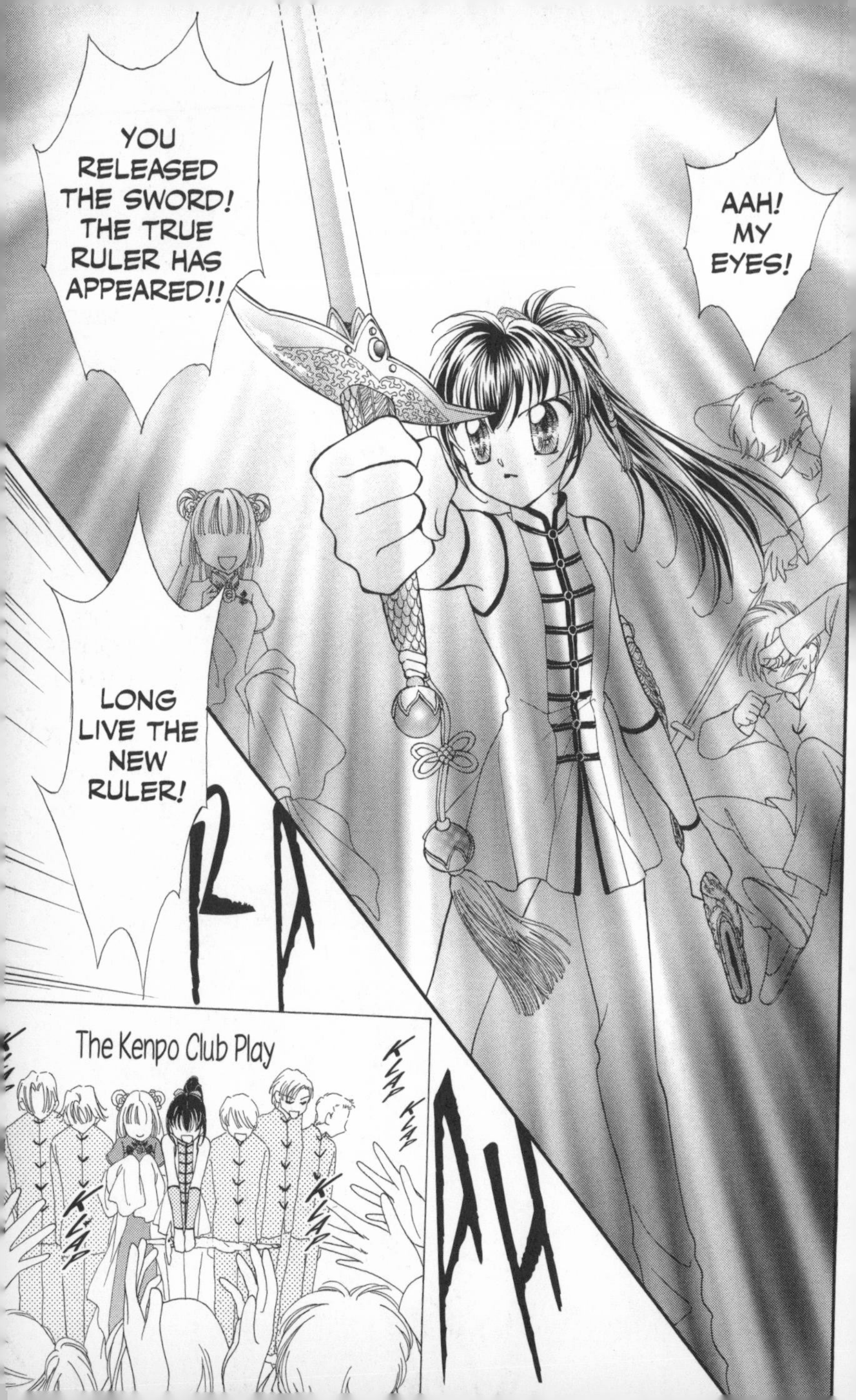
AAH! MY EYES!
YOU RELEASED THE SWORD! THE TRUE RULER HAS APPEARED!!
LONG LIVE THE NEW RULER!
The Kenpo Club Play

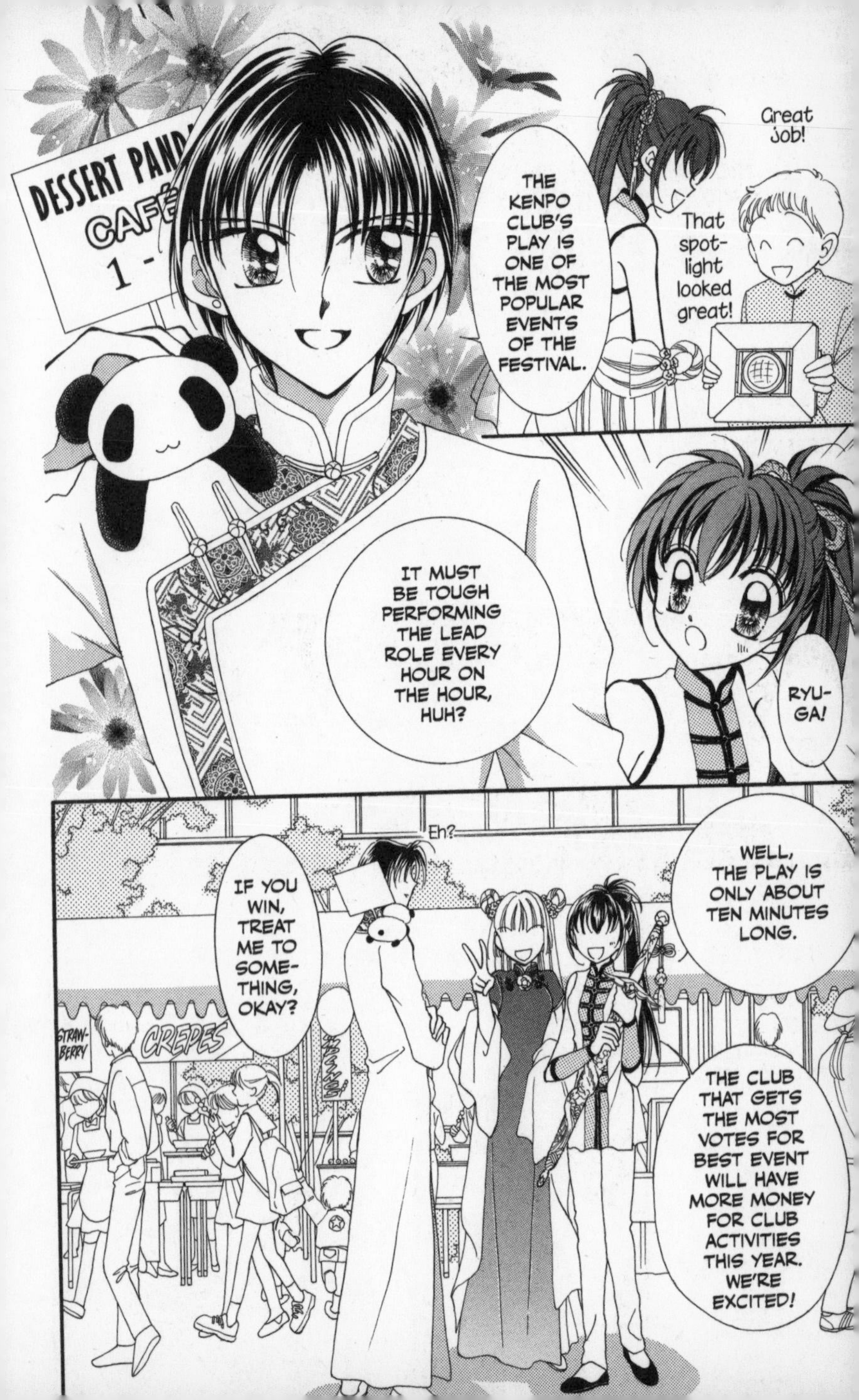
Great job!
That spot-light looked great!
THE KENPO CLUB'S PLAY IS ONE OF THE MOST POPULAR EVENTS OF THE FESTIVAL.
RYU-GA!
DESSERT PAND
CAFÉ
1 -
IT MUST BE TOUGH PERFORMING THE LEAD ROLE EVERY HOUR ON THE HOUR, HUH?
WELL, THE PLAY IS ONLY ABOUT TEN MINUTES LONG.
THE CLUB THAT GETS THE MOST VOTES FOR BEST EVENT WILL HAVE MORE MONEY FOR CLUB ACTIVITIES THIS YEAR. WE'RE EXCITED!
Eh?
IF YOU WIN, TREAT ME TO SOME-THING, OKAY?
STRAW-BERRY
CREPES

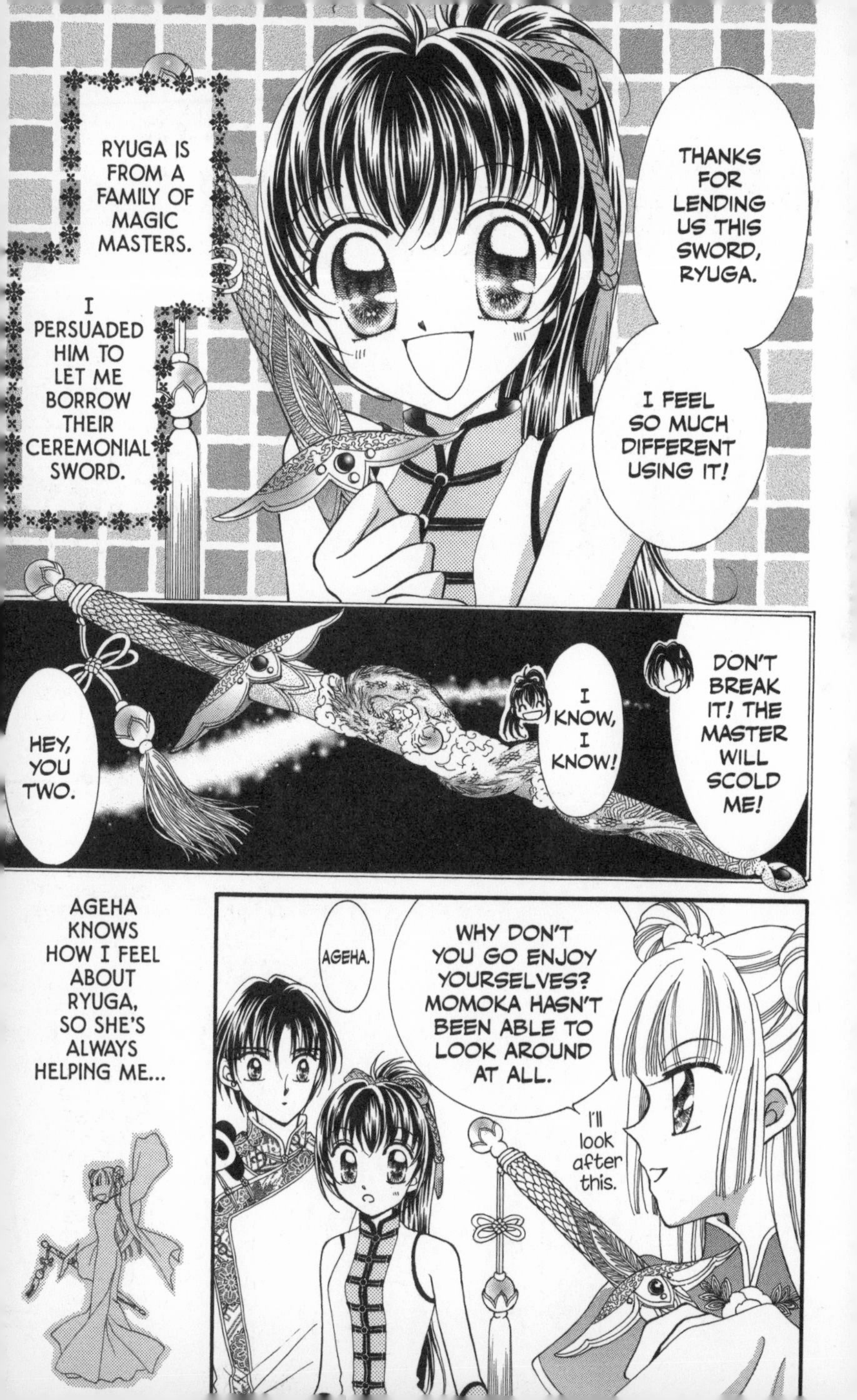

THANKS FOR LENDING US THIS SWORD, RYUGA.
I FEEL SO MUCH DIFFERENT USING IT!
RYUGA IS FROM A FAMILY OF MAGIC MASTERS.
I PERSUADED HIM TO LET ME BORROW THEIR CEREMONIAL SWORD.
DON'T BREAK IT! THE MASTER WILL SCOLD ME!
I KNOW, I KNOW!
HEY, YOU TWO.
WHY DON'T YOU GO ENJOY YOURSELVES? MOMOKA HASN'T BEEN ABLE TO LOOK AROUND AT ALL.
AGEHA.
I'll look after this.
AGEHA KNOWS HOW I FEEL ABOUT RYUGA, SO SHE'S ALWAYS HELPING ME...

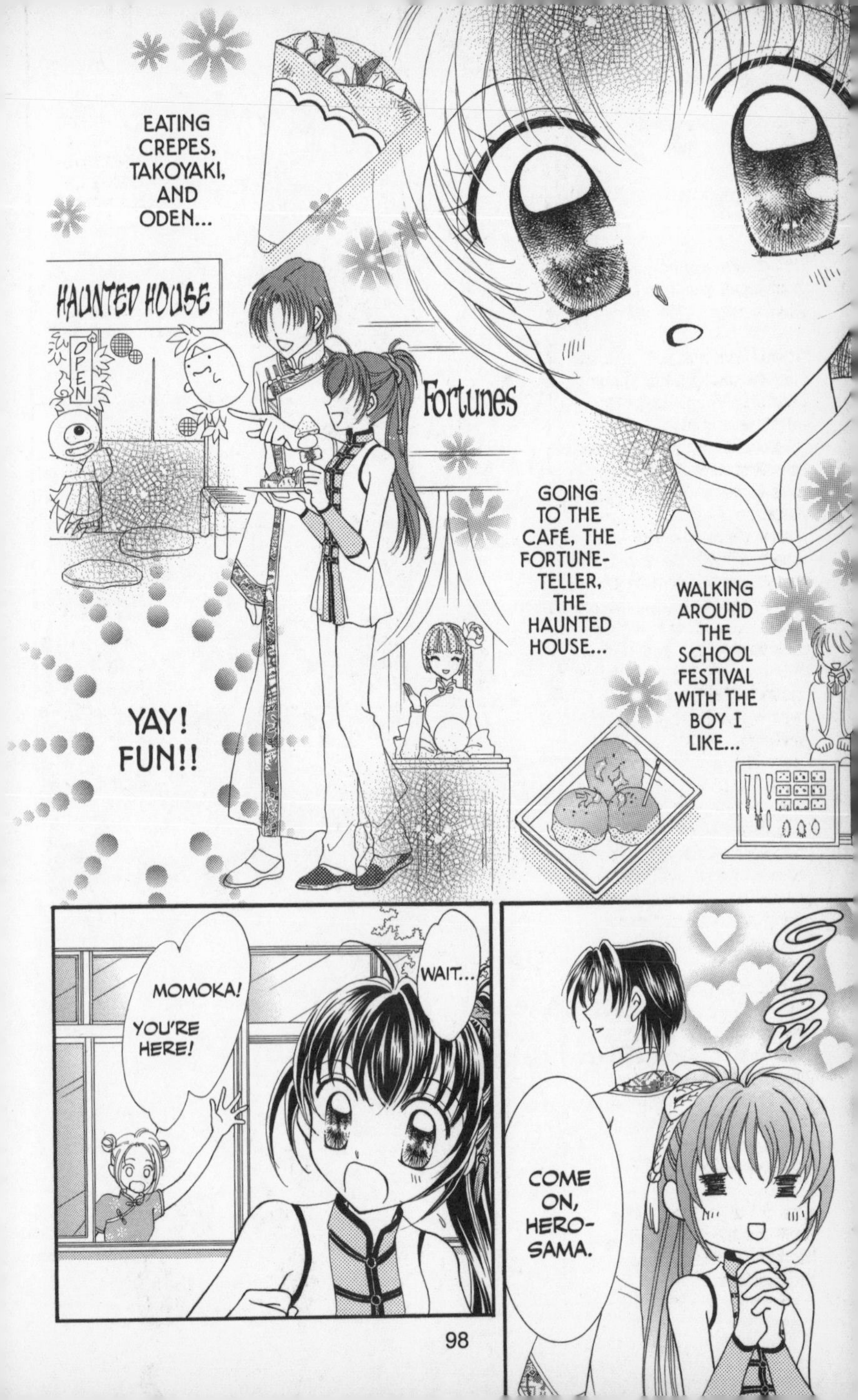
WALKING AROUND THE SCHOOL FESTIVAL WITH THE BOY I LIKE...
GOING TO THE CAFÉ, THE FORTUNE-TELLER, THE HAUNTED HOUSE...
Fortunes
EATING CREPES, TAKOYAKI, AND ODEN...
HAUNTED HOUSE
OPEN
YAY! FUN!!
GLOW
COME ON, HERO-SAMA.
WAIT...
MOMOKA!
YOU'RE HERE!

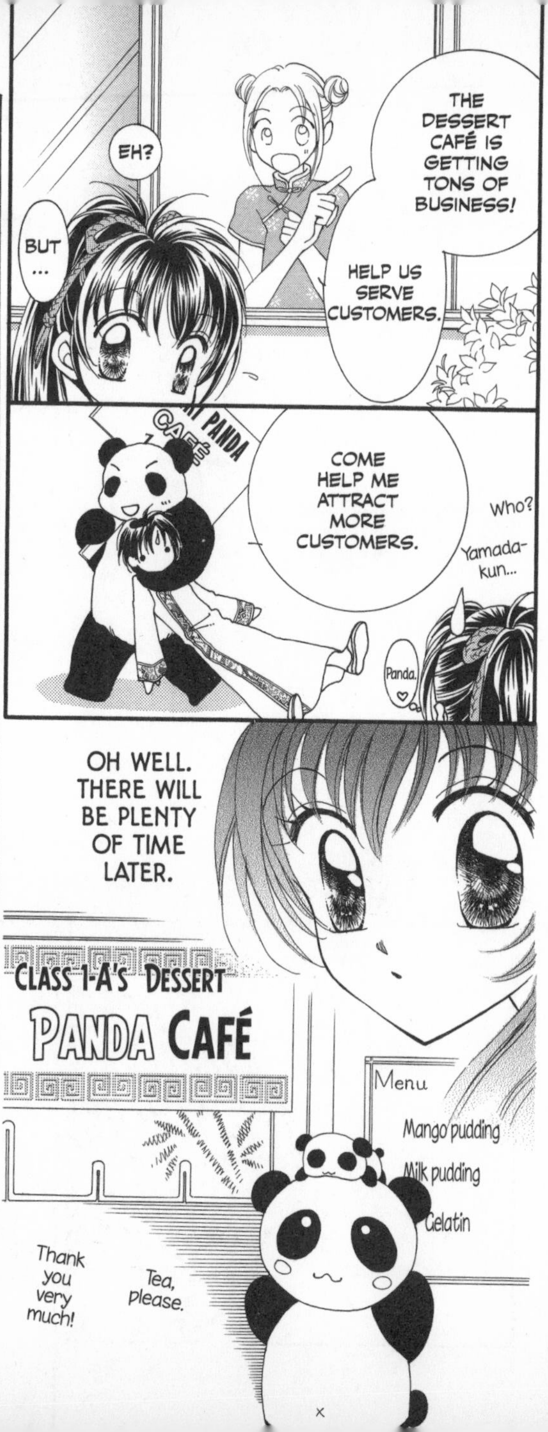
THE DESSERT CAFÉ IS GETTING TONS OF BUSINESS!
EH?
HELP US SERVE CUSTOMERS.
BUT ...
COME HELP ME ATTRACT MORE CUSTOMERS.
Who?
Yamada-kun...
Panda. ♡
OH WELL. THERE WILL BE PLENTY OF TIME LATER.
Menu
Mango pudding
Milk pudding
Gelatin
CLASS 1-A'S DESSERT
PANDA CAFÉ
Tea, please.
Thank you very much!

3

It's a little late now, but I'll talk about the "Beautiful Feng Shui Master Shion" story.

It was featured in the *Ribon* August special issue, "Super Fortune-Telling Manga 2000," which featured manga involving fortune-telling. It was the first time *St.♥Dragon Girl* was featured in a special issue, so I was really happy. I think the people who read the issue will understand, but it was the first time that *St.♥Dragon Girl* had numerous pages done in two colors. The cover page featured Momoka wearing red Chinese clothes, and Ryuga was wearing blue. The school uniforms, ribbons, and skirts were blue, and they had a really fun look to them. It wasn't my idea; my editor suggested we upgrade to two-color printing. So when I opened the special issue, I was so excited! The most popular thing at work was the red rose on Ryuga's back. (laugh)

In that story, Kouta-kun was really popular for some reason! I wonder why... He was such a pervert! (laugh) Actually, he was the most fun to draw for me. Another popular character was the old guy at the end. Another pervert!

I really like fortune-telling, so if another similar project comes up, I'd love to work on it, editor!

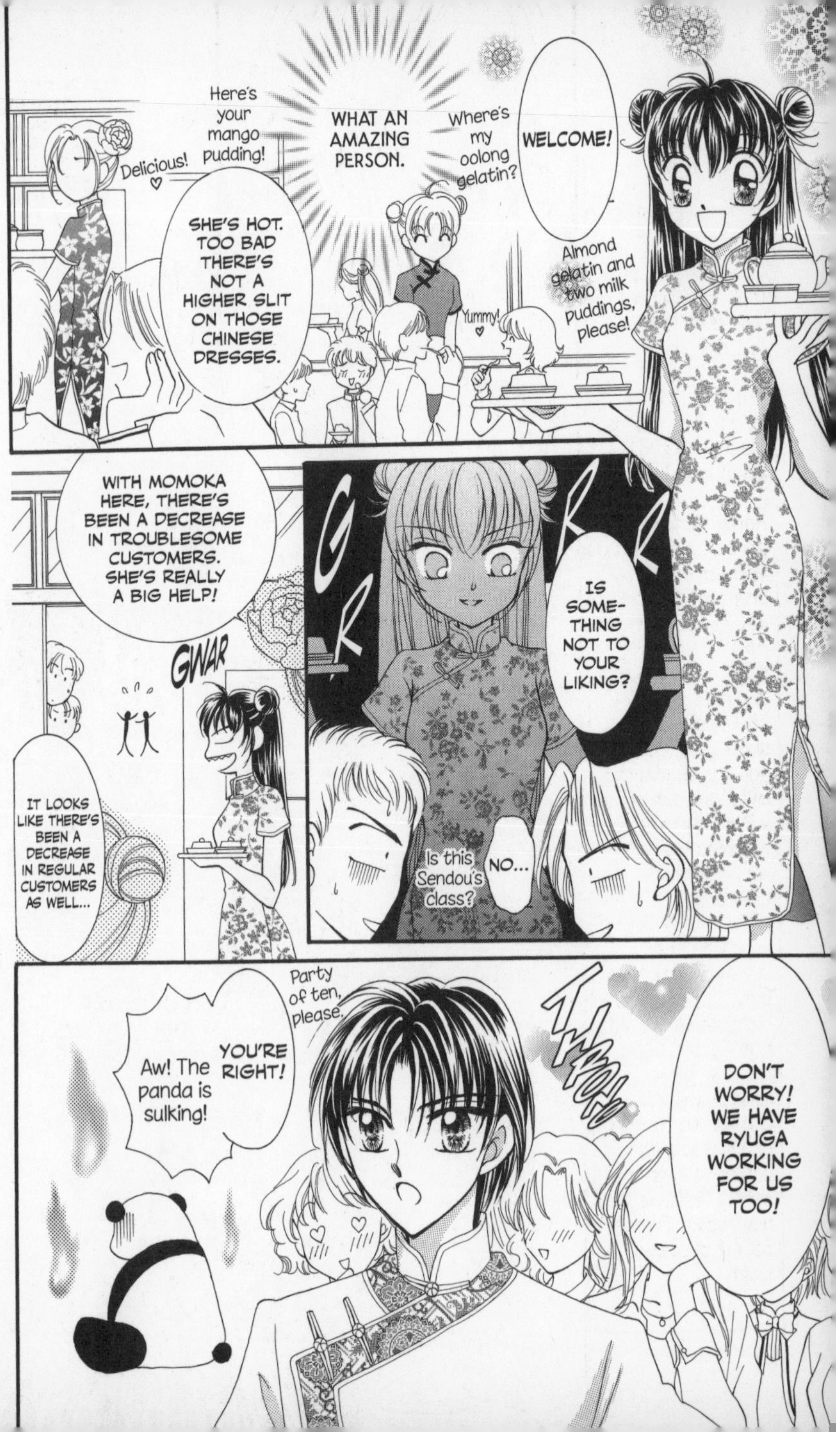
WELCOME!
Almond gelatin and two milk puddings, please!
Where's my oolong gelatin?
Yummy!
WHAT AN AMAZING PERSON.
Here's your mango pudding!
Delicious!
SHE'S HOT. TOO BAD THERE'S NOT A HIGHER SLIT ON THOSE CHINESE DRESSES.
IS SOMETHING NOT TO YOUR LIKING?
NO...
Is this Sendou's class?
WITH MOMOKA HERE, THERE'S BEEN A DECREASE IN TROUBLESOME CUSTOMERS. SHE'S REALLY A BIG HELP!
GWAR
IT LOOKS LIKE THERE'S BEEN A DECREASE IN REGULAR CUSTOMERS AS WELL...
DON'T WORRY! WE HAVE RYUGA WORKING FOR US TOO!
Party of ten, please.
YOU'RE RIGHT!
Aw! The panda is sulking!

4

I worked hard to make the school festival seem fun and lively.

The kenpo club's action play seems like it would be a lot of work!

However, the best part of a school festival is the preparation. You get to stay late at school making signs and billboards and preparing the stuff your club will show. Also, because you end up staying after sunset, a boy will usually walk you home! Being young was so great! (nostalgic)

In college, our class had an onigiri booth. In one girl's dorm room, we did nothing but cook rice! For some reason, we put curry in the onigiri, and it was quite popular. What are school festivals like nowadays? Please tell me all about them.

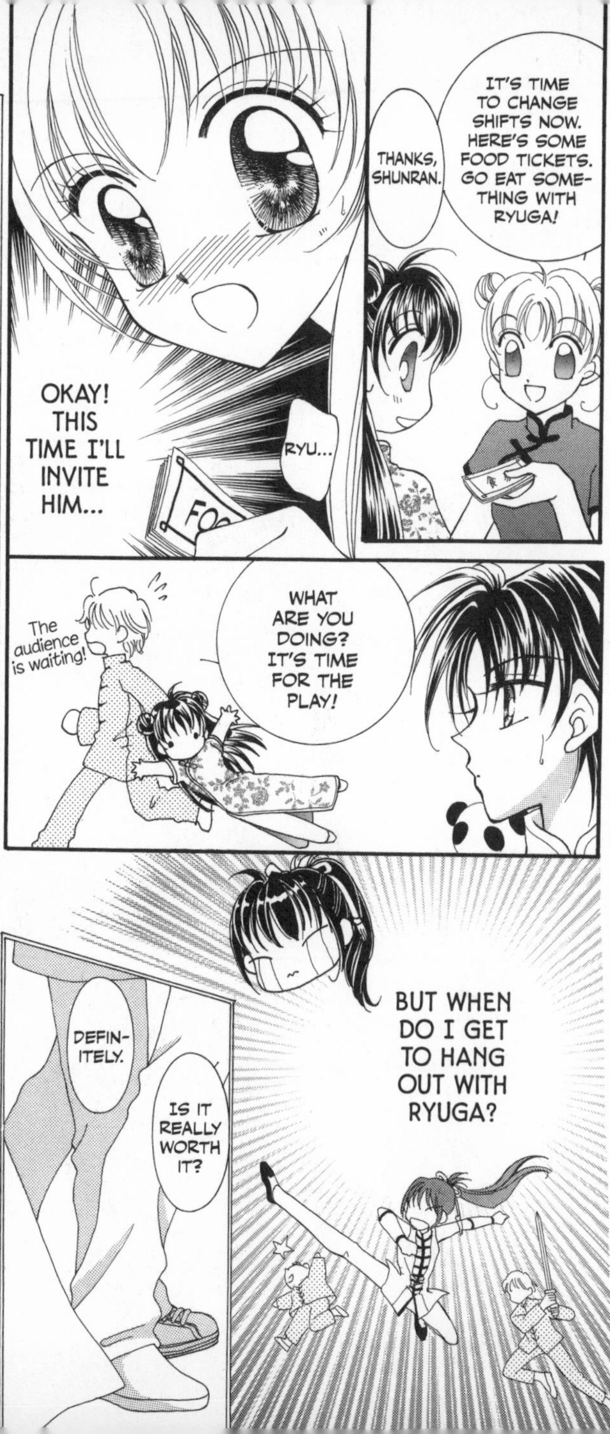

IT'S TIME TO CHANGE SHIFTS NOW. HERE'S SOME FOOD TICKETS. GO EAT SOME-THING WITH RYUGA!
THANKS, SHUNRAN.
RYU...
OKAY! THIS TIME I'LL INVITE HIM...
WHAT ARE YOU DOING? IT'S TIME FOR THE PLAY!
The audience is waiting!
BUT WHEN DO I GET TO HANG OUT WITH RYUGA?
IS IT REALLY WORTH IT?
DEFIN-ITELY.

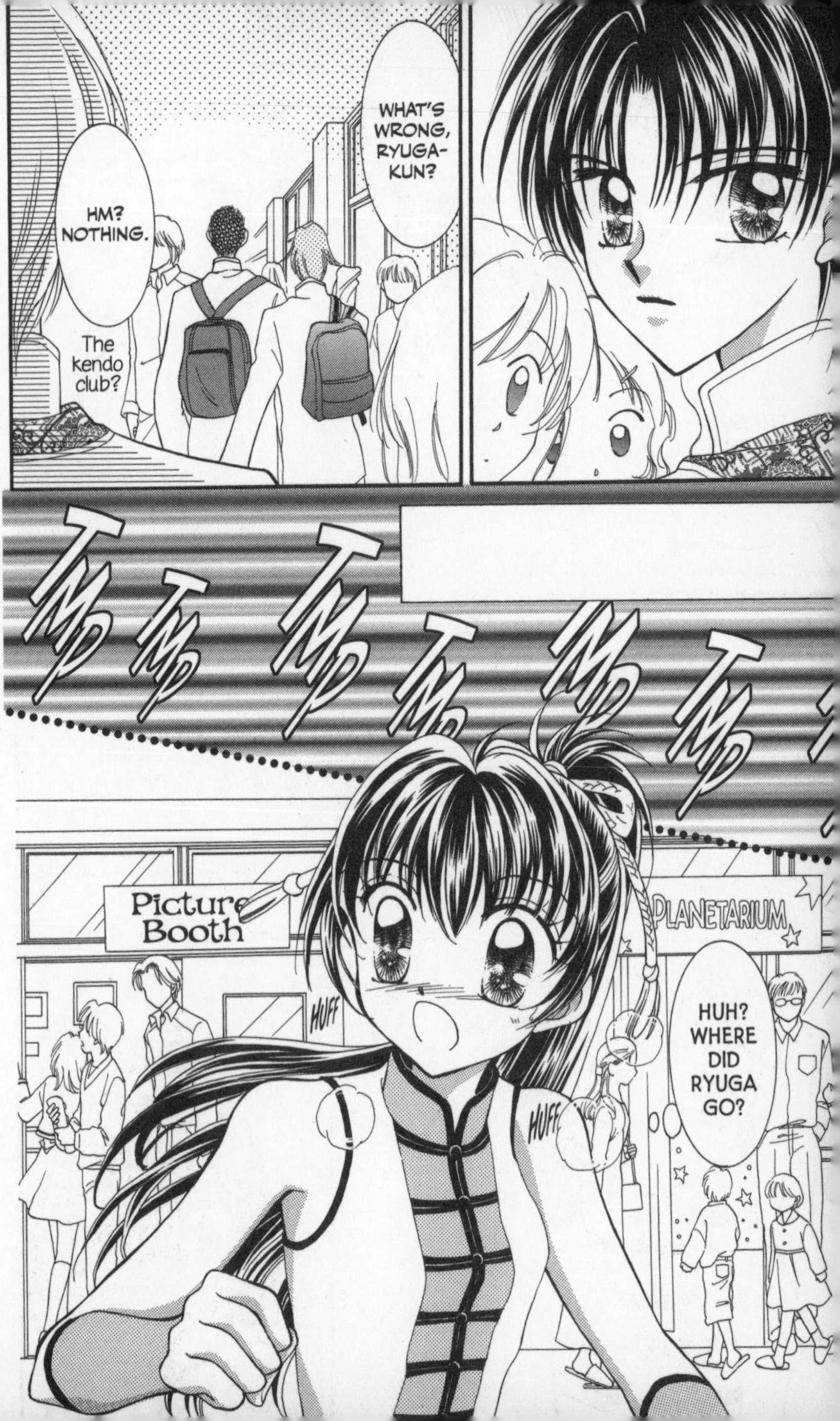
WHAT'S WRONG, RYUGA-KUN?
HM? NOTHING.
The kendo club?
TMP
TMP
TMP
TMP
TMP
TMP
TMP
PLANETARIUM
Picture Booth
HUFF
HUFF
HUH? WHERE DID RYUGA GO?

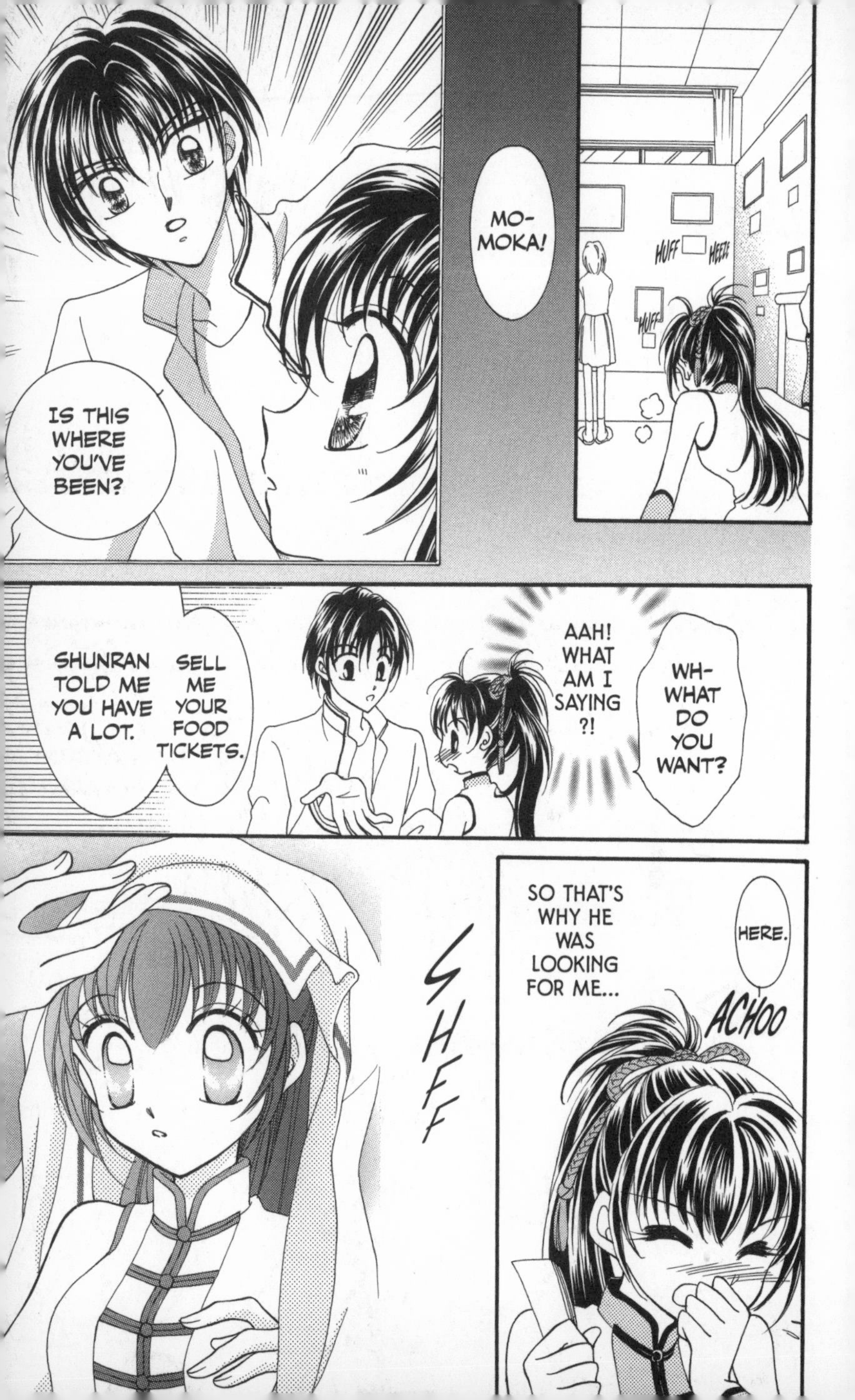
MO-MOKA!
HEEZE
HUFF
HUFF
IS THIS WHERE YOU'VE BEEN?
WH-WHAT DO YOU WANT?
AAH! WHAT AM I SAYING?!
SELL ME YOUR FOOD TICKETS.
SHUNRAN TOLD ME YOU HAVE A LOT.
HERE.
SO THAT'S WHY HE WAS LOOKING FOR ME...
ACHOO
SHFF

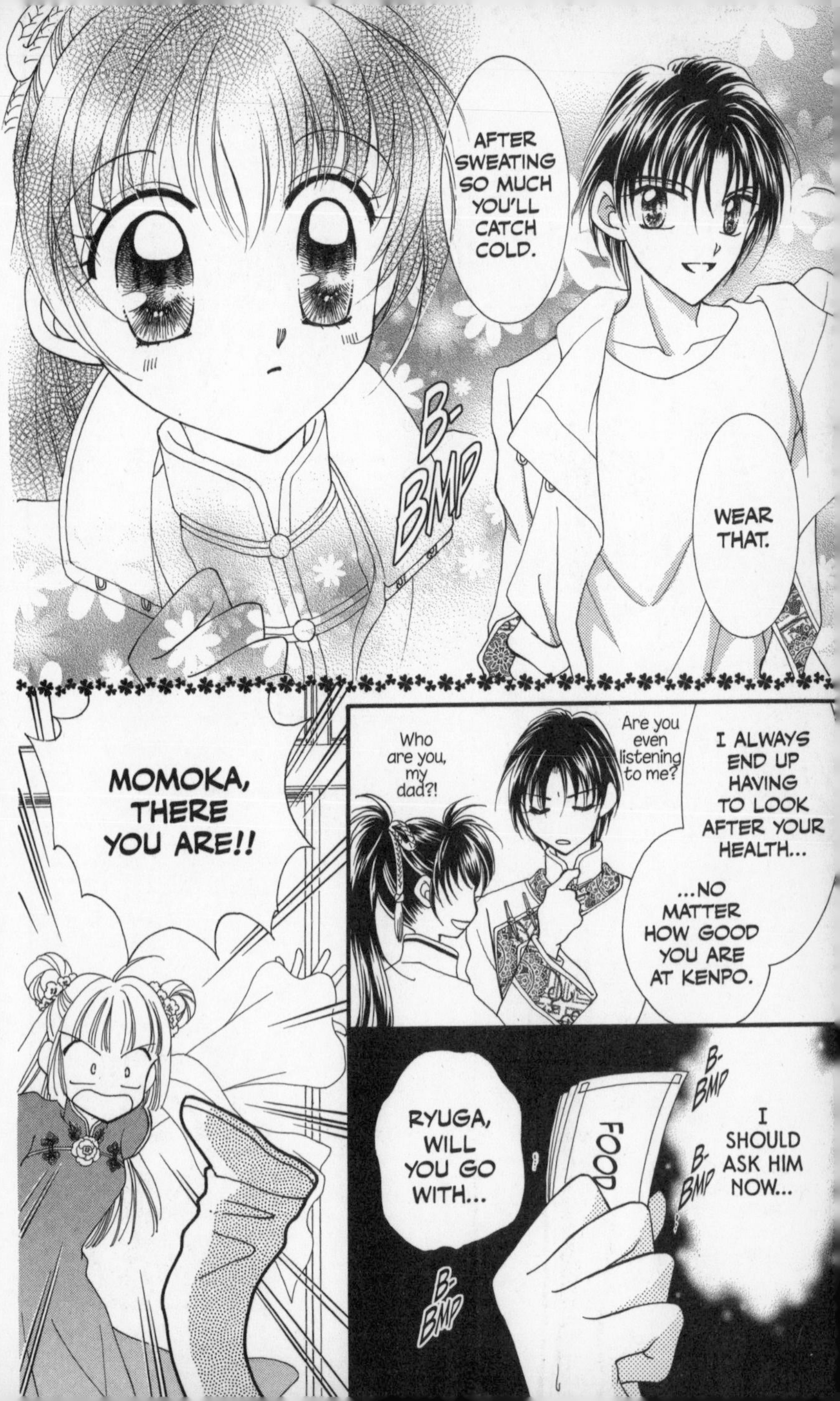
AFTER SWEATING SO MUCH YOU'LL CATCH COLD.
WEAR THAT.
B-BMP
I ALWAYS END UP HAVING TO LOOK AFTER YOUR HEALTH...
...NO MATTER HOW GOOD YOU ARE AT KENPO.
Are you even listening to me?
Who are you, my dad?!
B-BMP
I SHOULD ASK HIM NOW...
B-BMP
RYUGA, WILL YOU GO WITH...
FOOD
B-BMP
MOMOKA, THERE YOU ARE!!

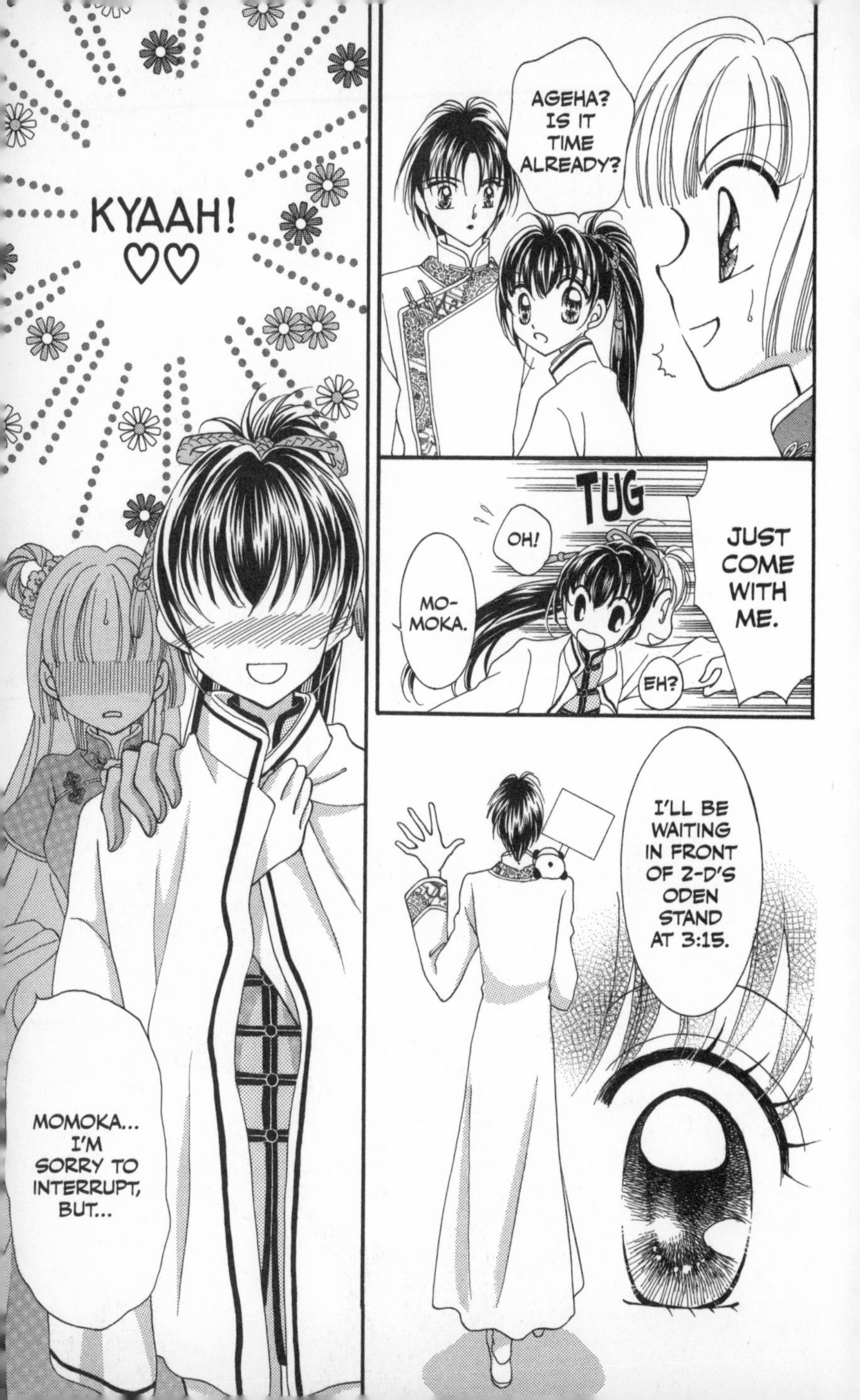
AGEHA? IS IT TIME ALREADY?
JUST COME WITH ME.
TUG
OH!
MO-MOKA.
EH?
I'LL BE WAITING IN FRONT OF 2-D'S ODEN STAND AT 3:15.
KYAAH! ♡♡
MOMOKA... I'M SORRY TO INTERRUPT, BUT...

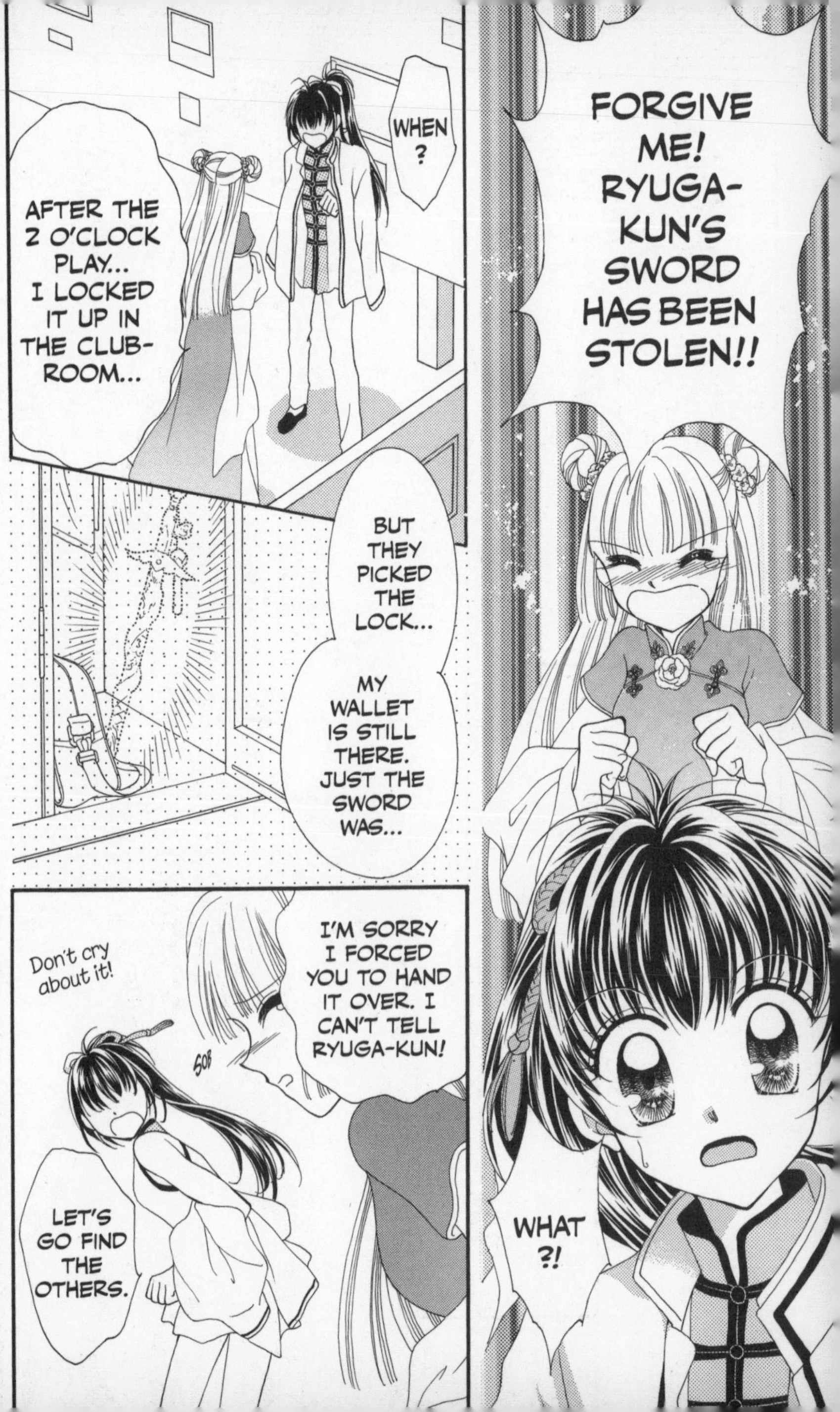
FORGIVE ME! RYUGA-KUN'S SWORD HAS BEEN STOLEN!!
WHAT?!
WHEN?
AFTER THE 2 O'CLOCK PLAY... I LOCKED IT UP IN THE CLUB-ROOM...
BUT THEY PICKED THE LOCK...
MY WALLET IS STILL THERE. JUST THE SWORD WAS...
I'M SORRY I FORCED YOU TO HAND IT OVER. I CAN'T TELL RYUGA-KUN!
SOB
Don't cry about it!
LET'S GO FIND THE OTHERS.

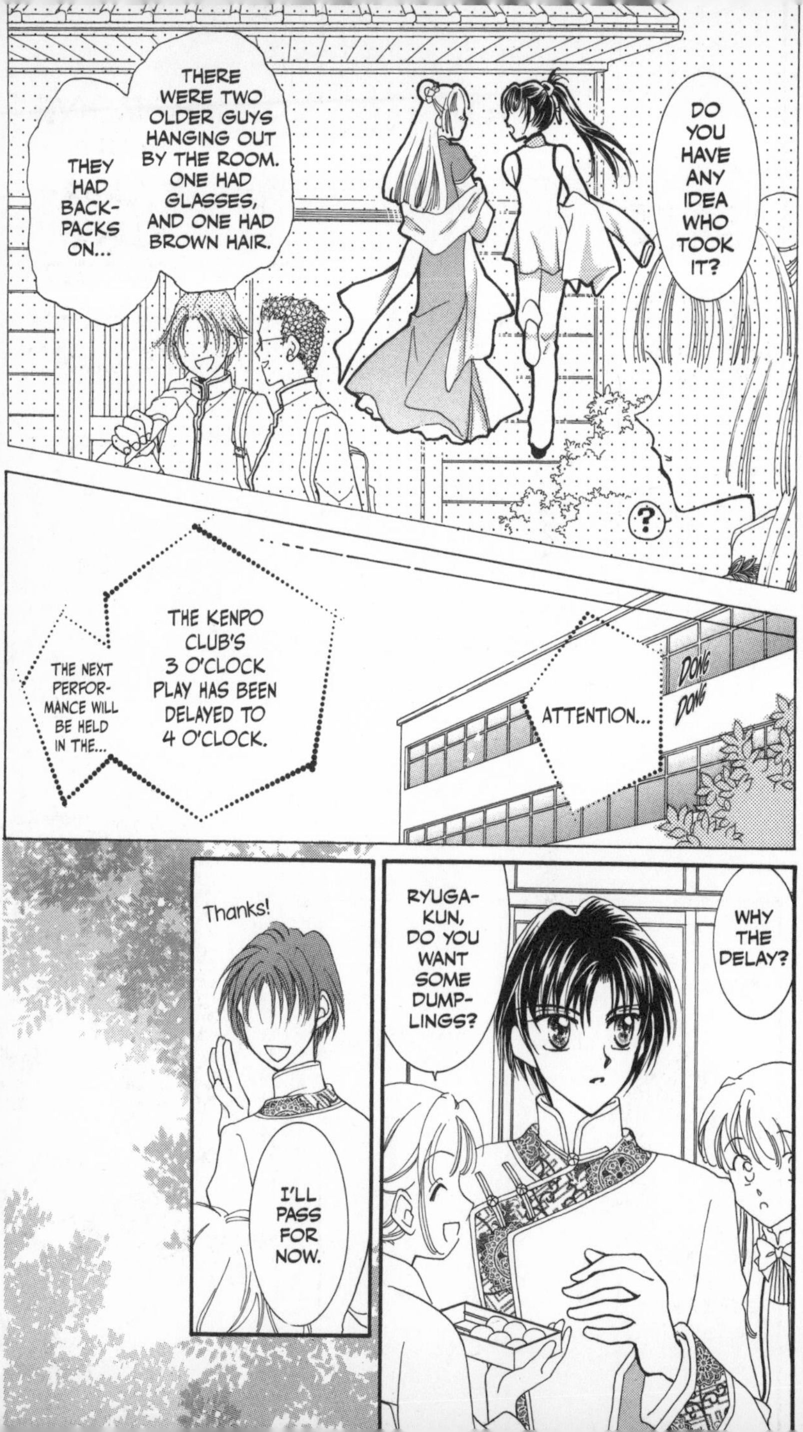
DO YOU HAVE ANY IDEA WHO TOOK IT?
THERE WERE TWO OLDER GUYS HANGING OUT BY THE ROOM. ONE HAD GLASSES, AND ONE HAD BROWN HAIR.
THEY HAD BACK-PACKS ON...
?
DONG DONG
ATTENTION...
THE KENPO CLUB'S 3 O'CLOCK PLAY HAS BEEN DELAYED TO 4 O'CLOCK.
THE NEXT PERFOR-MANCE WILL BE HELD IN THE...
WHY THE DELAY?
RYUGA-KUN, DO YOU WANT SOME DUMP-LINGS?
Thanks!
I'LL PASS FOR NOW.

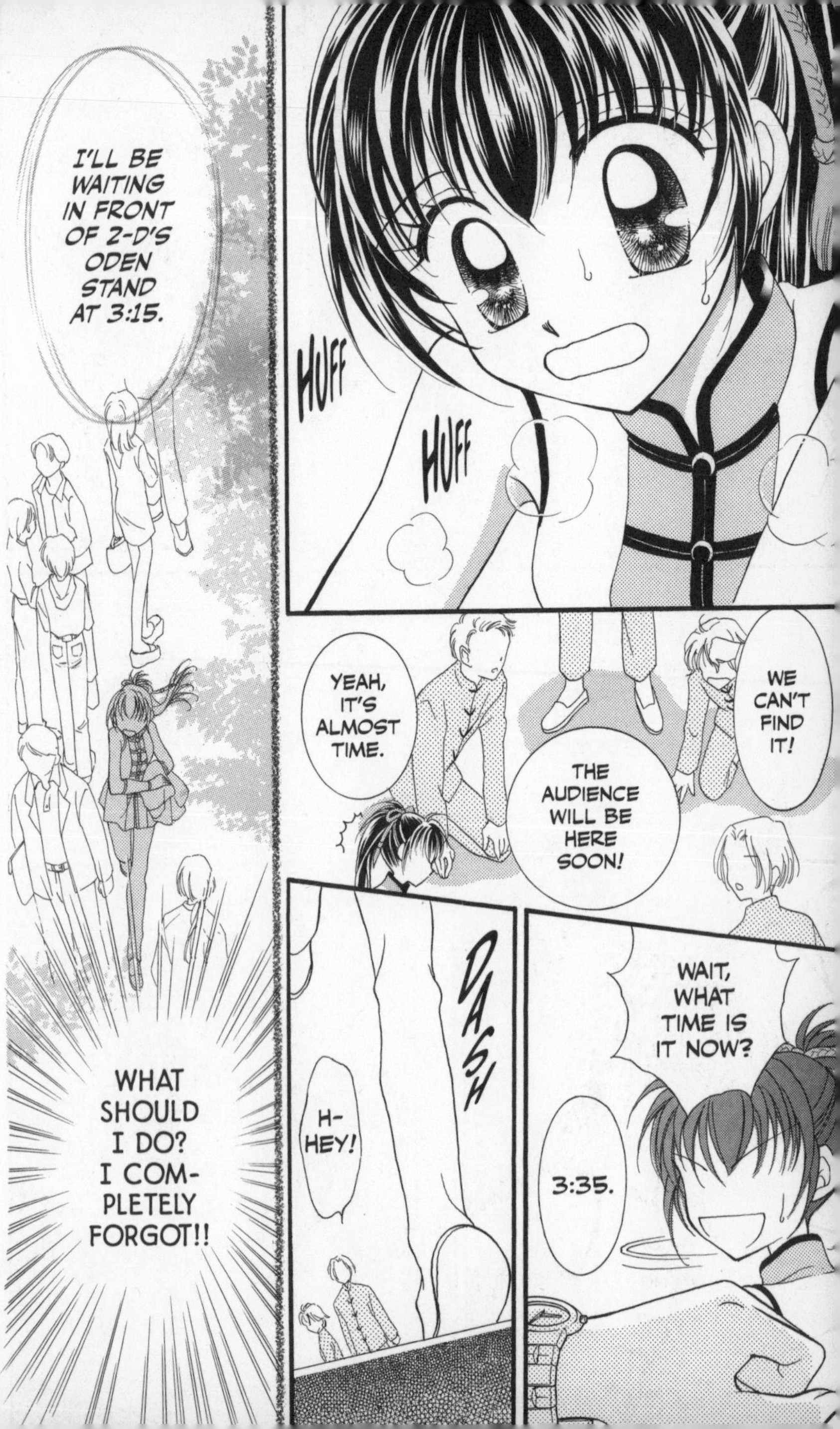
HUFF
HUFF
WE CAN'T FIND IT!
THE AUDIENCE WILL BE HERE SOON!
YEAH, IT'S ALMOST TIME.
WAIT, WHAT TIME IS IT NOW?
3:35.
DASH
H-HEY!
I'LL BE WAITING IN FRONT OF 2-D'S ODEN STAND AT 3:15.
WHAT SHOULD I DO? I COM-PLETELY FORGOT!!

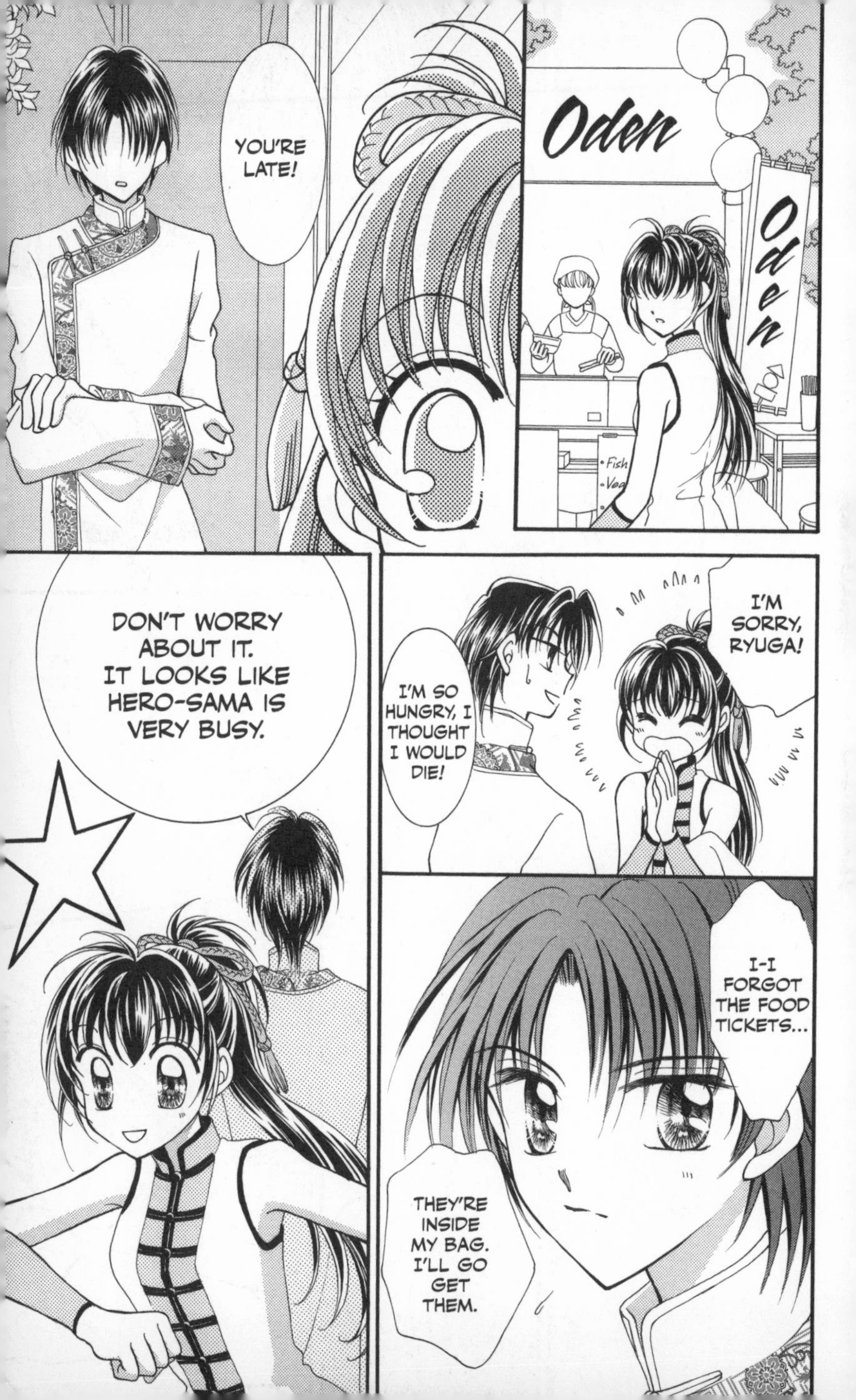
Oden
Oden
Fish
YOU'RE LATE!
I'M SORRY, RYUGA!
I'M SO HUNGRY, I THOUGHT I WOULD DIE!
I-I FORGOT THE FOOD TICKETS...
THEY'RE INSIDE MY BAG. I'LL GO GET THEM.
DON'T WORRY ABOUT IT. IT LOOKS LIKE HERO-SAMA IS VERY BUSY.

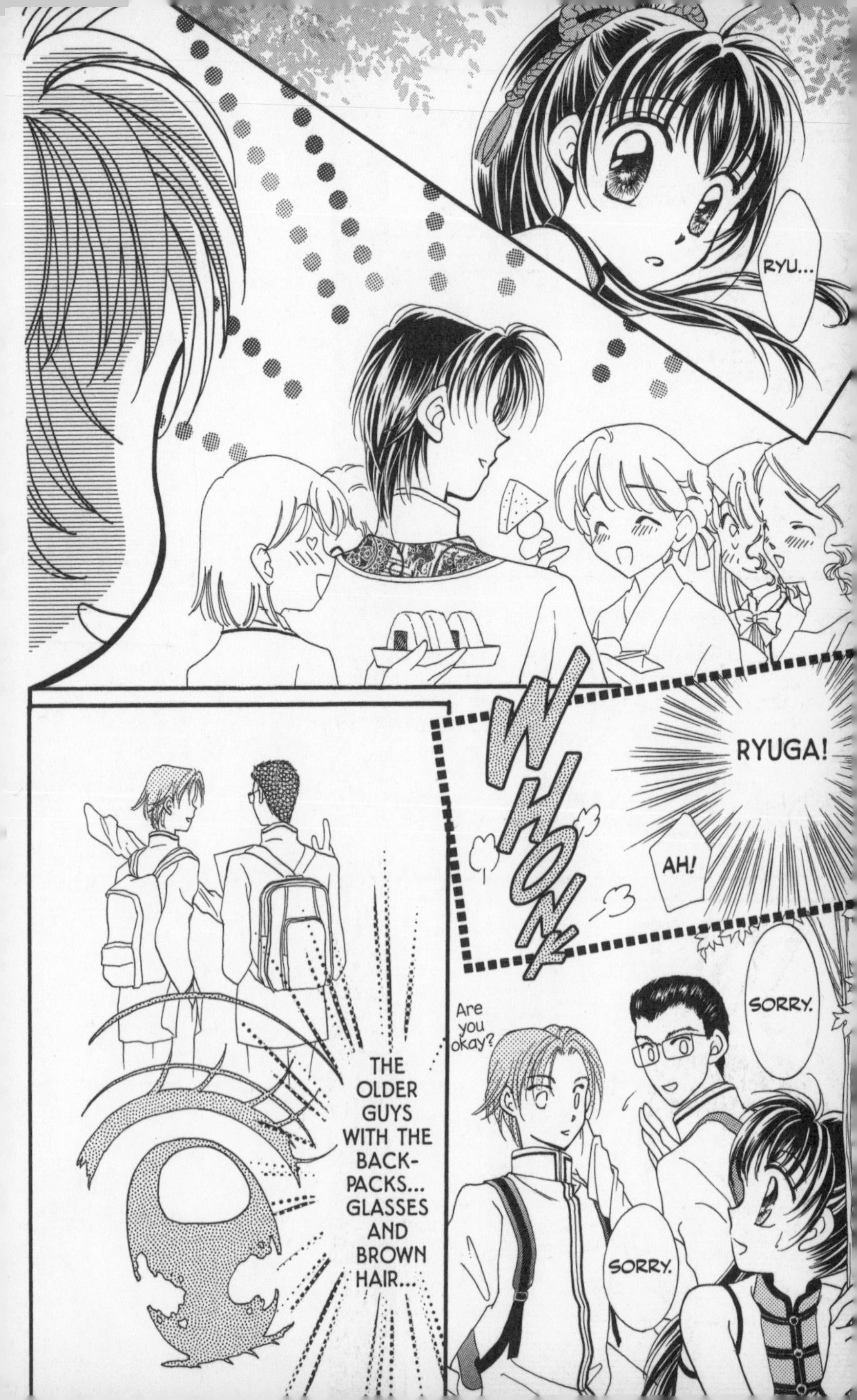
RYU...
RYUGA!
AH!
WHOMP
SORRY.
SORRY.
Are you okay?
THE OLDER GUYS WITH THE BACK-PACKS... GLASSES AND BROWN HAIR...

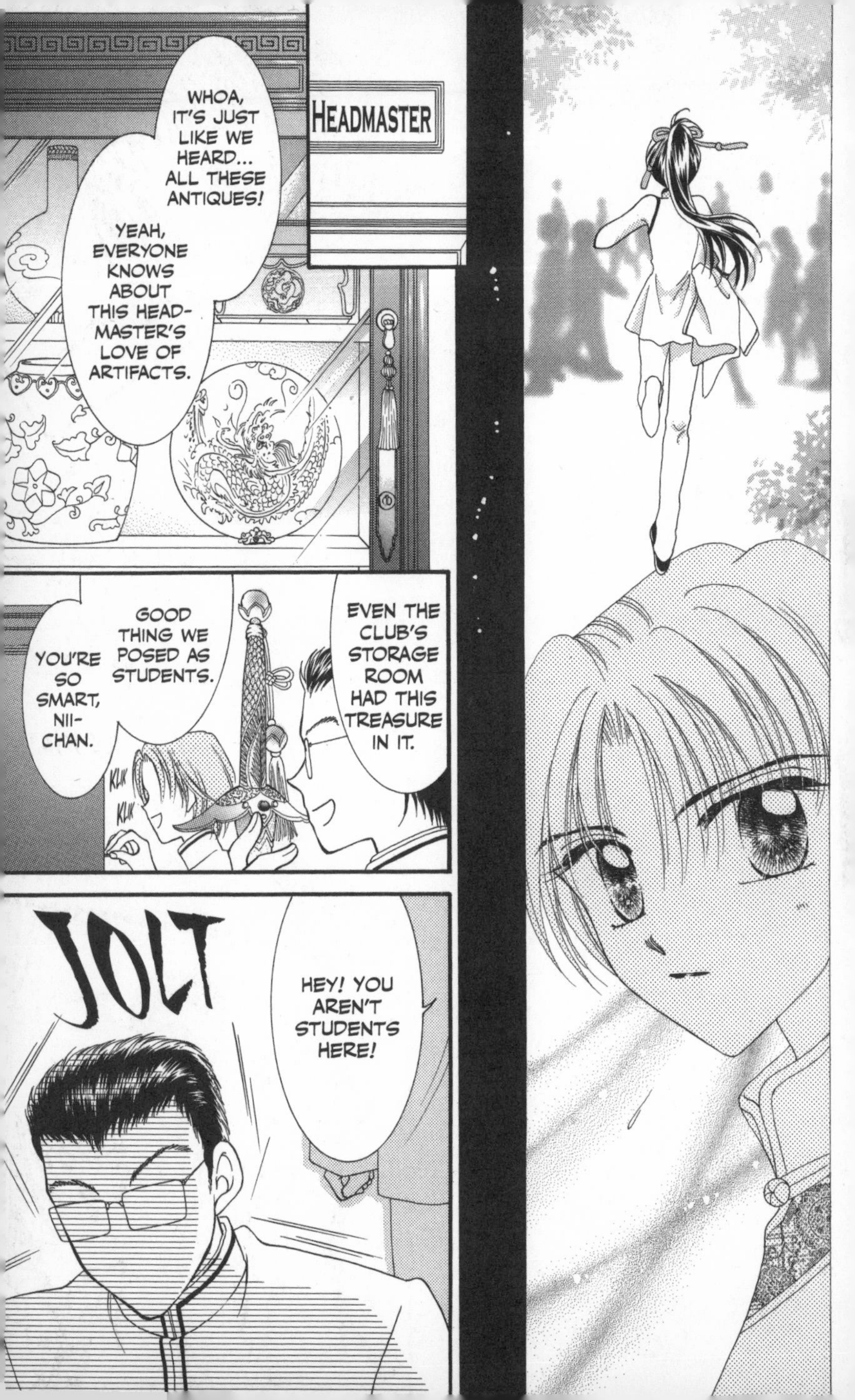
HEADMASTER
WHOA, IT'S JUST LIKE WE HEARD... ALL THESE ANTIQUES!
YEAH, EVERYONE KNOWS ABOUT THIS HEAD-MASTER'S LOVE OF ARTIFACTS.
EVEN THE CLUB'S STORAGE ROOM HAD THIS TREASURE IN IT.
GOOD THING WE POSED AS STUDENTS.
YOU'RE SO SMART, NII-CHAN.
KLIK
KLIK
HEY! YOU AREN'T STUDENTS HERE!
JOLT

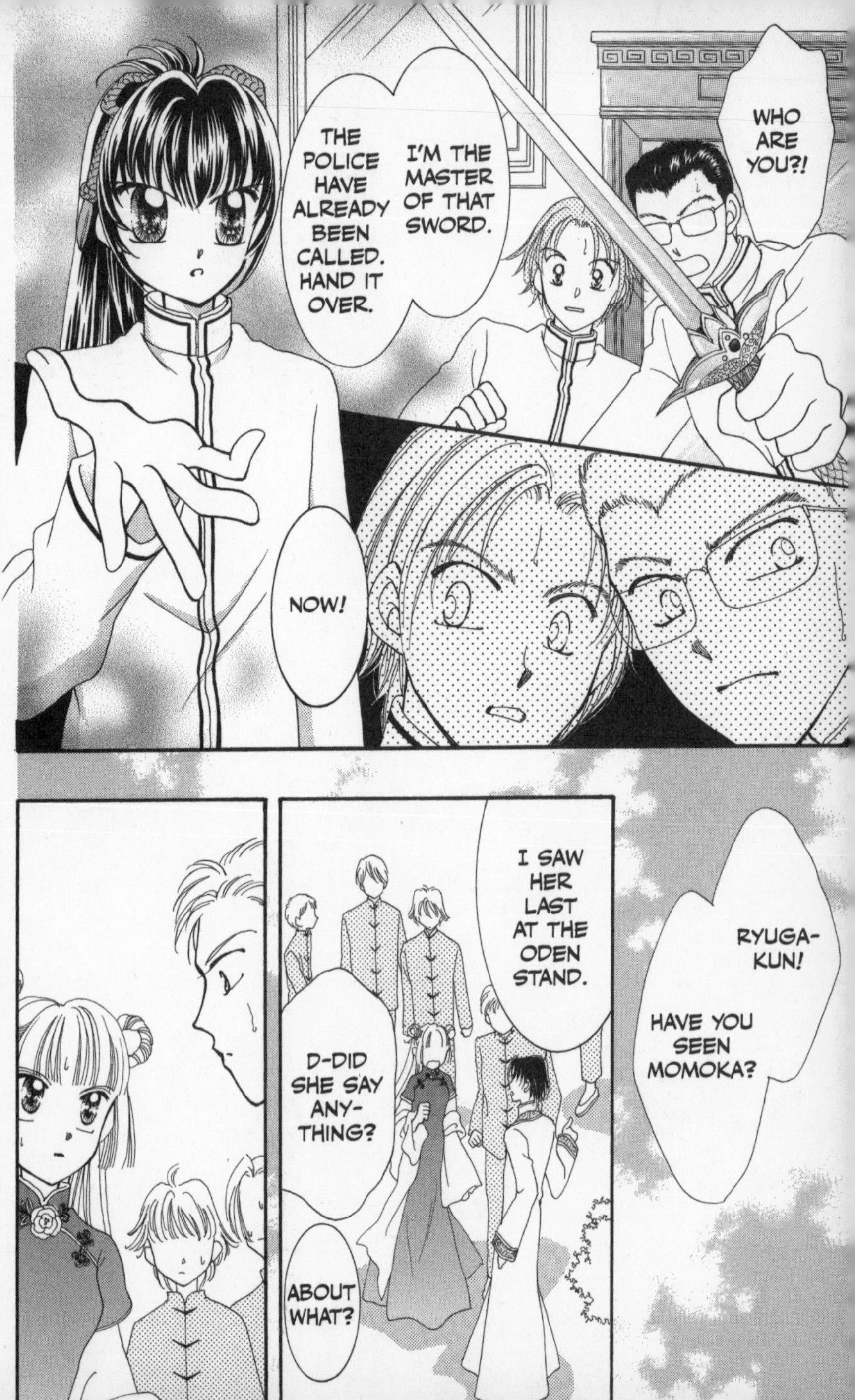
WHO ARE YOU?!
I'M THE MASTER OF THAT SWORD.
THE POLICE HAVE ALREADY BEEN CALLED. HAND IT OVER.
NOW!
RYUGA-KUN!
HAVE YOU SEEN MOMOKA?
I SAW HER LAST AT THE ODEN STAND.
D-DID SHE SAY ANY-THING?
ABOUT WHAT?

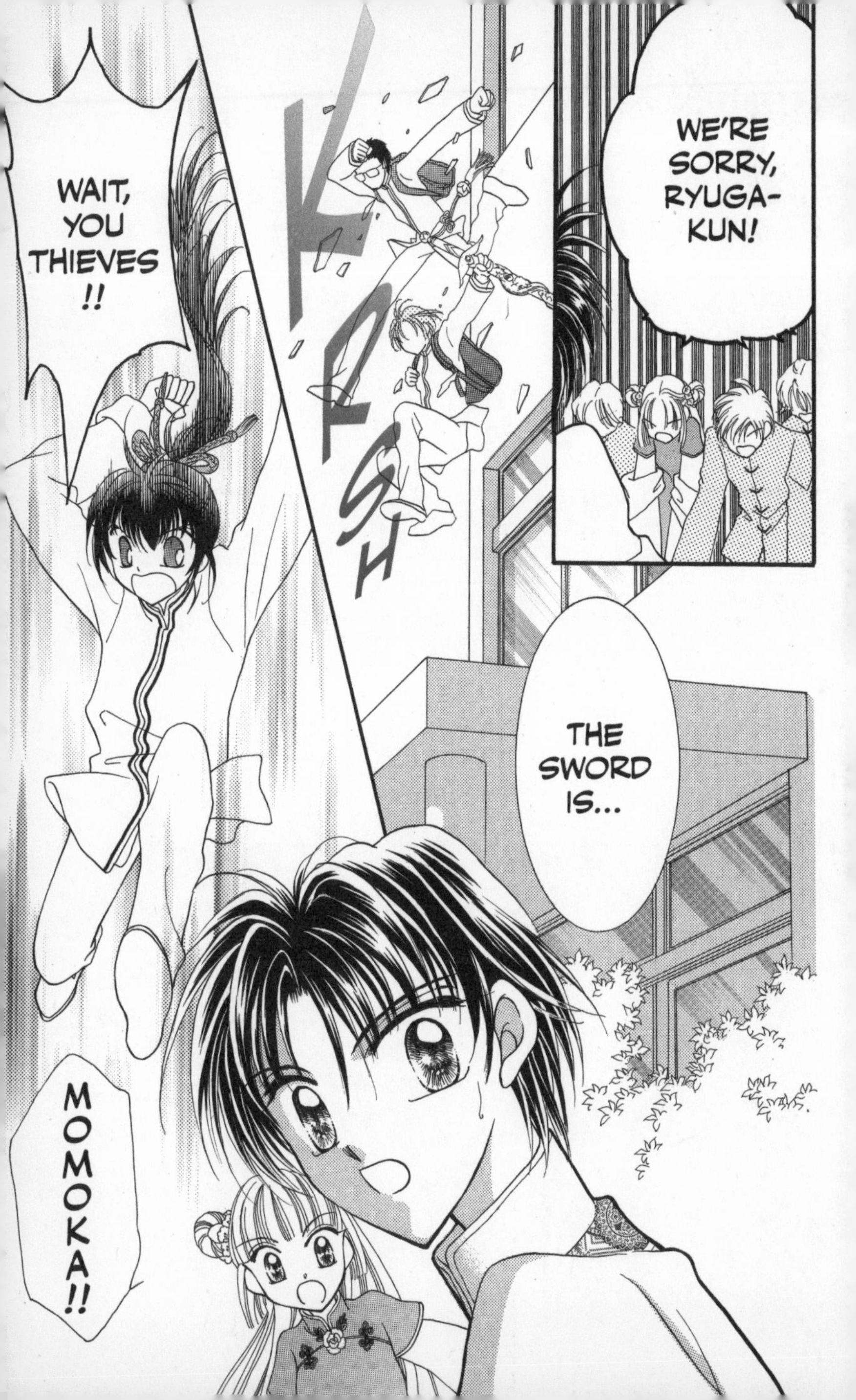
WE'RE SORRY, RYUGA-KUN!
KRASH
WAIT, YOU THIEVES!!
THE SWORD IS...
MOMOKA!!

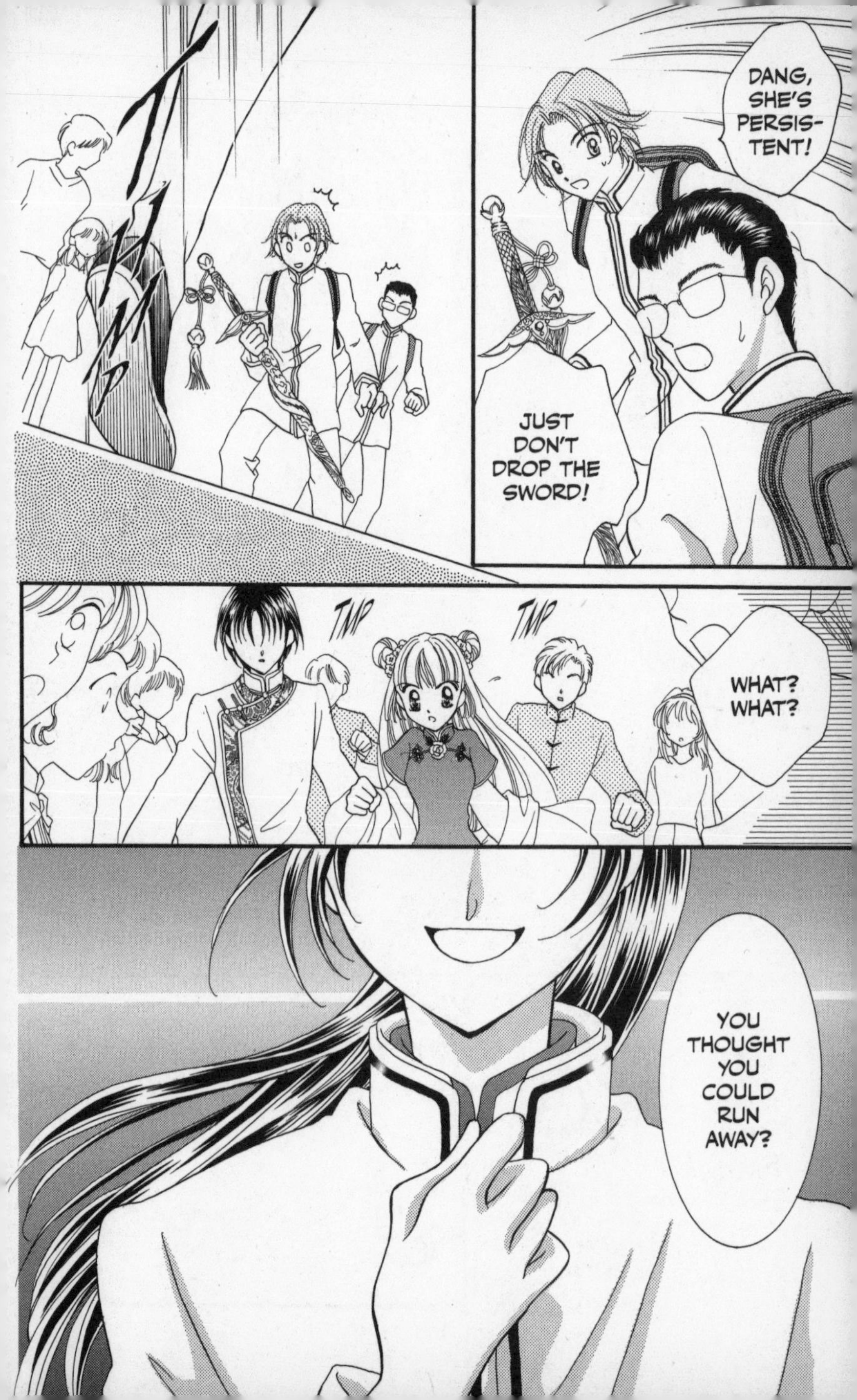
DANG, SHE'S PERSIS-TENT!
JUST DON'T DROP THE SWORD!
WHAT? WHAT?
TMP
TMP
YOU THOUGHT YOU COULD RUN AWAY?

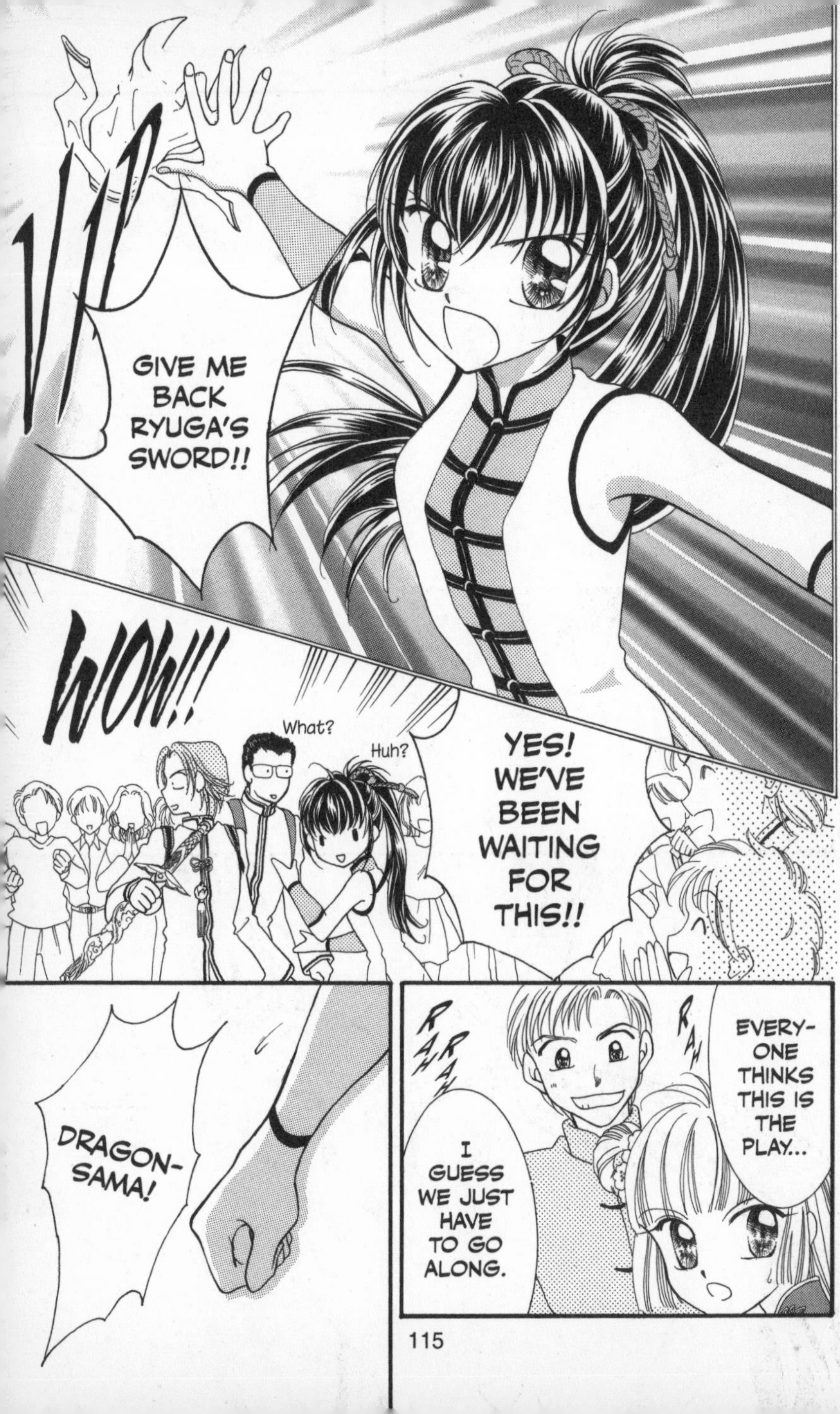
VIP
GIVE ME BACK RYUGA'S SWORD!!
YES! WE'VE BEEN WAITING FOR THIS!!
WOW!!
Huh?
What?
EVERY-ONE THINKS THIS IS THE PLAY...
RAH
I GUESS WE JUST HAVE TO GO ALONG.
RAH RAH
DRAGON-SAMA!

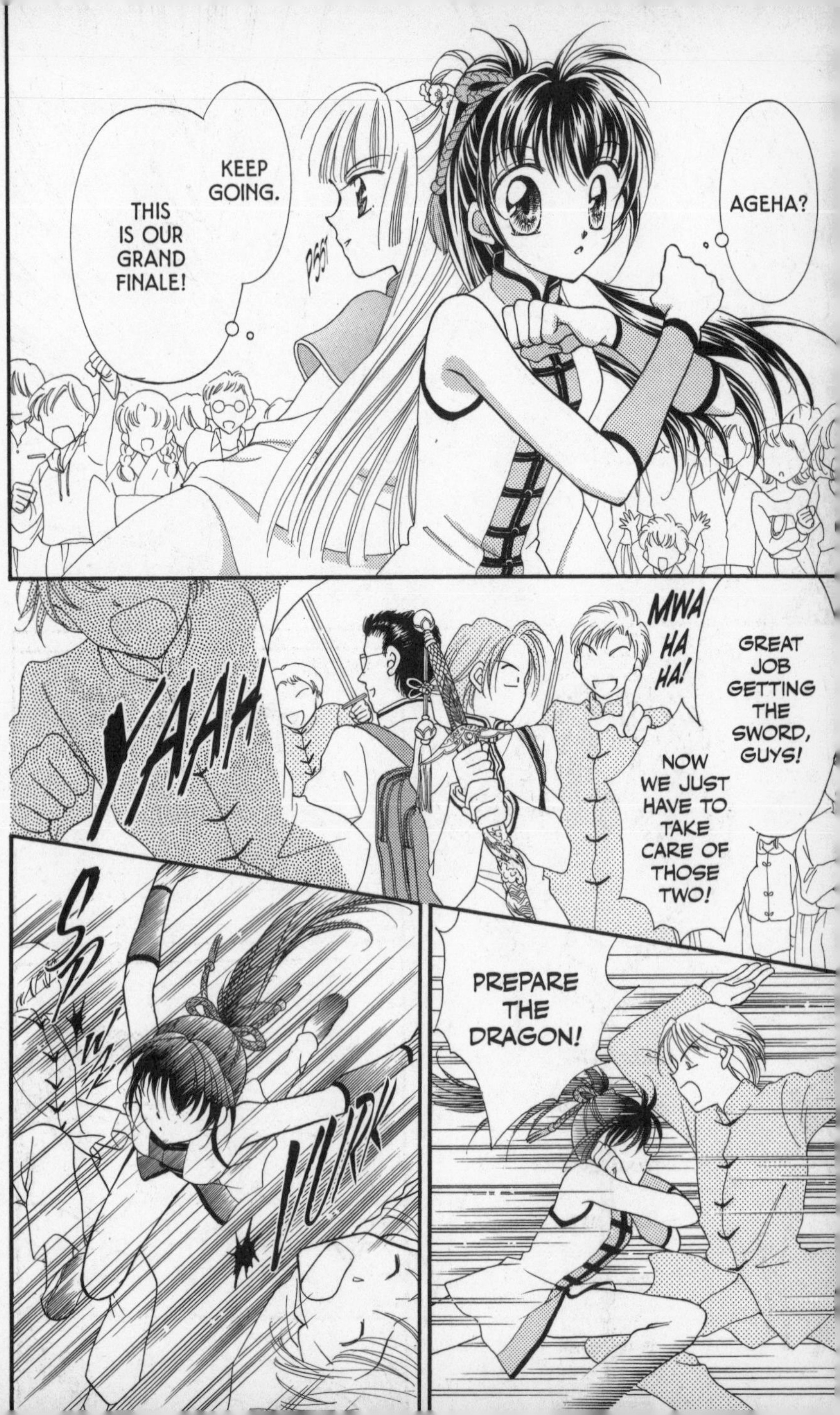
AGEHA?
KEEP GOING.
THIS IS OUR GRAND FINALE!
MWA HA HA!
GREAT JOB GETTING THE SWORD, GUYS!
NOW WE JUST HAVE TO TAKE CARE OF THOSE TWO!
YAAH
PREPARE THE DRAGON!
URK

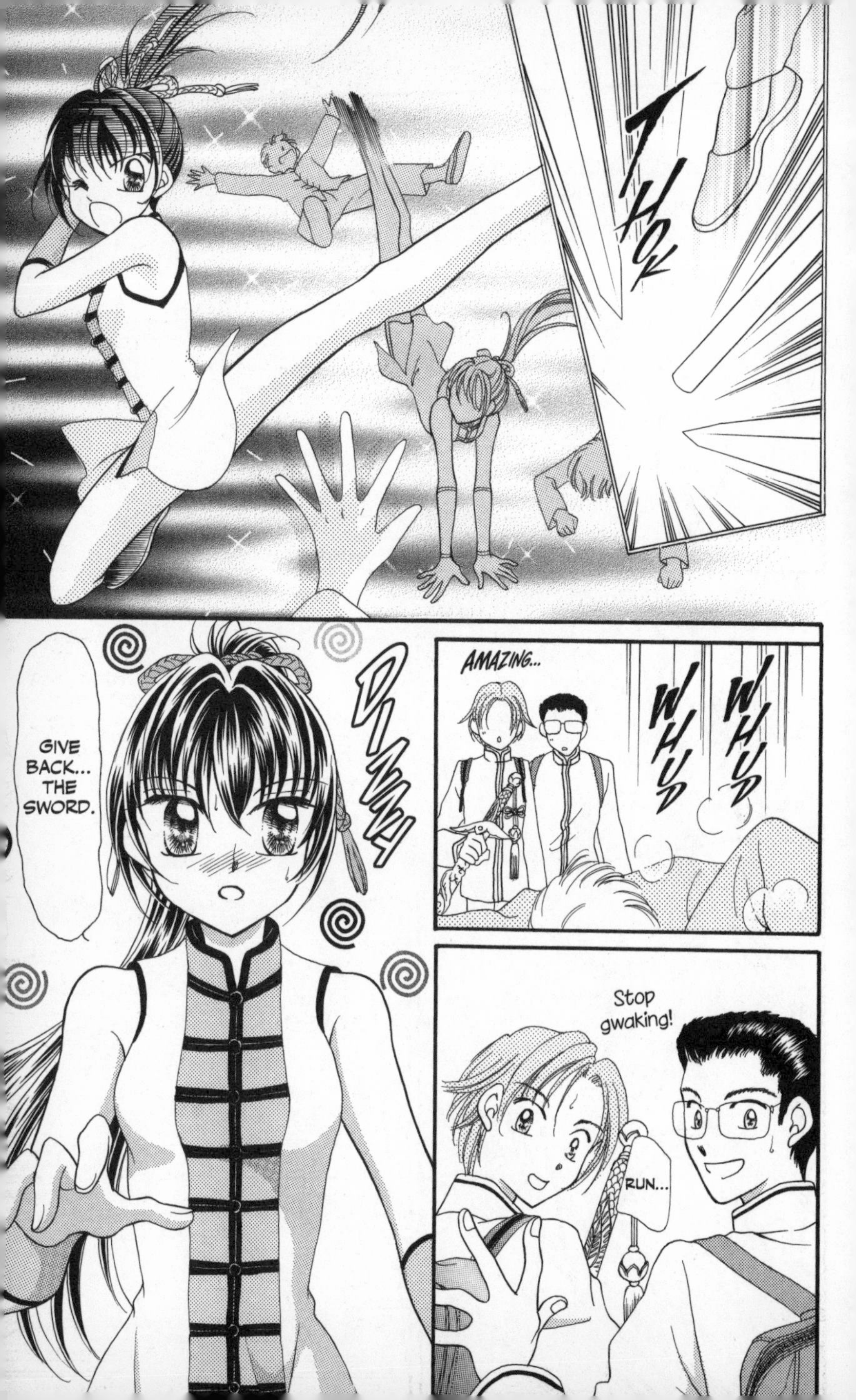
THOK
AMAZING...
WHUD
WHUD
DRAWWW
GIVE BACK... THE SWORD.
Stop gwaking!
RUN...

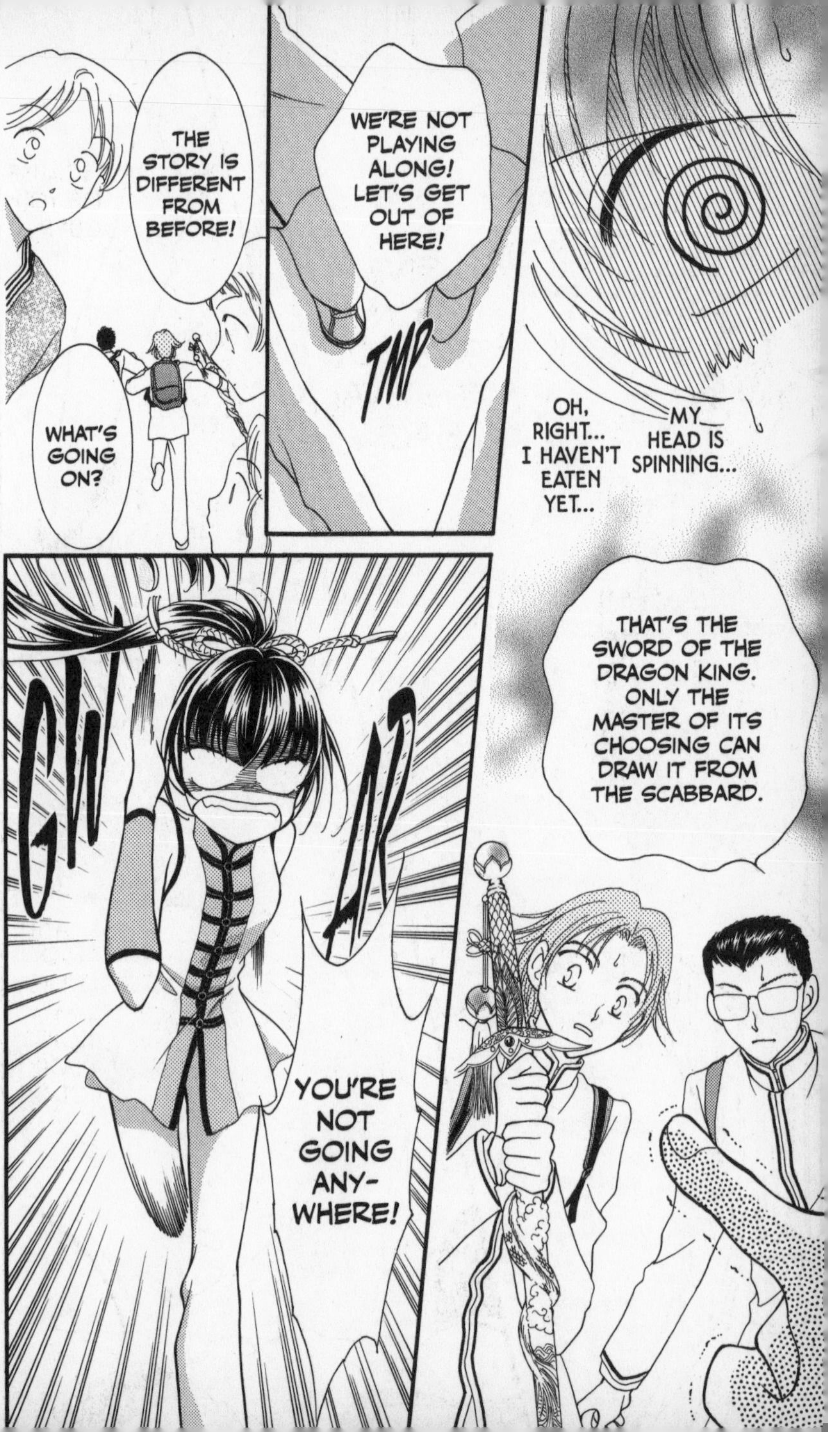

MY— HEAD IS SPINNING...
OH, RIGHT... I HAVEN'T EATEN YET...
WE'RE NOT PLAYING ALONG! LET'S GET OUT OF HERE!
TMP
THE STORY IS DIFFERENT FROM BEFORE!
WHAT'S GOING ON?
THAT'S THE SWORD OF THE DRAGON KING. ONLY THE MASTER OF ITS CHOOSING CAN DRAW IT FROM THE SCABBARD.
GWAK
YOU'RE NOT GOING ANYWHERE!

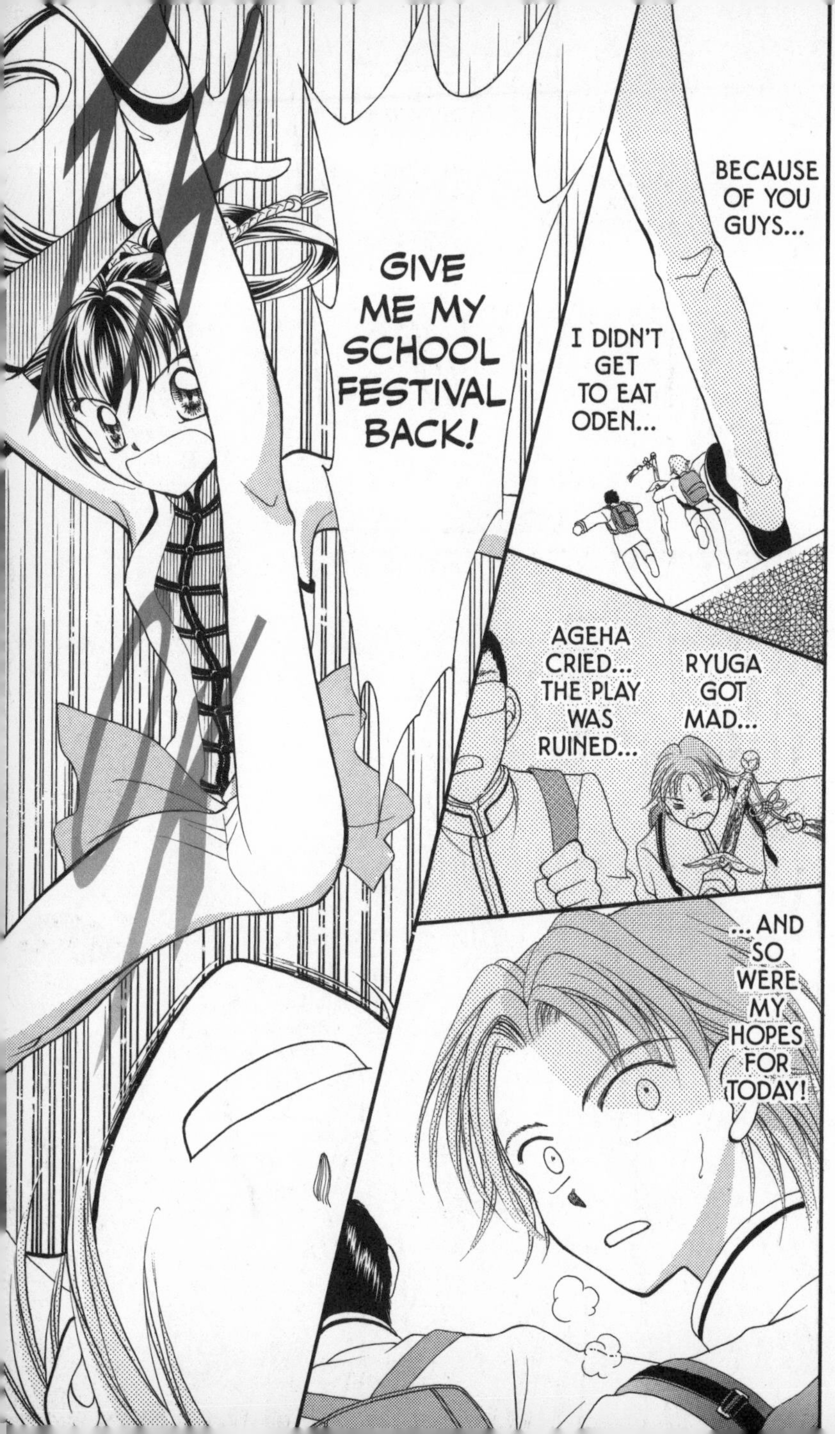
BECAUSE OF YOU GUYS...
I DIDN'T GET TO EAT ODEN...
RYUGA GOT MAD...
AGEHA CRIED... THE PLAY WAS RUINED...
...AND SO WERE MY HOPES FOR TODAY!
GIVE ME MY SCHOOL FESTIVAL BACK!

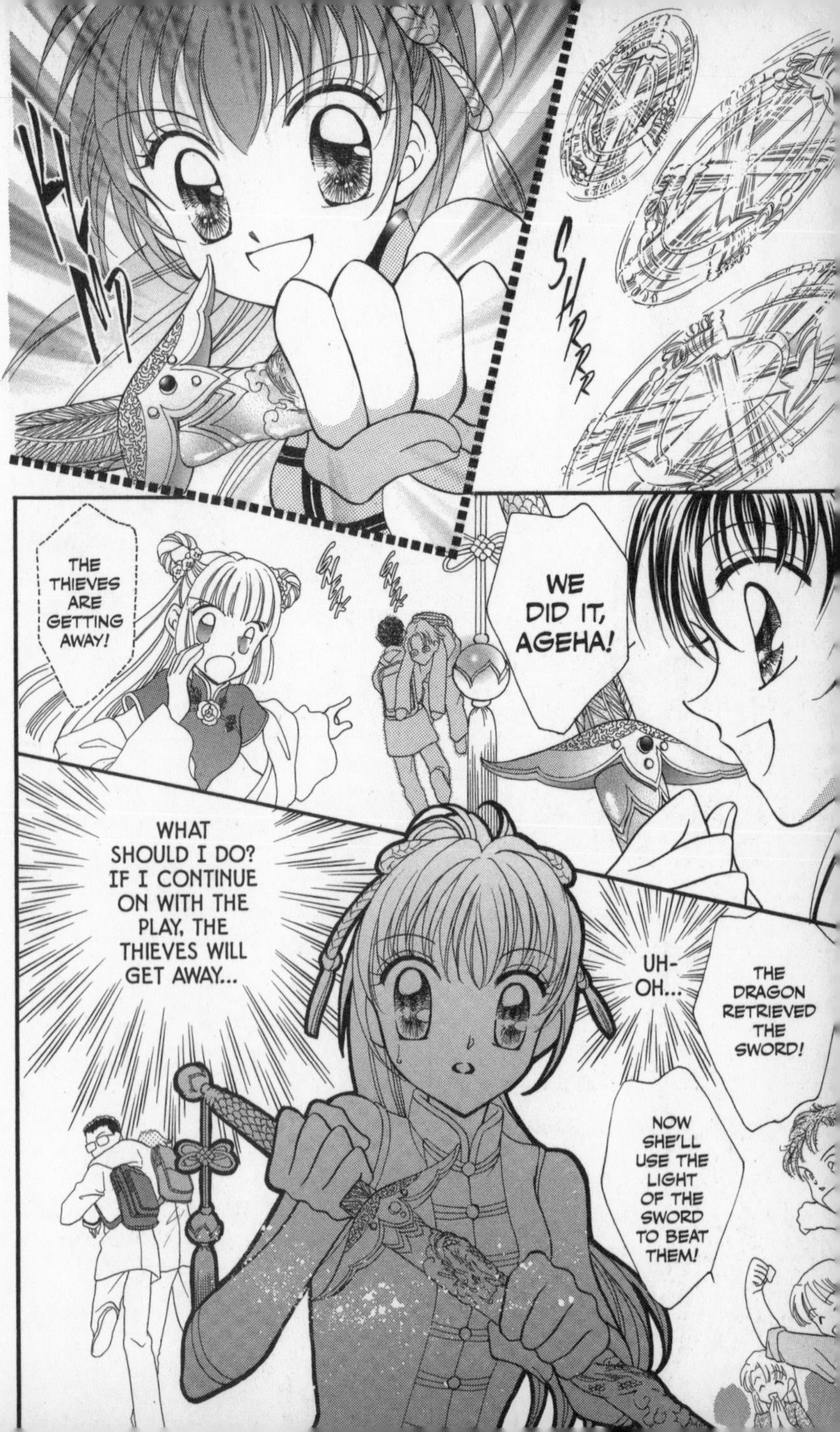
SHRRR
WE DID IT, AGEHA!
THE THIEVES ARE GETTING AWAY!
THE DRAGON RETRIEVED THE SWORD!
NOW SHE'LL USE THE LIGHT OF THE SWORD TO BEAT THEM!
UH-OH...
WHAT SHOULD I DO? IF I CONTINUE ON WITH THE PLAY, THE THIEVES WILL GET AWAY...

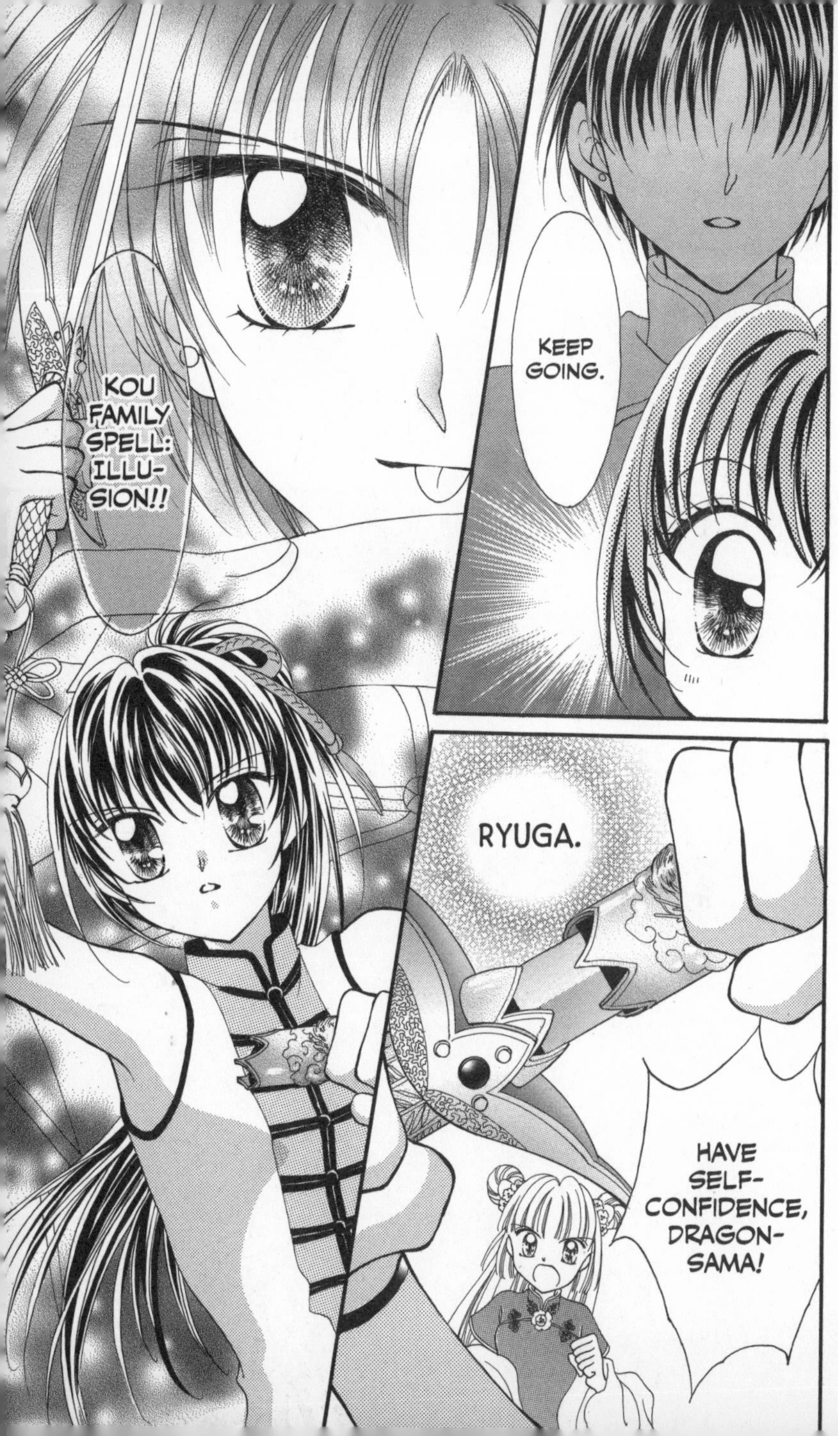
KEEP GOING.
RYUGA.
HAVE SELF-CONFIDENCE, DRAGON-SAMA!
KOU FAMILY SPELL: ILLUSION!!

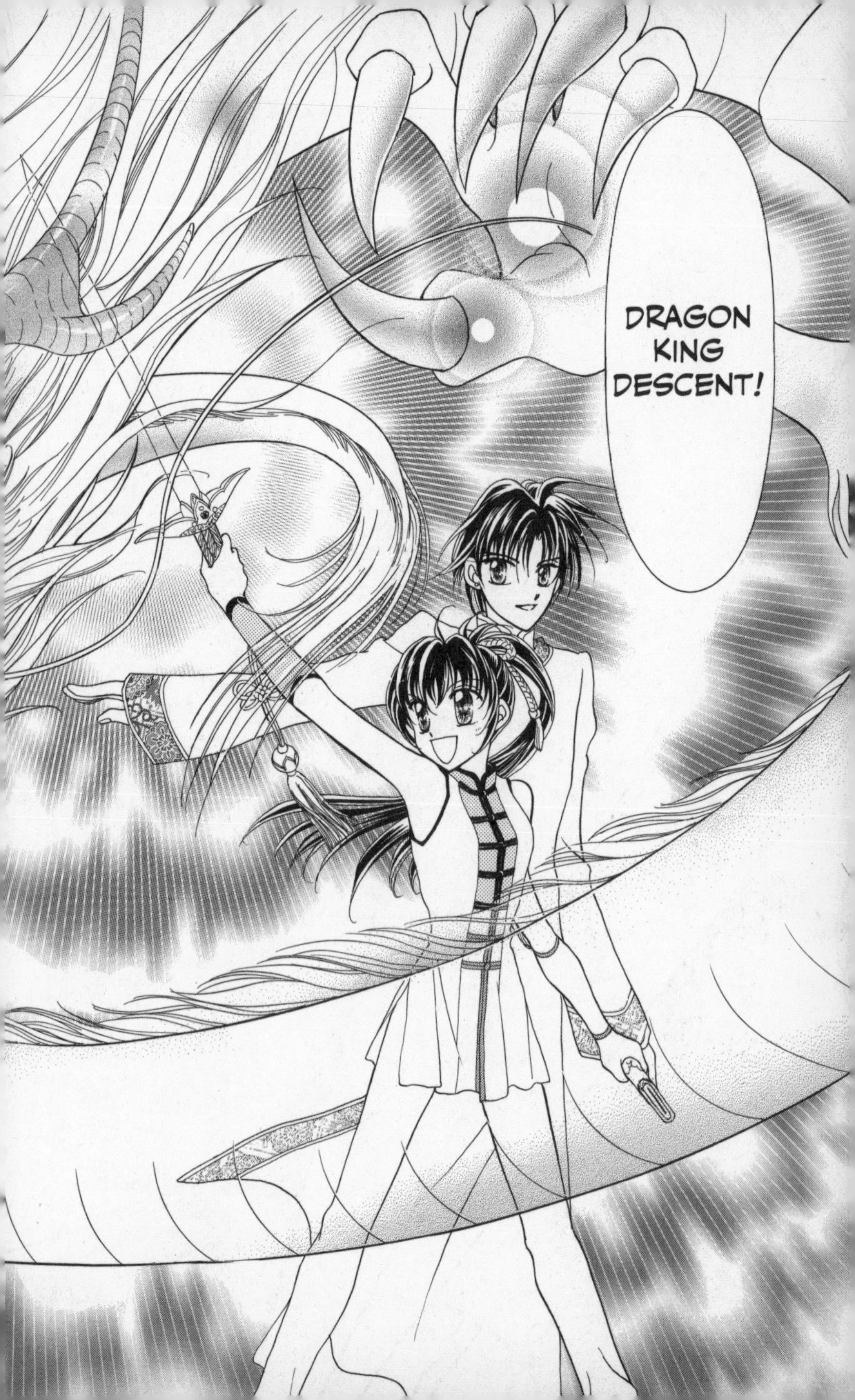
DRAGON KING DESCENT!

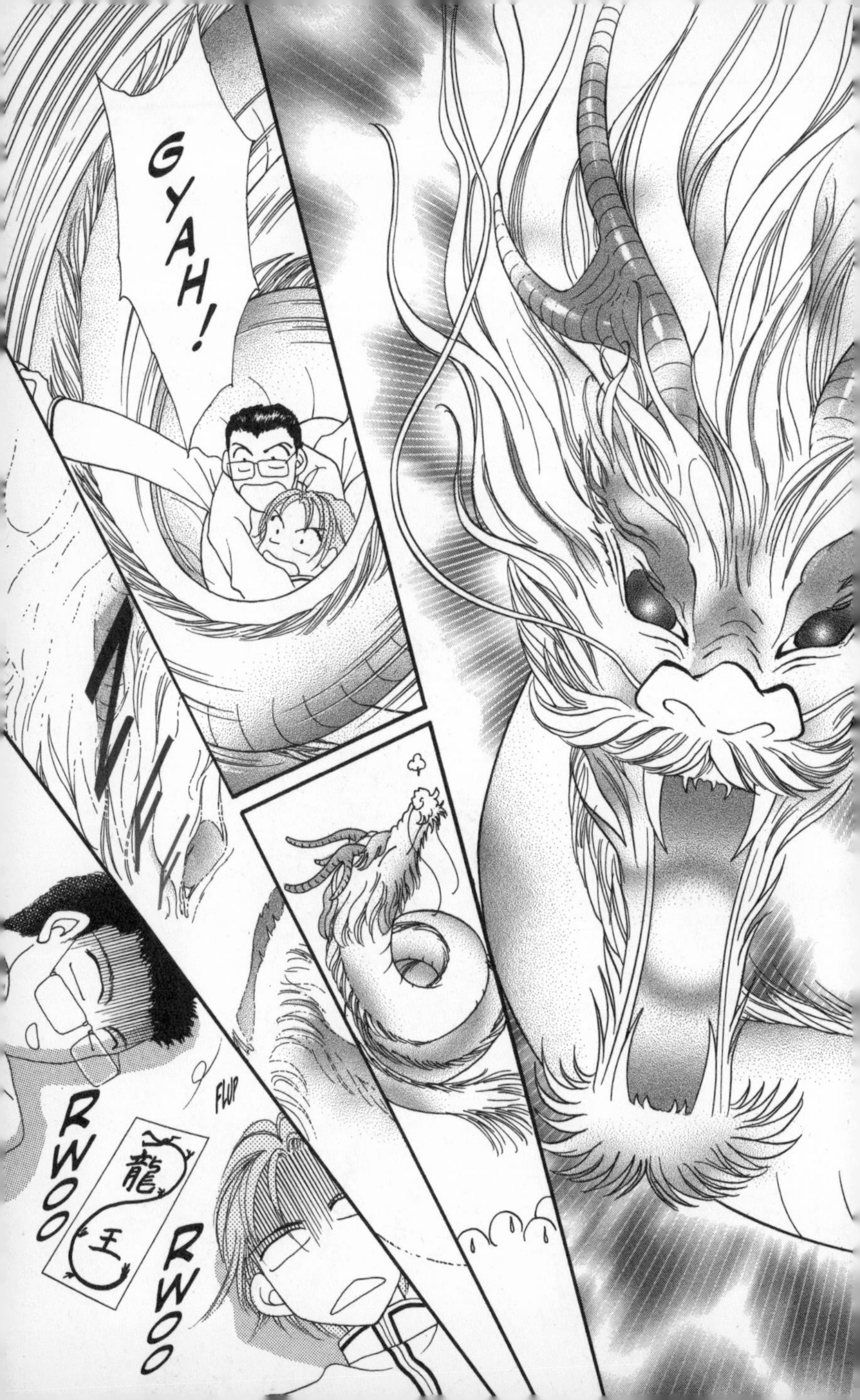
GYAH!
FLUP
RWOO
龍王
RWOO

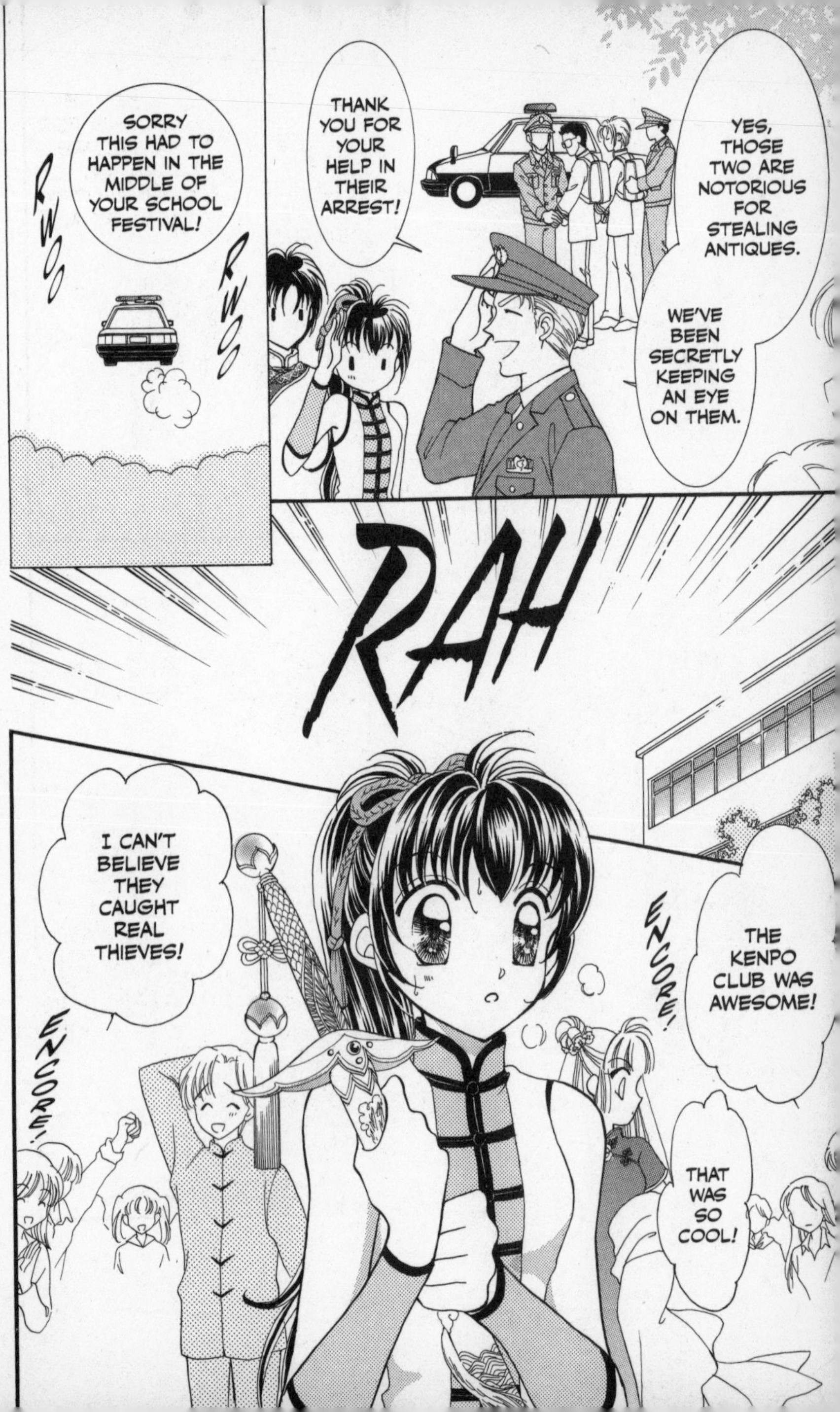
YES, THOSE TWO ARE NOTORIOUS FOR STEALING ANTIQUES.
WE'VE BEEN SECRETLY KEEPING AN EYE ON THEM.
THANK YOU FOR YOUR HELP IN THEIR ARREST!
RWOO
RWOO
SORRY THIS HAD TO HAPPEN IN THE MIDDLE OF YOUR SCHOOL FESTIVAL!
RAH
THE KENPO CLUB WAS AWESOME!
ENCORE!
THAT WAS SO COOL!
I CAN'T BELIEVE THEY CAUGHT REAL THIEVES!
ENCORE!

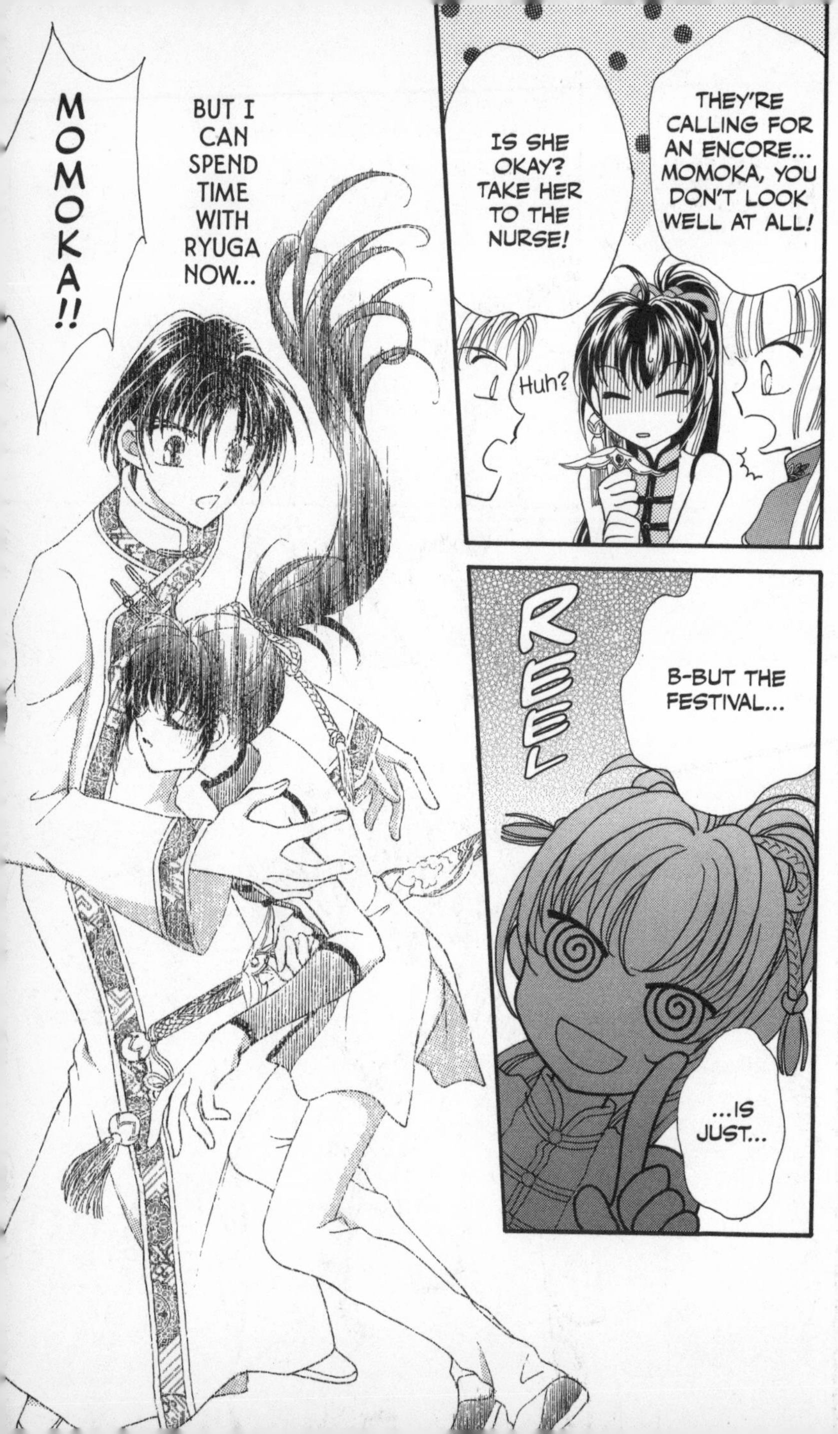
THEY'RE CALLING FOR AN ENCORE... MOMOKA, YOU DON'T LOOK WELL AT ALL!
IS SHE OKAY? TAKE HER TO THE NURSE!
Huh?
REEL
B-BUT THE FESTIVAL...
...IS JUST...
BUT I CAN SPEND TIME WITH RYUGA NOW...
MOMOKA!!

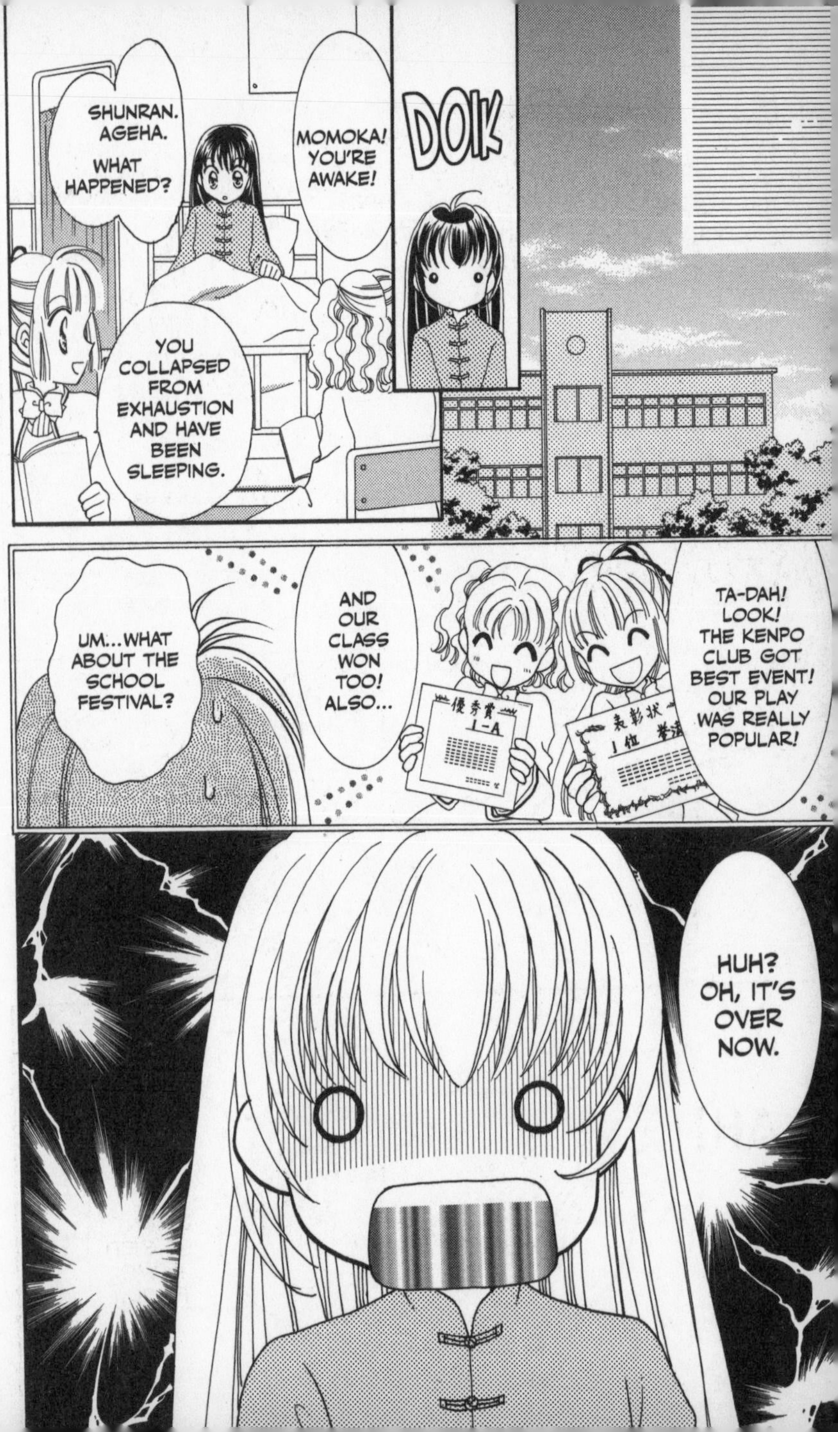
DOIK
MOMOKA! YOU'RE AWAKE!
SHUNRAN. AGEHA.
WHAT HAPPENED?
YOU COLLAPSED FROM EXHAUSTION AND HAVE BEEN SLEEPING.
TA-DAH! LOOK! THE KENPO CLUB GOT BEST EVENT! OUR PLAY WAS REALLY POPULAR!
表彰状
AND OUR CLASS WON TOO! ALSO...
優秀賞
1-A
UM...WHAT ABOUT THE SCHOOL FESTIVAL?
HUH? OH, IT'S OVER NOW.

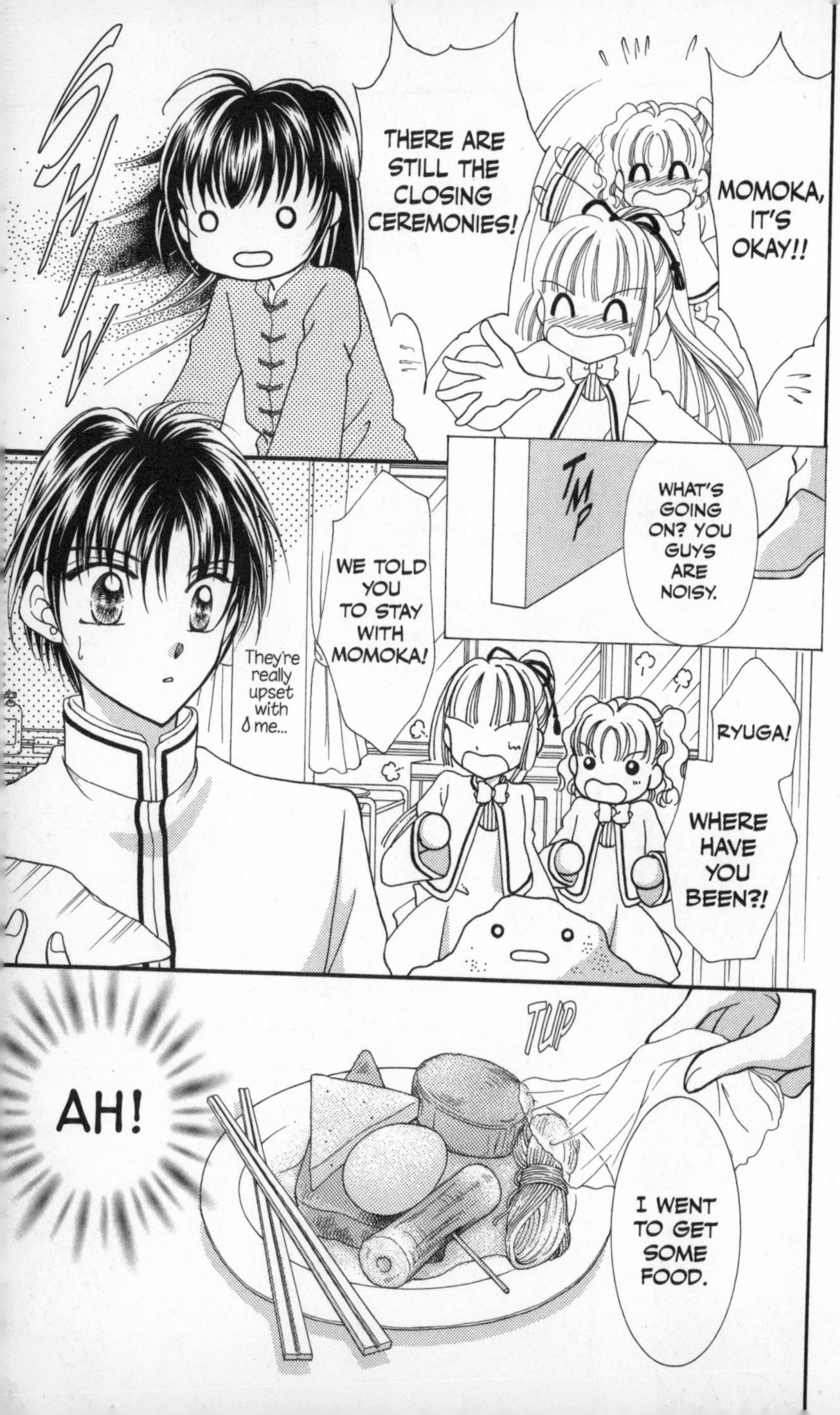
MOMOKA, IT'S OKAY!!
THERE ARE STILL THE CLOSING CEREMONIES!
TMP
WHAT'S GOING ON? YOU GUYS ARE NOISY.
RYUGA!
WHERE HAVE YOU BEEN?!
WE TOLD YOU TO STAY WITH MOMOKA!
They're really upset with me...
TUP
I WENT TO GET SOME FOOD.
AH!

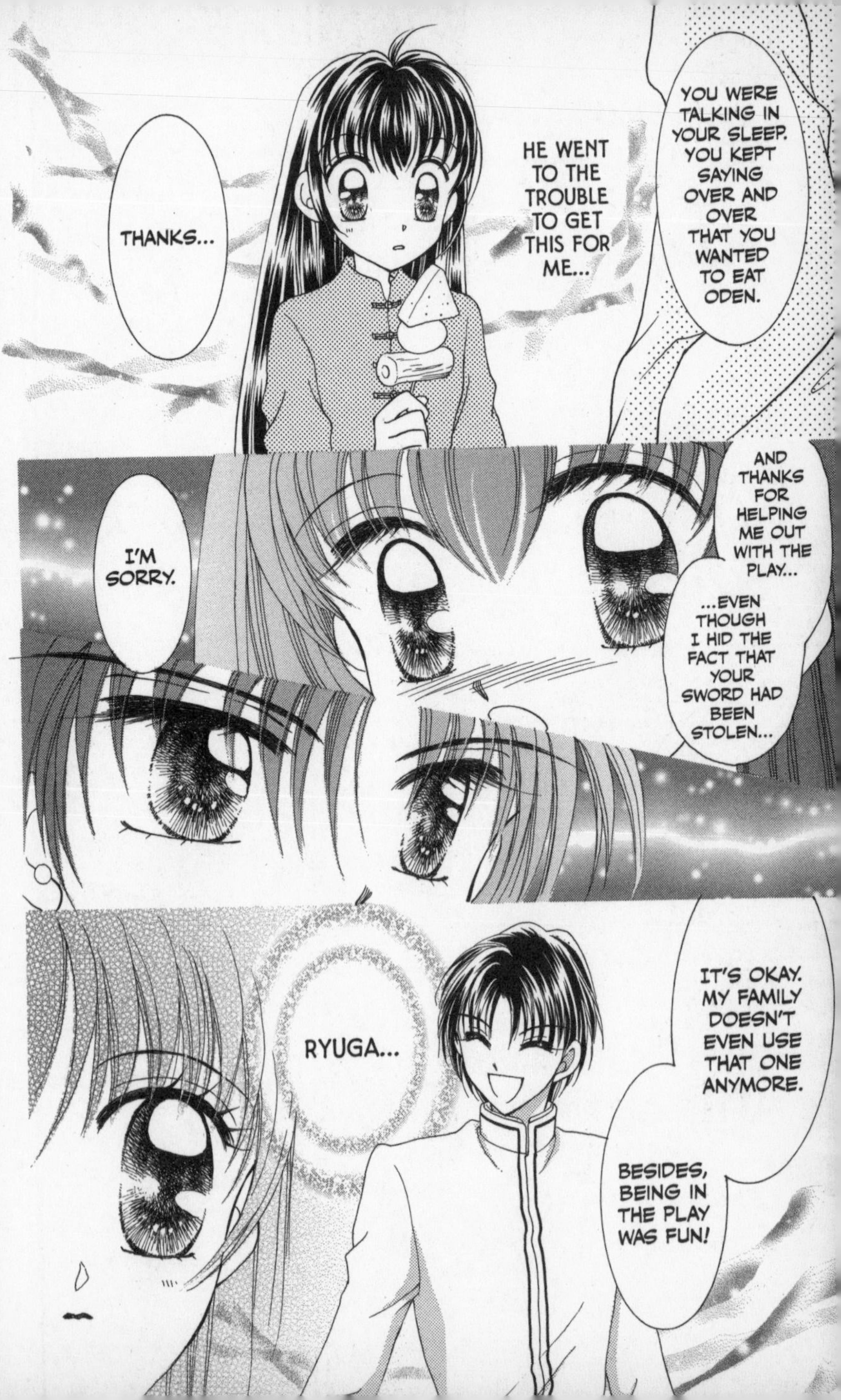

YOU WERE TALKING IN YOUR SLEEP. YOU KEPT SAYING OVER AND OVER THAT YOU WANTED TO EAT ODEN.
HE WENT TO THE TROUBLE TO GET THIS FOR ME...
THANKS...
AND THANKS FOR HELPING ME OUT WITH THE PLAY...
...EVEN THOUGH I HID THE FACT THAT YOUR SWORD HAD BEEN STOLEN...
I'M SORRY.
IT'S OKAY. MY FAMILY DOESN'T EVEN USE THAT ONE ANYMORE.
BESIDES, BEING IN THE PLAY WAS FUN!
RYUGA...

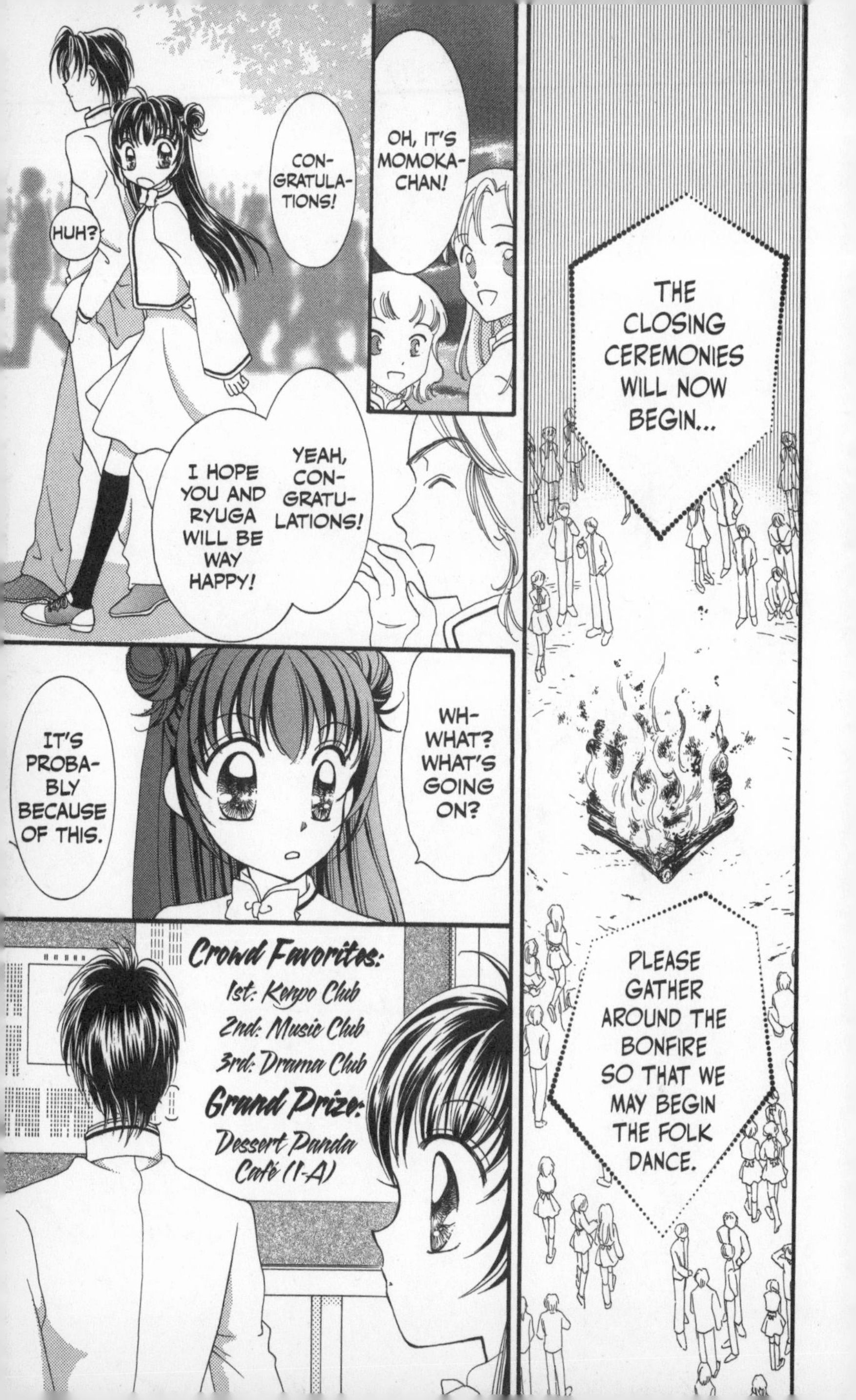
THE CLOSING CEREMONIES WILL NOW BEGIN...
PLEASE GATHER AROUND THE BONFIRE SO THAT WE MAY BEGIN THE FOLK DANCE.
OH, IT'S MOMOKA-CHAN!
CON-GRATULA-TIONS!
HUH?
YEAH, CON-GRATU-LATIONS!
I HOPE YOU AND RYUGA WILL BE WAY HAPPY!
WH-WHAT? WHAT'S GOING ON?
IT'S PROBA-BLY BECAUSE OF THIS.
Crowd Favorites:
1st: Kenpo Club
2nd: Music Club
3rd: Drama Club
Grand Prize:
Dessert Panda Café (1-A)

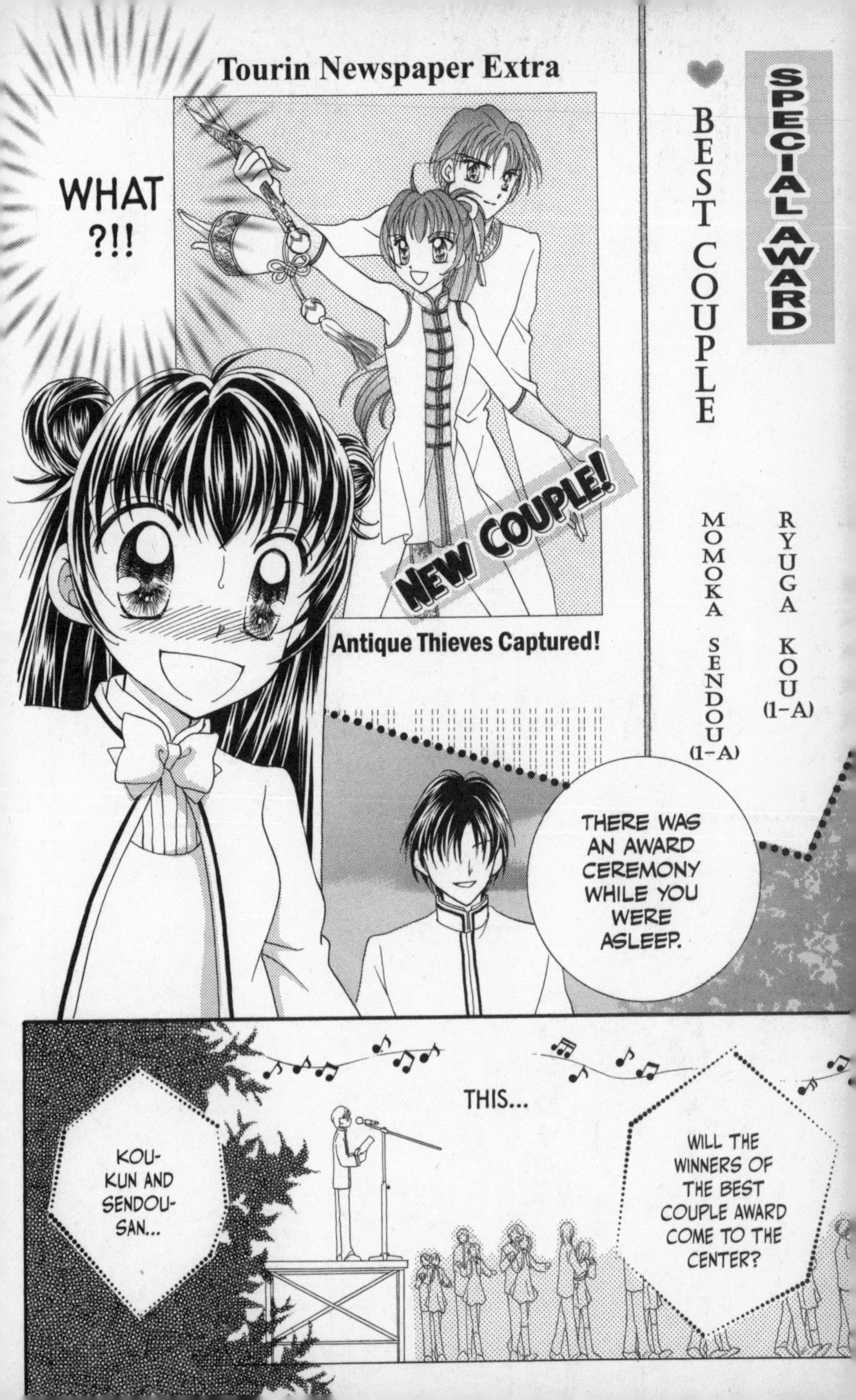
SPECIAL AWARD
BEST COUPLE
RYUGA KOU (1-A)
MOMOKA SENDOU (1-A)
Tourin Newspaper Extra
NEW COUPLE!
Antique Thieves Captured!
WHAT ?!!
THERE WAS AN AWARD CEREMONY WHILE YOU WERE ASLEEP.
WILL THE WINNERS OF THE BEST COUPLE AWARD COME TO THE CENTER?
THIS...
KOU-KUN AND SENDOU-SAN...

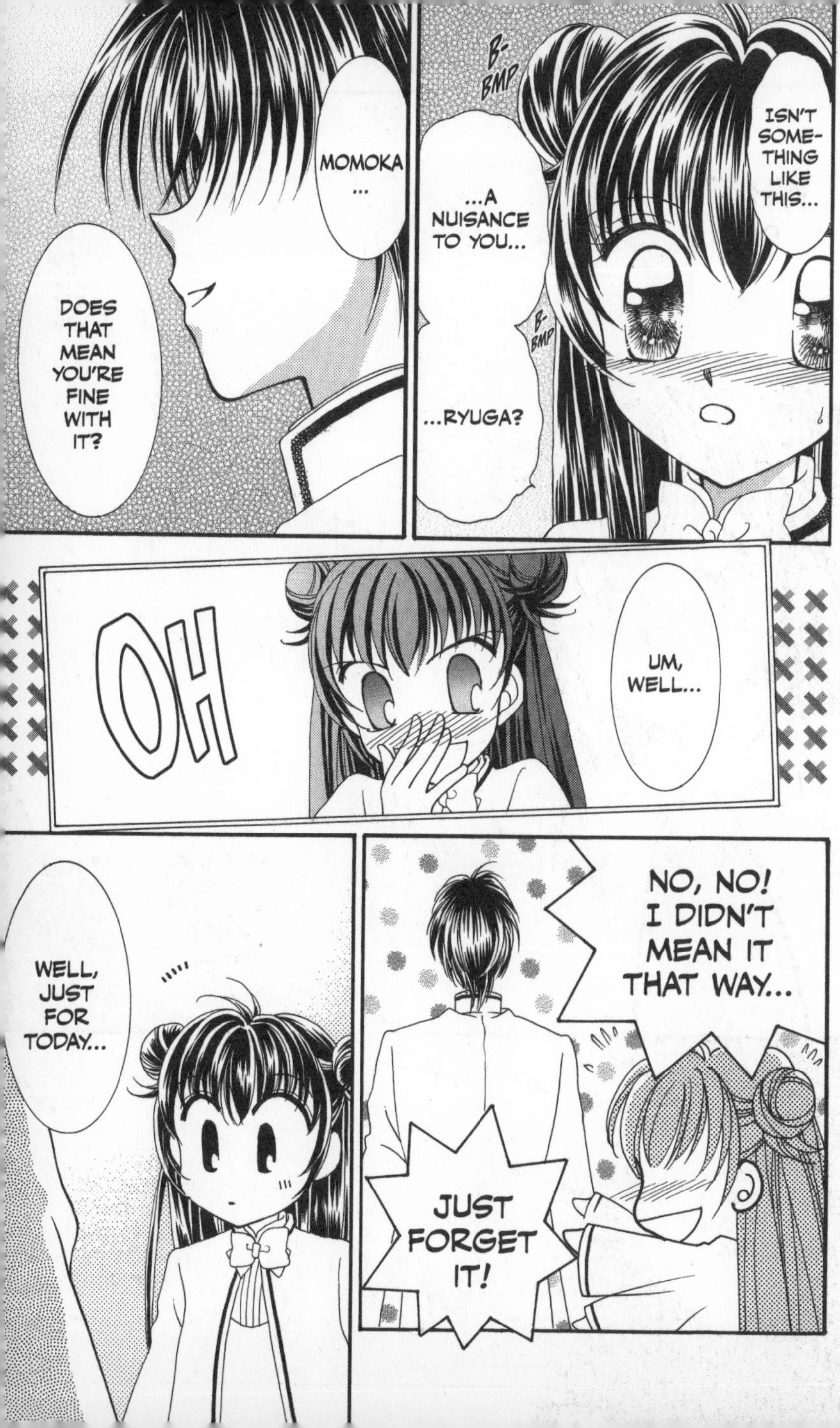
B-BMP
ISN'T SOMETHING LIKE THIS...
...A NUISANCE TO YOU...
B-BMP
...RYUGA?
MOMOKA...
DOES THAT MEAN YOU'RE FINE WITH IT?
UM, WELL...
OH
NO, NO! I DIDN'T MEAN IT THAT WAY...
JUST FORGET IT!
WELL, JUST FOR TODAY...

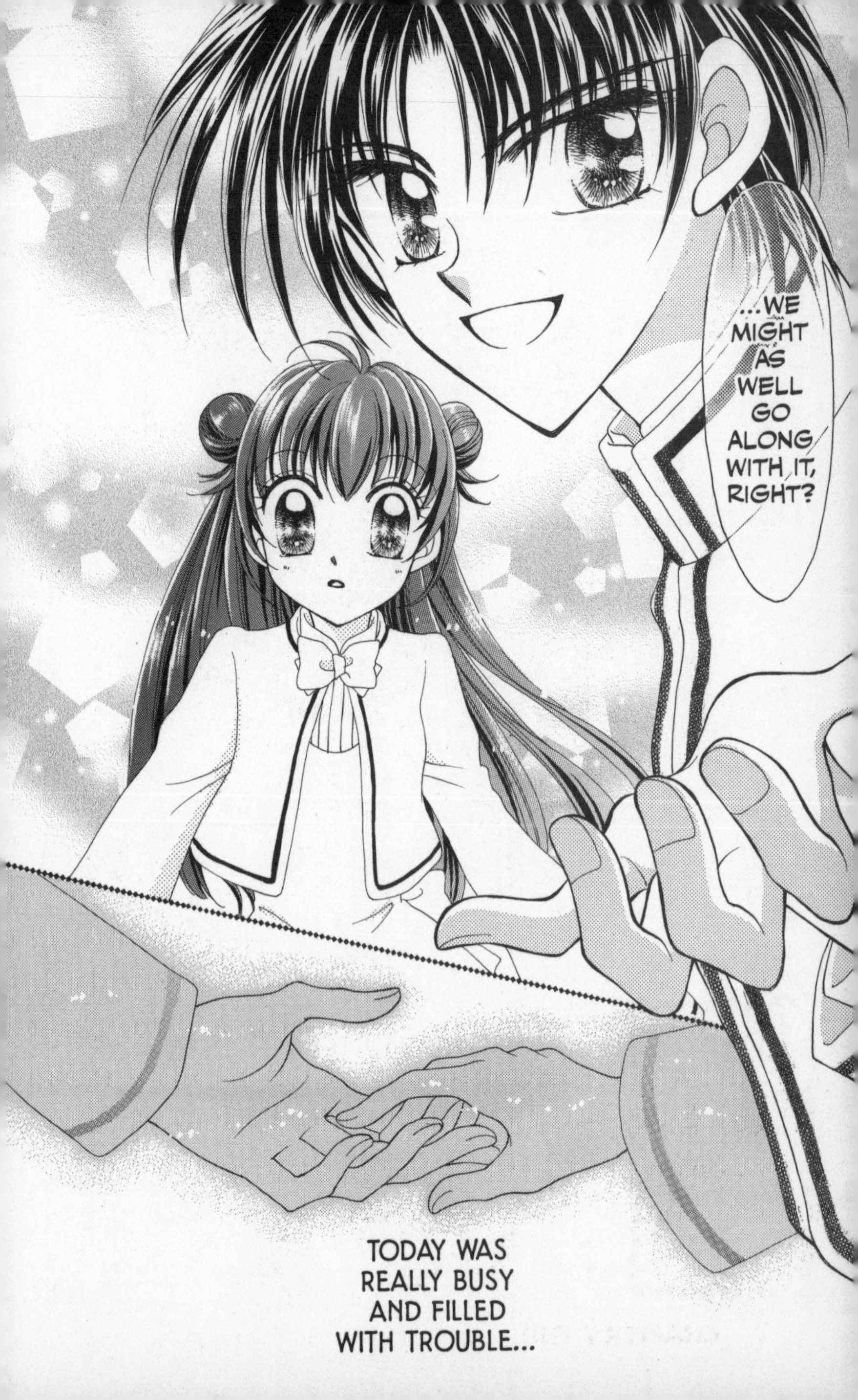
...WE MIGHT AS WELL GO ALONG WITH IT, RIGHT?
TODAY WAS REALLY BUSY AND FILLED WITH TROUBLE...

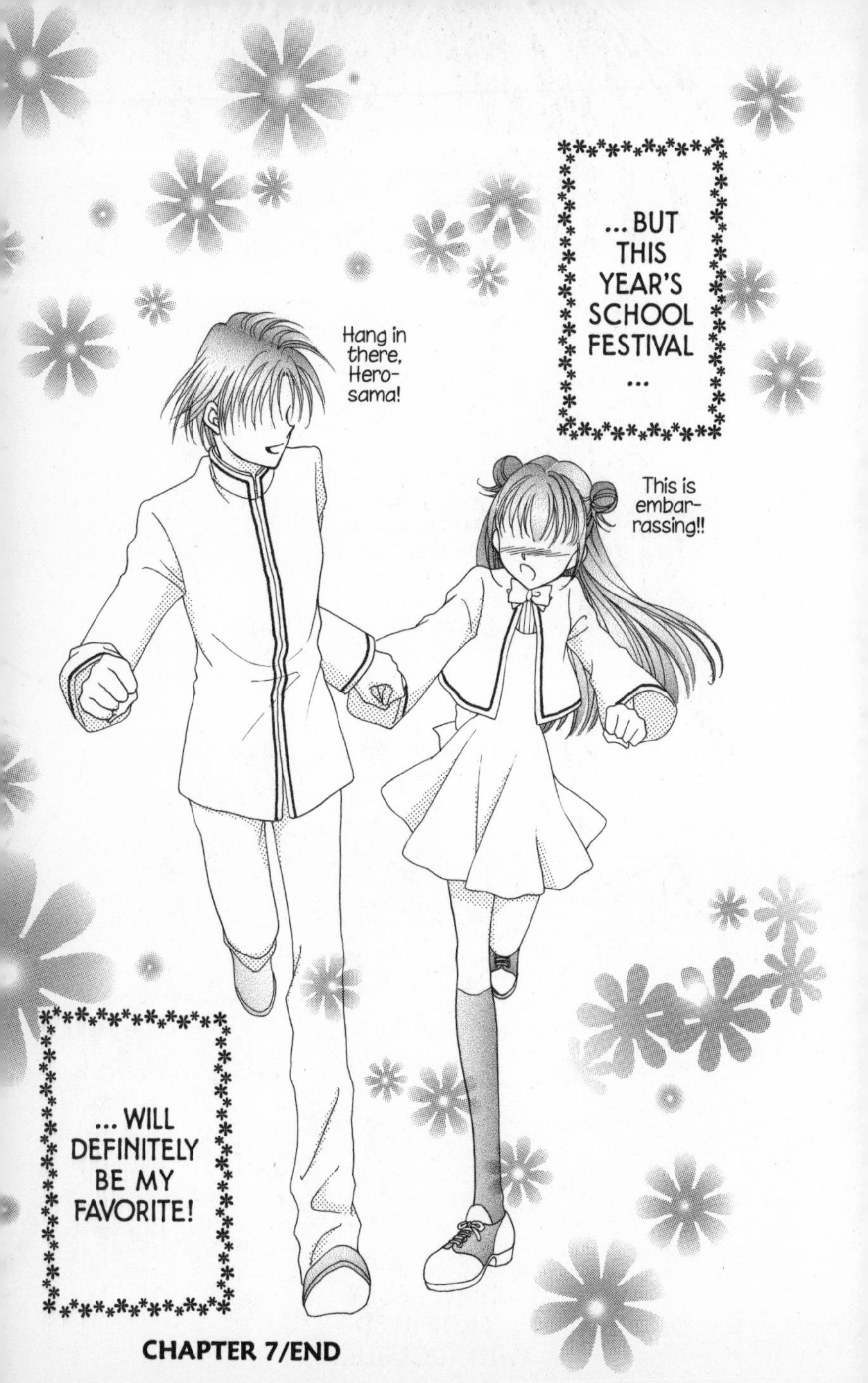
... BUT THIS YEAR'S SCHOOL FESTIVAL ...
Hang in there, Hero-sama!
This is embarrassing!!
... WILL DEFINITELY BE MY FAVORITE!

CHAPTER 7/END

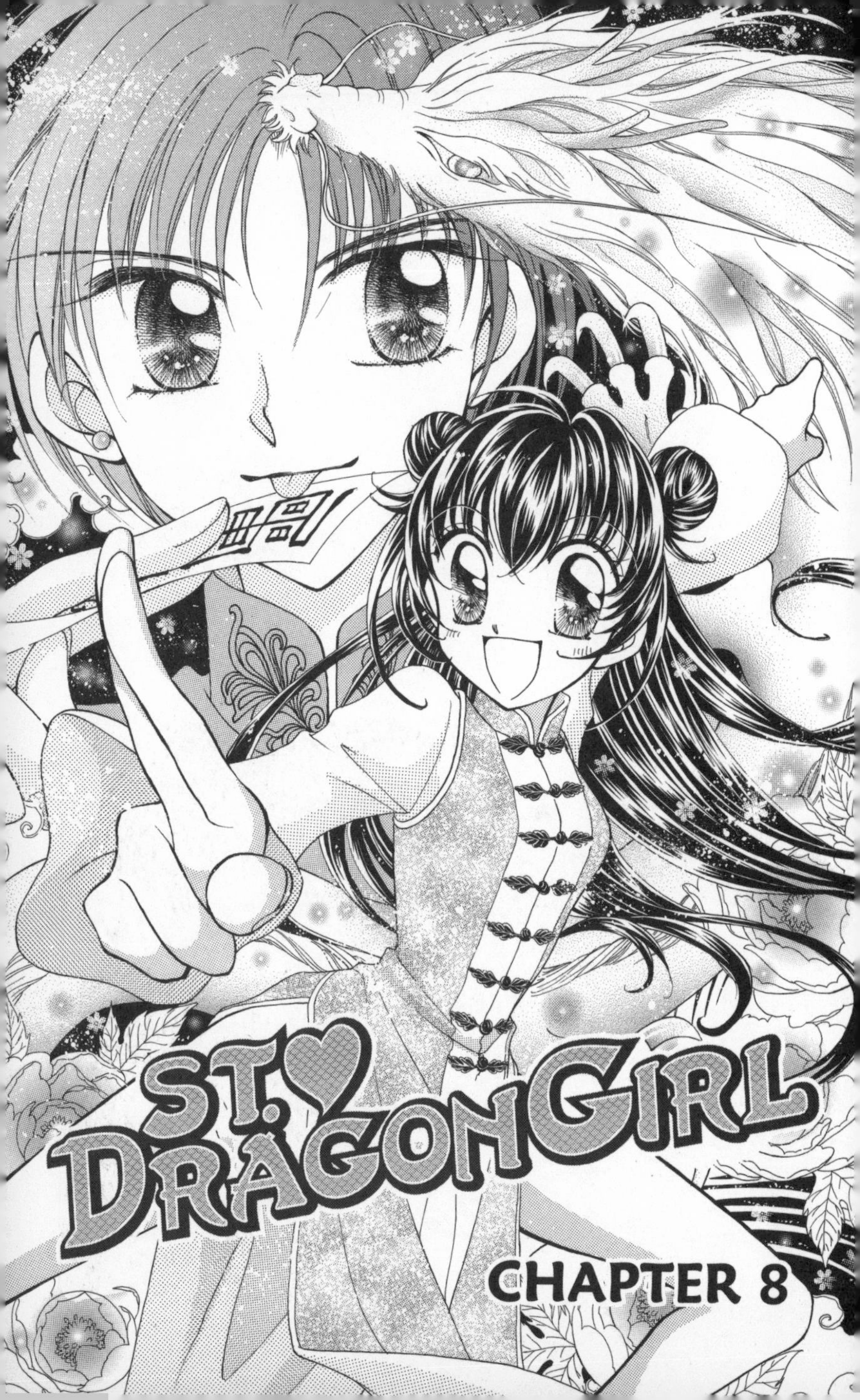
ST. DRAGON GIRL
CHAPTER 8

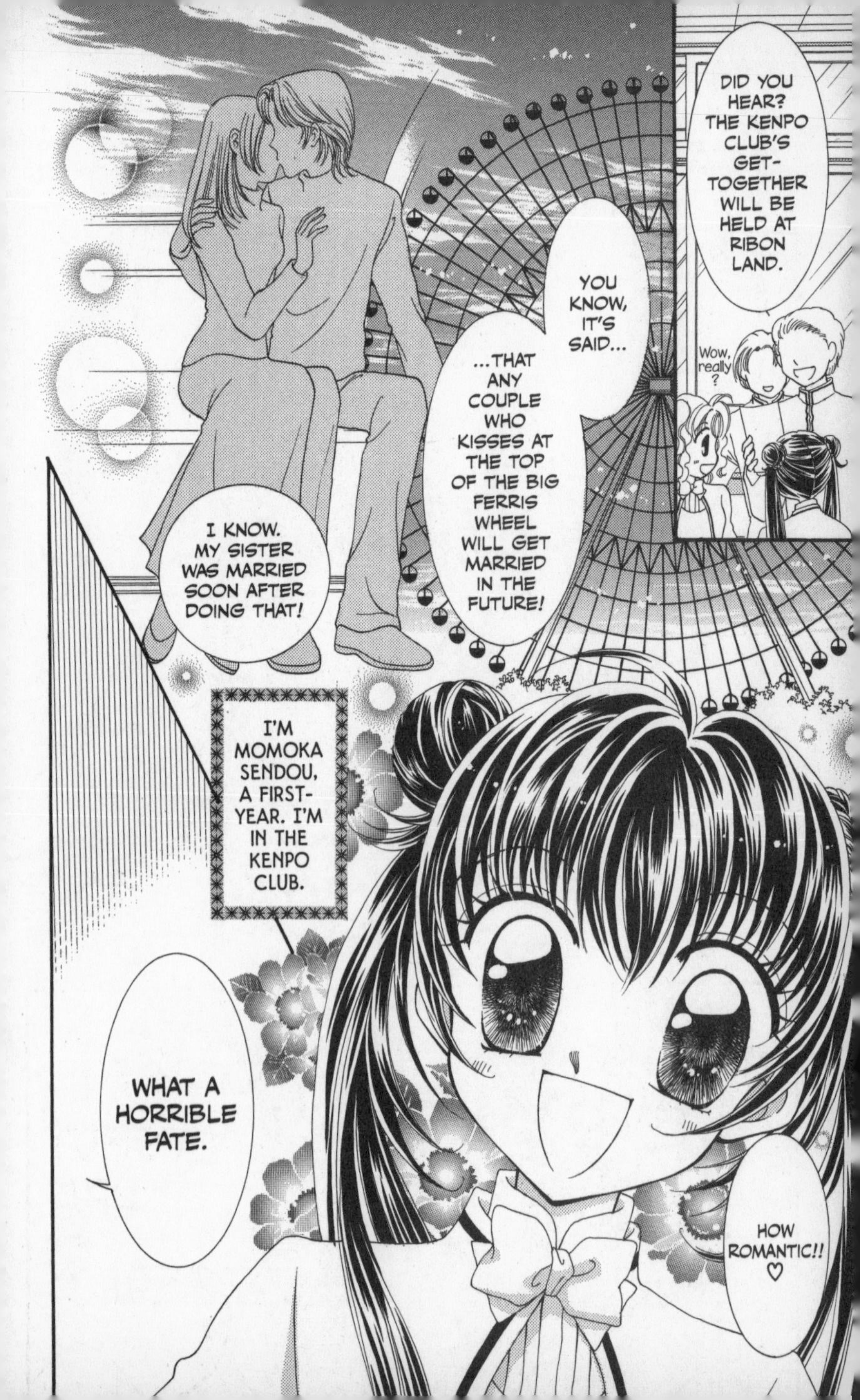
DID YOU HEAR? THE KENPO CLUB'S GET-TOGETHER WILL BE HELD AT RIBON LAND.
Wow, really?
YOU KNOW, IT'S SAID...
...THAT ANY COUPLE WHO KISSES AT THE TOP OF THE BIG FERRIS WHEEL WILL GET MARRIED IN THE FUTURE!
I KNOW. MY SISTER WAS MARRIED SOON AFTER DOING THAT!
I'M MOMOKA SENDOU, A FIRST-YEAR. I'M IN THE KENPO CLUB.
HOW ROMANTIC!! ♡
WHAT A HORRIBLE FATE.

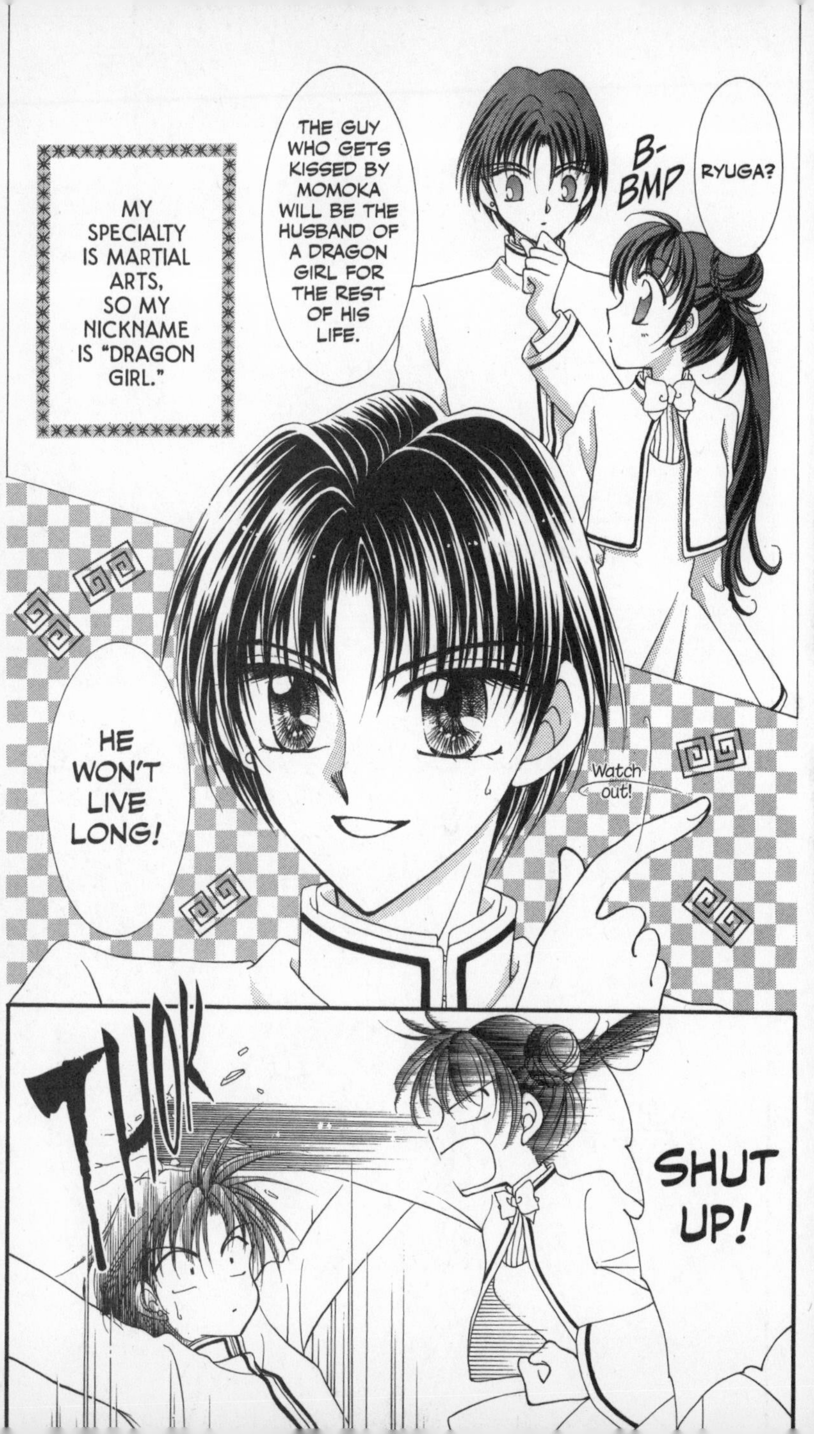
RYUGA?
B-BMP
THE GUY WHO GETS KISSED BY MOMOKA WILL BE THE HUSBAND OF A DRAGON GIRL FOR THE REST OF HIS LIFE.
MY SPECIALTY IS MARTIAL ARTS, SO MY NICKNAME IS "DRAGON GIRL."
Watch out!
HE WON'T LIVE LONG!
SHUT UP!
THOK

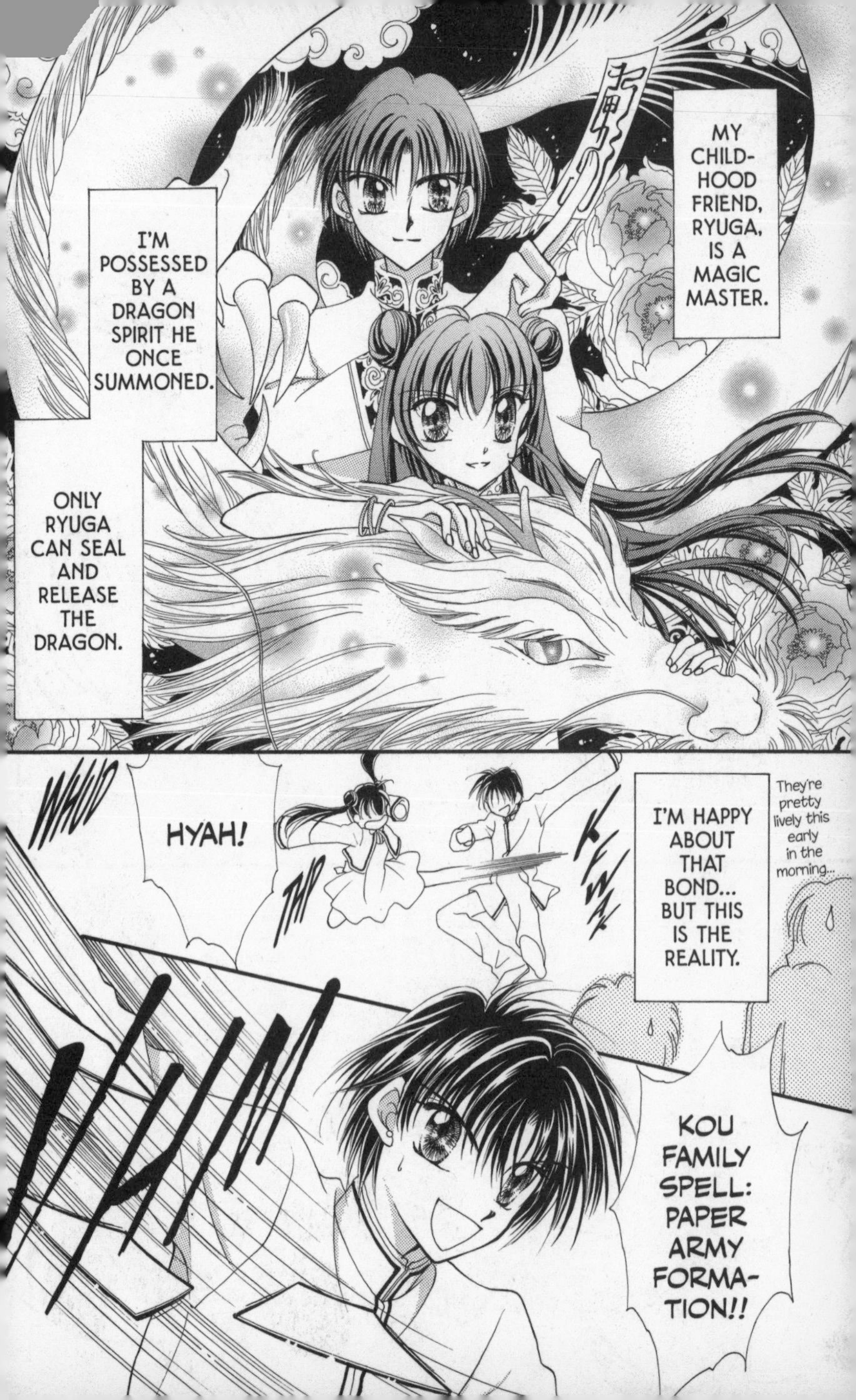
MY CHILDHOOD FRIEND, RYUGA, IS A MAGIC MASTER.
I'M POSSESSED BY A DRAGON SPIRIT HE ONCE SUMMONED.
ONLY RYUGA CAN SEAL AND RELEASE THE DRAGON.
They're pretty lively this early in the morning...
I'M HAPPY ABOUT THAT BOND... BUT THIS IS THE REALITY.
HYAH!
KOU FAMILY SPELL: PAPER ARMY FORMATION!!

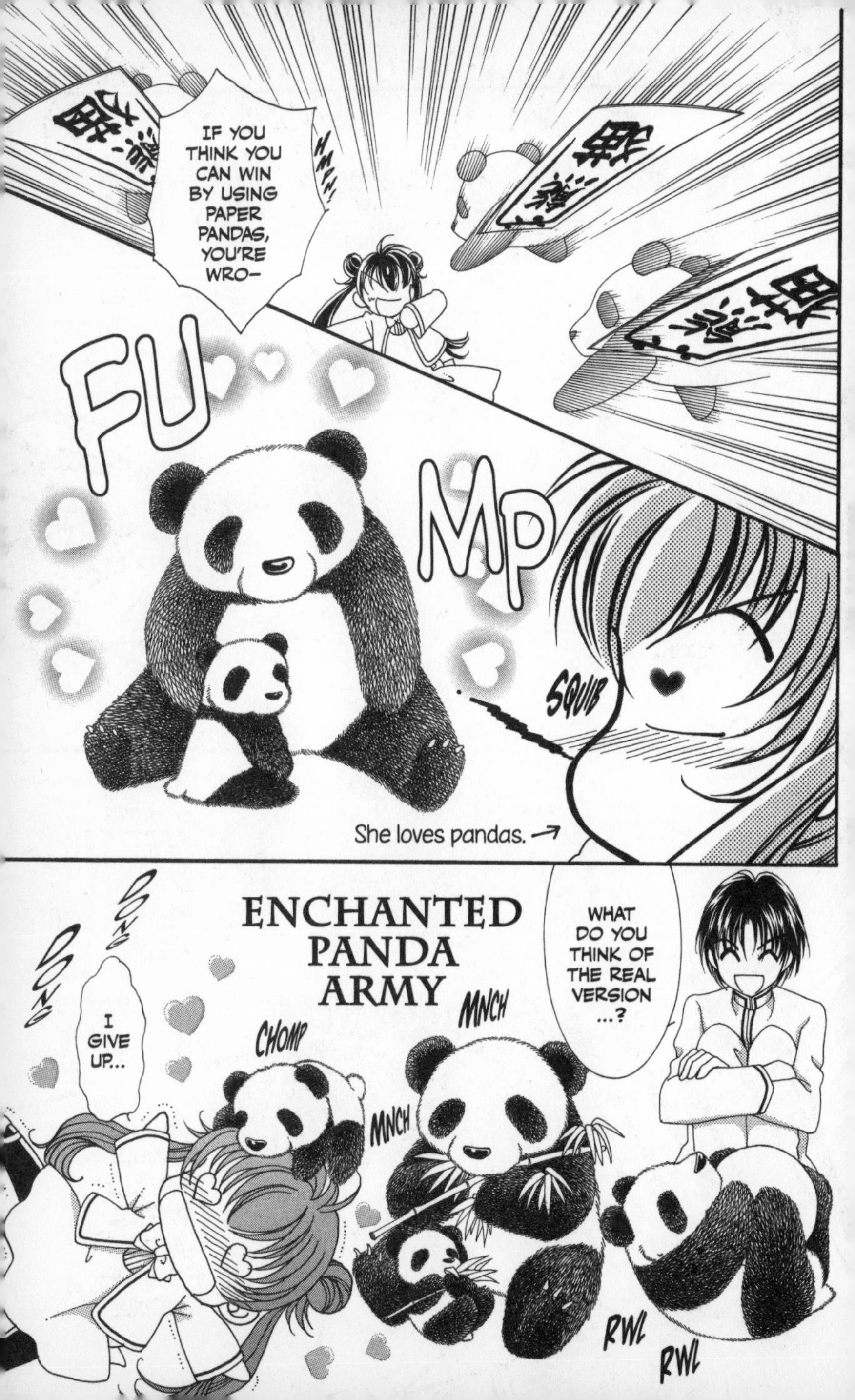
HMPH!
IF YOU THINK YOU CAN WIN BY USING PAPER PANDAS, YOU'RE WRO–
FUMP
SQUIB
She loves pandas.
WHAT DO YOU THINK OF THE REAL VERSION ...?
ENCHANTED PANDA ARMY
MNCH
MNCH
CHOMP
RWL
RWL
I GIVE UP...
GONG
GONG

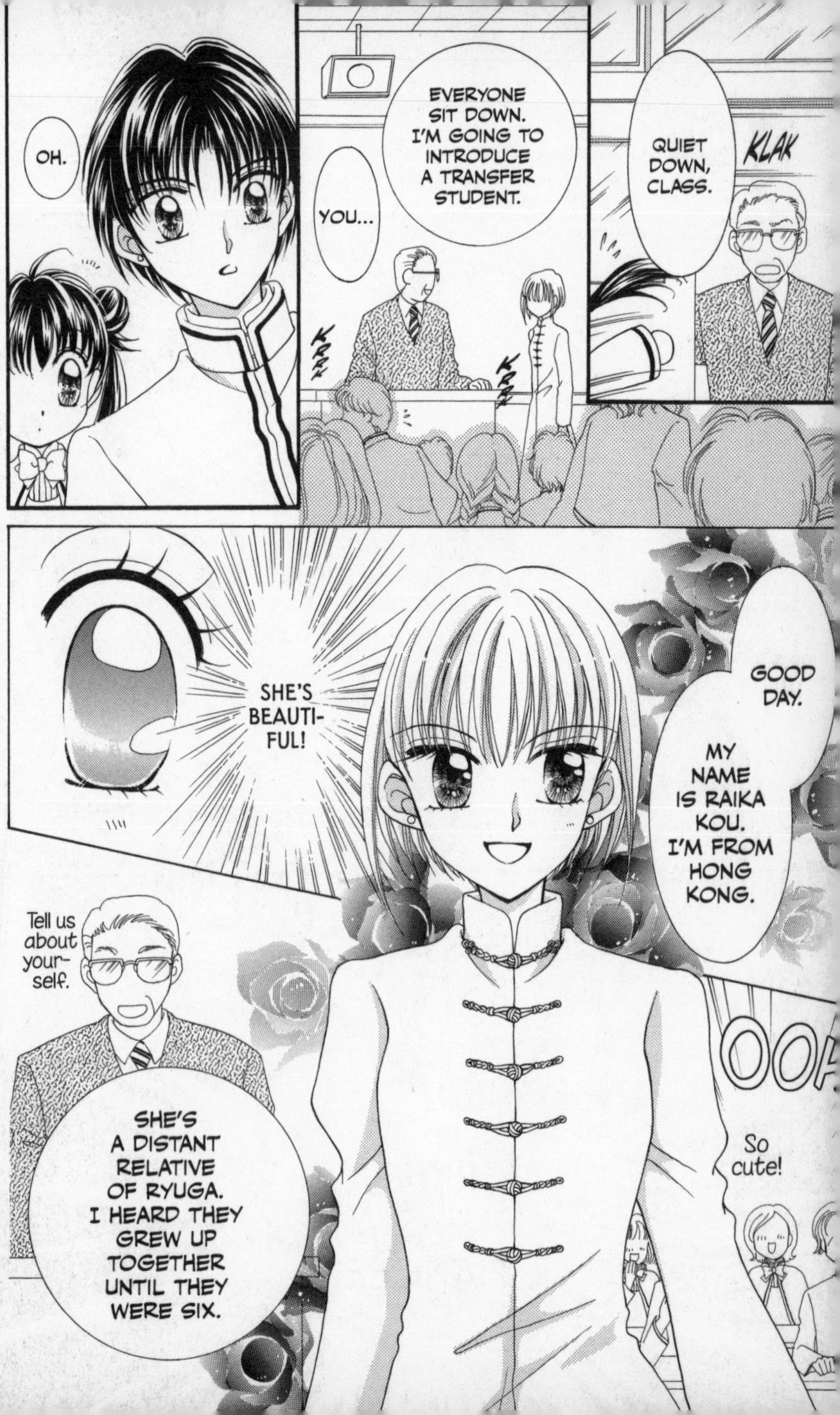
KLAK
QUIET DOWN, CLASS.
EVERYONE SIT DOWN. I'M GOING TO INTRODUCE A TRANSFER STUDENT.
YOU...
OH.
GOOD DAY.
MY NAME IS RAIKA KOU. I'M FROM HONG KONG.
SHE'S BEAUTI-FUL!
OOH
So cute!
Tell us about your-self.
SHE'S A DISTANT RELATIVE OF RYUGA. I HEARD THEY GREW UP TOGETHER UNTIL THEY WERE SIX.

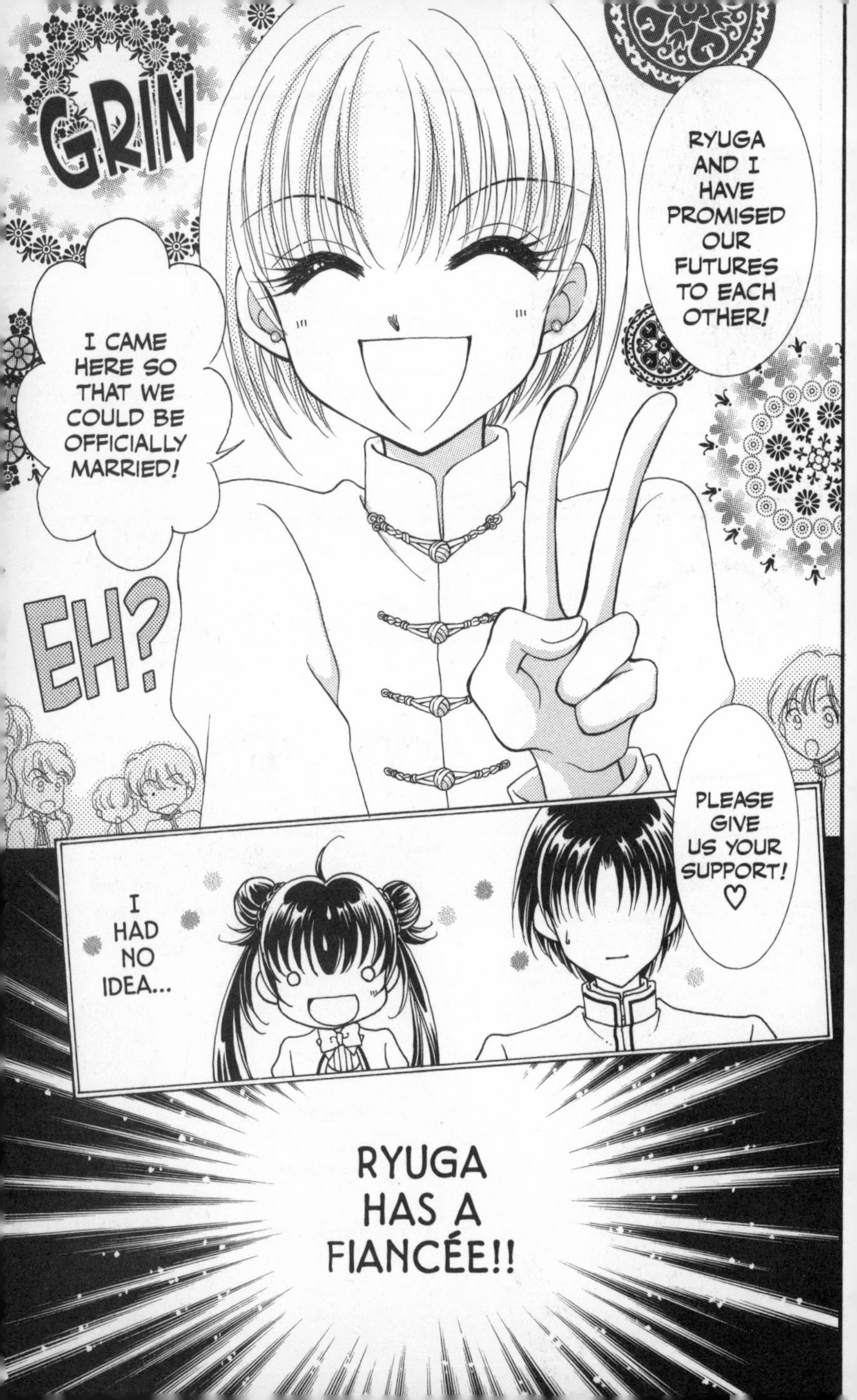
RYUGA AND I HAVE PROMISED OUR FUTURES TO EACH OTHER!
GRIN
I CAME HERE SO THAT WE COULD BE OFFICIALLY MARRIED!
EH?
PLEASE GIVE US YOUR SUPPORT! ♡
I HAD NO IDEA...
RYUGA HAS A FIANCÉE!!

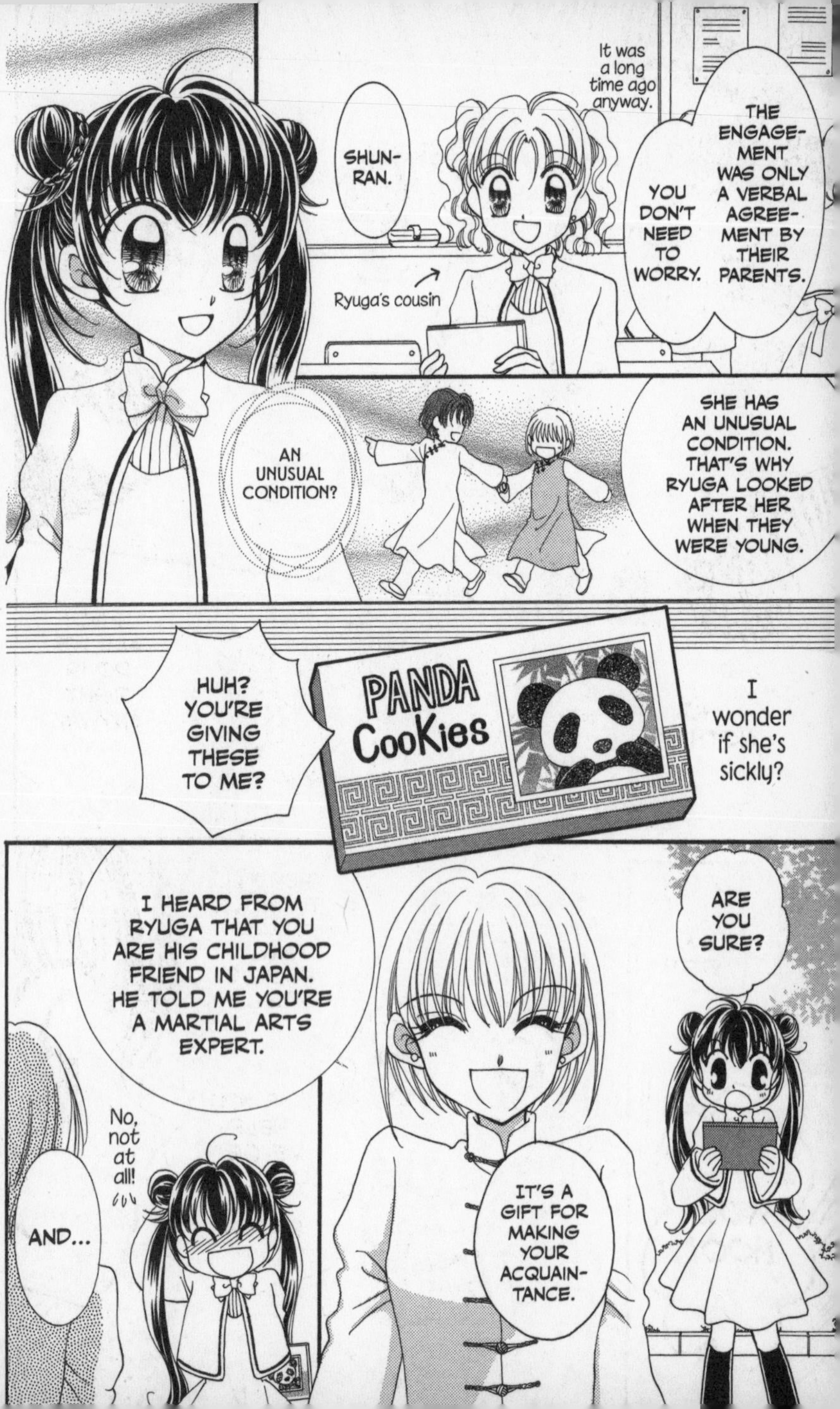
It was a long time ago anyway.
THE ENGAGEMENT WAS ONLY A VERBAL AGREEMENT BY THEIR PARENTS.
YOU DON'T NEED TO WORRY.
Ryuga's cousin
SHUN-RAN.
SHE HAS AN UNUSUAL CONDITION. THAT'S WHY RYUGA LOOKED AFTER HER WHEN THEY WERE YOUNG.
AN UNUSUAL CONDITION?
I wonder if she's sickly?
PANDA CooKies
HUH? YOU'RE GIVING THESE TO ME?
ARE YOU SURE?
IT'S A GIFT FOR MAKING YOUR ACQUAINTANCE.
I HEARD FROM RYUGA THAT YOU ARE HIS CHILDHOOD FRIEND IN JAPAN. HE TOLD ME YOU'RE A MARTIAL ARTS EXPERT.
No, not at all!
AND...

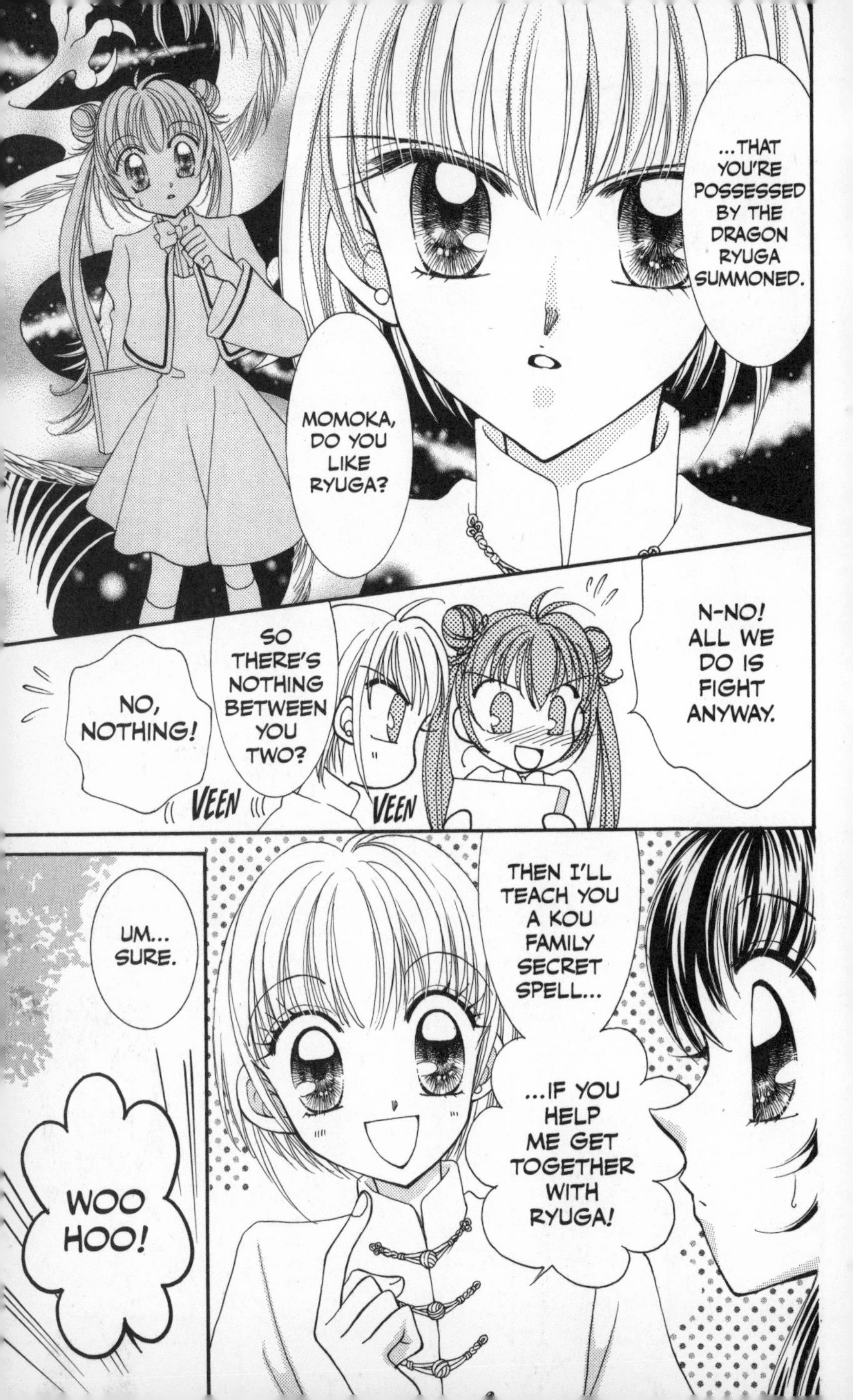
...THAT YOU'RE POSSESSED BY THE DRAGON RYUGA SUMMONED.
MOMOKA, DO YOU LIKE RYUGA?
N-NO! ALL WE DO IS FIGHT ANYWAY.
VEEN
SO THERE'S NOTHING BETWEEN YOU TWO?
VEEN
NO, NOTHING!
THEN I'LL TEACH YOU A KOU FAMILY SECRET SPELL...
...IF YOU HELP ME GET TOGETHER WITH RYUGA!
UM... SURE.
WOO HOO!

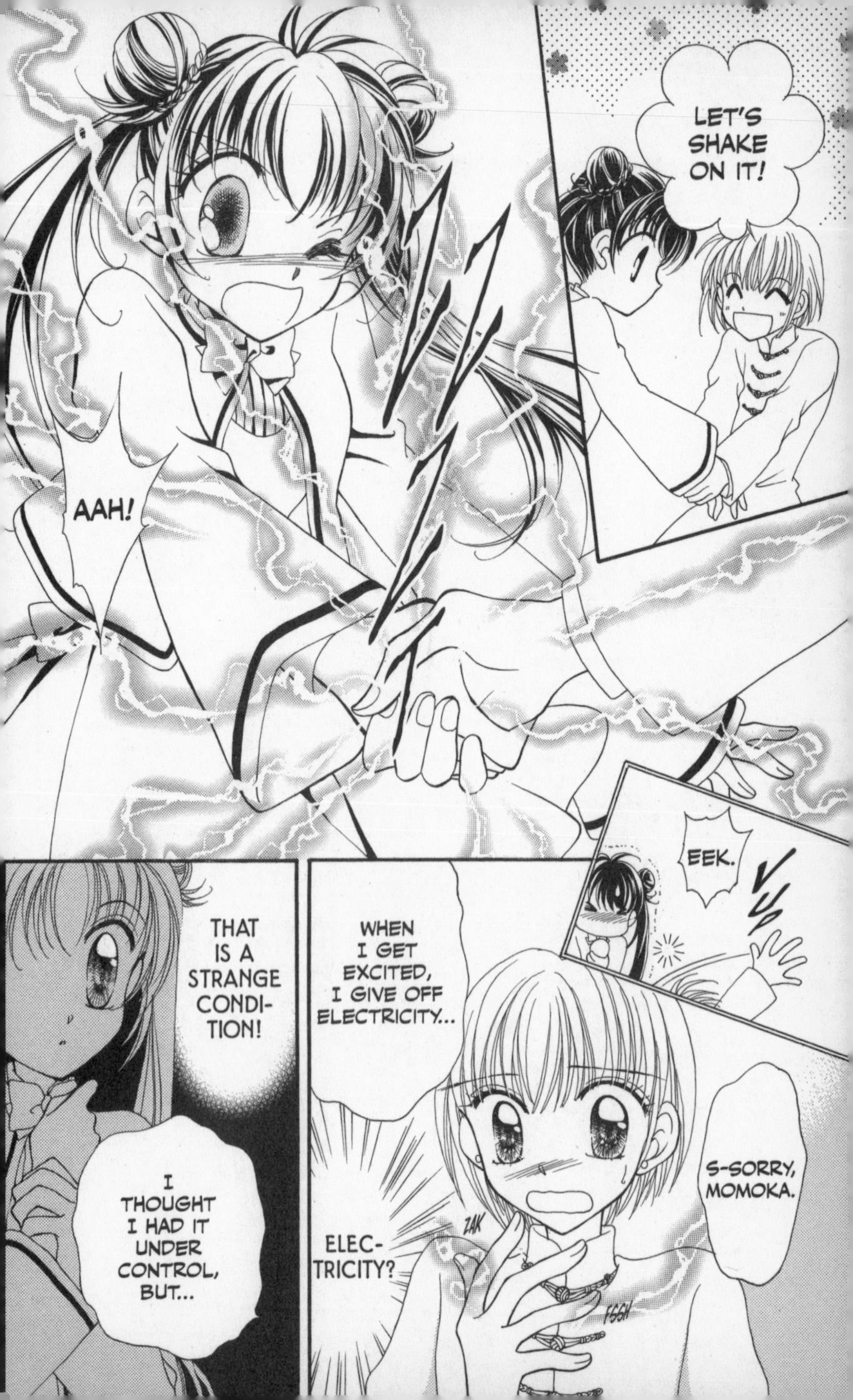
LET'S SHAKE ON IT!
AAH!
EEK.
S-SORRY, MOMOKA.
ELEC-TRICITY?
ZAK
FSSH
WHEN I GET EXCITED, I GIVE OFF ELECTRICITY...
THAT IS A STRANGE CONDI-TION!
I THOUGHT I HAD IT UNDER CONTROL, BUT...

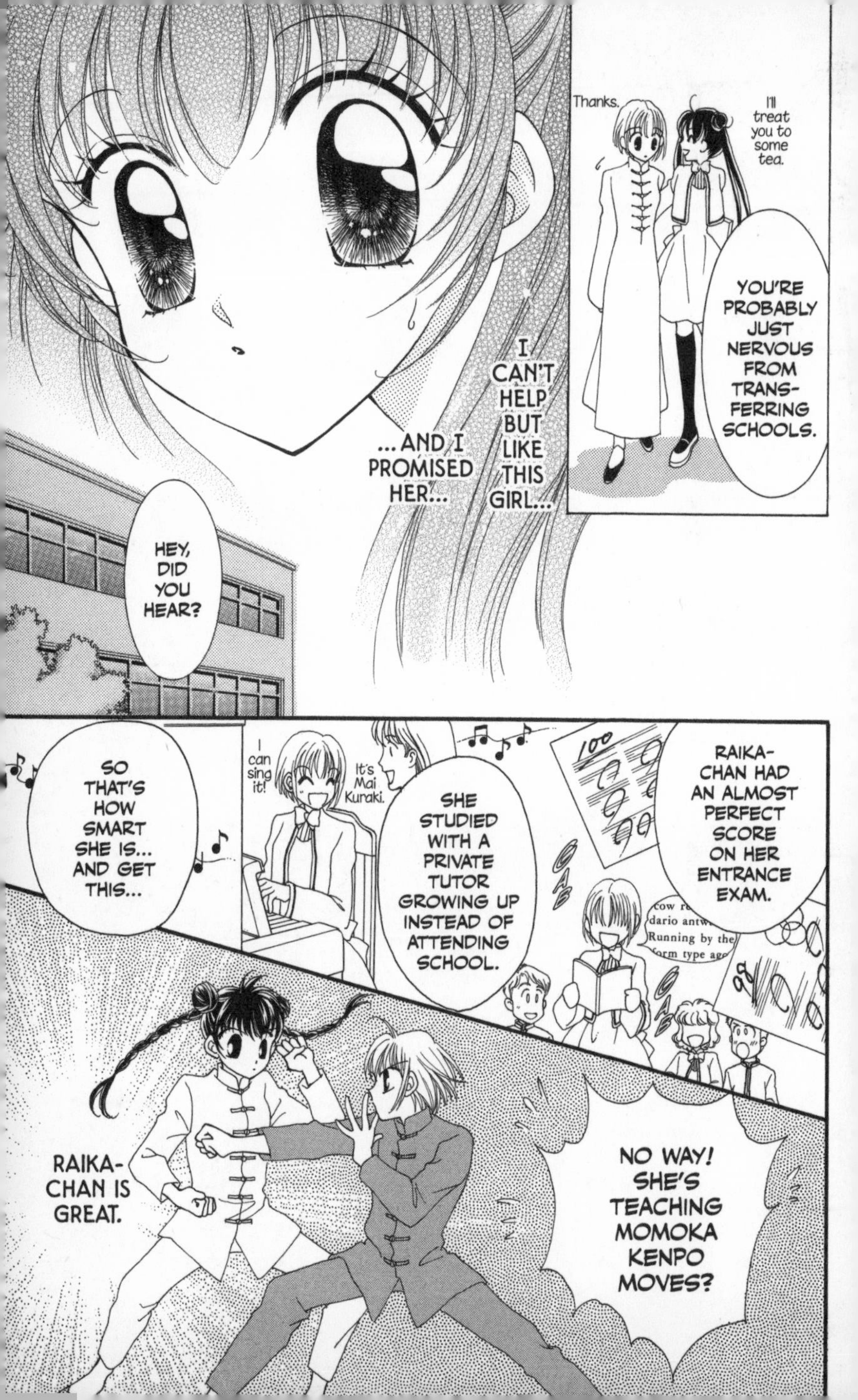
I'll treat you to some tea.
Thanks.
YOU'RE PROBABLY JUST NERVOUS FROM TRANS-FERRING SCHOOLS.
I CAN'T HELP BUT LIKE THIS GIRL...
...AND I PROMISED HER...
HEY, DID YOU HEAR?
100
RAIKA-CHAN HAD AN ALMOST PERFECT SCORE ON HER ENTRANCE EXAM.
SHE STUDIED WITH A PRIVATE TUTOR GROWING UP INSTEAD OF ATTENDING SCHOOL.
It's Mai Kuraki.
I can sing it!
SO THAT'S HOW SMART SHE IS... AND GET THIS...
NO WAY! SHE'S TEACHING MOMOKA KENPO MOVES?
RAIKA-CHAN IS GREAT.

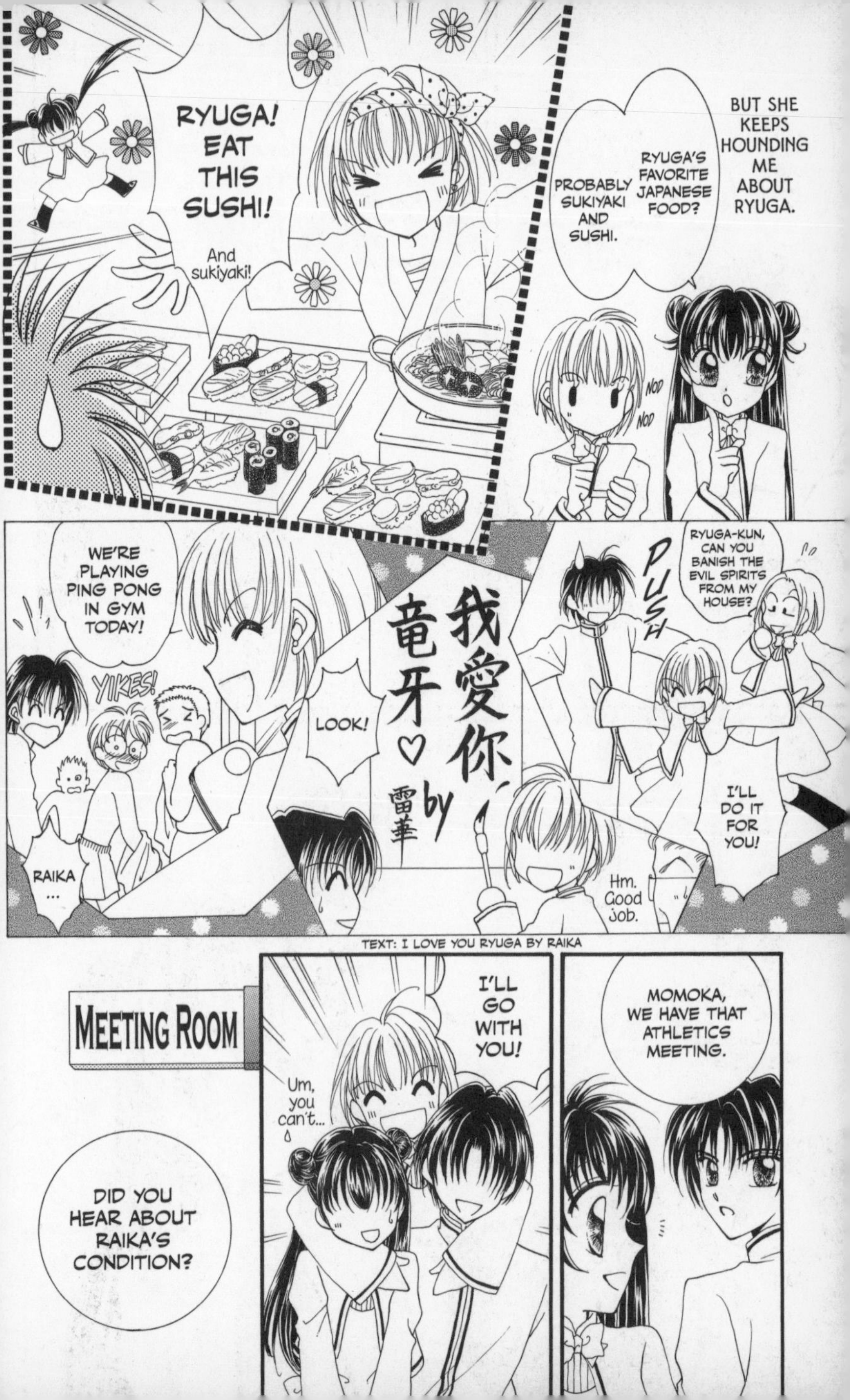
BUT SHE KEEPS HOUNDING ME ABOUT RYUGA.
RYUGA'S FAVORITE JAPANESE FOOD?
PROBABLY SUKIYAKI AND SUSHI.
NOD NOD
RYUGA! EAT THIS SUSHI!
And sukiyaki!
RYUGA-KUN, CAN YOU BANISH THE EVIL SPIRITS FROM MY HOUSE?
PUSH
I'LL DO IT FOR YOU!
Hm. Good job.
我愛你
竜牙♡
by 雷華
LOOK!
WE'RE PLAYING PING PONG IN GYM TODAY!
YIKES!
RAIKA ...
TEXT: I LOVE YOU RYUGA BY RAIKA
MOMOKA, WE HAVE THAT ATHLETICS MEETING.
I'LL GO WITH YOU!
Um, you can't...
MEETING ROOM
DID YOU HEAR ABOUT RAIKA'S CONDITION?

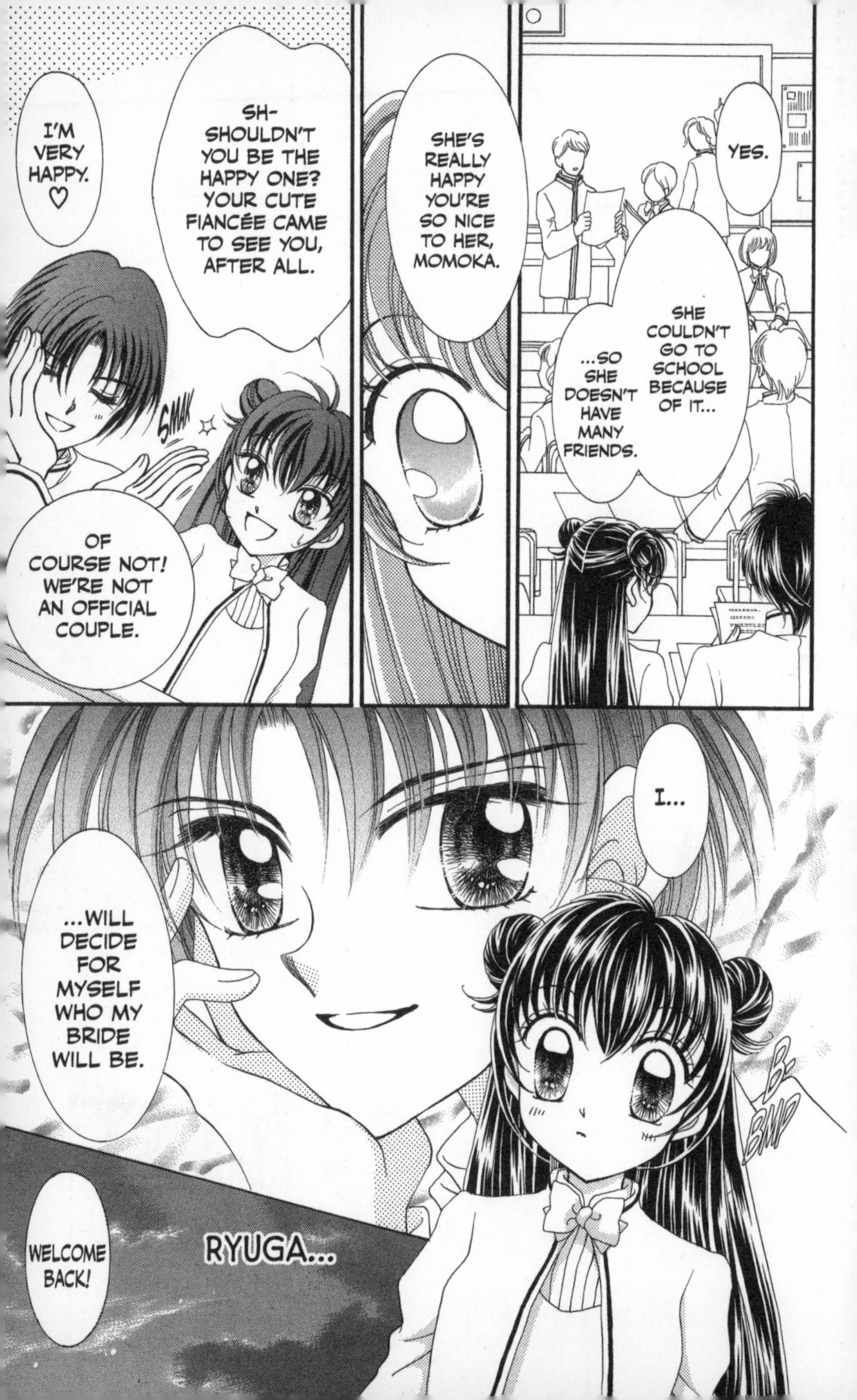
YES.
SHE COULDN'T GO TO SCHOOL BECAUSE OF IT...
...SO SHE DOESN'T HAVE MANY FRIENDS.
SHE'S REALLY HAPPY YOU'RE SO NICE TO HER, MOMOKA.
SH-SHOULDN'T YOU BE THE HAPPY ONE? YOUR CUTE FIANCÉE CAME TO SEE YOU, AFTER ALL.
I'M VERY HAPPY. ♡
SMAK
OF COURSE NOT! WE'RE NOT AN OFFICIAL COUPLE.
I...
...WILL DECIDE FOR MYSELF WHO MY BRIDE WILL BE.
B-BMP
RYUGA...
WELCOME BACK!

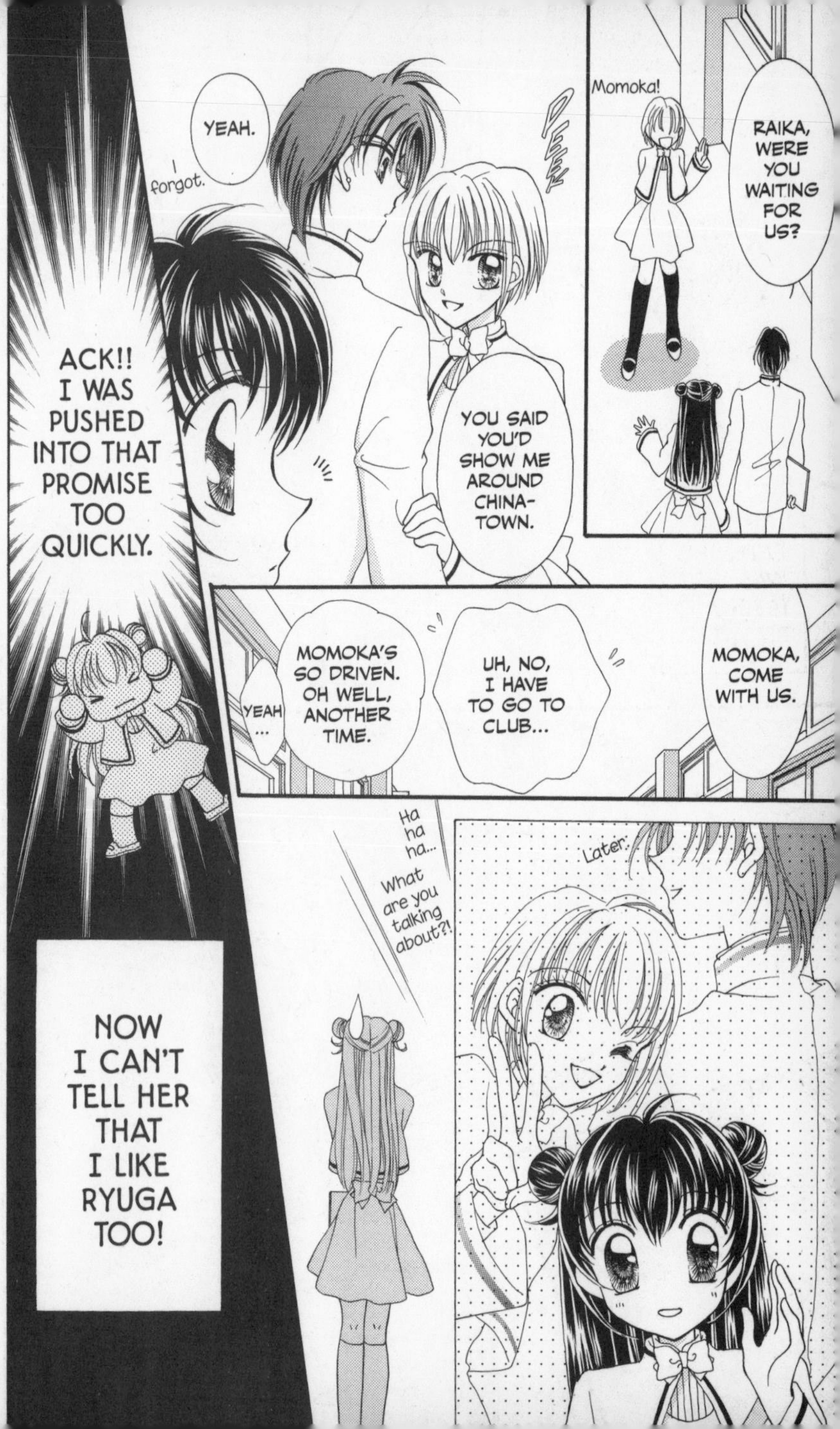
Momoka!
RAIKA, WERE YOU WAITING FOR US?
YOU SAID YOU'D SHOW ME AROUND CHINATOWN.
YEAH.
I forgot.
MOMOKA, COME WITH US.
UH, NO, I HAVE TO GO TO CLUB...
MOMOKA'S SO DRIVEN. OH WELL, ANOTHER TIME.
YEAH...
Later:
Ha ha ha... What are you talking about?!
ACK!! I WAS PUSHED INTO THAT PROMISE TOO QUICKLY.
NOW I CAN'T TELL HER THAT I LIKE RYUGA TOO!

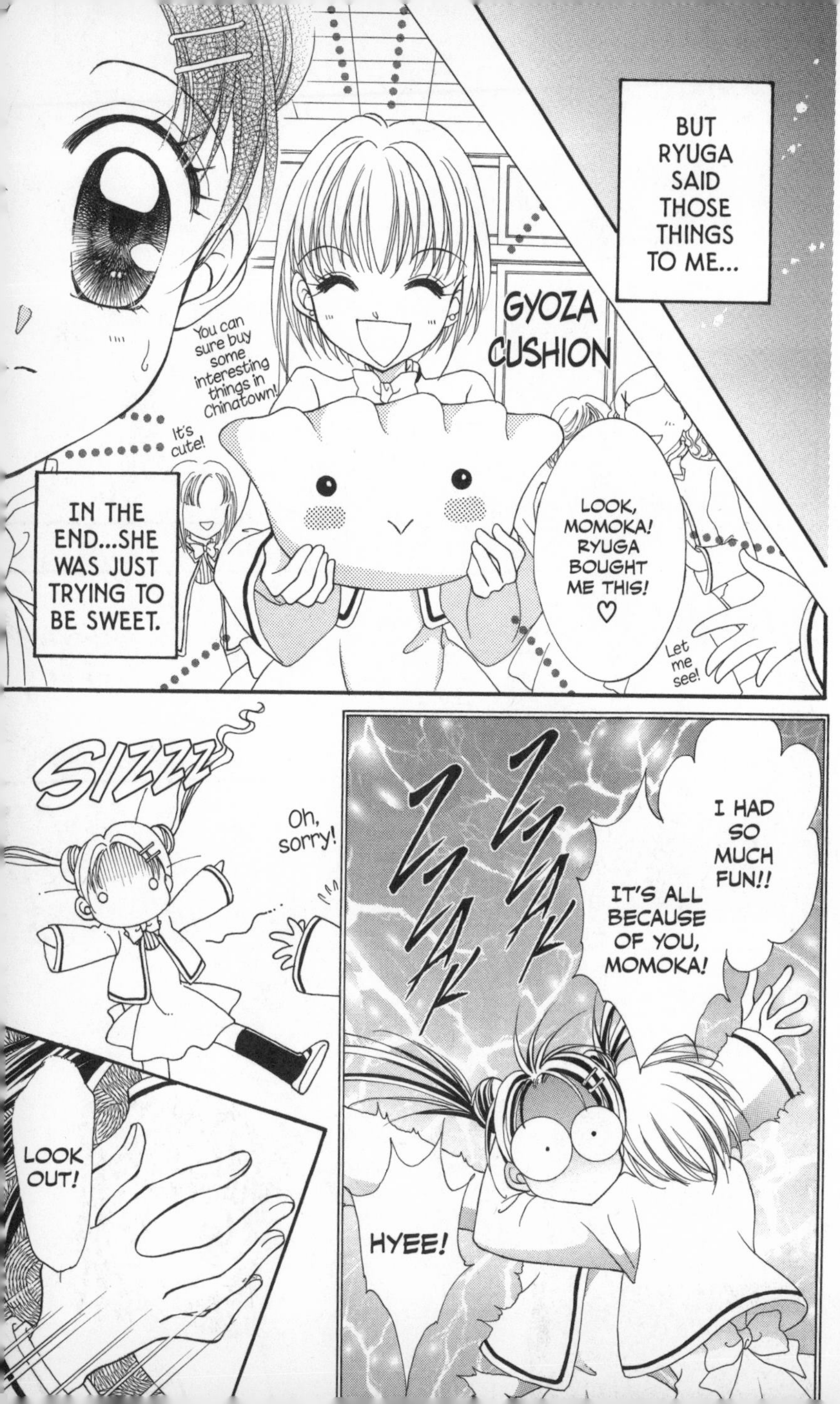
BUT RYUGA SAID THOSE THINGS TO ME...
GYOZA CUSHION
LOOK, MOMOKA! RYUGA BOUGHT ME THIS! ♡
Let me see!
You can sure buy some interesting things in Chinatown!
It's cute!
IN THE END...SHE WAS JUST TRYING TO BE SWEET.
I HAD SO MUCH FUN!!
IT'S ALL BECAUSE OF YOU, MOMOKA!
HYEE!
SIZZZ
Oh, sorry!
LOOK OUT!

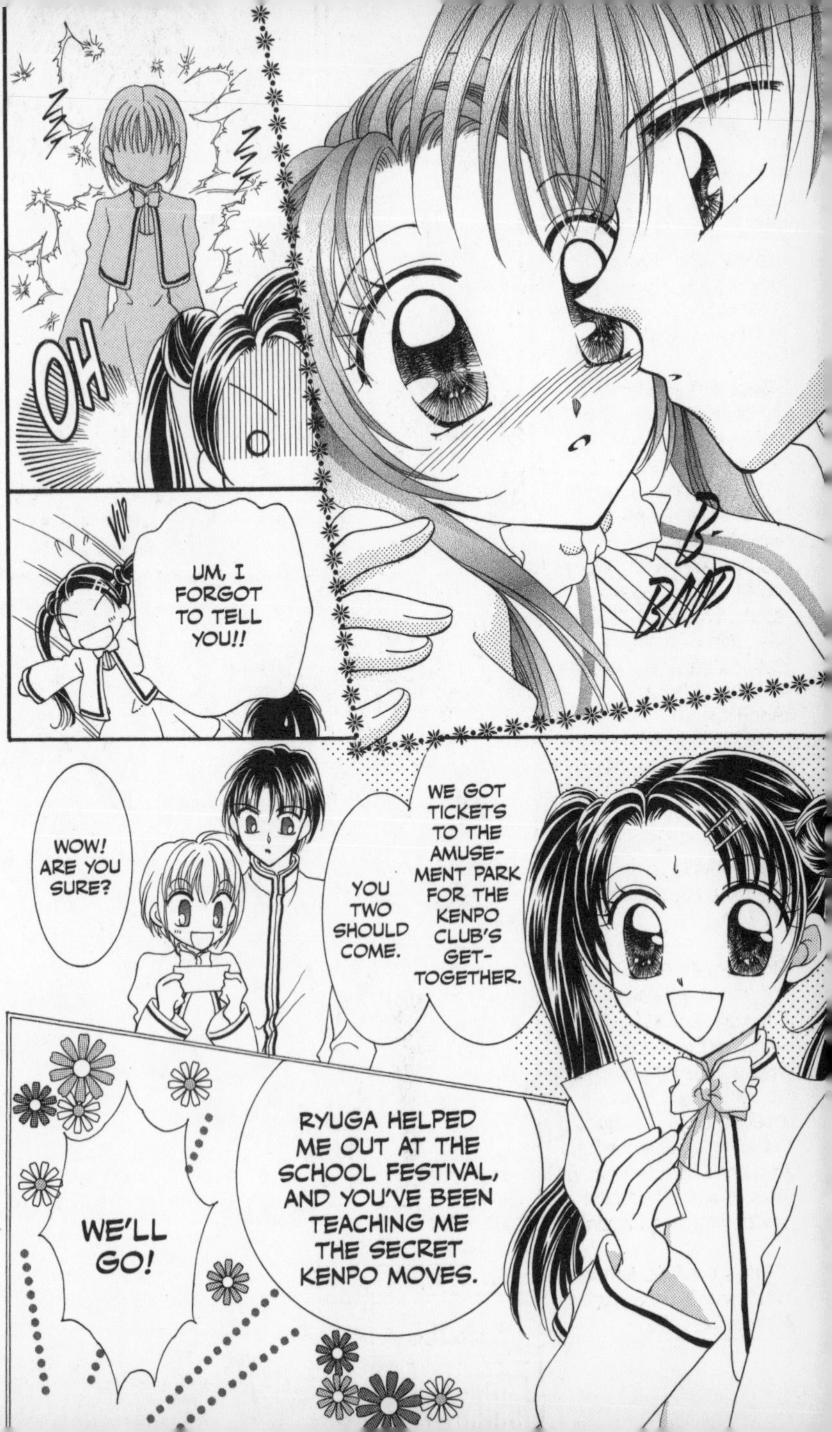
B-
BMP
OH
VUP
UM, I FORGOT TO TELL YOU!!
WE GOT TICKETS TO THE AMUSE-MENT PARK FOR THE KENPO CLUB'S GET-TOGETHER.
YOU TWO SHOULD COME.
WOW! ARE YOU SURE?
RYUGA HELPED ME OUT AT THE SCHOOL FESTIVAL, AND YOU'VE BEEN TEACHING ME THE SECRET KENPO MOVES.
WE'LL GO!

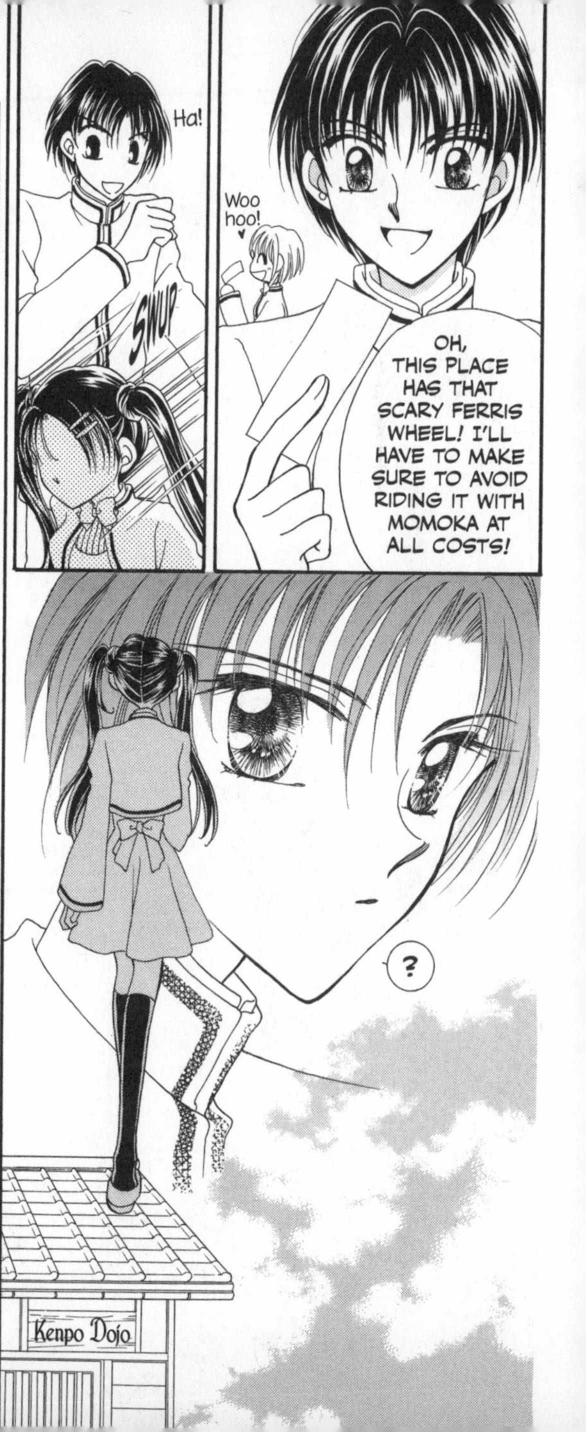
Woo hoo!
OH, THIS PLACE HAS THAT SCARY FERRIS WHEEL! I'LL HAVE TO MAKE SURE TO AVOID RIDING IT WITH MOMOKA AT ALL COSTS!
Ha!
SWUP
?
Kenpo Dojo

5

Here is the chapter in which Raika appears. This story also appeared in *Ribon* magazine.

Raika was supposed to appear in the first volume as Kouryu's younger sister. However, the readers of the magazine wouldn't know who Kouryu was, and I was told I wouldn't get the space to explain the situation. So then I turned her into Ryuga's childhood friend from Hong Kong.

When people heard that Ryuga's fiancée would be showing up, they assumed that she would be a girly-girl—the opposite of Momoka.

But somehow she turned out to be a tomboy. The way she hangs around Momoka also seems pretty boyish! (laugh) She's so intense that I thought readers would hate her, but she's pretty popular. Also, it was decided that she'd remain in Japan!

It looks like the number of characters keeps on increasing...

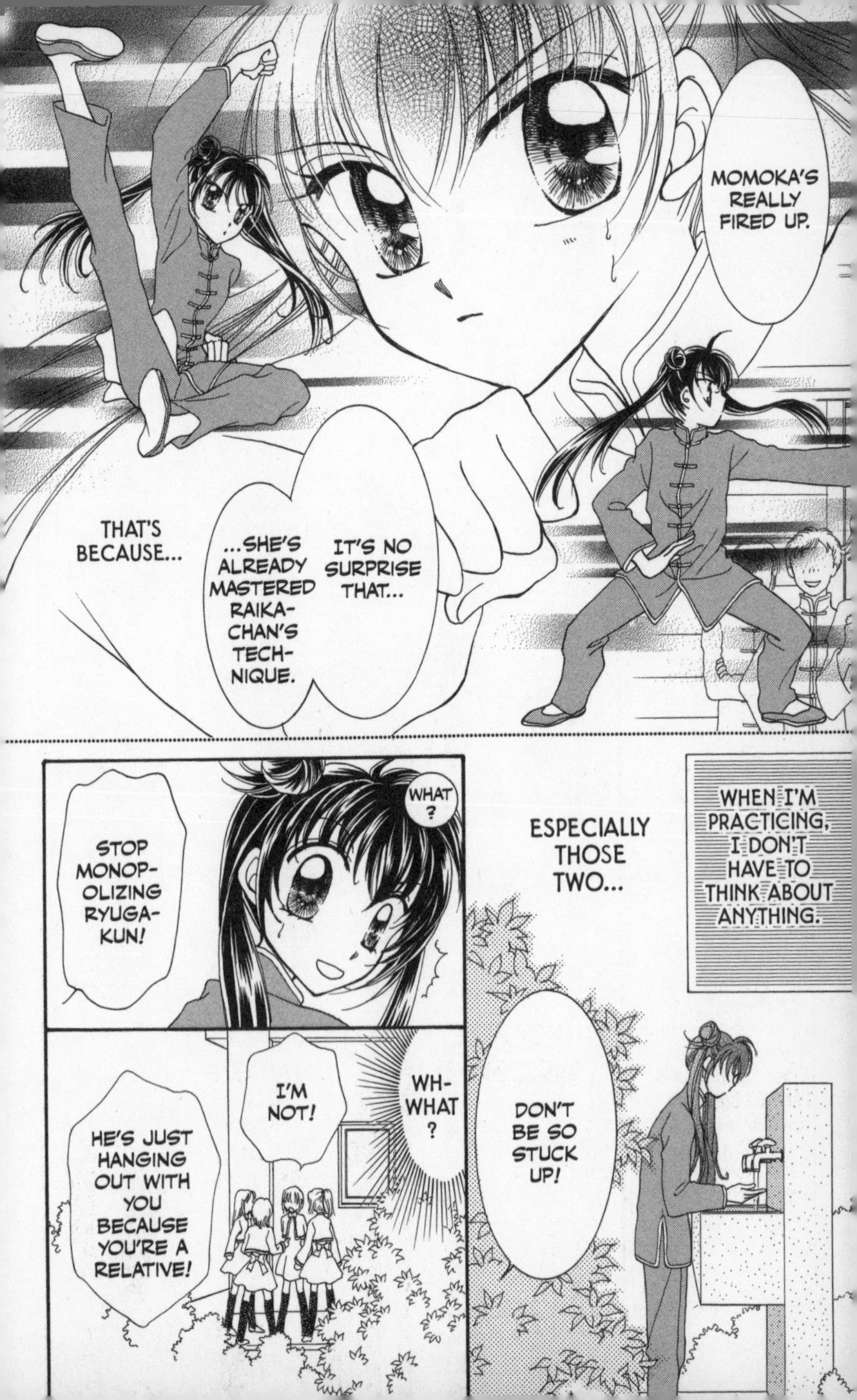
MOMOKA'S REALLY FIRED UP.
IT'S NO SURPRISE THAT...
...SHE'S ALREADY MASTERED RAIKA-CHAN'S TECH-NIQUE.
THAT'S BECAUSE...
WHEN I'M PRACTICING, I DON'T HAVE TO THINK ABOUT ANYTHING.
ESPECIALLY THOSE TWO...
DON'T BE SO STUCK UP!
WHAT?
STOP MONOP-OLIZING RYUGA-KUN!
WH-WHAT?
I'M NOT!
HE'S JUST HANGING OUT WITH YOU BECAUSE YOU'RE A RELATIVE!

6

Sometimes I get letters from people saying that their dad got mad at them after seeing a kiss scene. The dads say, "You shouldn't be reading that kind of comic book!" For some reason, kissing upsets dads a lot. Moms usually write to say they read the manga along with their daughters. Maybe it's because dads are usually more stubborn? I once had a similar experience myself. I was reading a manga with a kiss scene in it, and I got lectured! (laugh)

Well, just try to look at it from your dad's perspective; he's just worried about you. Try to keep it on the down low! (laugh)
Then again, maybe I should take the dads' advice and make *St.♥ Dragon Girl* a manga the whole family can enjoy? Just kidding.

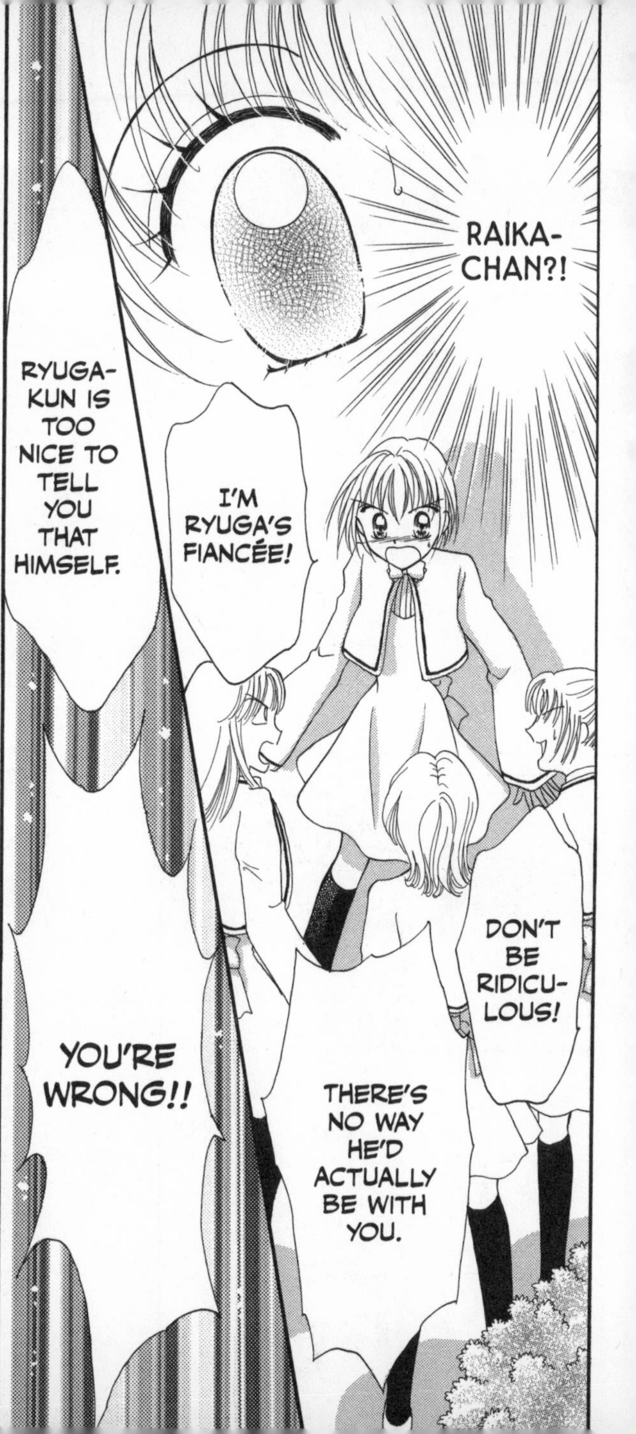
RAIKA-CHAN?!
I'M RYUGA'S FIANCÉE!
RYUGA-KUN IS TOO NICE TO TELL YOU THAT HIMSELF.
DON'T BE RIDICULOUS!
THERE'S NO WAY HE'D ACTUALLY BE WITH YOU.
YOU'RE WRONG!!

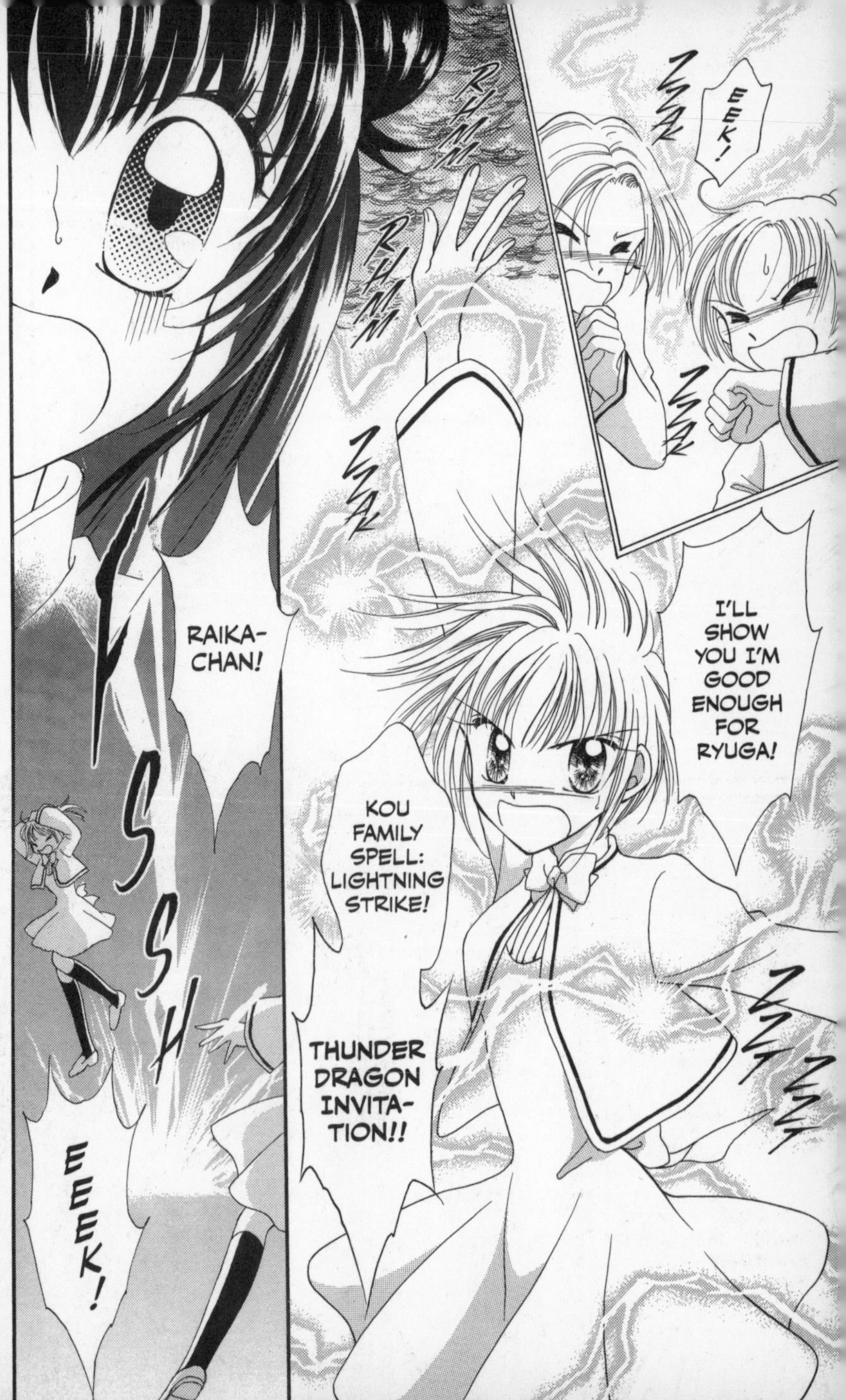
ZZZAK
EEK!
ZZZAK
RHMMM
RHMMM
ZZZAK
I'LL SHOW YOU I'M GOOD ENOUGH FOR RYUGA!
KOU FAMILY SPELL: LIGHTNING STRIKE!
THUNDER DRAGON INVITA-TION!!
ZZZZT
RAIKA-CHAN!
FSSSH
EEEK!

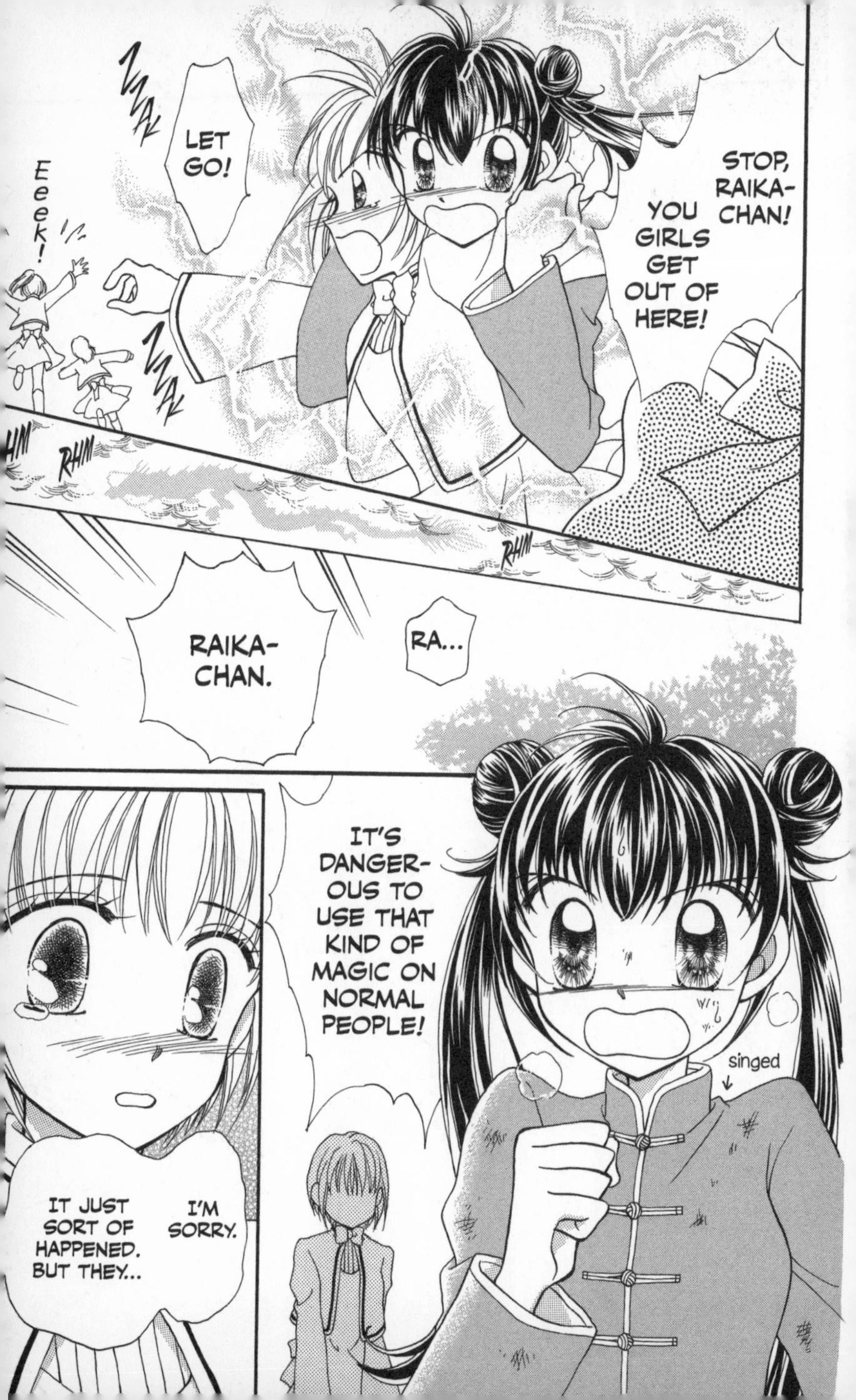
STOP, RAIKA-CHAN!
YOU GIRLS GET OUT OF HERE!
LET GO!
Eeeek!
RHM
RHM
RHM
RA...
RAIKA-CHAN.
IT'S DANGEROUS TO USE THAT KIND OF MAGIC ON NORMAL PEOPLE!
singed
I'M SORRY.
IT JUST SORT OF HAPPENED. BUT THEY...

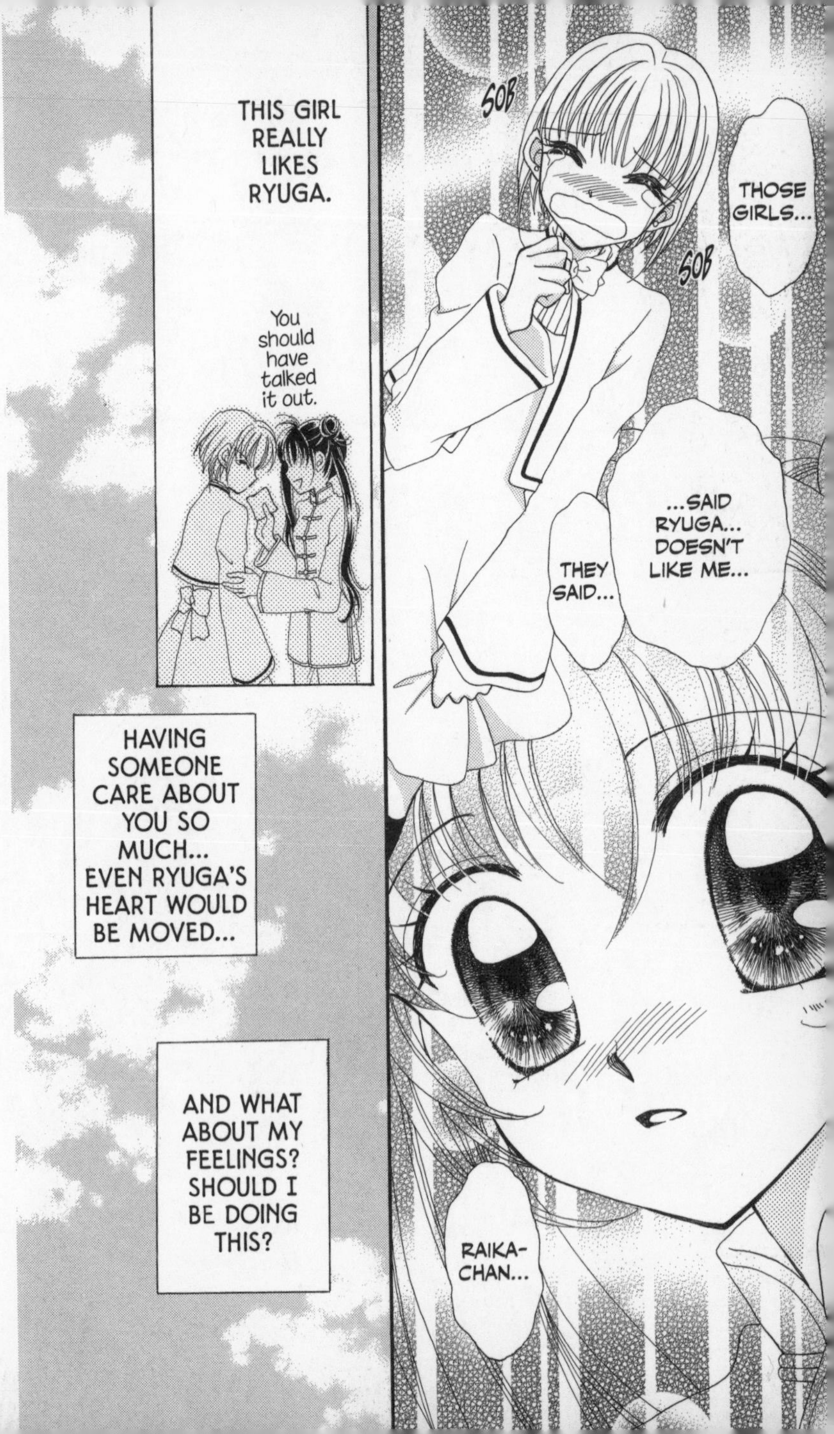
SOB
THOSE GIRLS...
SOB
...SAID RYUGA... DOESN'T LIKE ME...
THEY SAID...
RAIKA-CHAN...
THIS GIRL REALLY LIKES RYUGA.
You should have talked it out.
HAVING SOMEONE CARE ABOUT YOU SO MUCH... EVEN RYUGA'S HEART WOULD BE MOVED...
AND WHAT ABOUT MY FEELINGS? SHOULD I BE DOING THIS?

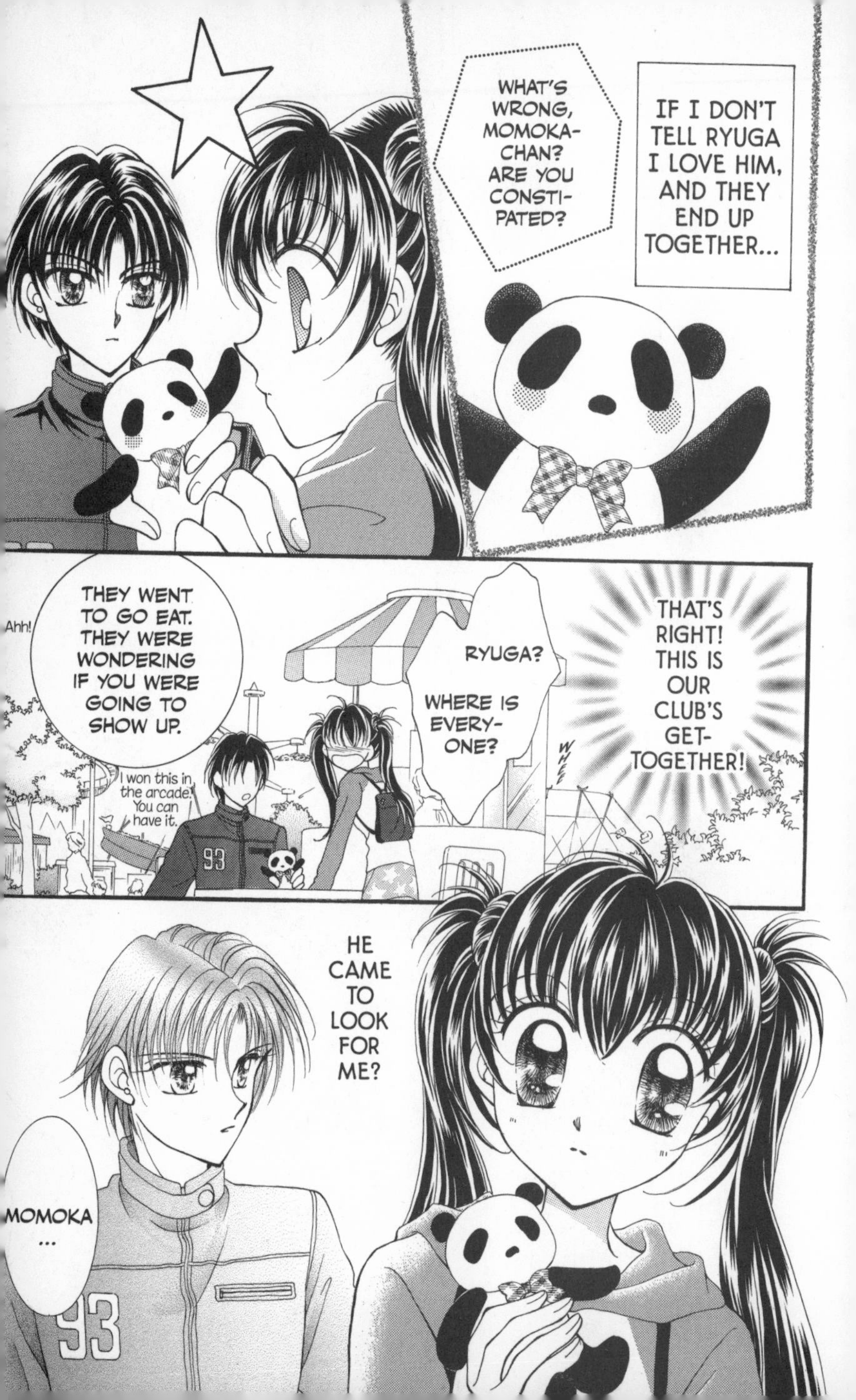
IF I DON'T TELL RYUGA I LOVE HIM, AND THEY END UP TOGETHER...
WHAT'S WRONG, MOMOKA-CHAN? ARE YOU CONSTI-PATED?
THAT'S RIGHT! THIS IS OUR CLUB'S GET-TOGETHER!
WHEE
RYUGA?
WHERE IS EVERY-ONE?
I won this in the arcade. You can have it.
THEY WENT TO GO EAT. THEY WERE WONDERING IF YOU WERE GOING TO SHOW UP.
Ahh!
HE CAME TO LOOK FOR ME?
MOMOKA ...

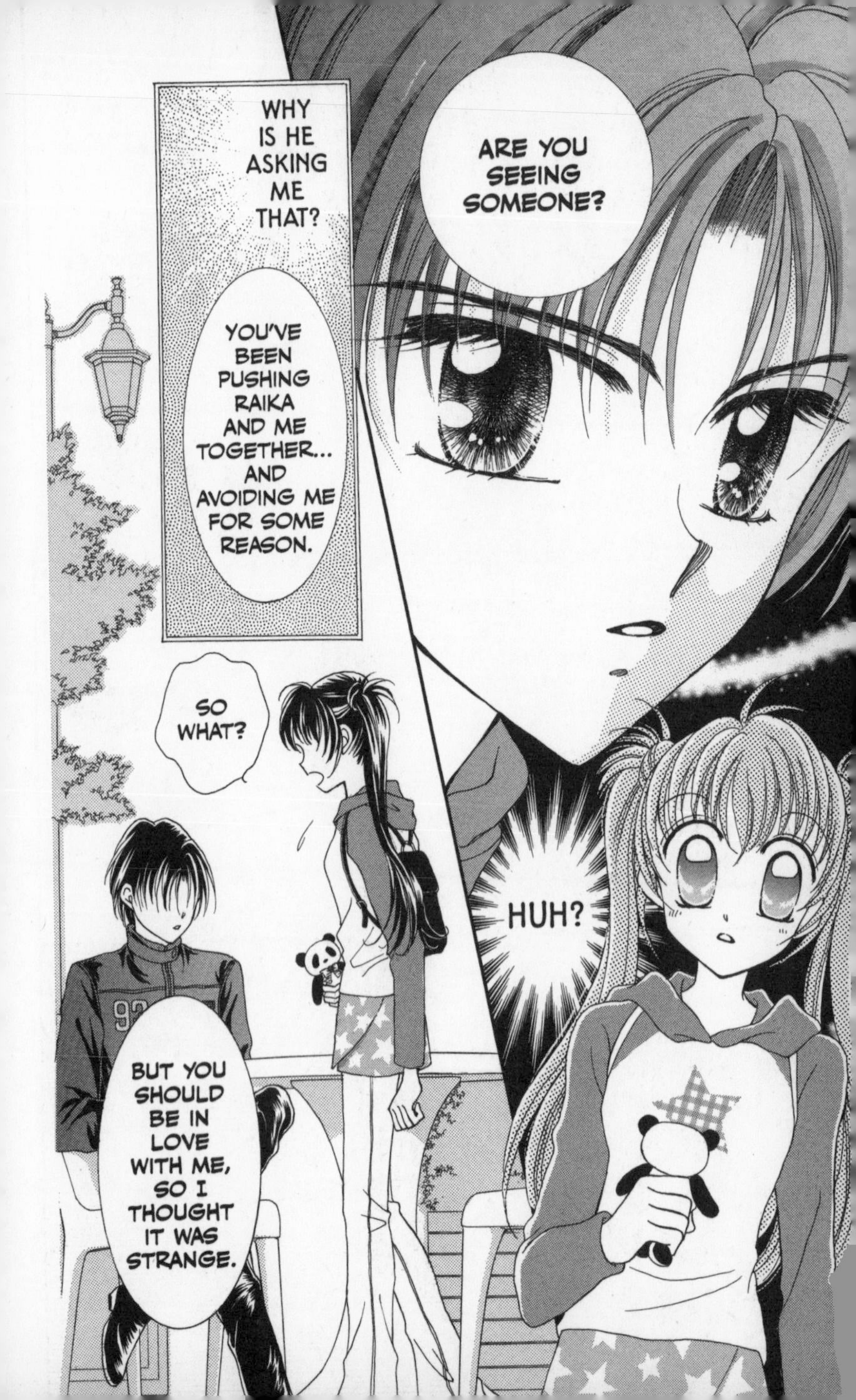

ARE YOU SEEING SOMEONE?
HUH?
WHY IS HE ASKING ME THAT?
YOU'VE BEEN PUSHING RAIKA AND ME TOGETHER... AND AVOIDING ME FOR SOME REASON.
SO WHAT?
BUT YOU SHOULD BE IN LOVE WITH ME, SO I THOUGHT IT WAS STRANGE.

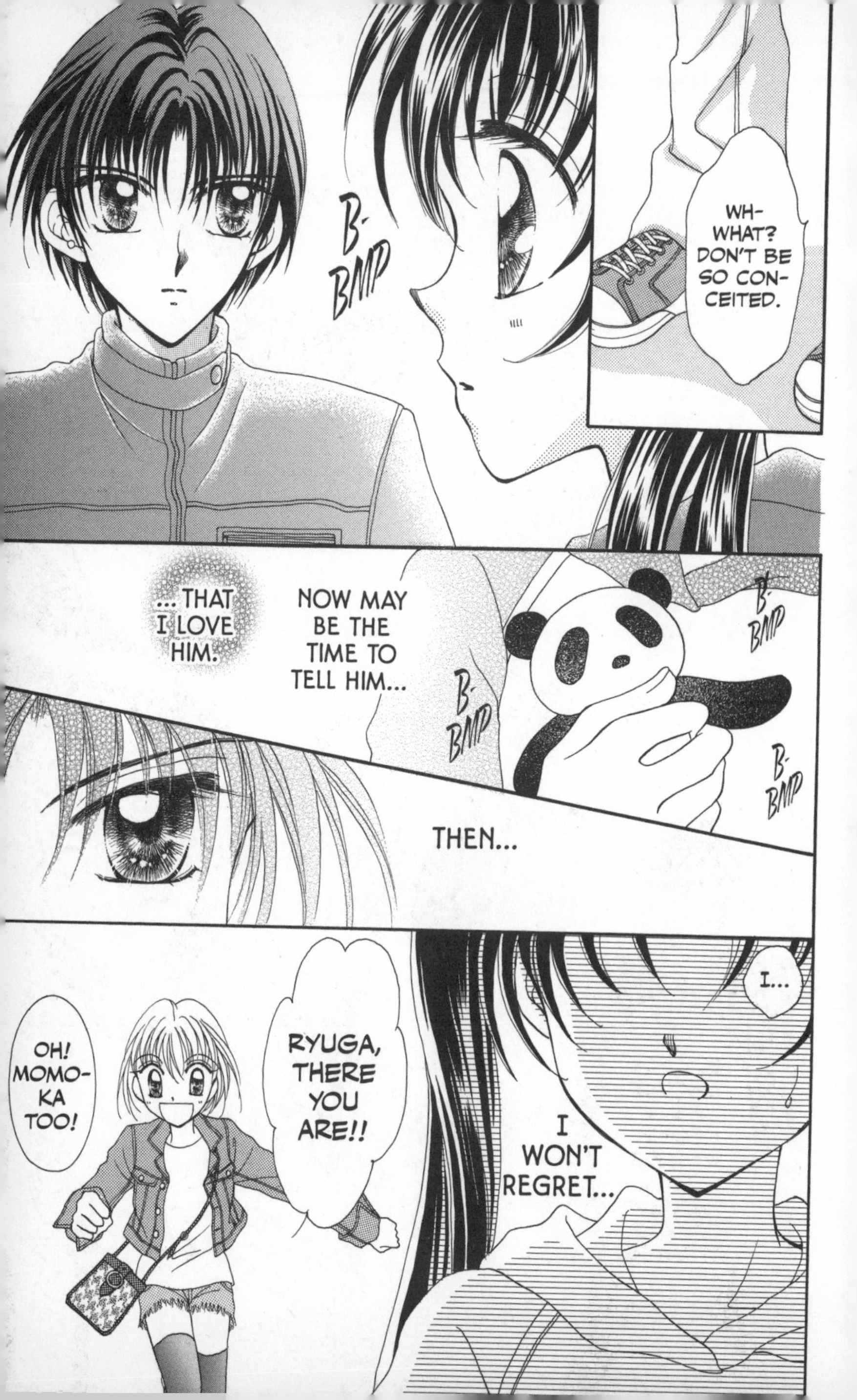
WH-WHAT? DON'T BE SO CONCEITED.
B-BMP
B-BMP
NOW MAY BE THE TIME TO TELL HIM...
... THAT I LOVE HIM.
B-BMP
B-BMP
THEN...
I...
I WON'T REGRET...
RYUGA, THERE YOU ARE!!
OH! MOMOKA TOO!

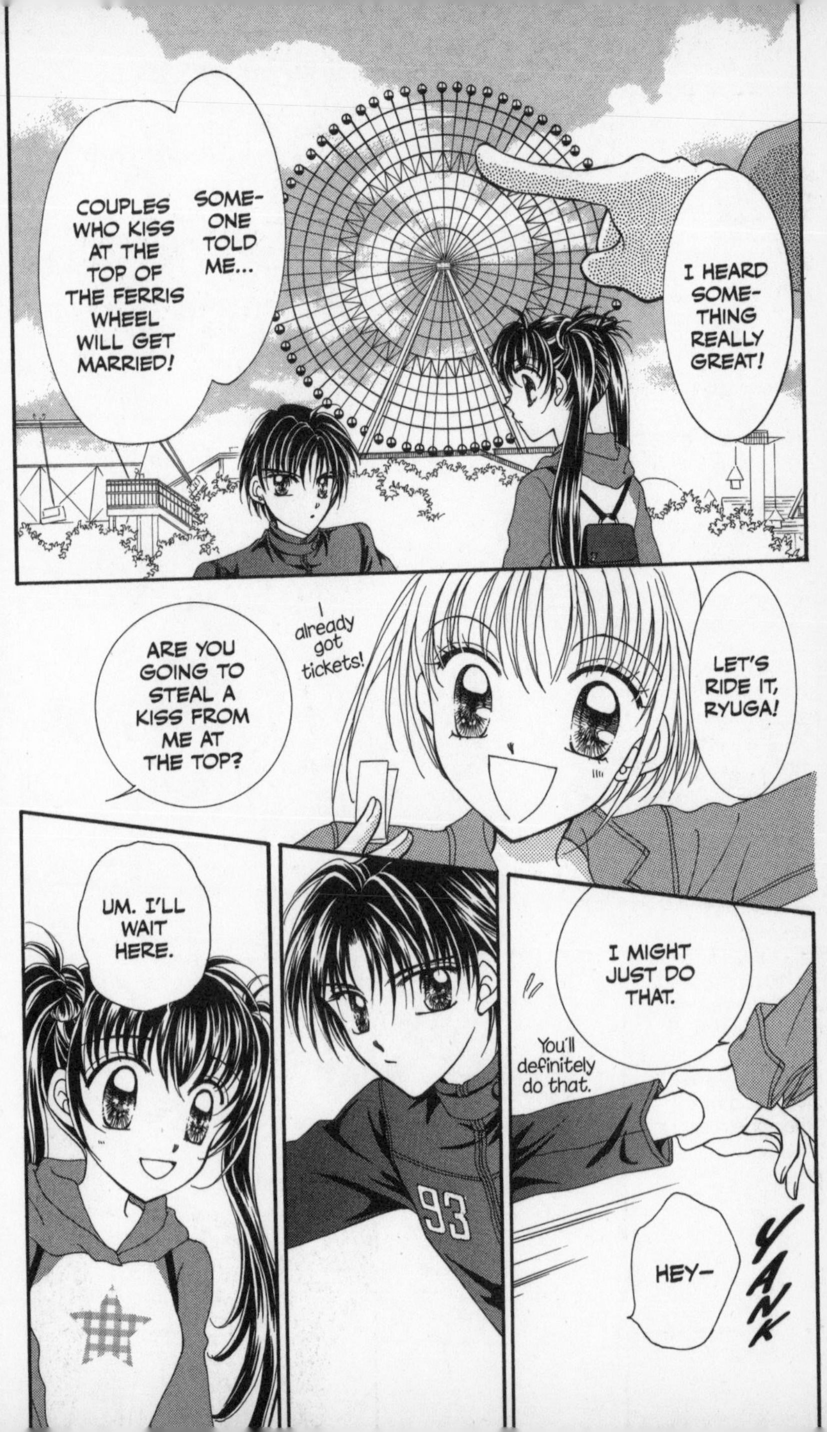
I HEARD SOMETHING REALLY GREAT!
SOMEONE TOLD ME...
COUPLES WHO KISS AT THE TOP OF THE FERRIS WHEEL WILL GET MARRIED!
LET'S RIDE IT, RYUGA!
I already got tickets!
ARE YOU GOING TO STEAL A KISS FROM ME AT THE TOP?
I MIGHT JUST DO THAT.
You'll definitely do that.
HEY—
YANK
UM. I'LL WAIT HERE.

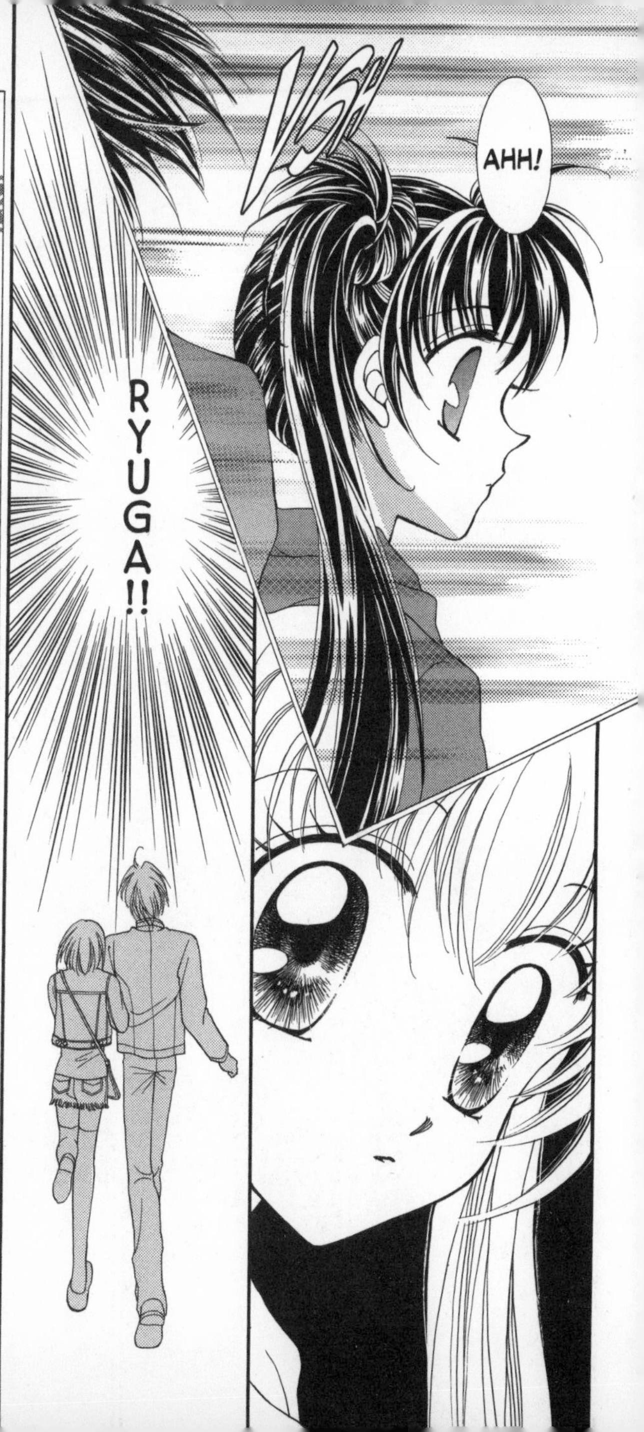
AHH!
RYUGA!!

7

This is the last column for this volume.

I'll write about the bonus story in this volume: "Far East Working Girl."

It appeared in the special Winter 2000 issue.

For the first time in a long time, I worked on it myself. It was only twelve pages, so I thought I'd be fine without having to ask assistants to help...

However, I drew and drew and inked and inked, and it never seemed to end! In the middle of it all, I considered asking someone to help me, but I'm stubborn, so I finished it myself. It holds a lot of memories for me.

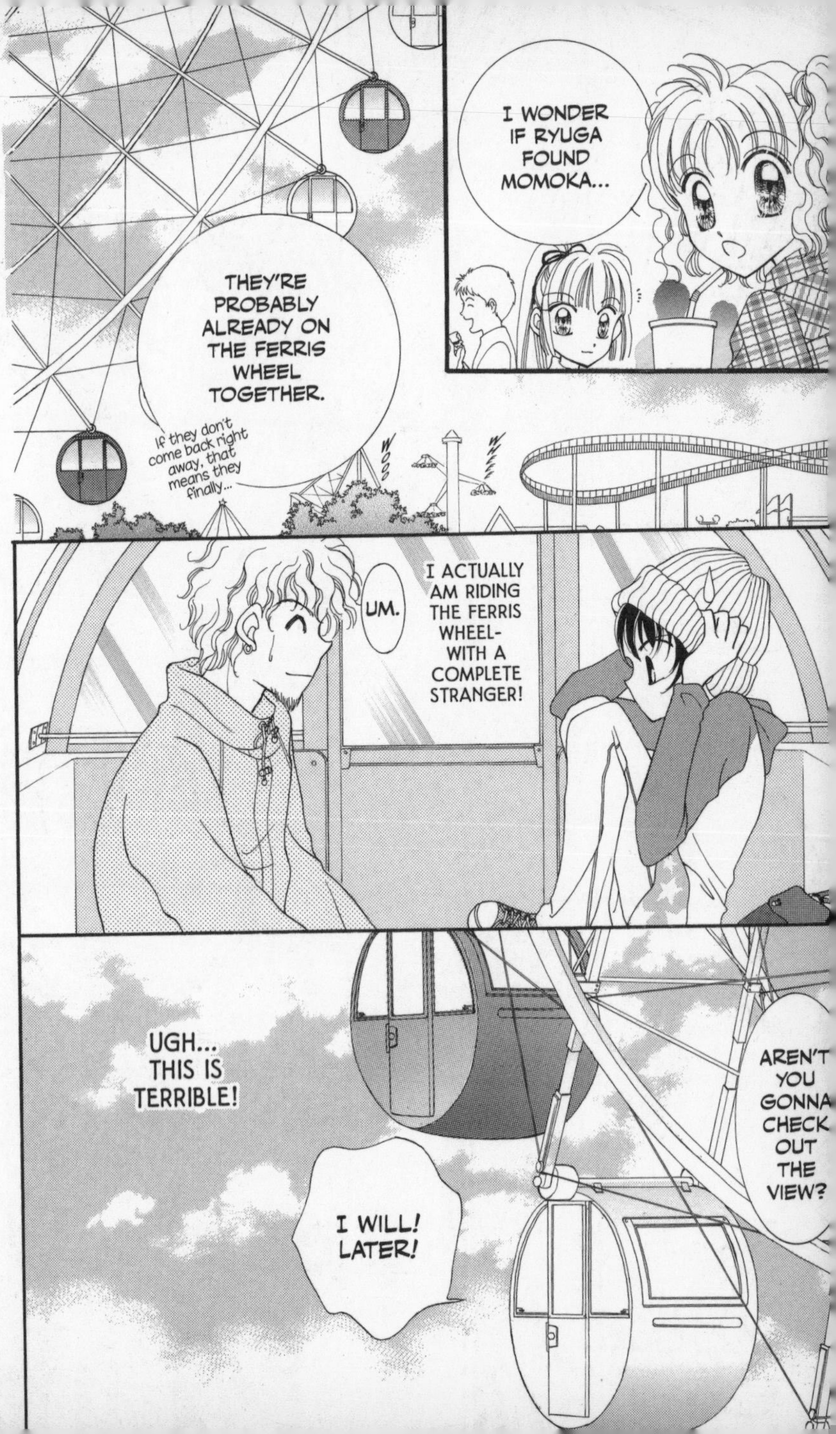
I WONDER IF RYUGA FOUND MOMOKA...
THEY'RE PROBABLY ALREADY ON THE FERRIS WHEEL TOGETHER.
If they don't come back right away, that means they finally...
WHEEE
WOOO
I ACTUALLY AM RIDING THE FERRIS WHEEL- WITH A COMPLETE STRANGER!
UM.
AREN'T YOU GONNA CHECK OUT THE VIEW?
UGH... THIS IS TERRIBLE!
I WILL! LATER!

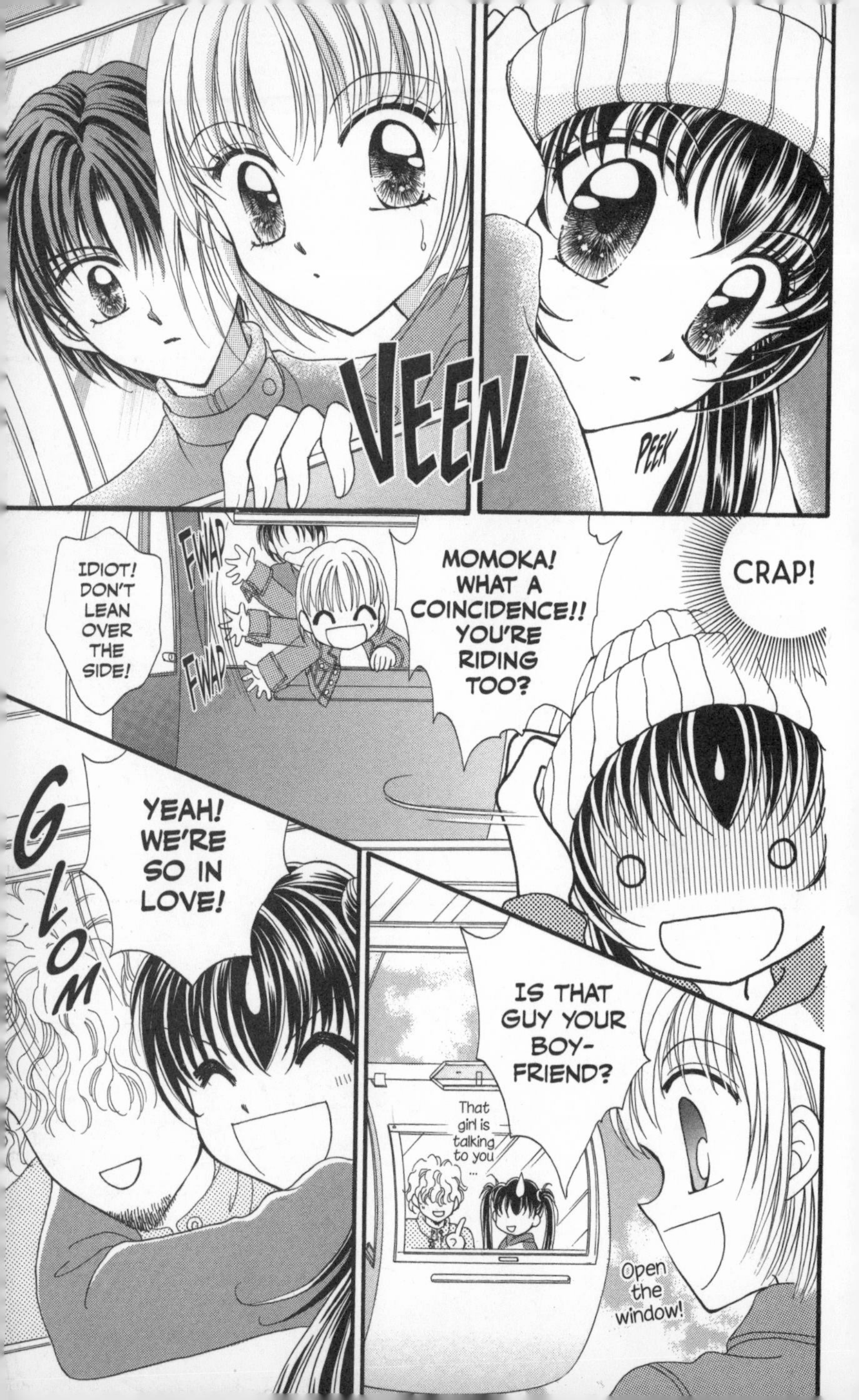
PEEK
VEEN
CRAP!
MOMOKA! WHAT A COINCIDENCE!! YOU'RE RIDING TOO?
FWAP
FWAP
IDIOT! DON'T LEAN OVER THE SIDE!
IS THAT GUY YOUR BOY-FRIEND?
That girl is talking to you ...
Open the window!
YEAH! WE'RE SO IN LOVE!
GLOM

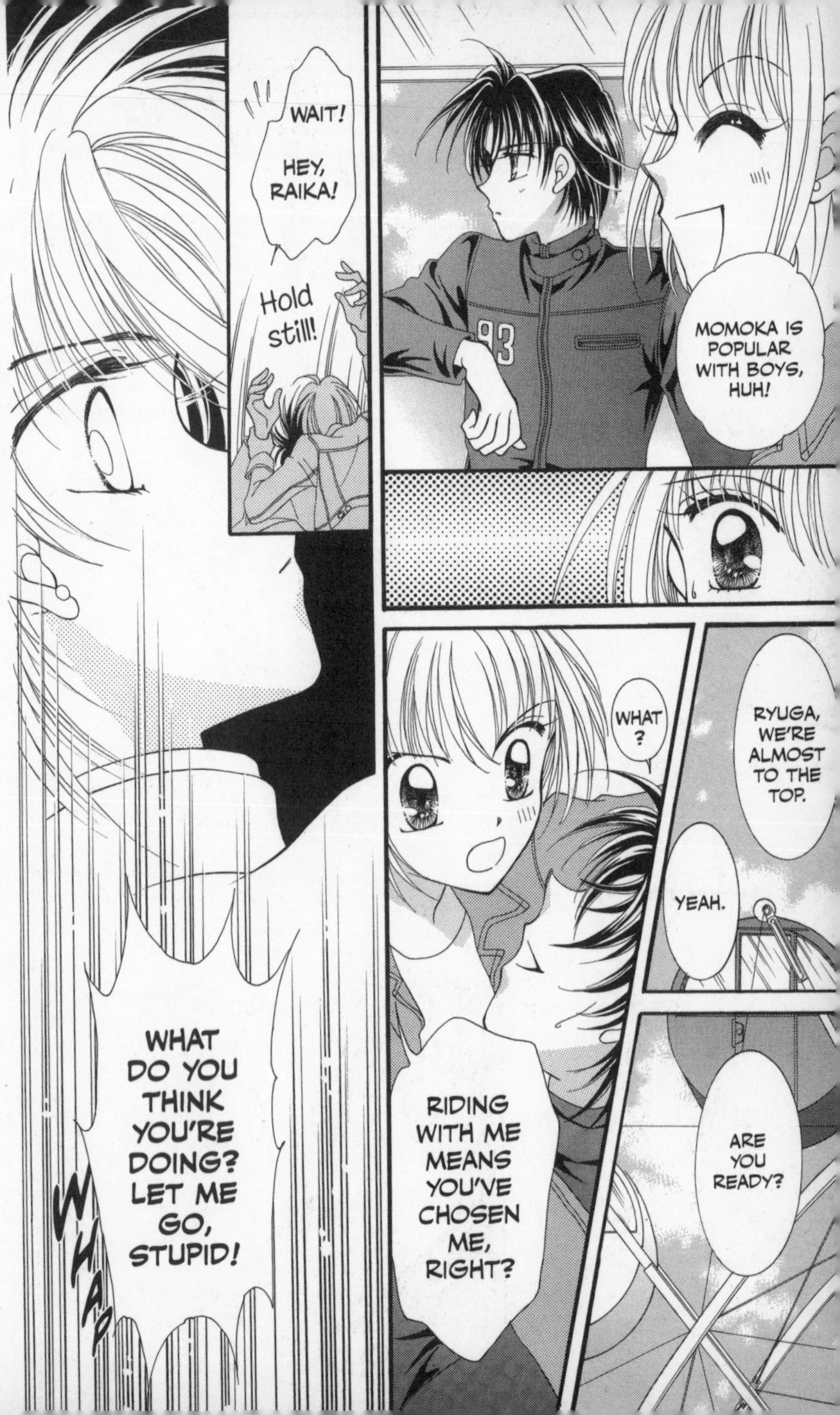
MOMOKA IS POPULAR WITH BOYS, HUH!
RYUGA, WE'RE ALMOST TO THE TOP.
YEAH.
ARE YOU READY?
WHAT?
RIDING WITH ME MEANS YOU'VE CHOSEN ME, RIGHT?
WAIT!
HEY, RAIKA!
Hold still!
WHAT DO YOU THINK YOU'RE DOING? LET ME GO, STUPID!
WHAP

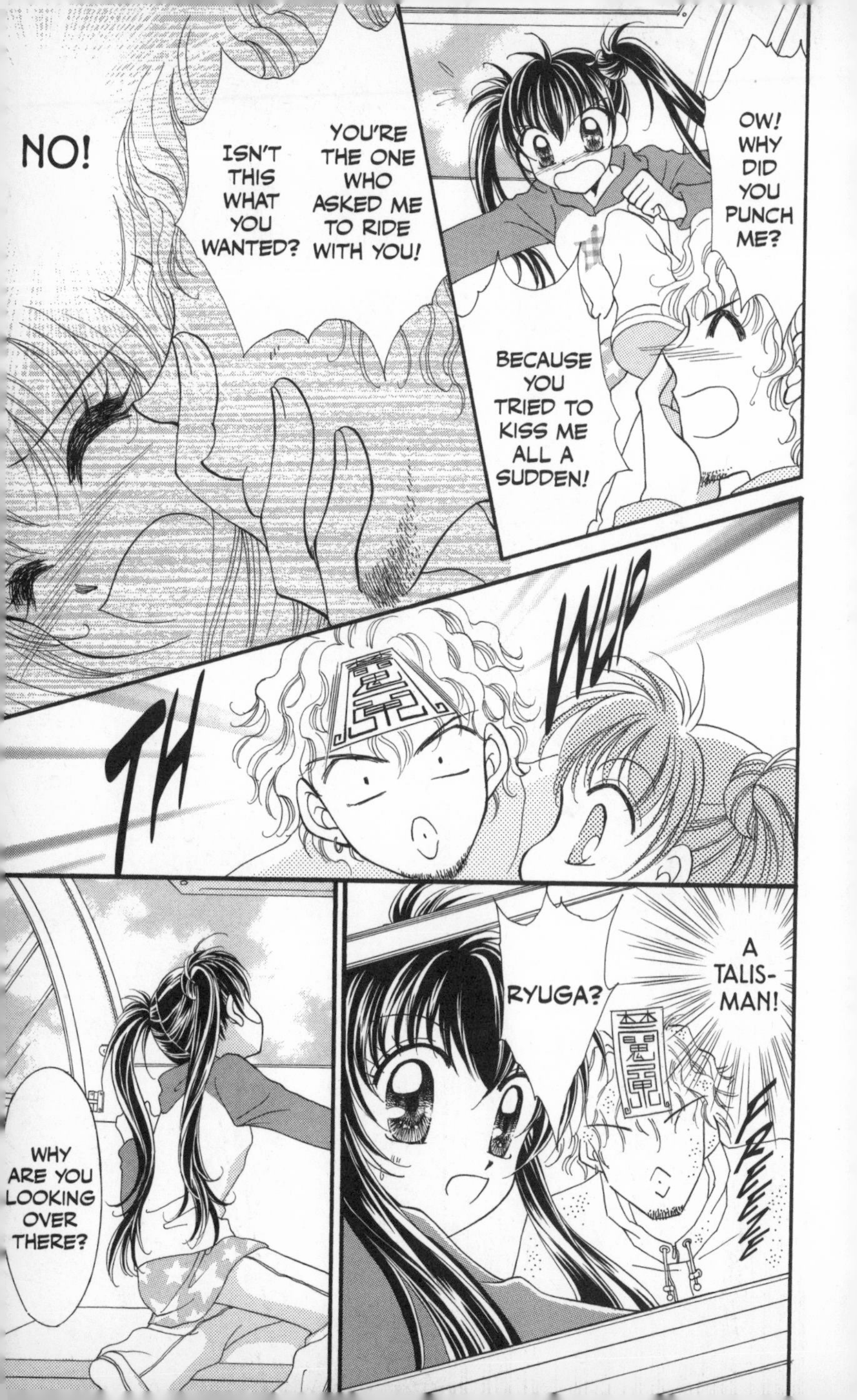
OW! WHY DID YOU PUNCH ME?
BECAUSE YOU TRIED TO KISS ME ALL A SUDDEN!
YOU'RE THE ONE WHO ASKED ME TO RIDE WITH YOU!
ISN'T THIS WHAT YOU WANTED?
NO!
WHIP
TH
A TALIS-MAN!
RYUGA?
WHY ARE YOU LOOKING OVER THERE?

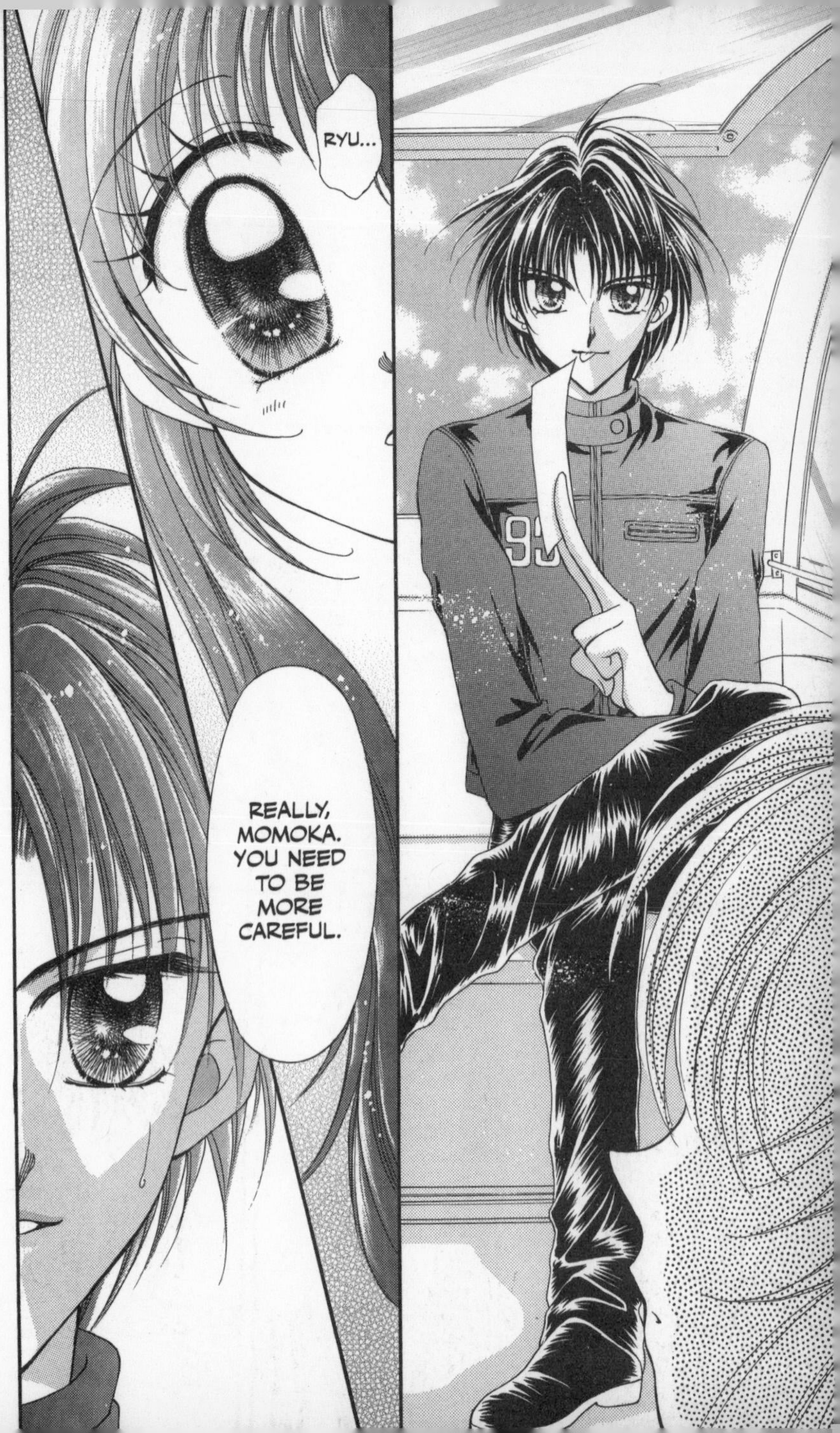
RYU...
REALLY, MOMOKA. YOU NEED TO BE MORE CAREFUL.

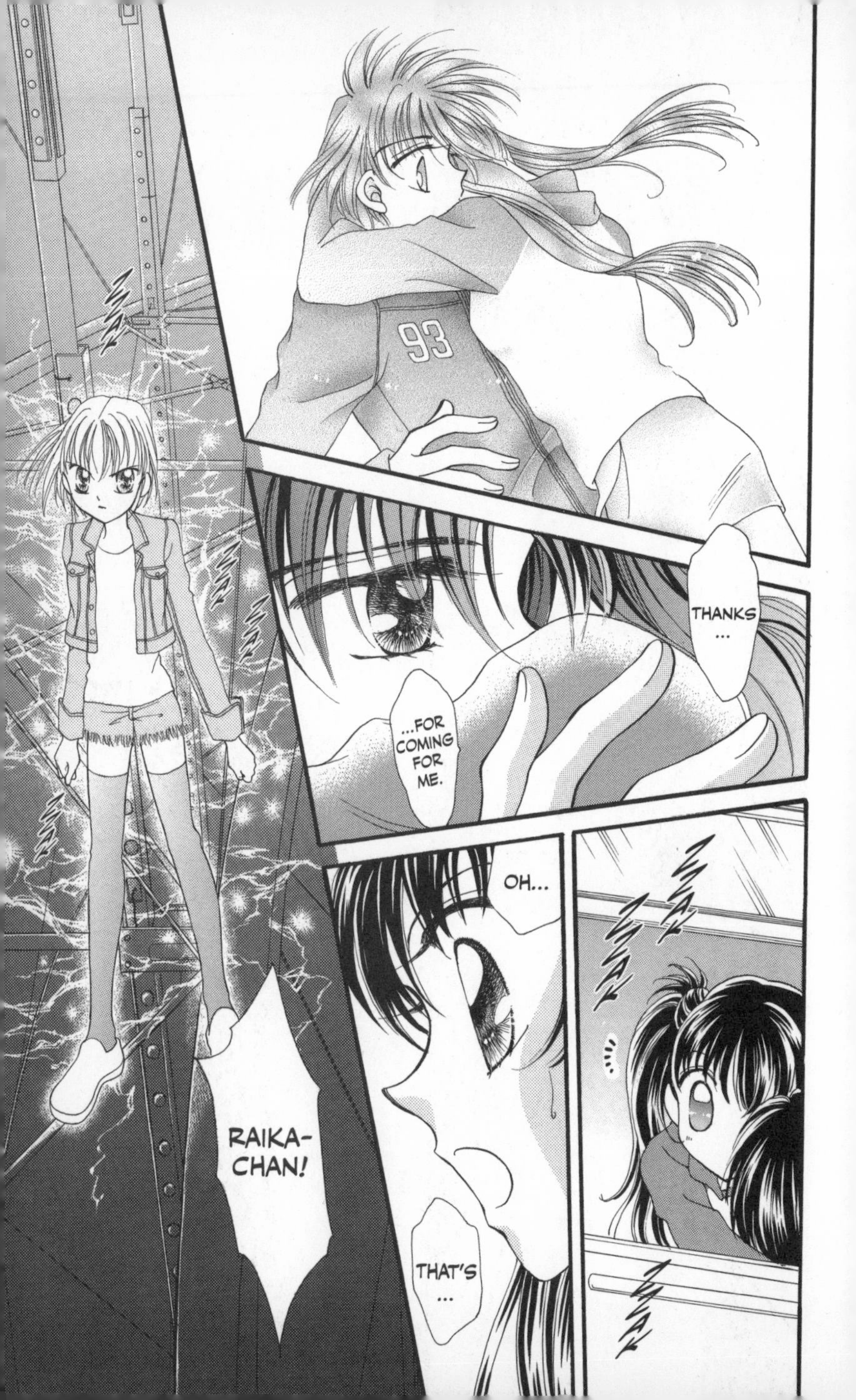
THANKS ...
...FOR COMING FOR ME.
OH...
THAT'S ...
RAIKA-CHAN!

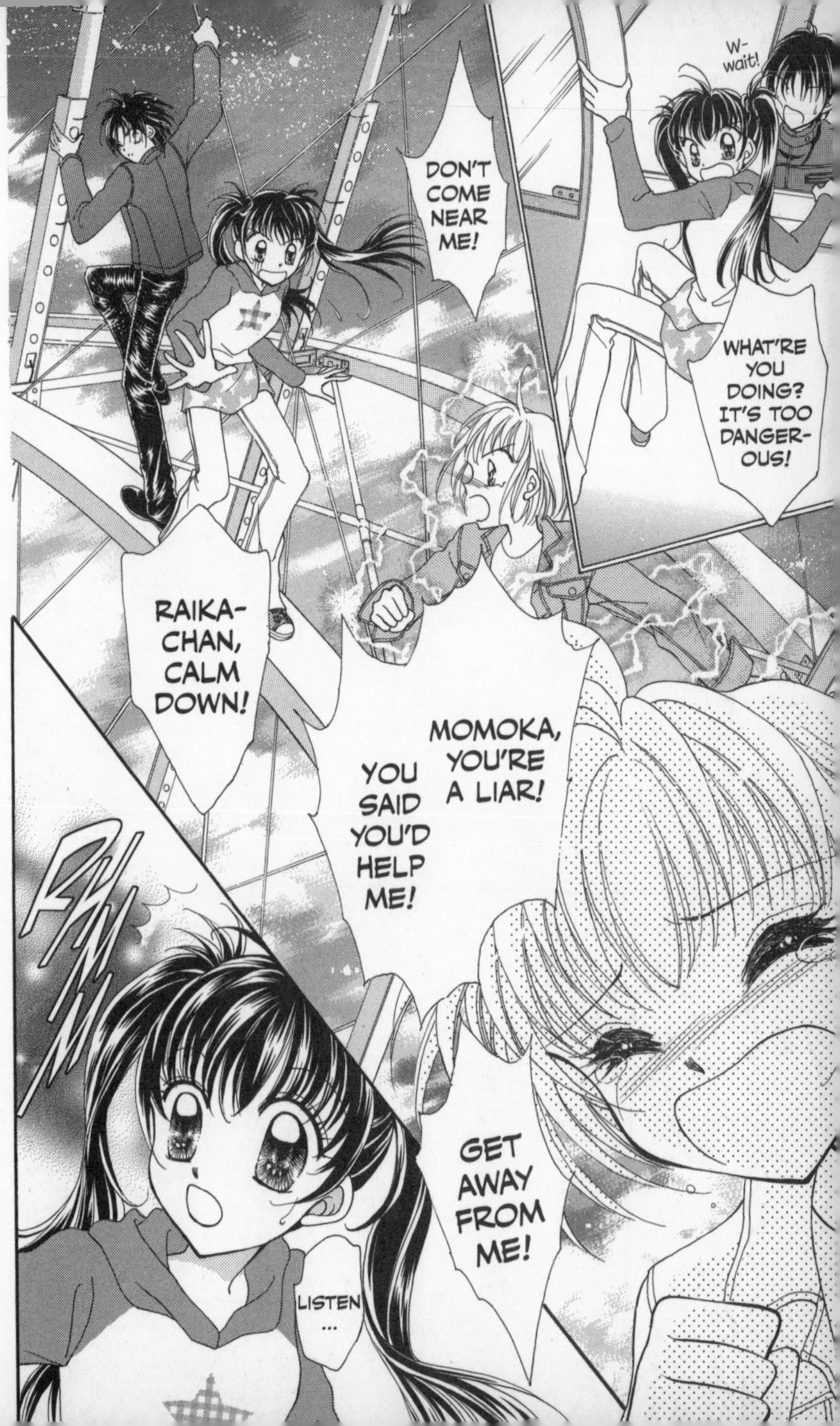
W-wait!
WHAT'RE YOU DOING? IT'S TOO DANGER-OUS!
DON'T COME NEAR ME!
RAIKA-CHAN, CALM DOWN!
MOMOKA, YOU'RE A LIAR!
YOU SAID YOU'D HELP ME!
GET AWAY FROM ME!
LISTEN ...

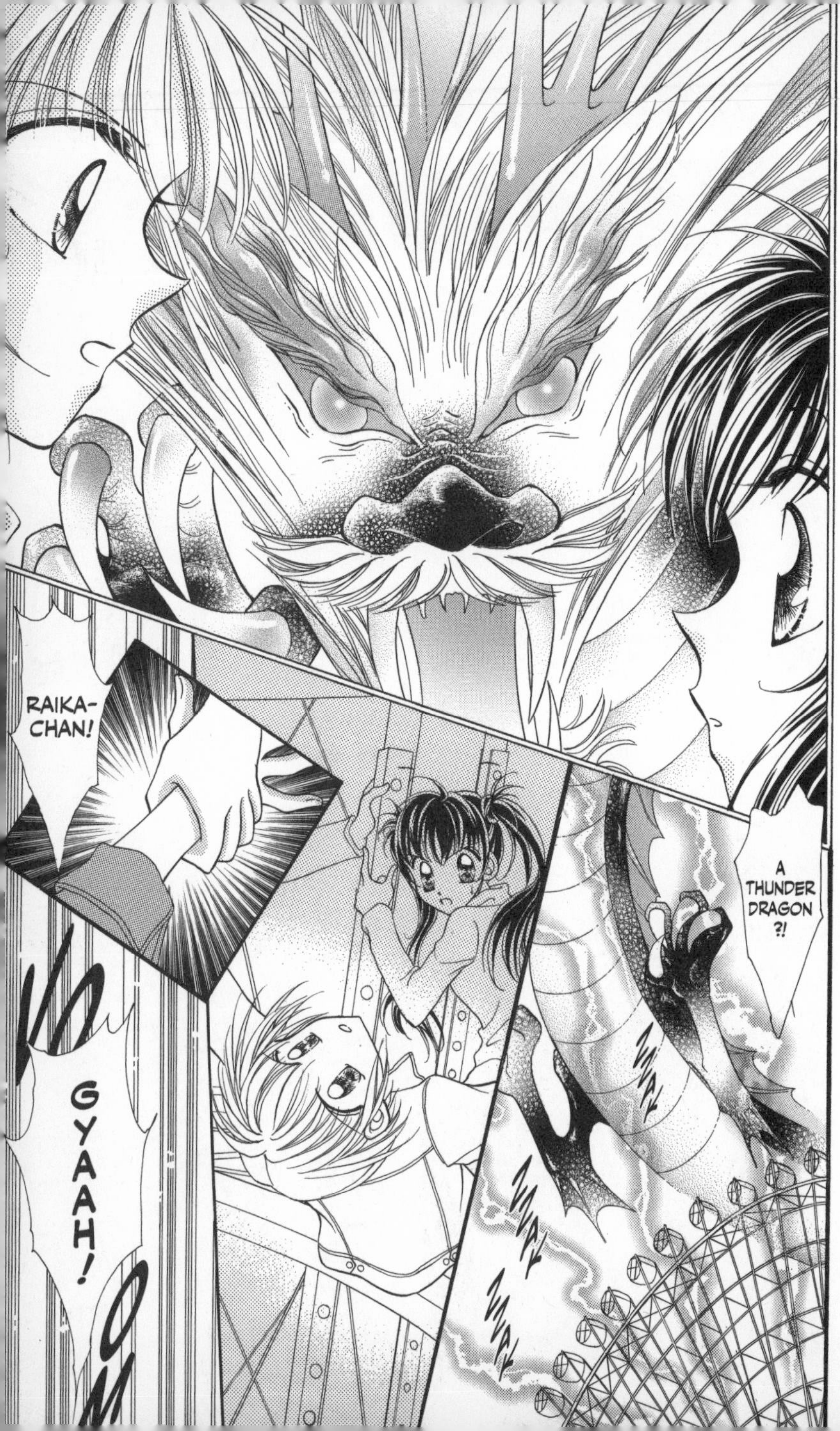
A THUNDER DRAGON ?!
RAIKA-CHAN!
GYAAH!

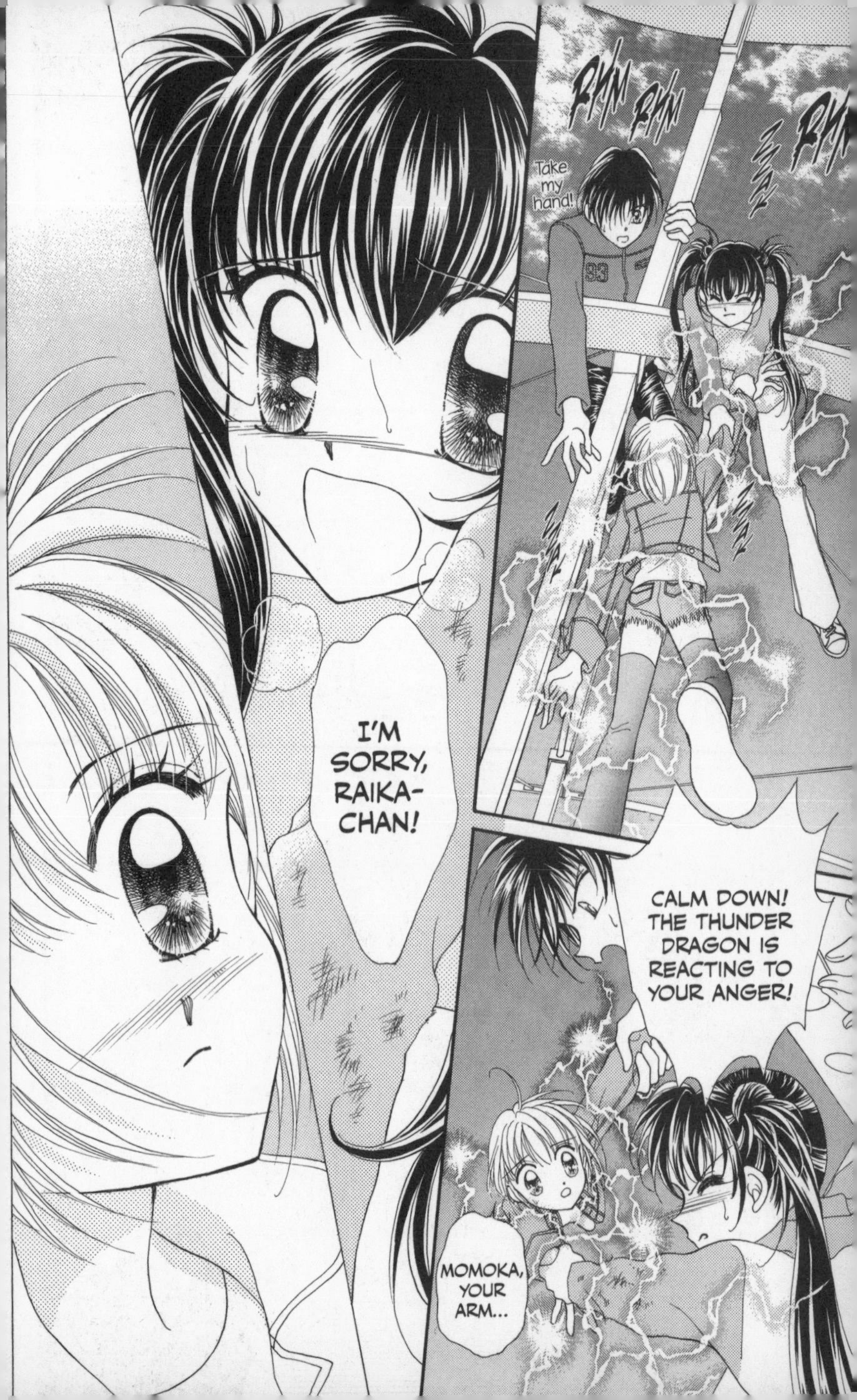
Take my hand!
CALM DOWN! THE THUNDER DRAGON IS REACTING TO YOUR ANGER!
MOMOKA, YOUR ARM...
I'M SORRY, RAIKA-CHAN!

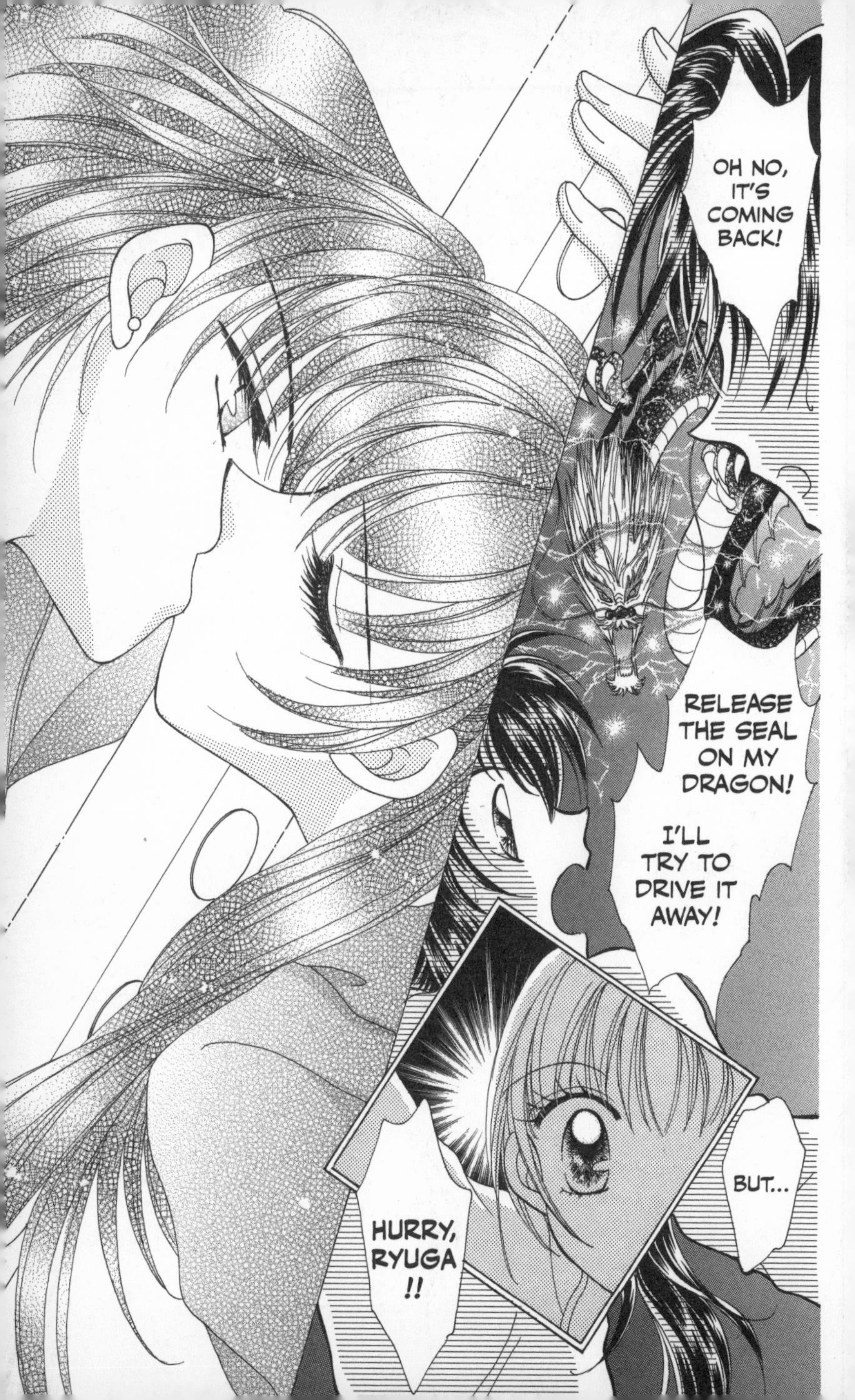
OH NO, IT'S COMING BACK!
RELEASE THE SEAL ON MY DRAGON!
I'LL TRY TO DRIVE IT AWAY!
BUT...
HURRY, RYUGA !!

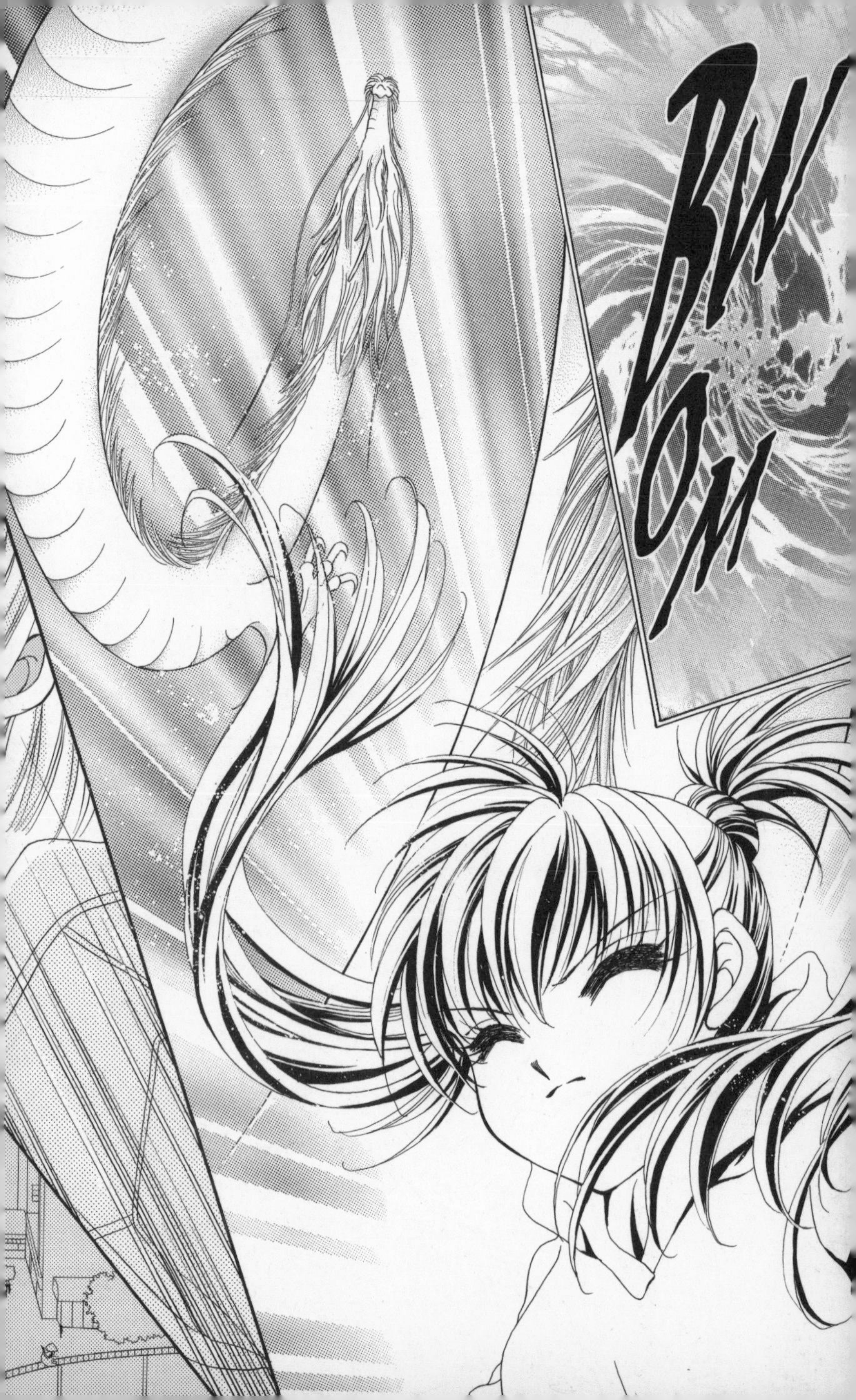
BWOOM

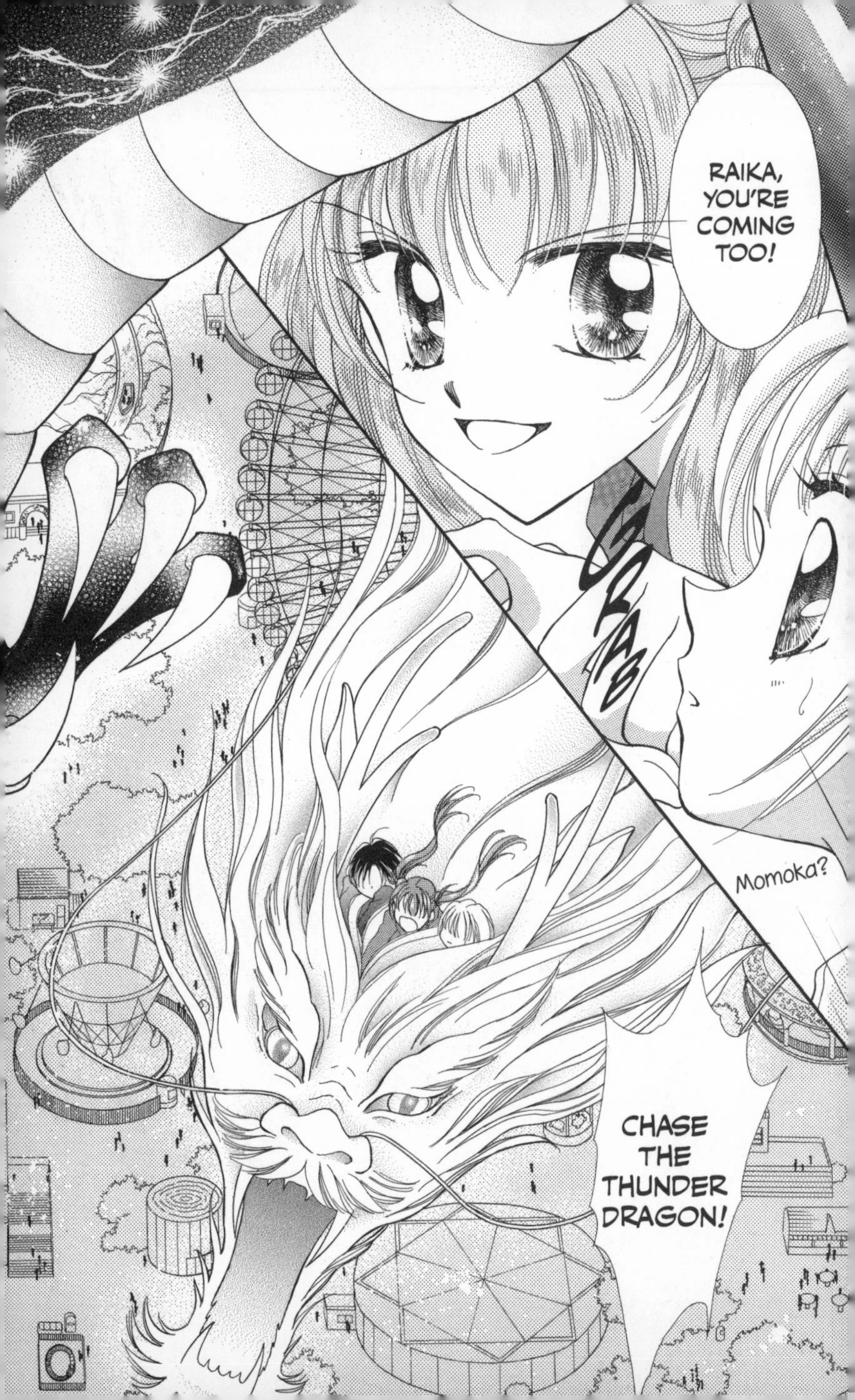
RAIKA, YOU'RE COMING TOO!
Momoka?
CHASE THE THUNDER DRAGON!

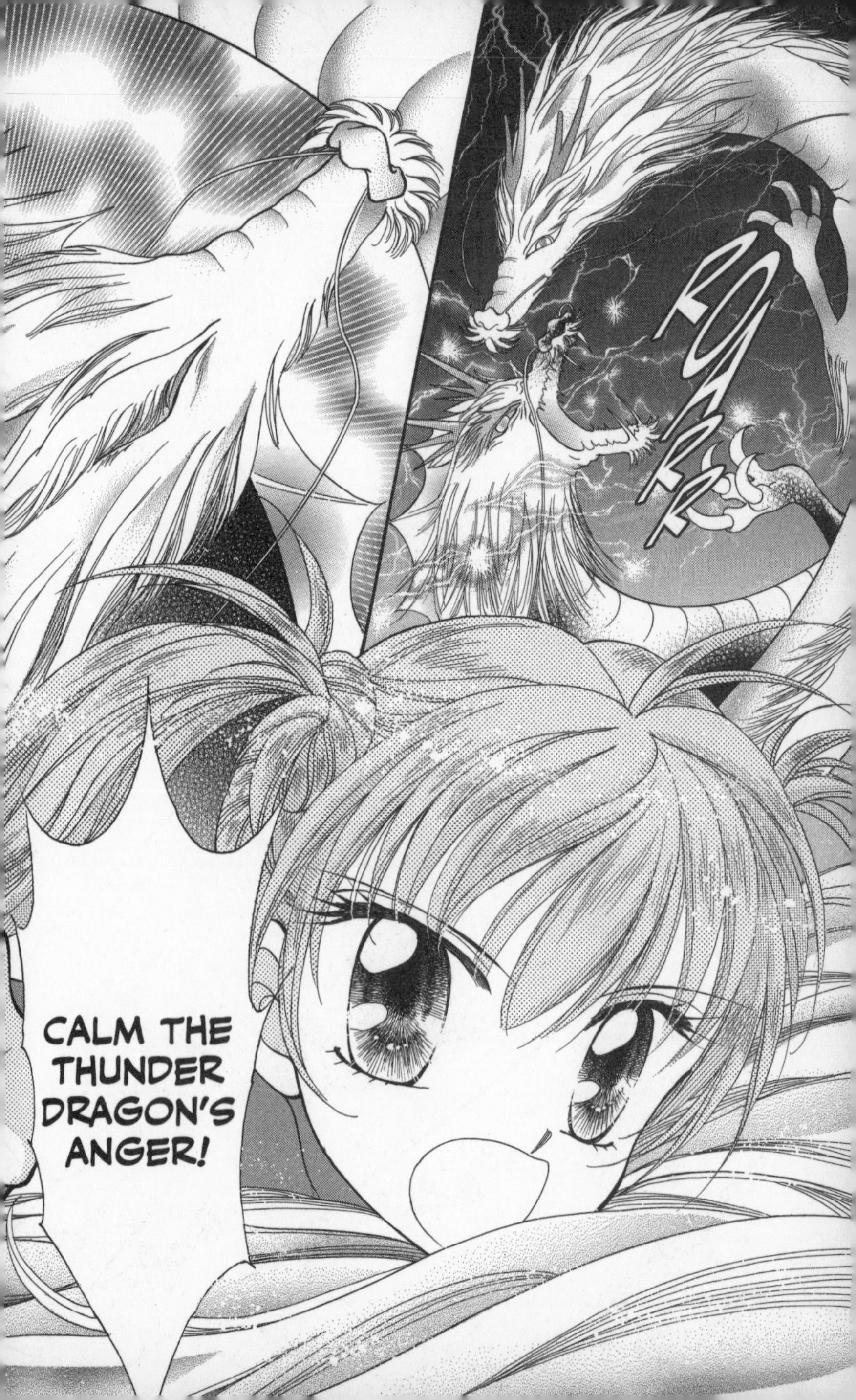
ROARRR
CALM THE THUNDER DRAGON'S ANGER!

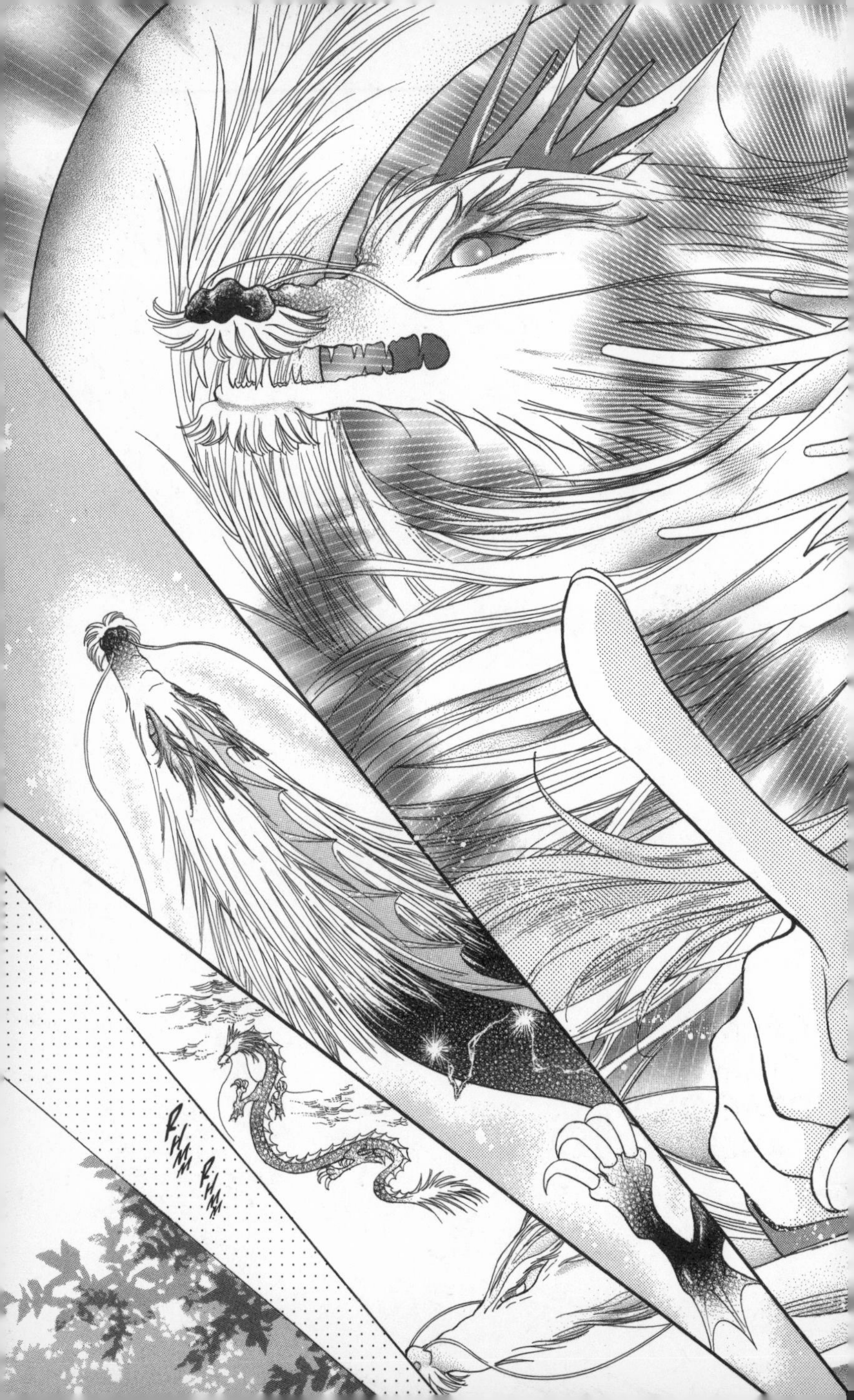
RINN RINN

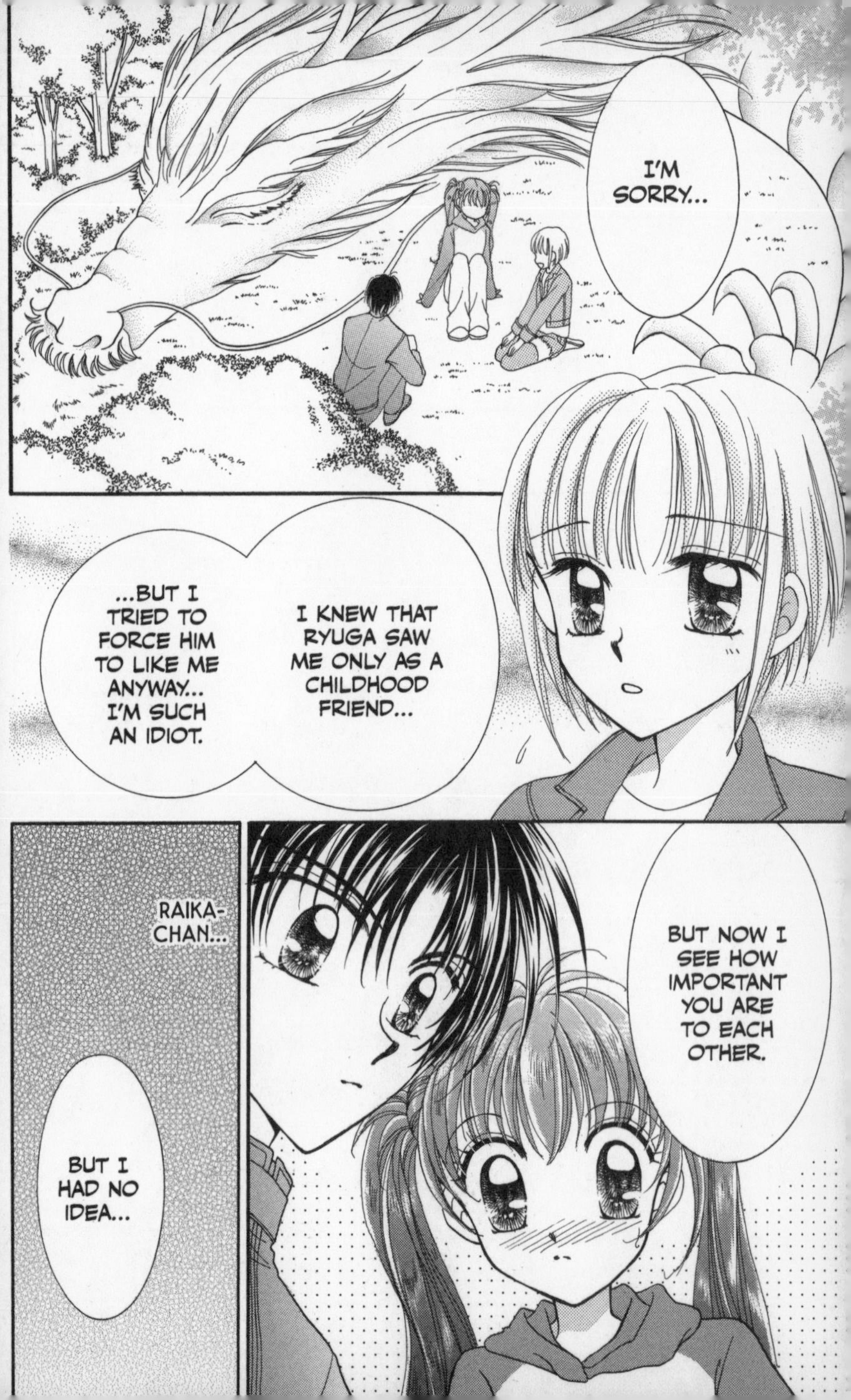
I'M SORRY...
I KNEW THAT RYUGA SAW ME ONLY AS A CHILDHOOD FRIEND...
...BUT I TRIED TO FORCE HIM TO LIKE ME ANYWAY... I'M SUCH AN IDIOT.
BUT NOW I SEE HOW IMPORTANT YOU ARE TO EACH OTHER.
RAIKA-CHAN...
BUT I HAD NO IDEA...

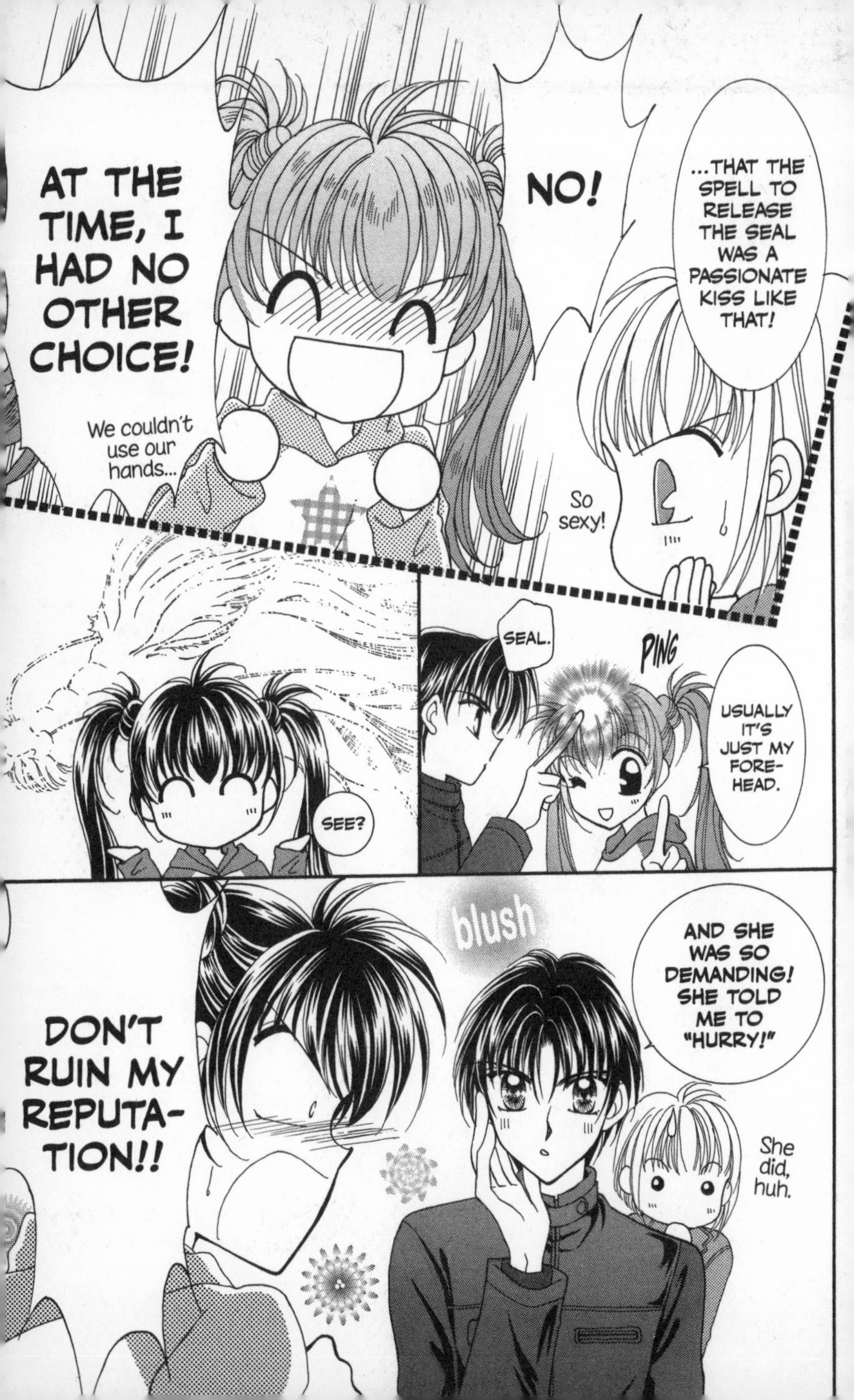
...THAT THE SPELL TO RELEASE THE SEAL WAS A PASSIONATE KISS LIKE THAT!
So sexy!
NO!
AT THE TIME, I HAD NO OTHER CHOICE!
We couldn't use our hands...
SEAL.
PING
USUALLY IT'S JUST MY FORE-HEAD.
SEE?
AND SHE WAS SO DEMANDING! SHE TOLD ME TO "HURRY!"
blush
She did, huh.
DON'T RUIN MY REPUTA-TION!!

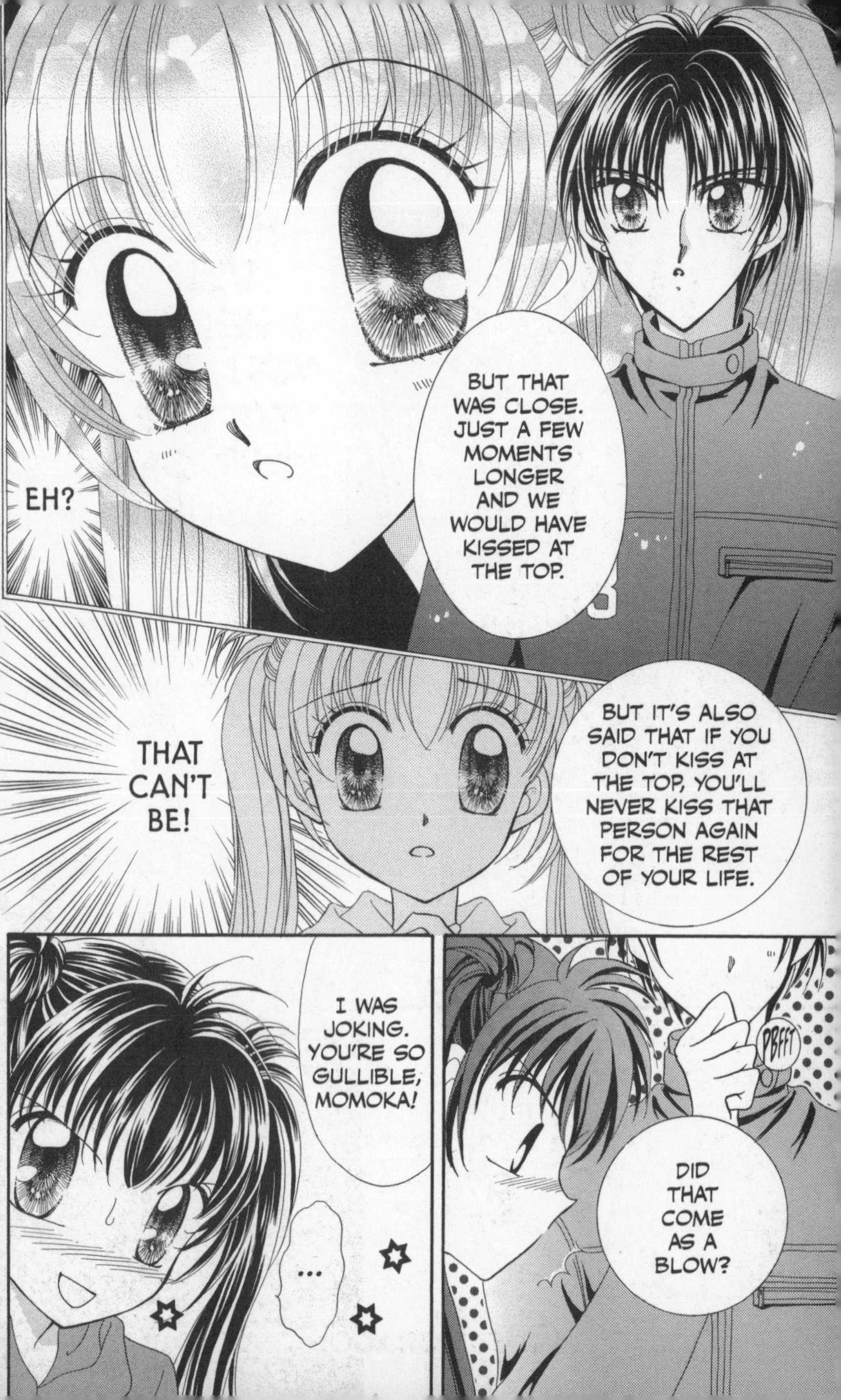
BUT THAT WAS CLOSE. JUST A FEW MOMENTS LONGER AND WE WOULD HAVE KISSED AT THE TOP.
EH?
BUT IT'S ALSO SAID THAT IF YOU DON'T KISS AT THE TOP, YOU'LL NEVER KISS THAT PERSON AGAIN FOR THE REST OF YOUR LIFE.
THAT CAN'T BE!
PBFFT
DID THAT COME AS A BLOW?
I WAS JOKING. YOU'RE SO GULLIBLE, MOMOKA!
...

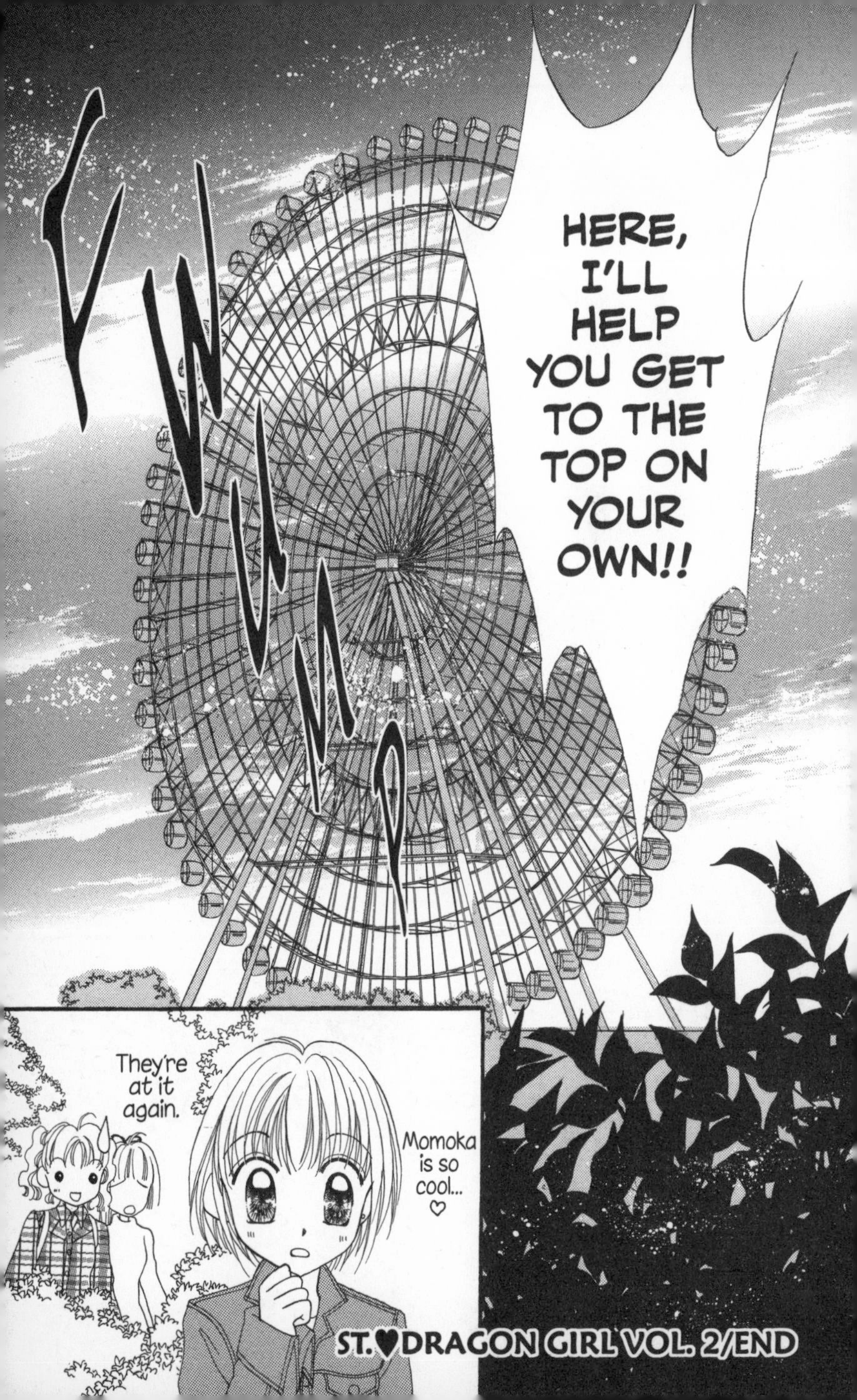
HERE, I'LL HELP YOU GET TO THE TOP ON YOUR OWN!!
They're at it again.
Momoka is so cool... ♡
ST.♥DRAGON GIRL VOL. 2/END

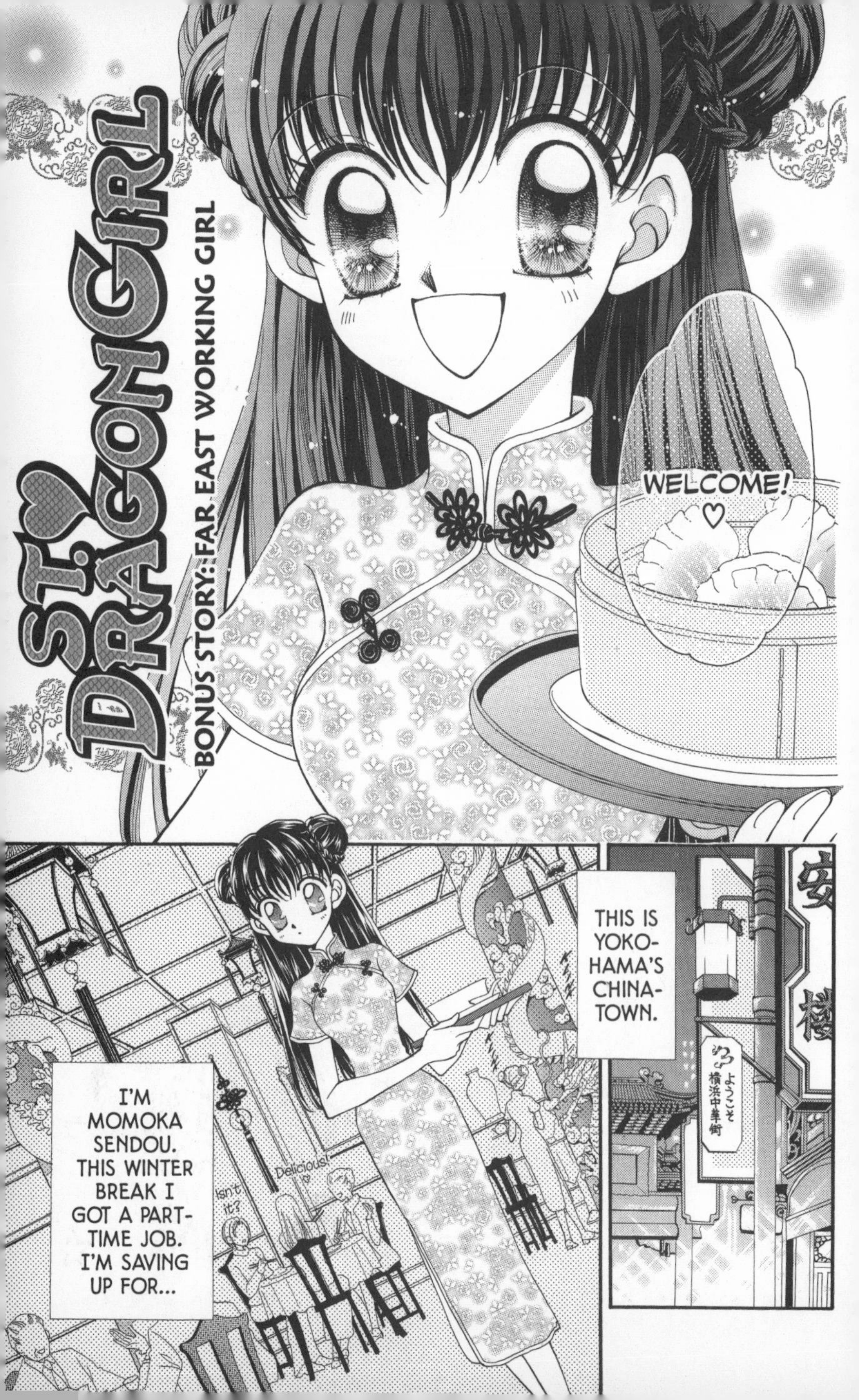
ST. DRAGON GIRL
BONUS STORY: FAR EAST WORKING GIRL
WELCOME! ♡
THIS IS YOKOHAMA'S CHINATOWN.
ようこそ横浜中華街
I'M MOMOKA SENDOU. THIS WINTER BREAK I GOT A PART-TIME JOB. I'M SAVING UP FOR...
Delicious! ♡
Isn't it?

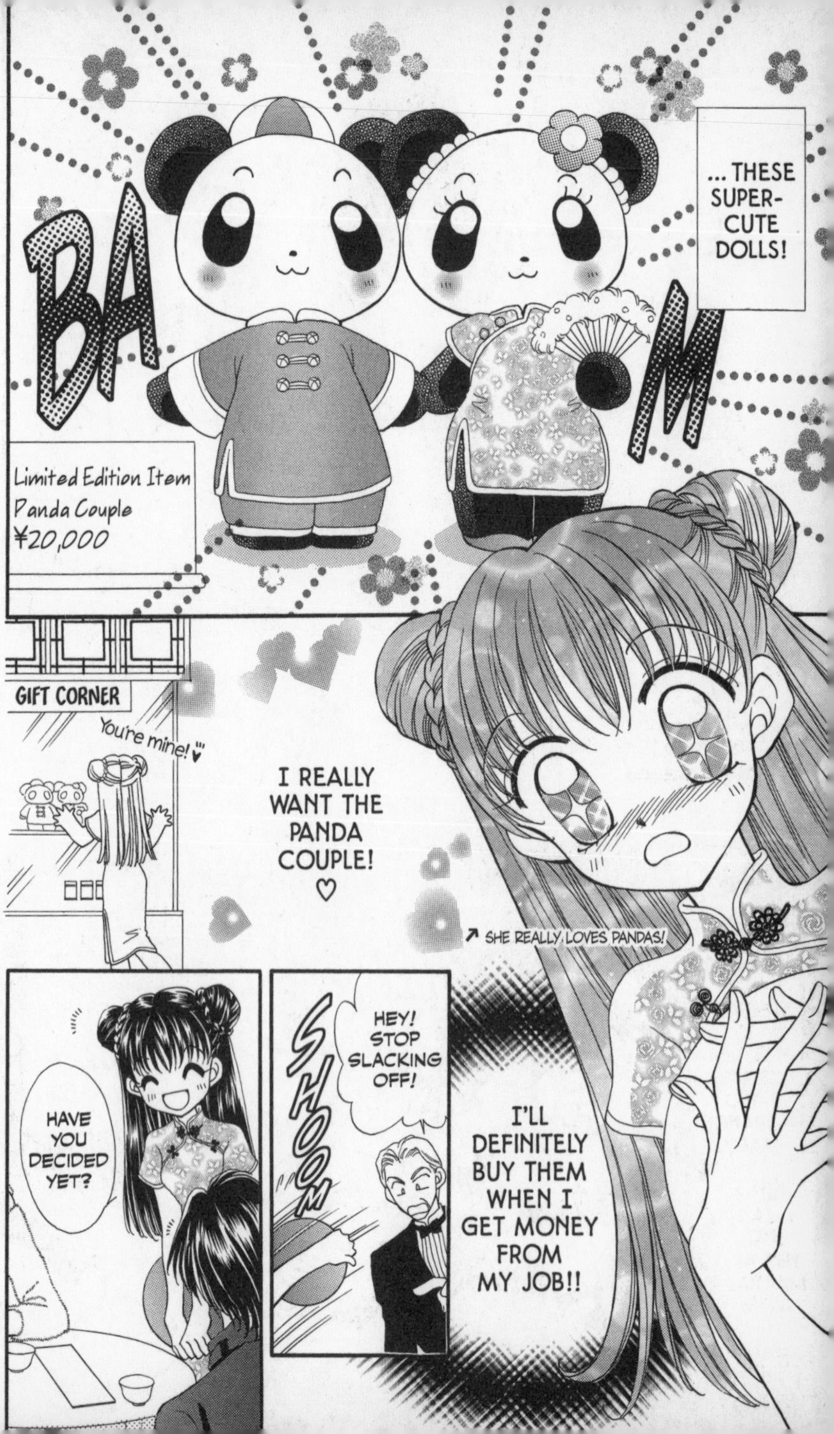
... THESE SUPER-CUTE DOLLS!
BAM
Limited Edition Item
Panda Couple
¥20,000
I REALLY WANT THE PANDA COUPLE! ♡
SHE REALLY LOVES PANDAS!
I'LL DEFINITELY BUY THEM WHEN I GET MONEY FROM MY JOB!!
GIFT CORNER
You're mine! ♥
HEY! STOP SLACKING OFF!
SHOOOM
HAVE YOU DECIDED YET?

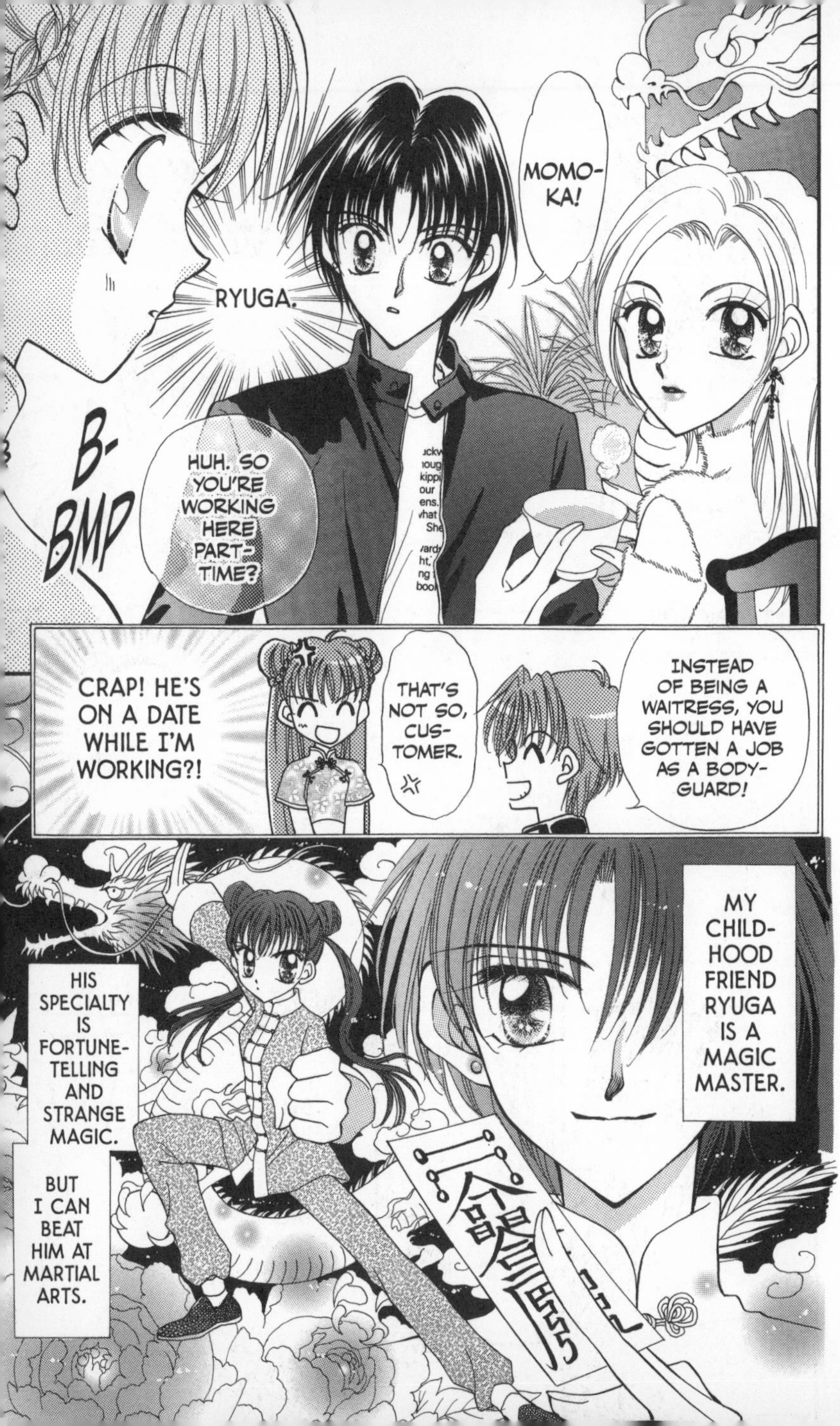
MOMO-KA!
RYUGA.
HUH. SO YOU'RE WORKING HERE PART-TIME?
B-BMP
INSTEAD OF BEING A WAITRESS, YOU SHOULD HAVE GOTTEN A JOB AS A BODY-GUARD!
THAT'S NOT SO, CUS-TOMER.
CRAP! HE'S ON A DATE WHILE I'M WORKING?!
MY CHILD-HOOD FRIEND RYUGA IS A MAGIC MASTER.
HIS SPECIALTY IS FORTUNE-TELLING AND STRANGE MAGIC.
BUT I CAN BEAT HIM AT MARTIAL ARTS.

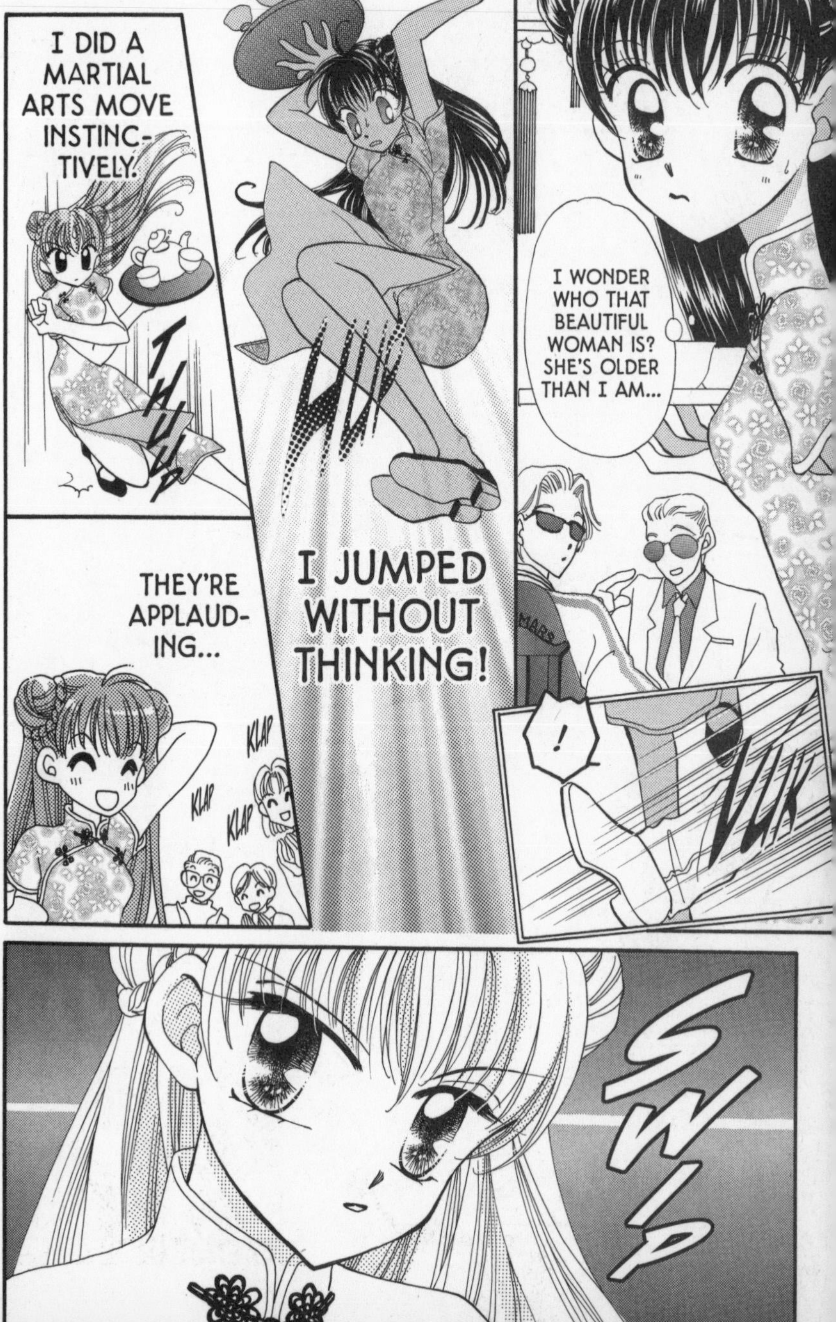
I WONDER WHO THAT BEAUTIFUL WOMAN IS? SHE'S OLDER THAN I AM...
!
VUK
I JUMPED WITHOUT THINKING!
I DID A MARTIAL ARTS MOVE INSTINCTIVELY.
THWUP
THEY'RE APPLAUDING...
KLAP
KLAP
KLAP
SWIP

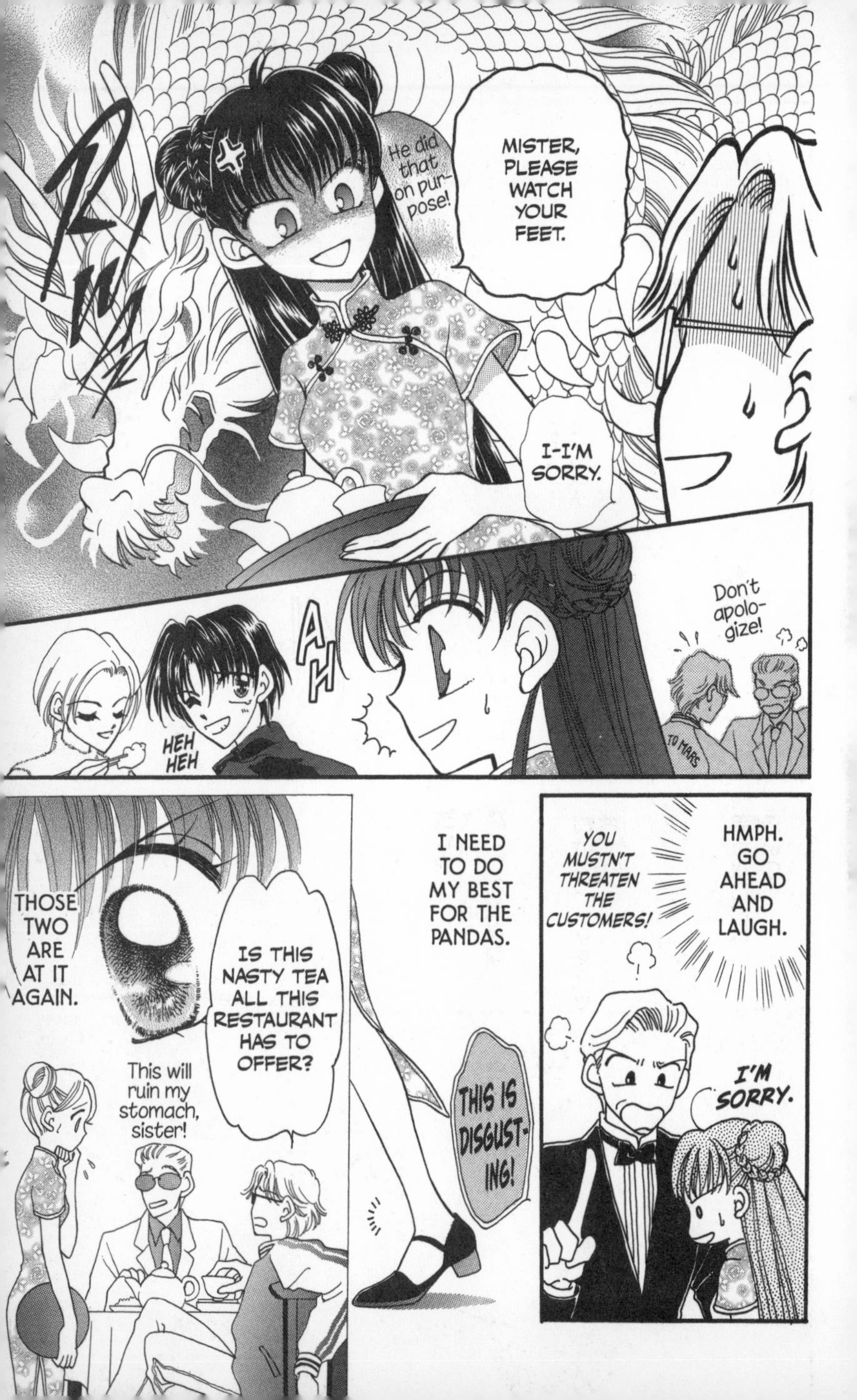
MISTER, PLEASE WATCH YOUR FEET.
He did that on purpose!
I-I'M SORRY.
Don't apologize!
TO MARS
AH
HEH HEH
HMPH. GO AHEAD AND LAUGH.
YOU MUSTN'T THREATEN THE CUSTOMERS!
I'M SORRY.
I NEED TO DO MY BEST FOR THE PANDAS.
IS THIS NASTY TEA ALL THIS RESTAURANT HAS TO OFFER?
THOSE TWO ARE AT IT AGAIN.
THIS IS DISGUSTING!
This will ruin my stomach, sister!

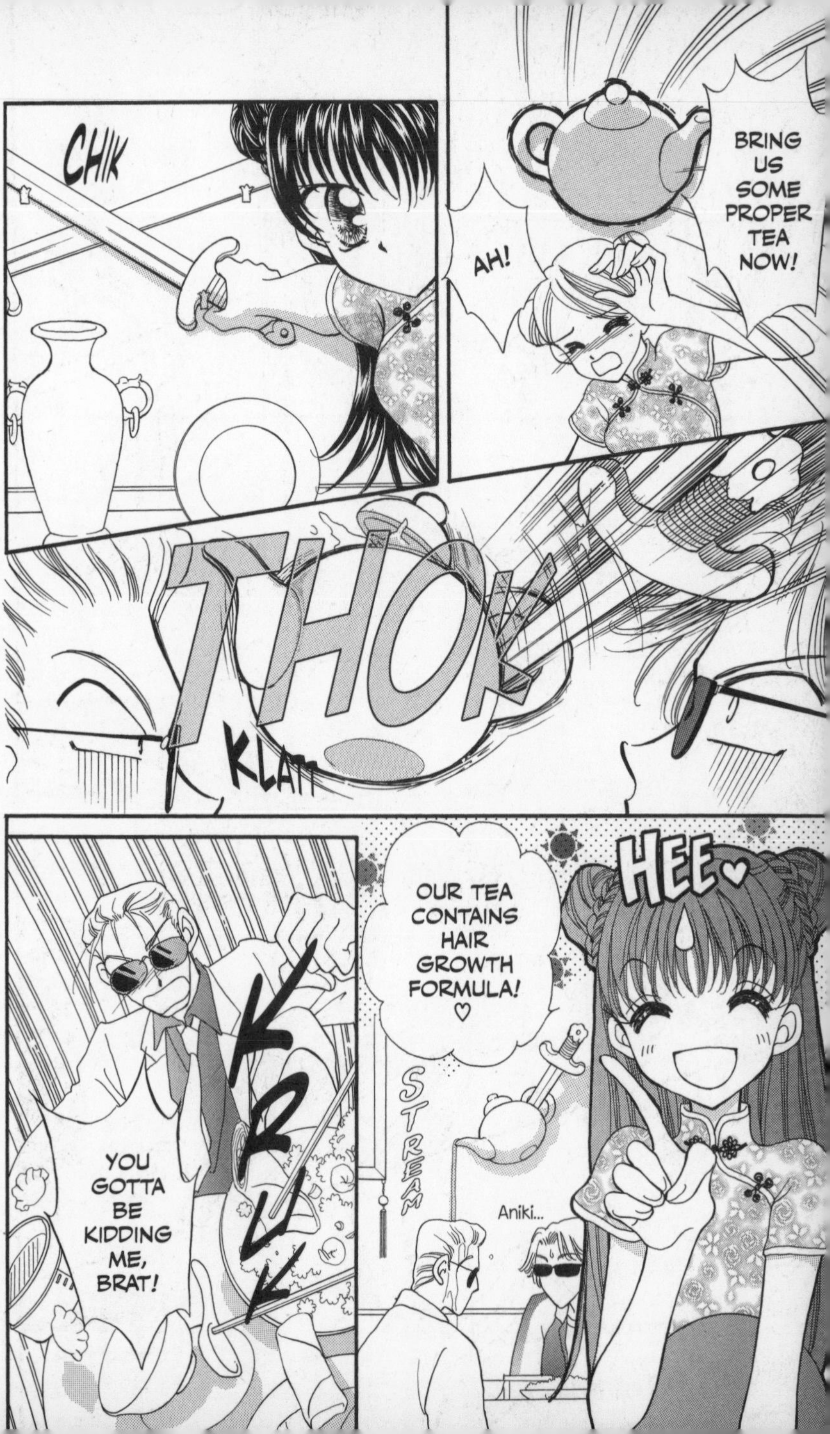

BRING US SOME PROPER TEA NOW!
AH!
CHIK
THOK
KLATT
HEE♥
OUR TEA CONTAINS HAIR GROWTH FORMULA! ♡
STREAM
Aniki...
YOU GOTTA BE KIDDING ME, BRAT!

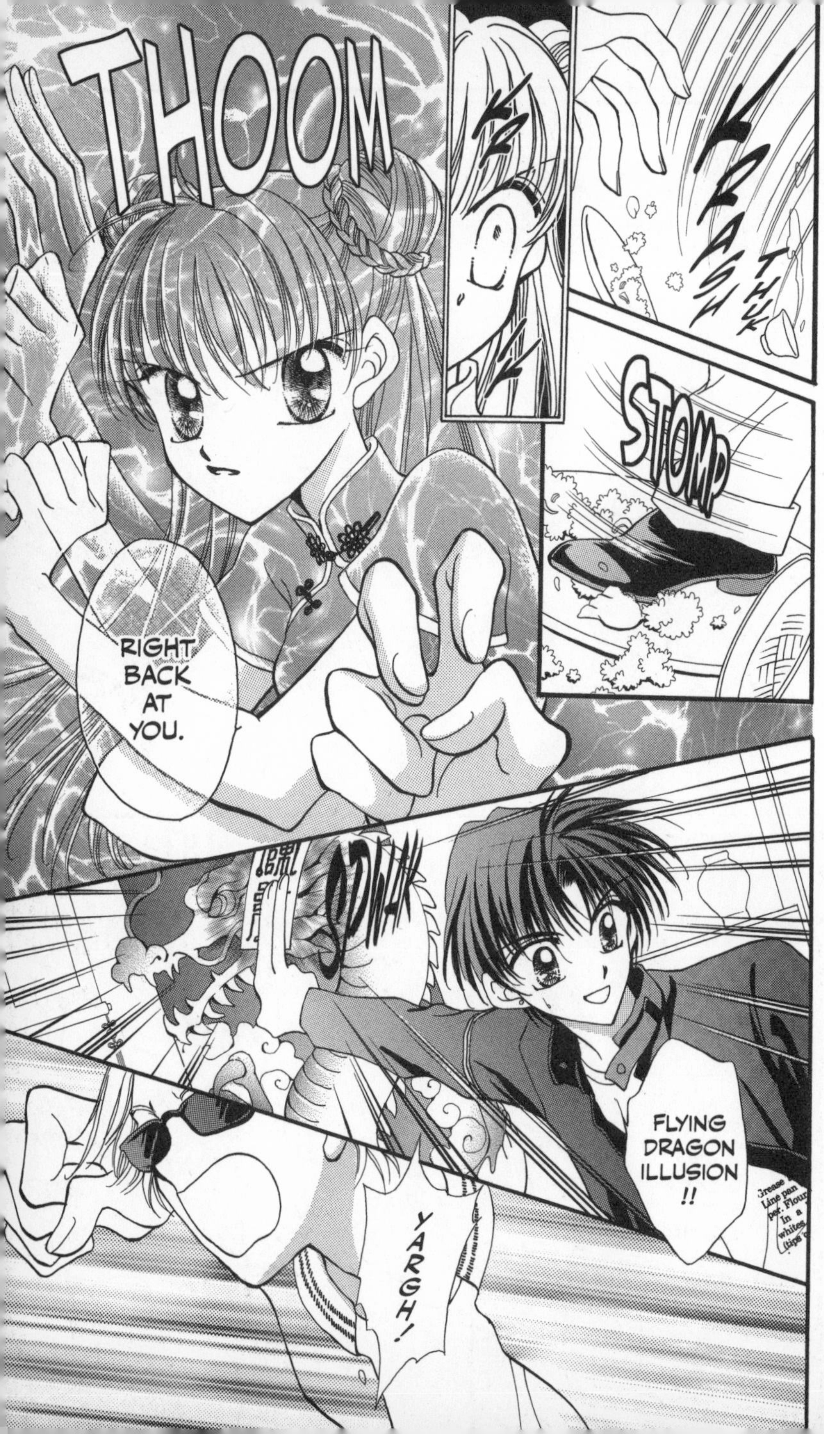

KRASH
THUK
STOMP
THOOM
RIGHT BACK AT YOU.
SPWAK
FLYING DRAGON ILLUSION!!
YARGH!

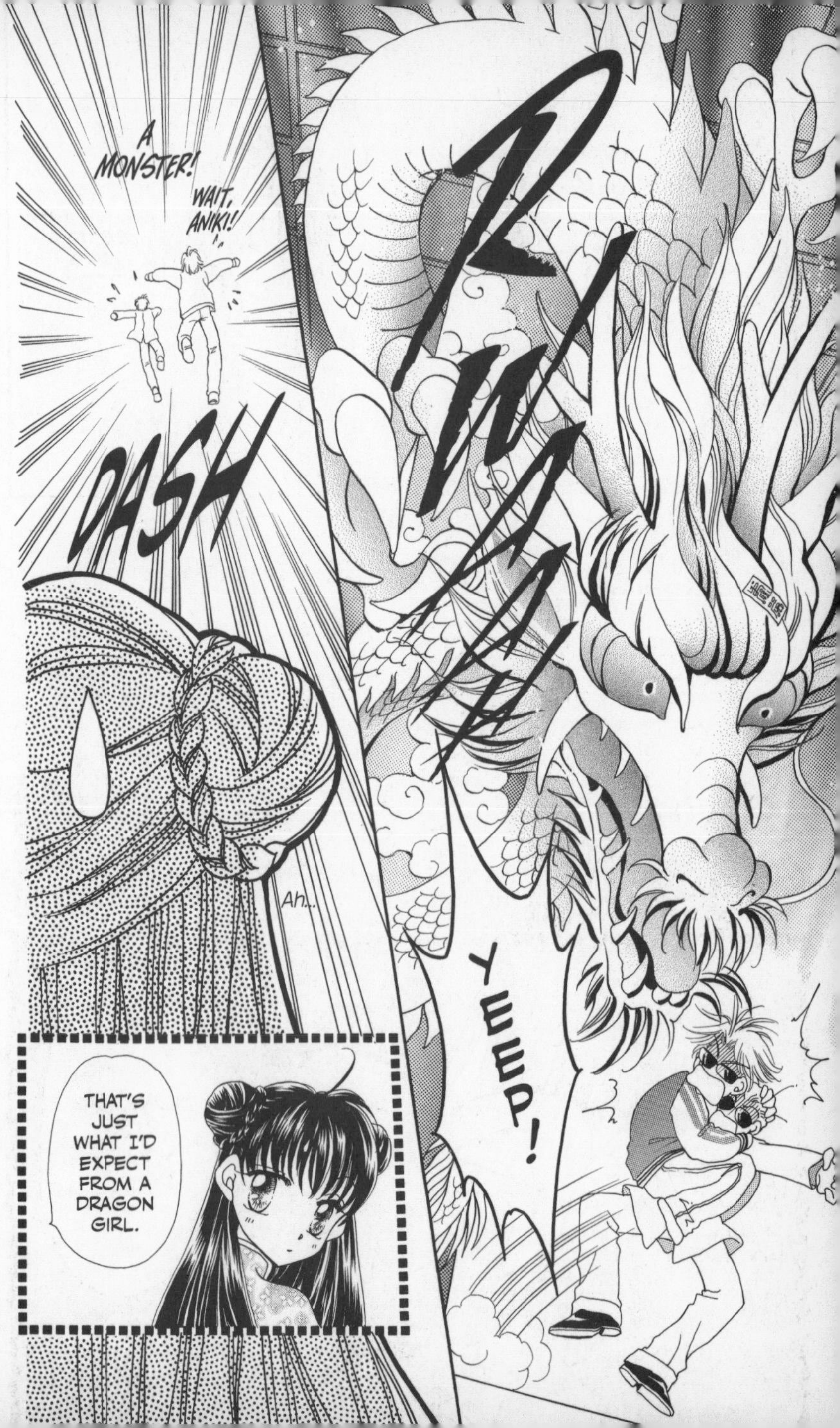
YEEP!
A MONSTER!
WAIT, ANIKI!
DASH
Ah...
THAT'S JUST WHAT I'D EXPECT FROM A DRAGON GIRL.

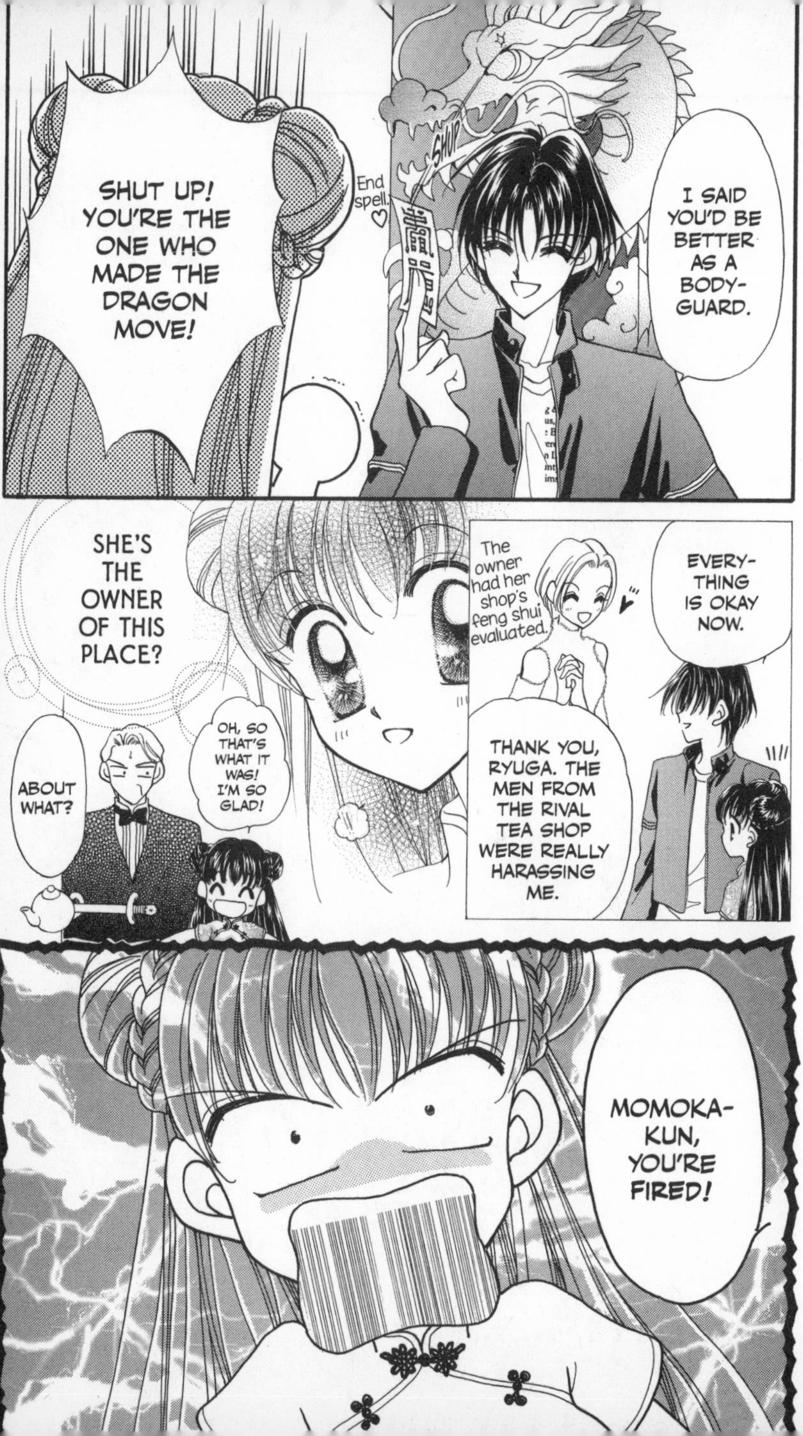
I SAID YOU'D BE BETTER AS A BODY-GUARD.
SHUP
End spell. ♡
SHUT UP! YOU'RE THE ONE WHO MADE THE DRAGON MOVE!
EVERY-THING IS OKAY NOW.
The owner had her shop's feng shui evaluated.
THANK YOU, RYUGA. THE MEN FROM THE RIVAL TEA SHOP WERE REALLY HARASSING ME.
SHE'S THE OWNER OF THIS PLACE?
OH, SO THAT'S WHAT IT WAS! I'M SO GLAD!
ABOUT WHAT?
MOMOKA-KUN, YOU'RE FIRED!

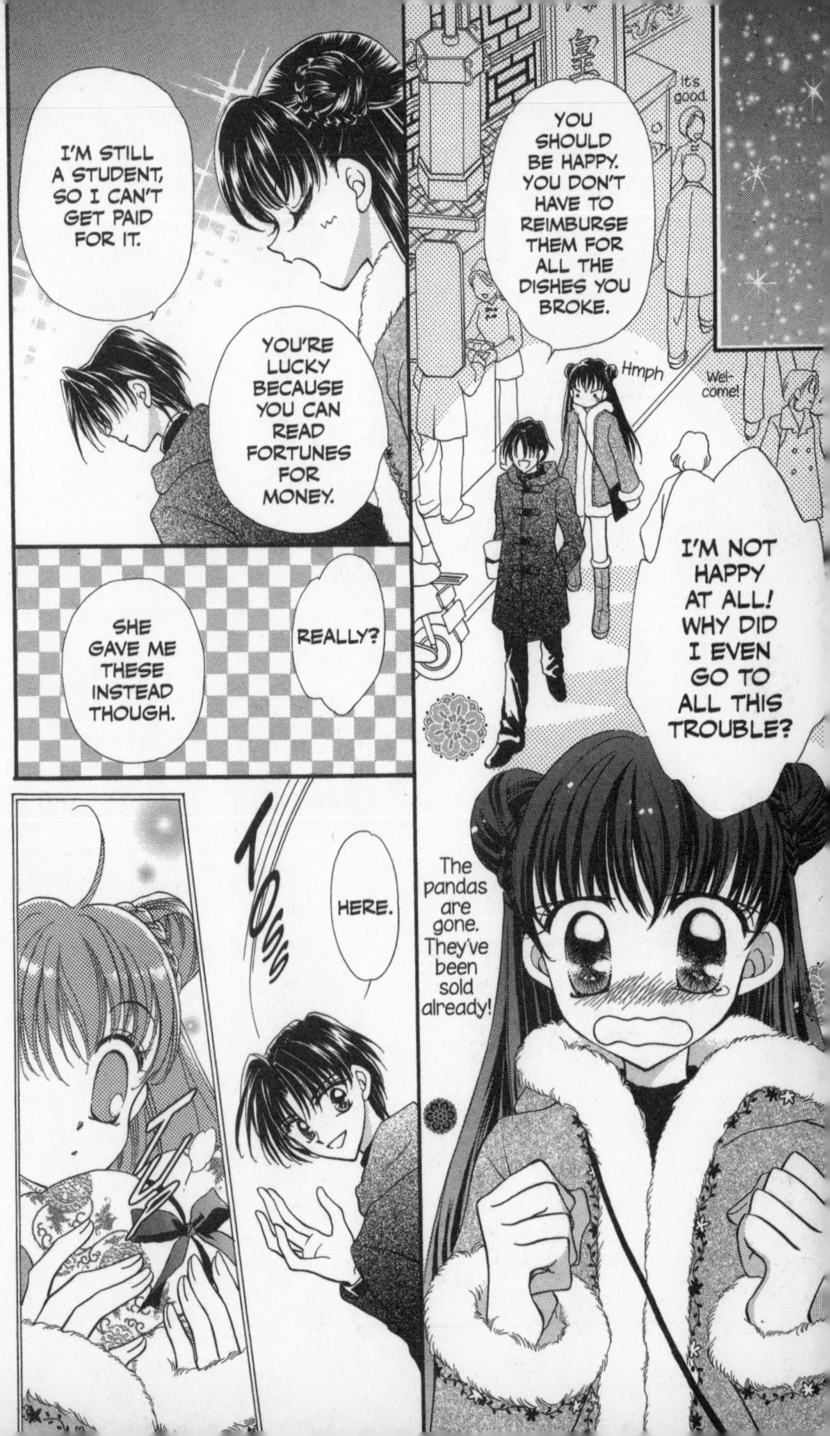
It's good.
YOU SHOULD BE HAPPY. YOU DON'T HAVE TO REIMBURSE THEM FOR ALL THE DISHES YOU BROKE.
Hmph
Wel-come!
I'M NOT HAPPY AT ALL! WHY DID I EVEN GO TO ALL THIS TROUBLE?
YOU'RE LUCKY BECAUSE YOU CAN READ FORTUNES FOR MONEY.
I'M STILL A STUDENT, SO I CAN'T GET PAID FOR IT.
SHE GAVE ME THESE INSTEAD THOUGH.
REALLY?
The pandas are gone. They've been sold already!
HERE.

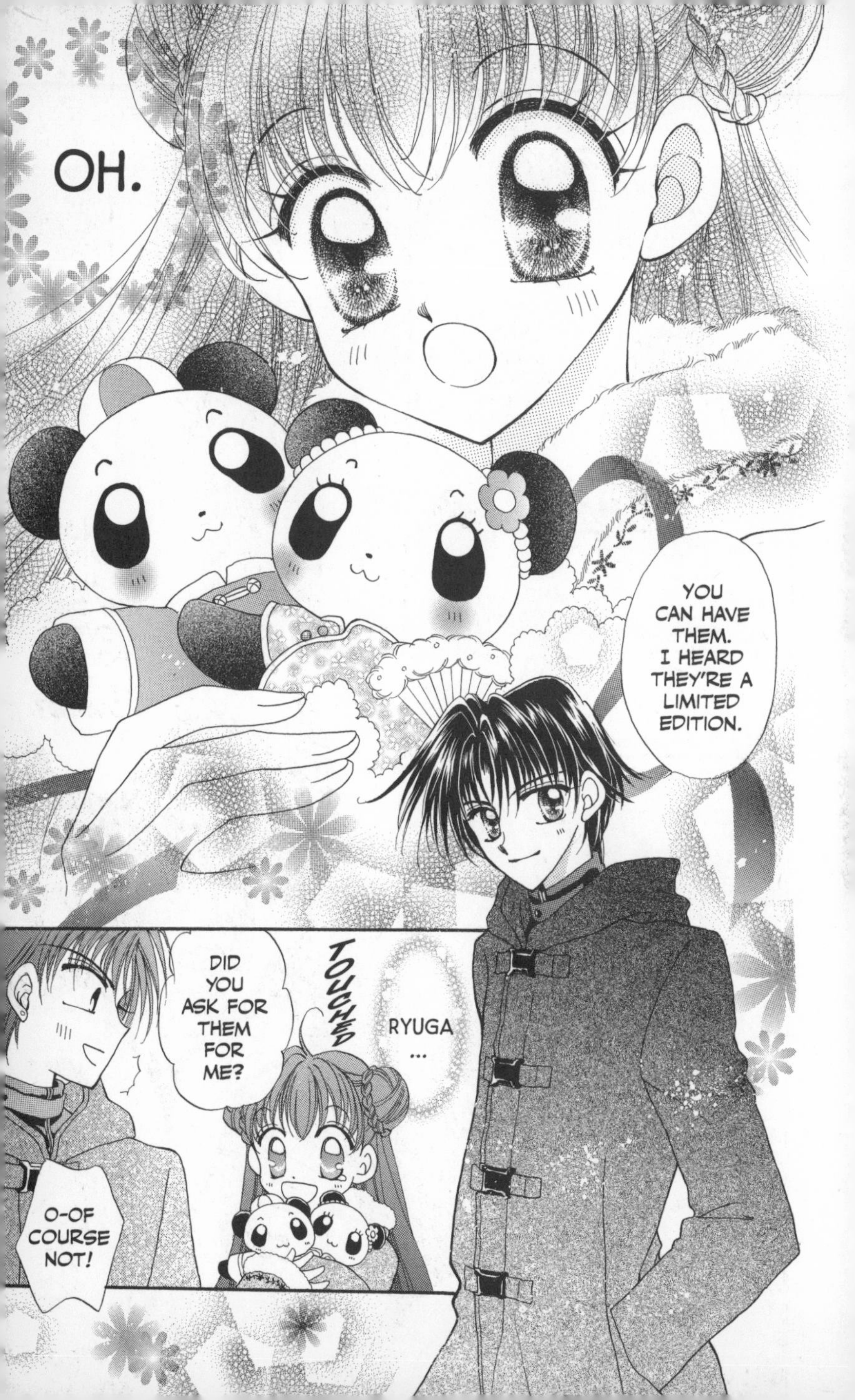
OH.
YOU CAN HAVE THEM. I HEARD THEY'RE A LIMITED EDITION.
RYUGA ...
TOUCHED
DID YOU ASK FOR THEM FOR ME?
O-OF COURSE NOT!

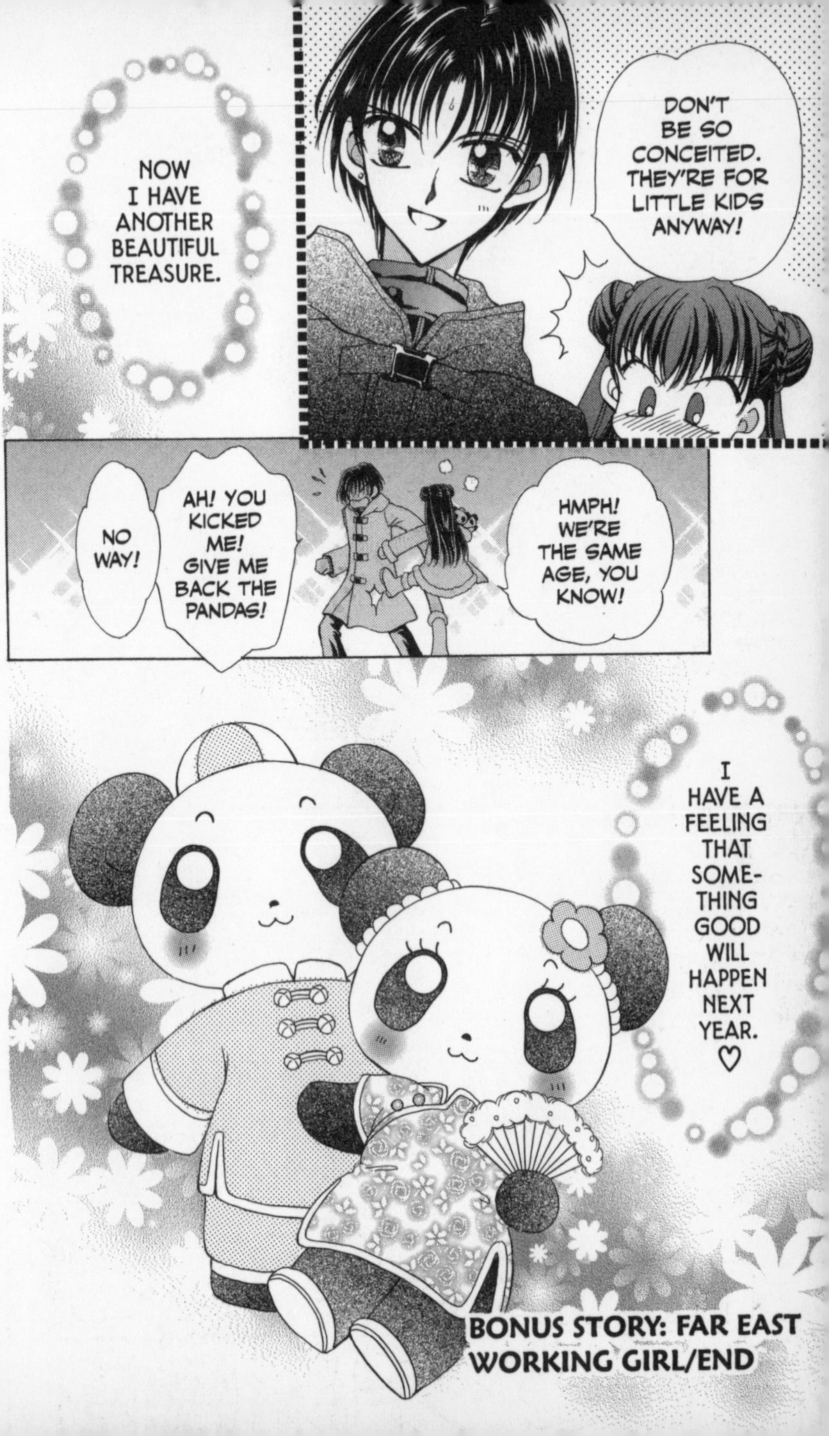
DON'T BE SO CONCEITED. THEY'RE FOR LITTLE KIDS ANYWAY!
NOW I HAVE ANOTHER BEAUTIFUL TREASURE.
HMPH! WE'RE THE SAME AGE, YOU KNOW!
AH! YOU KICKED ME! GIVE ME BACK THE PANDAS!
NO WAY!
I HAVE A FEELING THAT SOME-THING GOOD WILL HAPPEN NEXT YEAR. ♡
BONUS STORY: FAR EAST WORKING GIRL/END

Bonus Pages

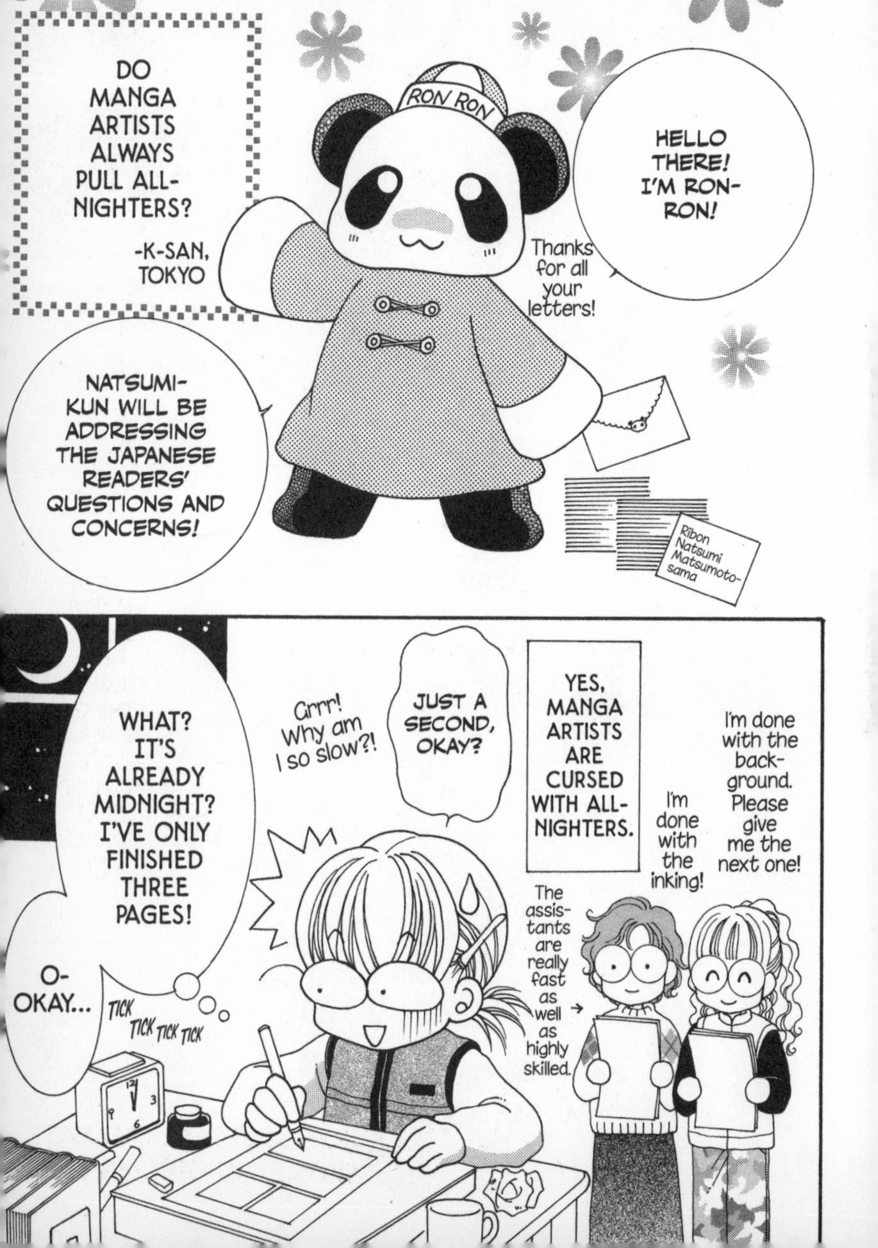
HELLO THERE! I'M RON-RON!
Thanks for all your letters!
RON RON
DO MANGA ARTISTS ALWAYS PULL ALL-NIGHTERS?
-K-SAN, TOKYO
NATSUMI-KUN WILL BE ADDRESSING THE JAPANESE READERS' QUESTIONS AND CONCERNS!
Ribon Natsumi Matsumoto-sama
I'm done with the background. Please give me the next one!
I'm done with the inking!
YES, MANGA ARTISTS ARE CURSED WITH ALL-NIGHTERS.
JUST A SECOND, OKAY?
Grrr! Why am I so slow?!
WHAT? IT'S ALREADY MIDNIGHT? I'VE ONLY FINISHED THREE PAGES!
The assistants are really fast as well as highly skilled.
O-OKAY...
TICK TICK TICK TICK

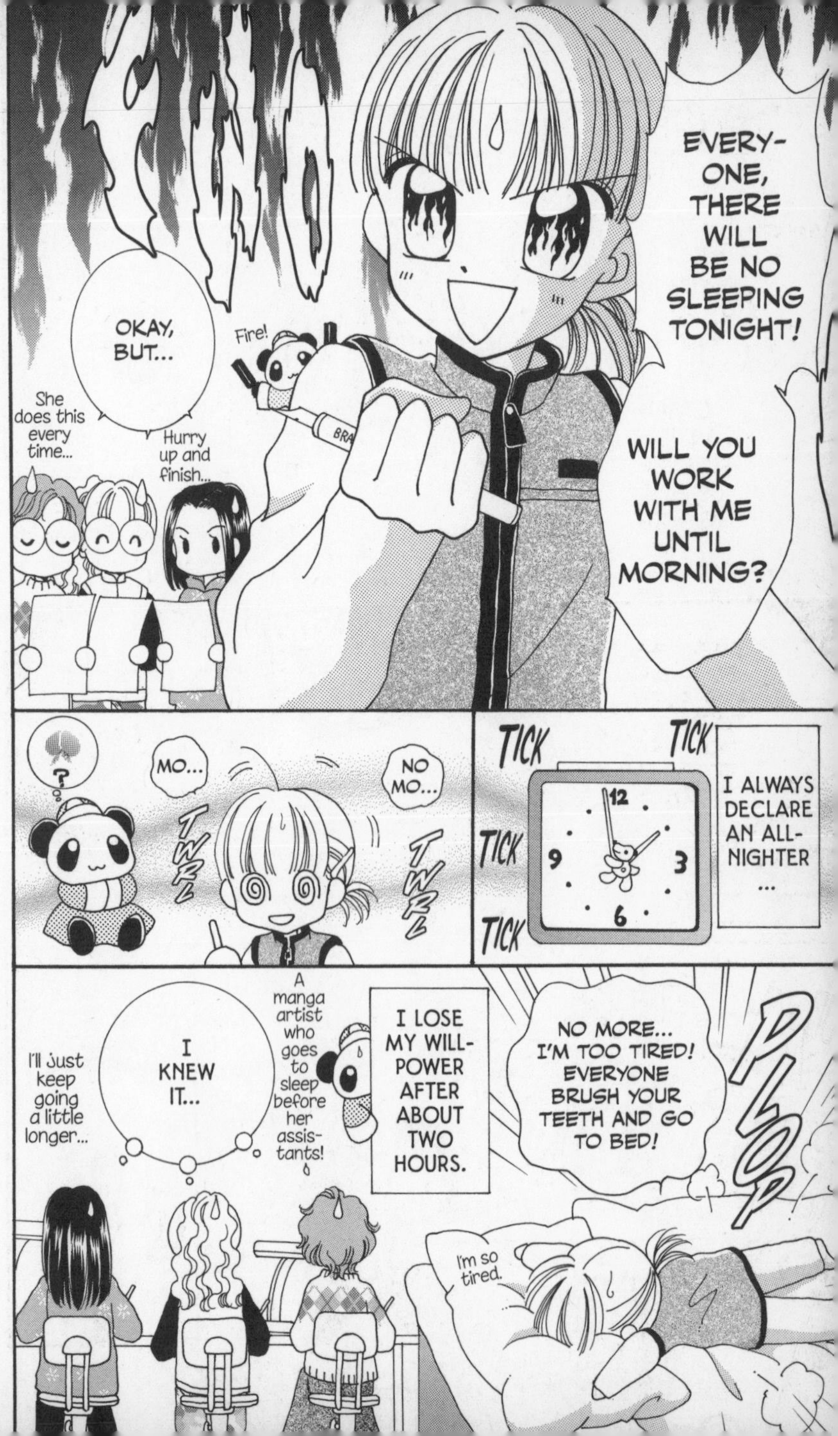
EVERYONE, THERE WILL BE NO SLEEPING TONIGHT!
WILL YOU WORK WITH ME UNTIL MORNING?
Fire!
OKAY, BUT...
Hurry up and finish...
She does this every time...
I ALWAYS DECLARE AN ALL-NIGHTER ...
TICK
TICK
TICK
TICK
NO MO...
TWRL
MO...
TWRL
?
PLOP
NO MORE... I'M TOO TIRED! EVERYONE BRUSH YOUR TEETH AND GO TO BED!
I'm so tired.
I LOSE MY WILL-POWER AFTER ABOUT TWO HOURS.
A manga artist who goes to sleep before her assistants!
I KNEW IT...
I'll just keep going a little longer...

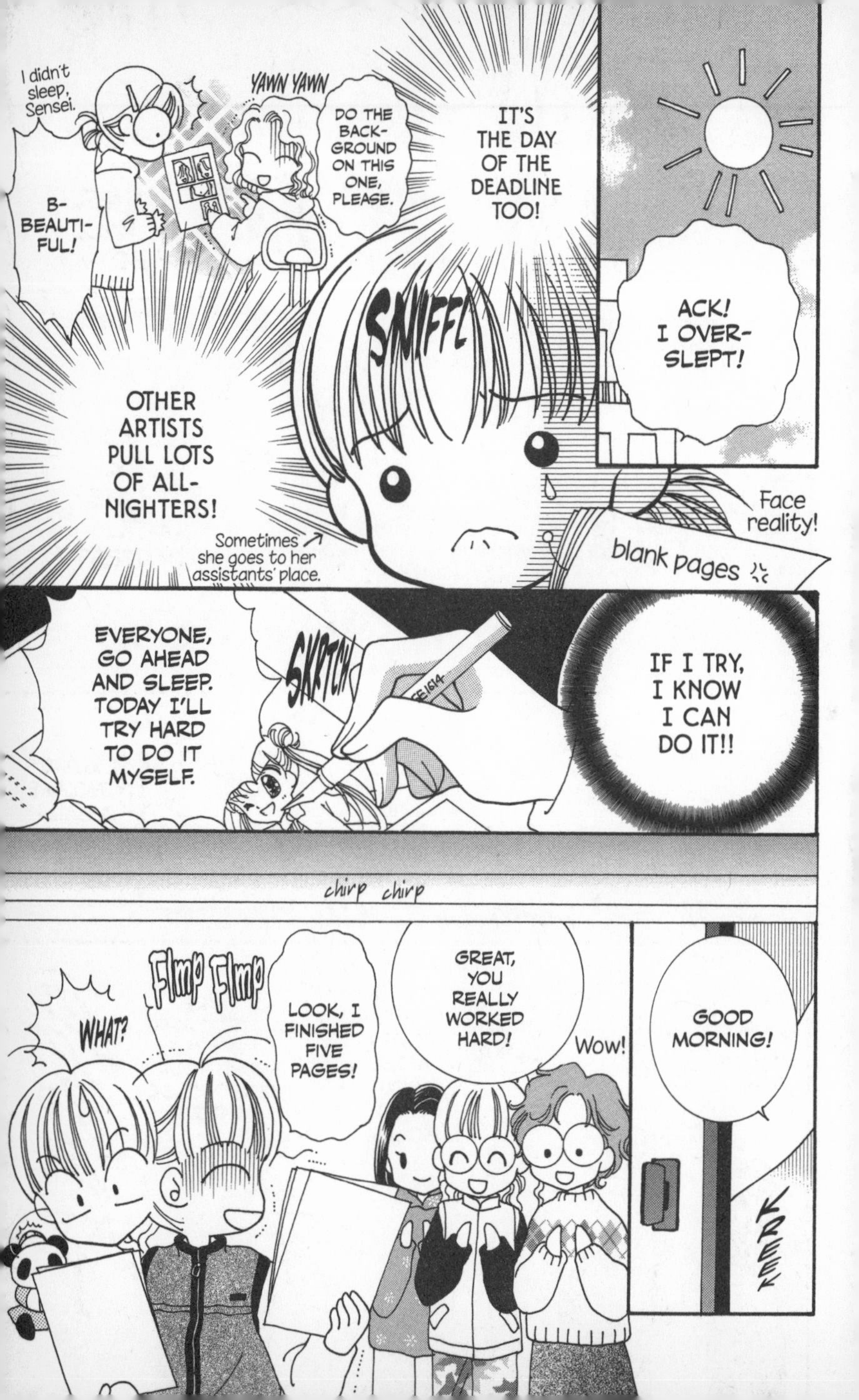
ACK! I OVER-SLEPT!
IT'S THE DAY OF THE DEADLINE TOO!
SNIFFL
Face reality!
blank pages
DO THE BACK-GROUND ON THIS ONE, PLEASE.
YAWN YAWN
I didn't sleep, Sensei.
B-BEAUTI-FUL!
OTHER ARTISTS PULL LOTS OF ALL-NIGHTERS!
Sometimes she goes to her assistants' place.
IF I TRY, I KNOW I CAN DO IT!!
SKRTCH
EVERYONE, GO AHEAD AND SLEEP. TODAY I'LL TRY HARD TO DO IT MYSELF.
chirp chirp
KREEE
GOOD MORNING!
Wow!
GREAT, YOU REALLY WORKED HARD!
LOOK, I FINISHED FIVE PAGES!
Flmp Flmp
WHAT?

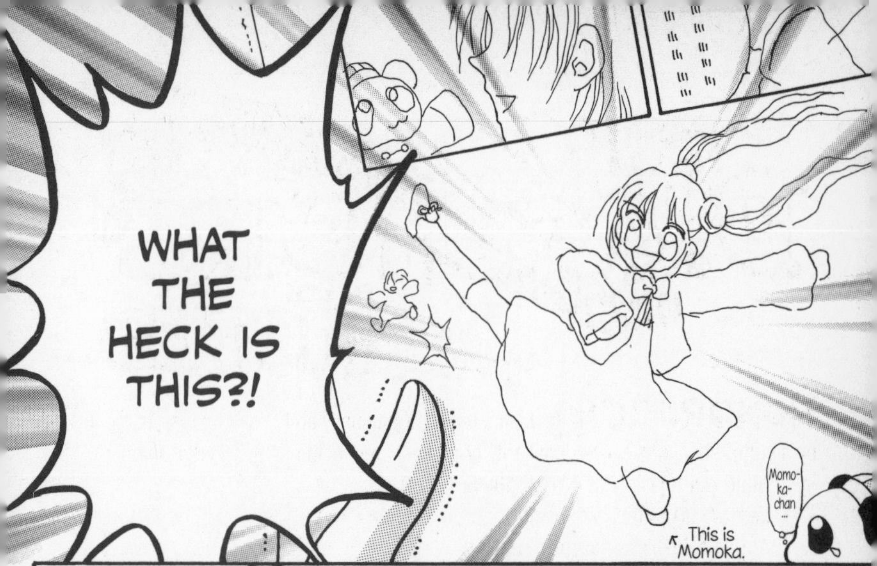
WHAT THE HECK IS THIS?!
Momo-ka-chan...
This is Momoka.

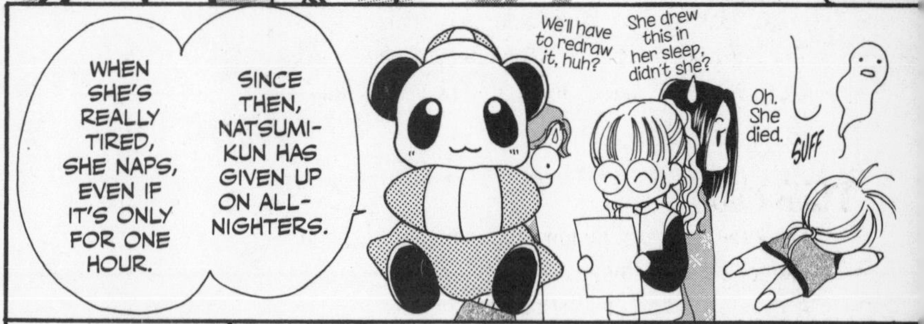
SUFF
Oh. She died.
She drew this in her sleep, didn't she?
We'll have to redraw it, huh?
SINCE THEN, NATSUMI-KUN HAS GIVEN UP ON ALL-NIGHTERS.
WHEN SHE'S REALLY TIRED, SHE NAPS, EVEN IF IT'S ONLY FOR ONE HOUR.

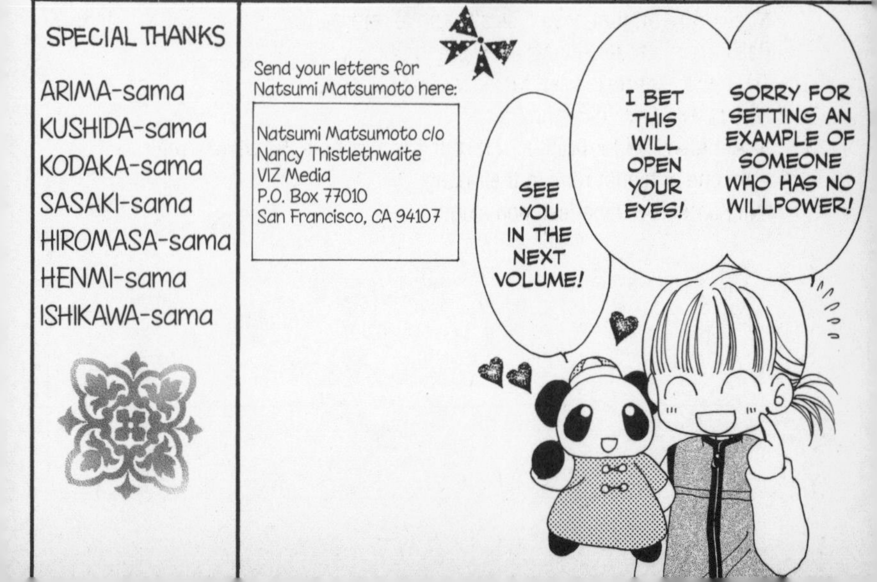
SORRY FOR SETTING AN EXAMPLE OF SOMEONE WHO HAS NO WILLPOWER!
I BET THIS WILL OPEN YOUR EYES!
SEE YOU IN THE NEXT VOLUME!

Send your letters for Natsumi Matsumoto here:

Natsumi Matsumoto c/o
Nancy Thistlethwaite
VIZ Media
P.O. Box 77010
San Francisco, CA 94107

SPECIAL THANKS

ARIMA-sama
KUSHIDA-sama
KODAKA-sama
SASAKI-sama
HIROMASA-sama
HENMI-sama
ISHIKAWA-sama

HONORIFICS
In Japan, people are usually addressed by their name followed by a suffix. The suffix shows familiarity or respect, depending on the relationship.

Male (familiar): first or last name + kun
Female (familiar): first or last name + chan
Adult (polite): last name + san
Upperclassman (polite): last name + senpai
Teacher or professional: last name + sensei
Close friends or lovers: first name only, no suffix

TERMS
The kanji for *ryu* in Ryuga's name means "dragon."
Momoka's name means "peach flower."
A *yukata* is a kimono worn in the summer.
Boku is a term that boys typically use to refer to themselves. The fact that Raika uses it means she's a bit of a tomboy.
The suffix *–sama* is used to show utmost respect.
Nii-chan means "older brother."
Aniki means "older brother" too, but it is also how the yakuza refer to someone of higher rank in their gang.
Mai Kuraki is a Japanese pop singer.

St.♥ Dragon Girl

Fan Art Submissions!

I'm looking for fan art to include in future volumes of the *St.♥ Dragon Girl* manga.
Please fill out the form on the next page and send it in with your fan art to:

Nancy Thistlethwaite, Editor
VIZ Media
P.O. Box 77010
San Francisco, CA 94107

Guidelines:

- All fan art will be presented in black and white, but you can send color art if you want.
- Submissions should be no bigger than 8 1/2" by 11".
- All submissions must have a completed release form (see next page) for consideration.

Please be sure to include the following with your fan art.

FAN ART RELEASE

In exchange for allowing the artwork I submitted with this Fan Art Release ("Fan Art") to be considered for inclusion in the *St. ♥ Dragon Girl* manga series and/or other publications, I hereby irrevocably authorize and grant a non-exclusive, transferable, worldwide, perpetual license to VIZ Media, LLC and others authorized by it, to use, copy, print, publicly display, broadcast and edit the Fan Art and my name, in whole or in part, with or without my name identification, in any and all media now known or hereinafter developed without time, territory or other restrictions and to refrain from doing any or all of the foregoing. I release them all from any claims, liability, costs, losses or damages of any kind in connection therewith, including but not limited to copyright infringement, right of publicity/privacy, blurring or optical distortion. I agree that I have no right to approve any use of the Fan Art or my name as licensed above or the content thereof.

I represent and warrant that I am of the age of majority in my state or province of residence (or, if not, that a parent or legal guardian will sign on my behalf) and that this release does not in any way conflict with any existing commitments on my part. I represent that no other person, firm or entity claiming or deriving rights through me is entitled to grant the rights in the Fan Art I've granted to you (or granted by my parent or legal guardian on my behalf) and that I have the right to license it as outlined herein. I further represent and warrant that I have the full right to enter into this agreement without violating the legal or equitable rights of any third party and that no payments shall be due to me or any third party in conjunction with the use of the Fan Art or my name as outlined herein.

ACCEPTED AND AGREED TO:

Print Name: _____

Signature: _____

(Sign or have your Parent or Legal Guardian do so, if you are a minor)

Address: _____

Date: _____

Because of all of you, I was able to continue the series. Thanks, everyone!! There were so many new characters in this volume. It was so busy it made me happy! I'm fond of every one of them, and I want them to interact with Momoka even more! Please tell me who your favorite character is!

—Natsumi Matsumoto

Natsumi Matsumoto debuted with the manga *Guuzen Janai Yo!* (No Coincidence!) in *Ribon Original* magazine. *St. ♥ Dragon Girl* was such a hit that it spawned a sequel, *St. ♥ Dragon Girl Miracle*. Her other series include *Angel Time* and *Alice kara Magic*. In her free time, Natsumi studies Chinese and practices tai chi. She also likes visiting aquariums and collecting the toy prizes that come with snack food in Japan.

St.♥ Dragon Girl

Vol. 2

The Shojo Beat Manga Edition

STORY AND ART BY | **Natsumi Matsumoto**

English Adaptation | **Heidi Vivolo**
Translation | **Andria Cheng**
Touch-up Art & Lettering | **Gia Cam Luc**
Design | **Fawn Lau**
Editor | **Nancy Thistlethwaite**

Editor in Chief, Books | **Alvin Lu**
Editor in Chief, Magazines | **Marc Weidenbaum**
VP, Publishing Licensing | **Rika Inouye**
VP, Sales & Product Marketing | **Gonzalo Ferreyra**
VP, Creative | **Linda Espinosa**
Publisher | **Hyoe Narita**

Printed in Canada

Published by VIZ Media, LLC
P.O. Box 77010
San Francisco, CA 94107

Shojo Beat Manga Edition
10 9 8 7 6 5 4 3 2 1
First printing, March 2009

RATED T FOR TEEN

PARENTAL ADVISORY
ST. ♥ DRAGON GIRL is rated T for Teen and is recommended for ages 13 and up. This volume contains mild violence.

ratings.viz.com

store.viz.com

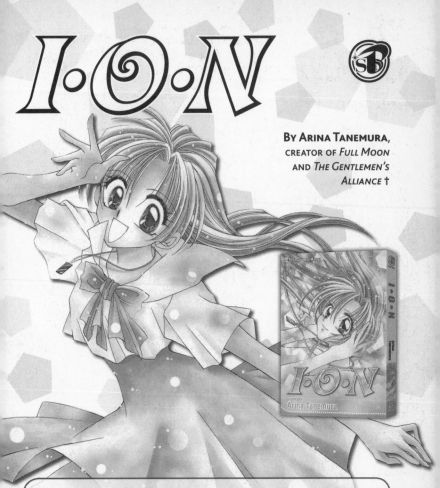

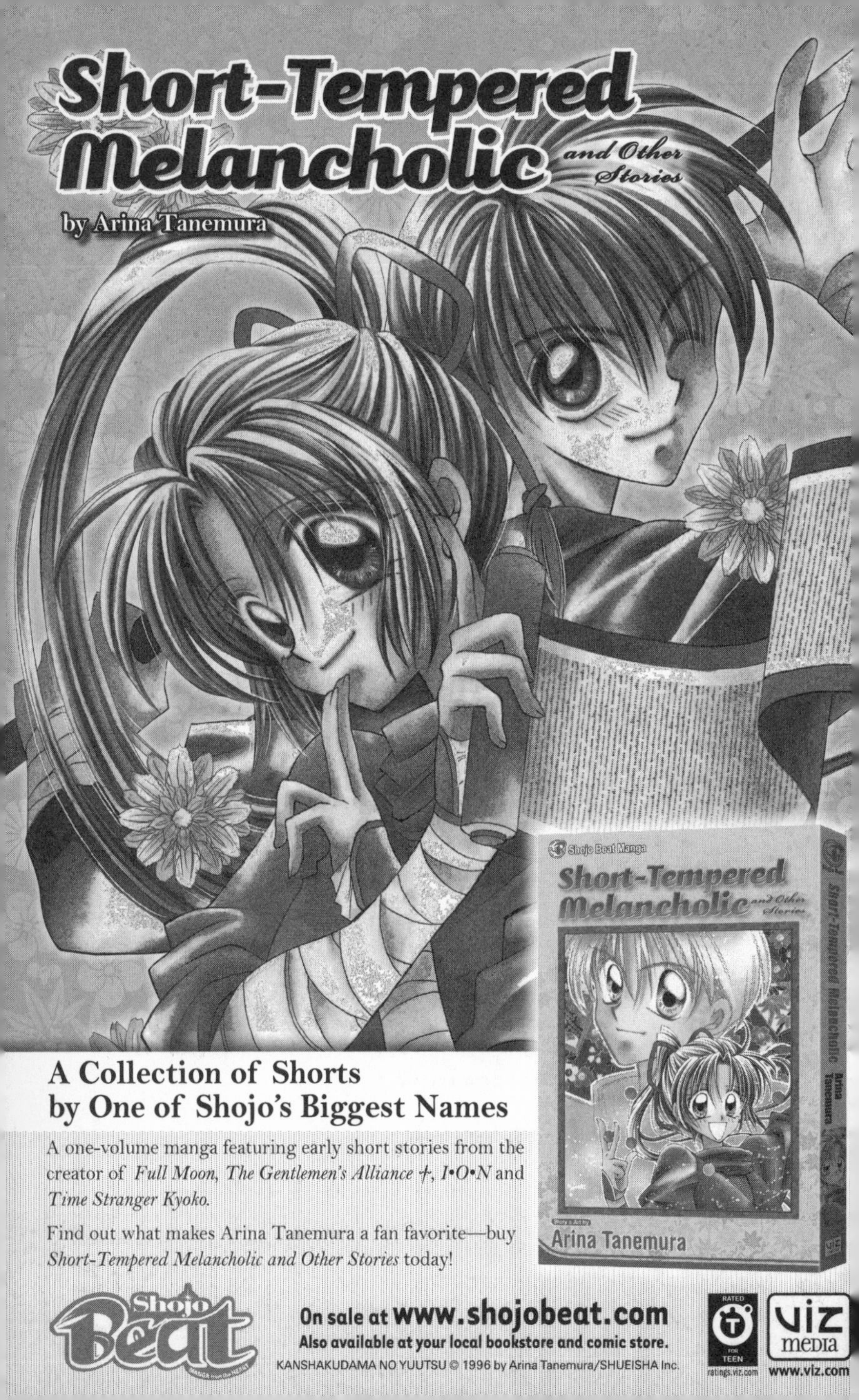

Short-Tempered Melancholic
and Other Stories
by Arina Tanemura
Shojo Beat Manga
Short-Tempered Melancholic and Other Stories
Arina Tanemura

High School DEBUT

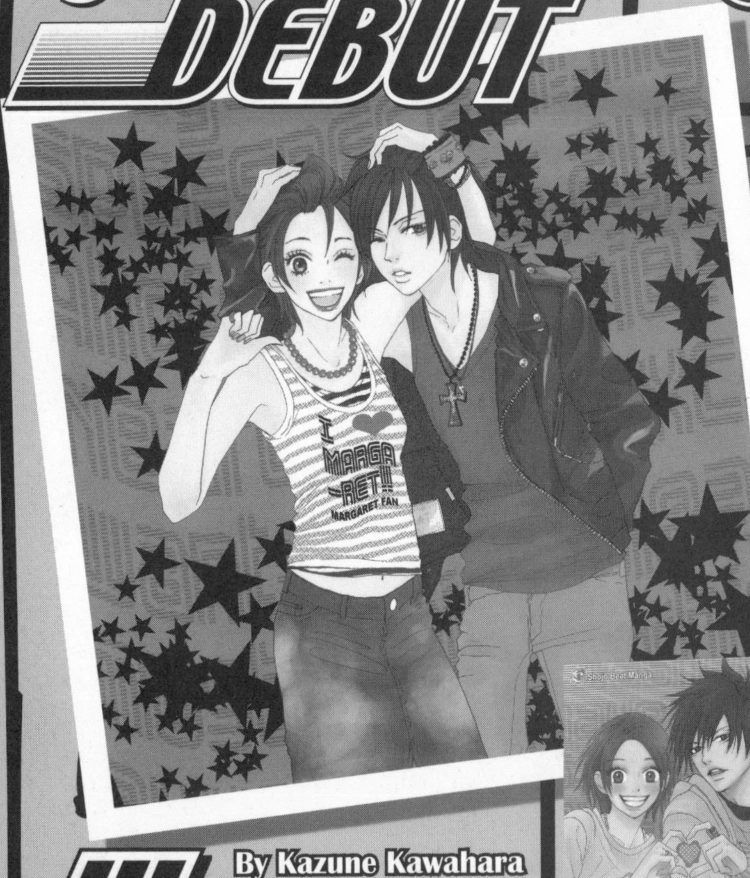

I ♥ MAGA-RET!!
MARGARET FAN

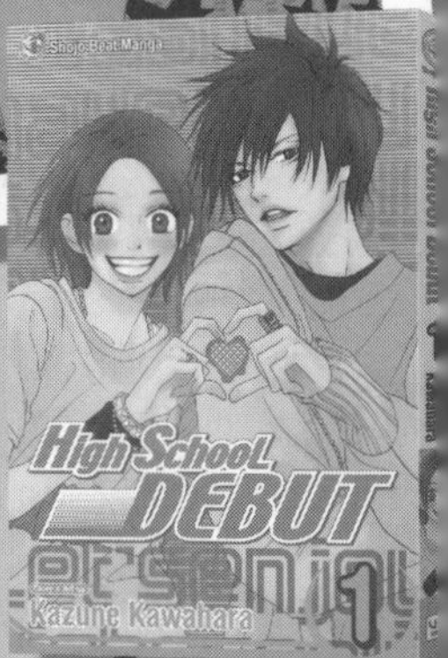

Shojo Beat Manga
High School DEBUT
Kazune Kawahara
1

By Kazune Kawahara

When Haruna Nagashima was in junior high, softball and comics were her life. Now that she's in high school, she's ready to find a boyfriend. But will hard work (and the right coach) be enough?

Find out in the *High School Debut* manga series—available now!

Tell us what you think about Shojo Beat Manga!

Our survey is now available online. Go to:

shojobeat.com/mangasurvey

Help us make our product offerings better!

Shojo Beat™

MANGA from the HEART

The Shojo Manga Authority

The most **ADDICTIVE** shojo manga stories from Japan **PLUS** unique editorial coverage on the arts, music, culture, fashion, and much more!

12 GIANT issues for ONLY $34.99*

That's 51% OFF the cover price!

Subscribe NOW and become a member of the ⓉB Sub Club!

- **SAVE** 51% OFF the cover price
- **ALWAYS** get every issue
- **ACCESS** exclusive areas of www.shojobeat.com
- **FREE** members-only gifts several times a year

Strictly VIP!